Building has been my favorite occupation ever since I can remember. I must have been 2 years old when I tried to enter a pillow in order to transform it into a shelter. This happened on the veranda of the house in Sent. One year later, in February, together with my brother Jon, I dug a tunnel under the snow in front of our house. The snow had fallen so high that winter that the fence of the garden had completely disappeared. We were digging in the snow for days. Even though it was dark in there, I could see light coming in from above. A blueish, cold light. The sound was damped. It was like being inside the belly of a large animal. My brother was at school in his first year & I could be inside the tunnel alone for most of the day, which I preferred. It was a sensation. The smell was also blue. From time to time I would eat some snow. I would eat my tunnel.

The Tunnel in Front
Not Vital, Switzerland, 2014

SCARCH
\ 'skärch \ noun
1: an artwork that bridges sculpture and architecture, typically monumental in scale and conceived to fulfill a single purpose, such as watching the sunset or hiding from sandstorms. First coined by Not Vital in 2009, SCARCH is when "sculpture and architecture scratch each other."

NOT VITAL — SCARCH

Hauser & Wirth Publishers

Contents

Project Sites

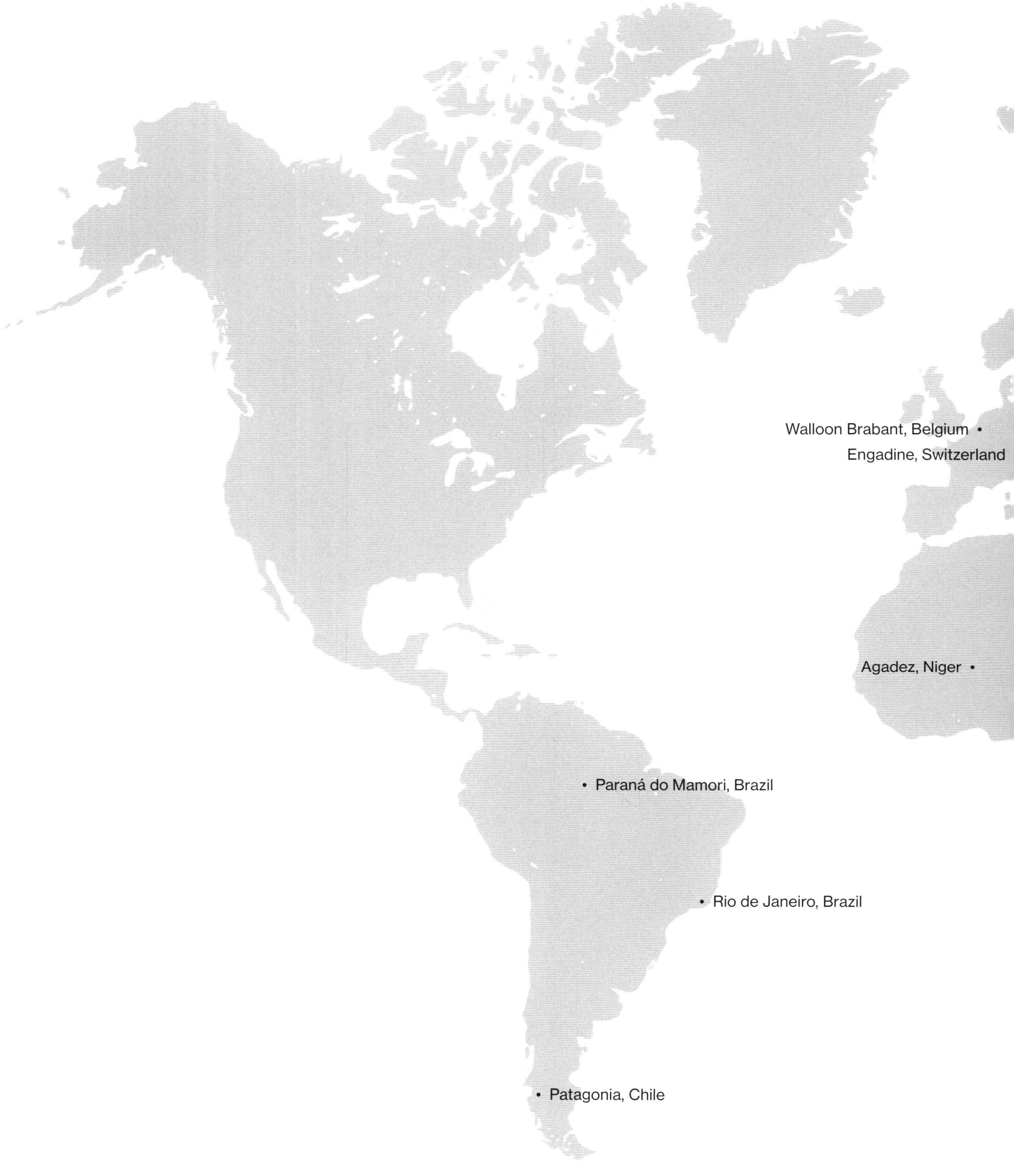

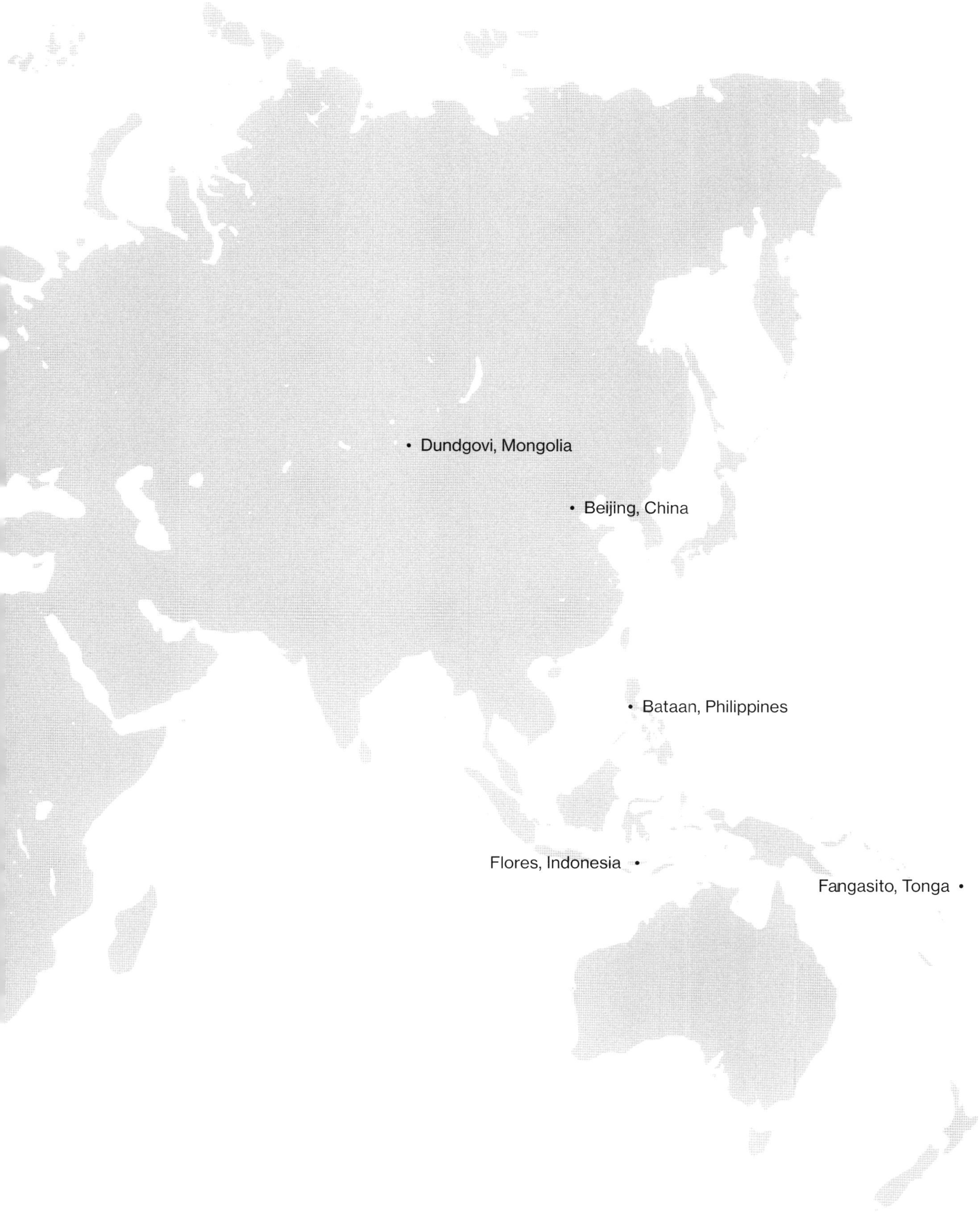
Dundgovi, Mongolia
Beijing, China
Bataan, Philippines
Flores, Indonesia
Fangasito, Tonga

Introduction
Olivier Renaud-Clément

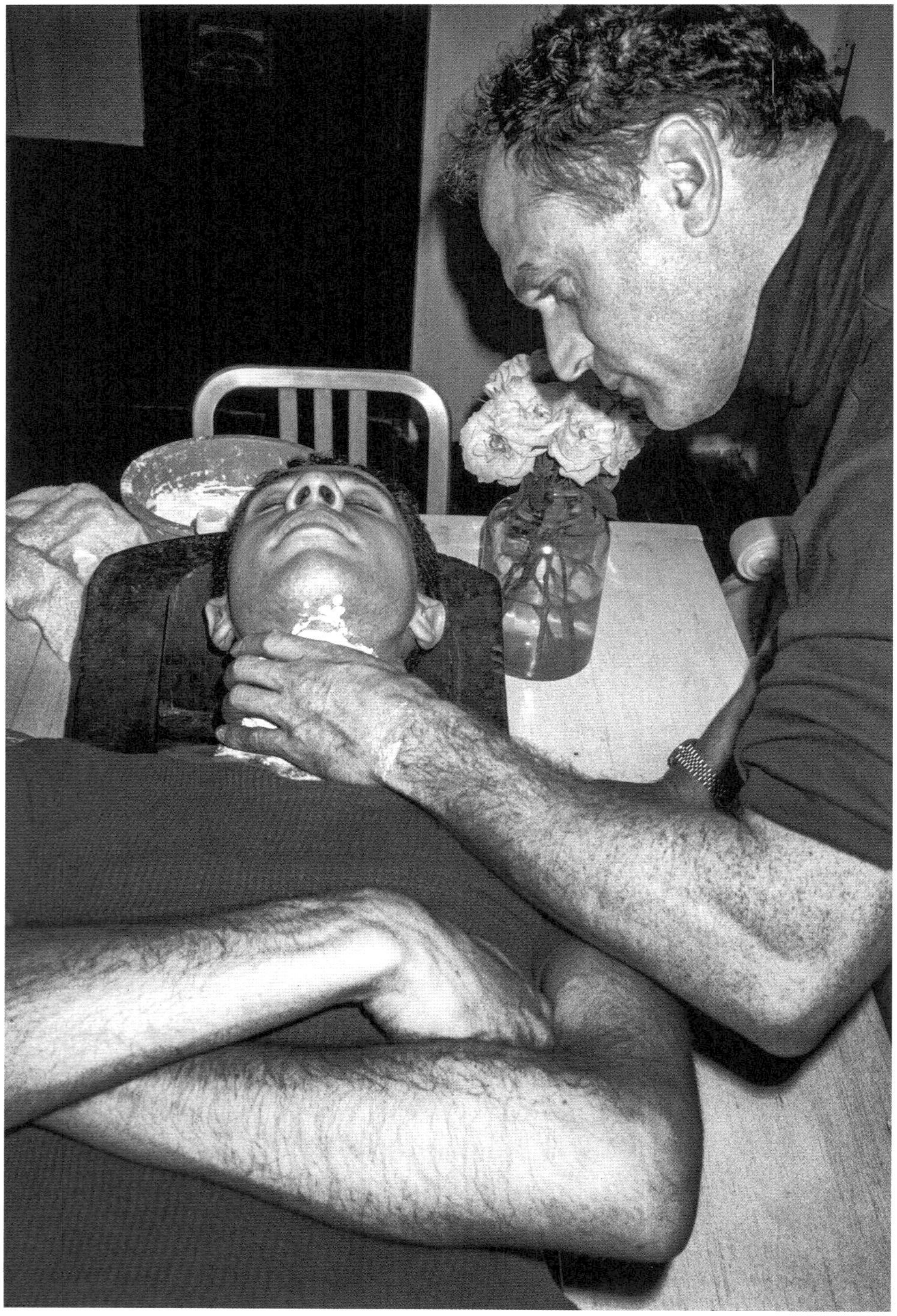

Making of *Adam One Afternoon*, 1993

In 1990, Not Vital's publisher asked me if I would meet him. The name was familiar to me, although I truly thought it was that of a collective. Not was looking for a prominent Adam's apple. I was twenty-six, very skinny, and had that required feature. We met nearly thirty years ago for dinner, which resulted in one of his most unusual, cryptic sculptures and a long-lasting friendship.

Following that first meeting, we frequently saw each other. At the time, we both lived in New York City: I in SoHo, and he near Washington Square on Broadway. We used to call him "the animal." Often, he behaved like one: he was hard to catch; he sometimes smelled people; he appeared and vanished. In those days, we'd find him in Egypt, or Thailand, or Italy. I was intrigued and disturbed by his work—it was unique and unusual. He was a sculptor, primarily.

Not briefly worked with Nature Morte Gallery, the now-mythical seminal East Village gallery, amongst friends and peers such as Peter Nagy. He very quickly ended up with Sperone Westwater in New York and Galerie Faust in Geneva. Not was dealing with unusual processes and figures that he wrought from and into abstractions suggesting body parts, animal remains, or memories of his birthplace.

Visiting Not's world in the Engadine, a mountainous region in eastern Switzerland, helps one to understand him and his work. I remember Not making a print with snow and, another time, a snowball trapped in glass. Not is permanently attached to his roots, and, at the same time, always fleeing and escaping them. The Engadine is where he needs to return to collect his thoughts and walk to the top of the *Piz*, or mountain peak. Speaking his native Romansh—a little-known Latin language spoken only in that part of Switzerland—taught Not to identify with faraway communities and express himself in unique ways.

Not Vital is in constant search of hidden lairs: remote sites and worlds. I've always been ready to follow or tag along with Not. I went to his house in Agadez, Niger, and slept on a cot in one of the seven rooms that he dedicated to each day of the week. Agadez is the location of one of his most achieved architectural sculpture ensembles, begun in 1999 and still underway. The world of the Peuls and Tuareg exhilarated Not. Their nomadic roots fascinated and motivated him—their custom of arriving and departing at all times, their caravans and camels. In an oasis near Agadez, he built the very first *House to Watch the Sunset* and declared that he would erect one on each continent.

Around the globe, Not builds his projects in the hidden locations he seeks out: the island *NotOna* in central Patagonia (2008–14); his studio in Beijing (2009); the *House to Watch the Sunset* and *House with No Doors* in the Brazilian Amazon forest (2016); the *House to Watch the 3 Volcanoes* on the Indonesian island of Flores (2017); and the *Chapel* in the Philippines (2016). Current projects are rising in both Tonga and Mongolia. Meanwhile, Not created a foundation in Ardez and acquired the historic Castle of Tarasp, both in the Engadine.

Few people have seen these mysterious wonders. It is difficult to get any information on how to find them. When I went to *NotOna* in Chile, I had to use my instincts and sense of direction to figure out where I was going. Not never gave any clues, instructions, or information beyond simply telling me: "Once in the village, ask for Chely."

Seeing Not's carved marble island for the first time, I understood what it means to marvel. *NotOna* is unreal and yet totally material—the way it towers over the water, the way that it filters light. It embodies what Not coined as SCARCH, a term he defines as sculptural architecture.

Not Vital: SCARCH presents a survey of the artist's works, putting Not's cloistered and far-flung creations within reach of readers. This is important because Not remains forever unfollowable. Even so, I keep trying to track him down, hoping to stumble into him or his projects somewhere unexpected. Maybe I'll discover a house in the shape of my Adam's apple one day, in some unfindable place.

Door + Window
1965

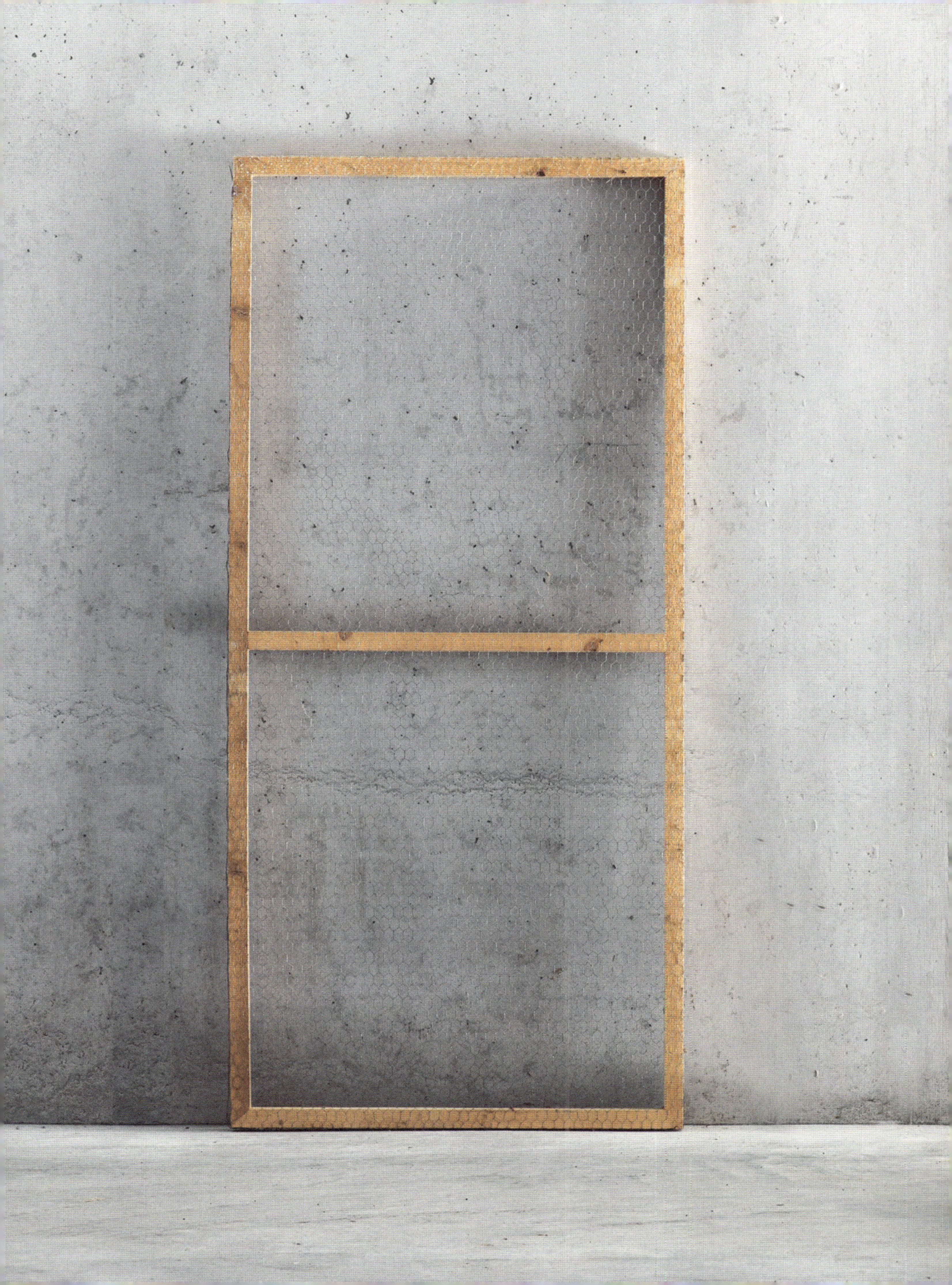

Leaping In and Out of Architecture

Giorgia von Albertini

"Houses everywhere but nowhere shut in, this is the motto of the dreamer of dwellings."
—Gaston Bachelard, *The Poetics of Space*[1]

Not Vital grew up in the midst of the raw, natural mountains of the lower Engadine in Switzerland. Because of the long cold winters, the houses there are extremely sheltering if not almost motherly: the thick walls are often slightly curved, with wood interiors and the windows so small that even the mountains hesitate in front of them.

Vital embarked on his first journeys of discovery in the narrow tunnels that he dug into the snow as a child. He caught his first views of challenging, barely accessible places that he wanted to explore from tree houses that he built in the woods around his hometown Sent. The first works Vital made when he turned to art in the mid-1960s testify to his interest in the concept of habitat and the formal idiom of architecture. The early work *Chanala da tet* (1964 [p. 13]) consists of a roof gutter that he found on the street in front of his parents' house. Vital promptly painted it white and turned it into a rectified readymade. For *Fatschada* (1965 [p. 14]), he applied acrylic and sand to his canvas to render the discoloring on the bottom of many houses in the Engadine caused by goats rubbing up against the façade. The work is whitish in color, reminiscent of monochromatic Minimal Art but much rougher in texture; it is neither picture, nor sculpture, but essentially an object. For *Chasa i bogn* (1970 [p. 14]), a two-part work consisting of the simplified shape of a house and a children's tub, Vital used found objects of zinc, their grey surfaces showing traces of use, dents, and scratches: an assisted readymade.

Although the readymade later yielded to sculpture, drawing, painting, and architecture, Vital's early work clearly prefigured what was to come. The Romansh titles of the works simply name the subject matter: *Chanala da tet* (*Rainwater Gutter*), *Fatschada* (*Façade*), and *Chasa i bogn* (*House and Bathtub*). This straightforward economy of means applies not only to language but also to the treatment of form that characterizes Vital's oeuvre. He has a penchant for liberating objects or organs—binoculars, a bone, or even a tongue—from their conventional, mundane use and transforming them sculpturally into surreal, minimal

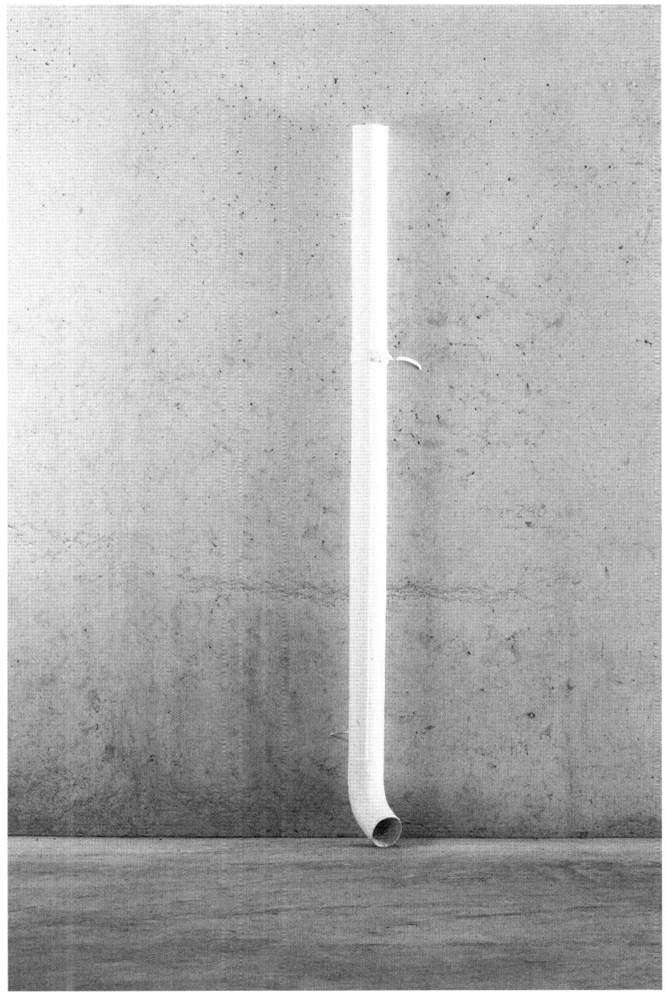

Chanala da tet, 1964

1. Gaston Bachelard, *The Poetics of Space*, trans. Maria Jolas (1958; repr., New York: Penguin Books, 2014), 62.

Fatschada, 1965

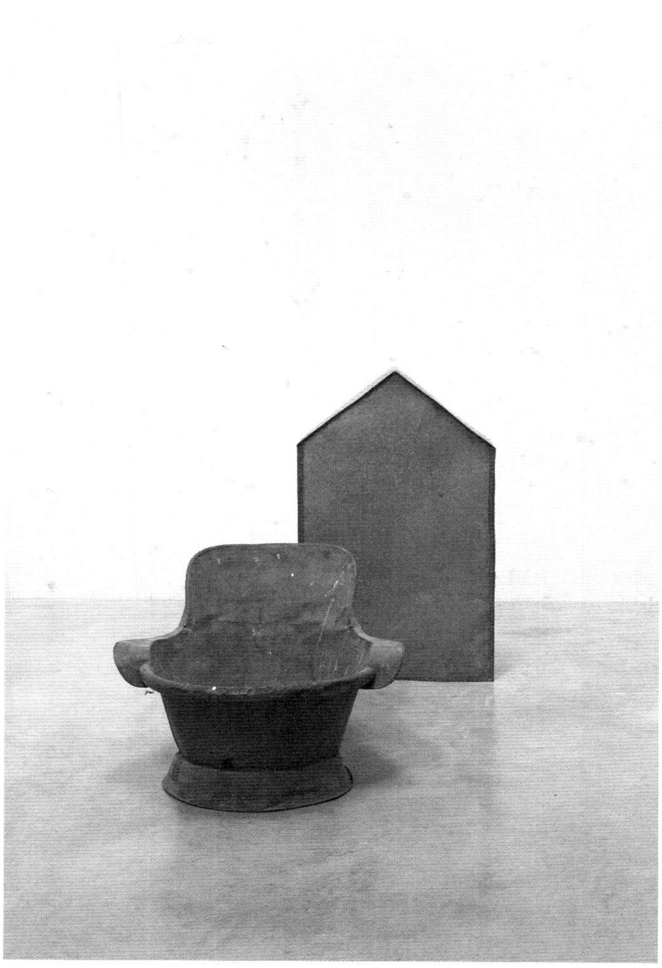

Chasa i bogn, 1970

objects. Often standing upright, propped against the wall or freestanding in space, these subliminally familiar objects confront us as alien newcomers. With disconcerting nonchalance, they realign our perception, their ineluctable presence nominating us to bear witness.

Not only did Vital's obsession with the concept of habitat, with questions of where and how we live, soon become manifest, other intensities emerged as well—the persuasive appeal of his charismatic native Engadine never stood in the way of the artist's energetic curiosity.

A NOMADIC WAY OF LIFE

For some 50 years Vital has been leading an essentially nomadic life, moving from one continent to the next. Driven by a seemingly unquenchable urge to explore remote places, their culture, and their handicrafts, he immerses himself in new worlds with astonishing ease. He carries out projects in regions that are usually remote and hard to reach. He collaborates with local craftspeople and sources regional means of production, enlisting a visual vocabulary and materials that are as mobile as he himself. The rhythm of Vital's ceaseless and extensive travels has led to building habitats that complement his native Sent, ranging as far afield as Beijing [p. 15], Rio de Janeiro, the Amazon, the Chilean part of Patagonia, Indonesia, the Philippines, New York, Lucca, and Agadez. Over the years, Italy, Niger, and China have become particularly important locations for the production of his sculptures.

The French writer Jean Lescure once wrote that an artist "does not create the way he lives, he lives the way he creates."[2] In Vital's case, it's probably a matter of the chicken and the egg. In the course of his nomadic lifestyle, the constant seeking and finding of habitats and places of production has become a maxim. The causal relationship between the two processes is not easily unraveled. Sometimes Vital is attracted by the beauty or difference of a place, and the discovery of a fascinating craft is a serendipitous

2. Jean Lescure, *Lapicque* (Paris: Galanis, 1956), 78.

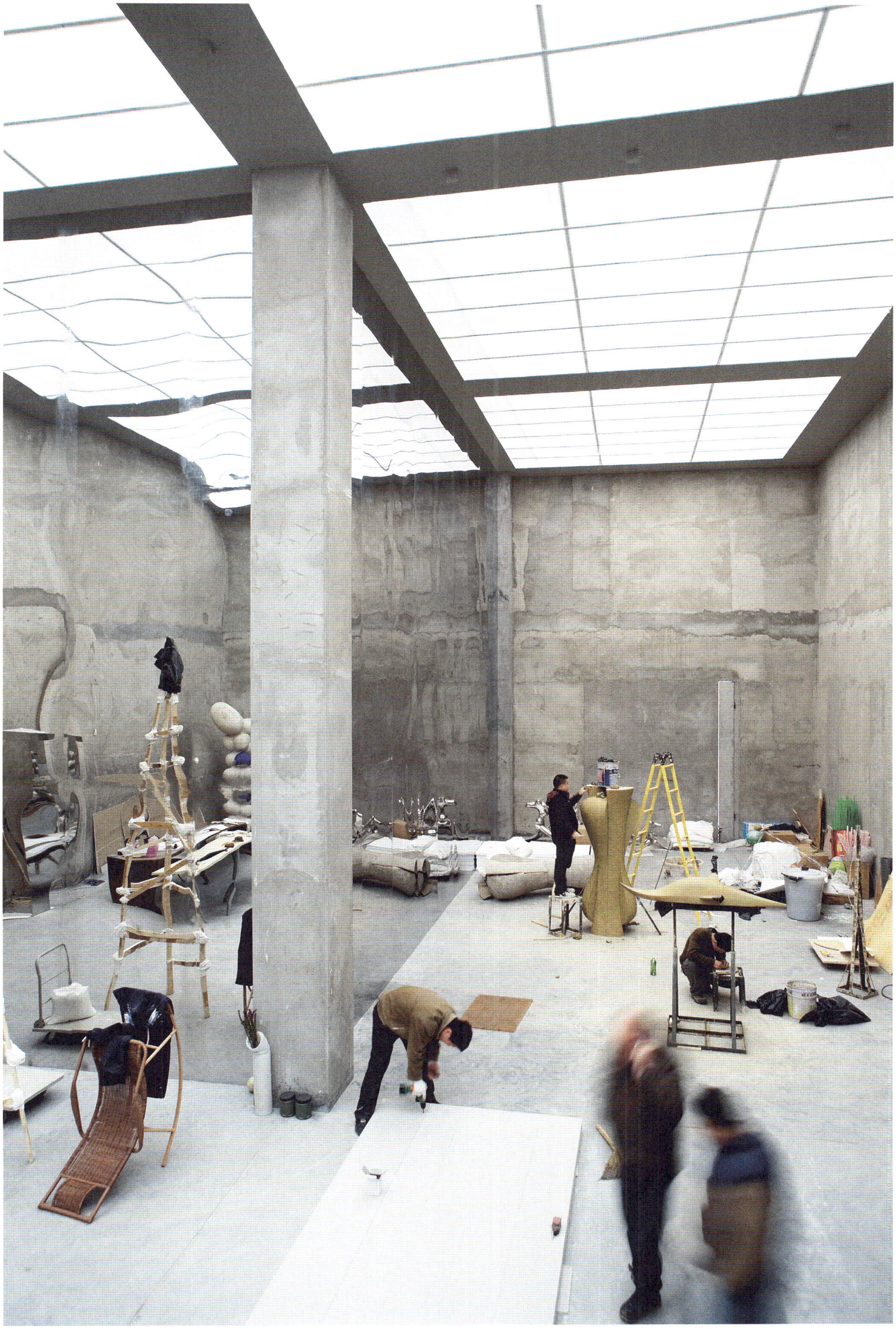

Not Vital's studio in Beijing, China

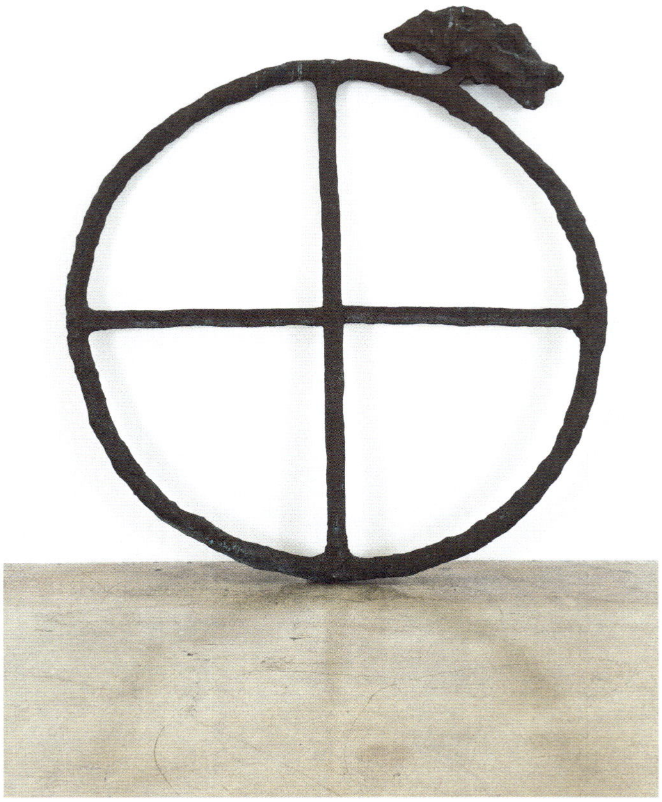

Wheel Animal, 1982

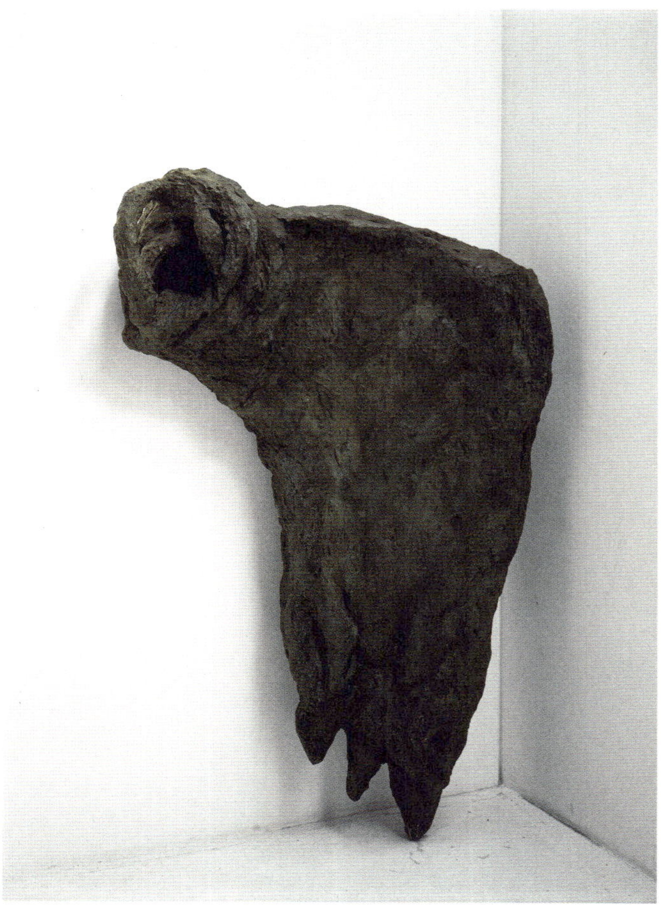

Paw Pow, 1984

by-product that he then incorporates into his work. After he began adapting the animal subject matter in the early 1980s, Vital went to Pietrasanta in Italy and there discovered bronze as a sculptural medium, upon which he created a number of suggestively archaic works in rapid succession; for instance, *Wheel Animal* (1982 [p. 16]), *Stone Eater* (1983), and *Paw Pow* (1984 [p. 16]). Vital's trip from New York to Italy had an unexpected and enduring influence on his oeuvre: he still works in bronze and the utopian, totemic syntax of the resulting sculptures has been of equally enduring relevance.

In addition to bronze, Vital discovered marble in Pietrasanta, a material that would become as important a vehicle for his sculptures as bronze, plaster, and stainless steel. He created his first marble sculpture in 1985 with Umberto Togni, a local artisan whose hair has since turned as white as the marble dust that clothes him like a second skin from his curly pate to his wooden clogs. The appearance of the two columns in *Arabia* (1985 [p. 17]), one a white marble and the other a greyish-green patinated bronze, varies with the seasons; in summer the white marble is luminous against the saturated green, while in winter the greenish patina of the bronze comes to the fore and the marble retires with dignity into the background.

Embellished with an Islamic dog motif, *Arabia* is a paradigm of Vital's virtuoso ability to transform cultural fragments into surreal, dreamlike constructs through decontextualization, reconfiguration, and relocation. The artist's mental and physical mobility are requisite to activating the three main ingredients of his light-footed alchemy. Having absorbed non-European signs and symbols while traveling through the Far East, he mentally recontextualizes and culturally reconfigures them while taking a rest elsewhere, and then implements them through the use of unexpected materials by specialized craftsmen. The last step in the process involves installing the sculpture in a different context—the Islamic dog motif thus suddenly plays hide and seek with us, assisted by the seasons in Europe.

In Pietrasanta, Vital also worked with Togni to create *Marble Tower* (2009 [pp. 186–89]), a monumental work that is just over thirty feet tall.

The minimalist and perfectly symmetrical tower reaches up majestically, its pointed roof piercing the sky. Even the making of this tower alone is indeed a miraculous achievement; it consists of one single block of Carrara marble. Togni spent years meticulously hollowing it out from the inside, carving the shape from the outside, and polishing the surfaces to perfection, both inside and out. Rising in the midst of grass and shrubs and trees, the tower appears pure and everlasting, as if standing guard, serenely dominant and nonjudgmental. Walking through the rectangular entry that is both door and window and turning your head to look up is quite literally breathtaking. It is a cathedral. Peter Handke, one of Vital's favorite writers, once wrote, "As soon as I see the incredible—I become a witness."[3]

Although monumentality and precious materials did not enter into Vital's oeuvre until the early 2000s, *Marble Tower* still clearly relates to his early work. Once again we encounter a reduction of form and content; the artist distills the essence of things with such immediacy, such clarity, that we truly begin to know. And once again we encounter Vital's manifest interest in architecture. However, unlike *Chanala da tet*, *Fatschada*, and also *Chasa i bogn*, *Marble Tower* is neither an architectural fragment nor a rendition in miniature of the architectural idiom. The work is a tower and it clearly formulates essential architectural principles. According to the great poet and philosopher Gaston Bachelard, towers and houses are vertical beings and speak to us as such, rising upward as concentrated creatures and appealing to our consciousness of centrality.[4]

One might therefore conclude that Vital's *Marble Tower* meets the basic criteria of architecture. But it is not that simple. Vital undoubtedly rebelled against the fullness of the house.[5] Traditionally, houses are full of beds, carpets, bathrooms, towels, frying pans, plates, and even cats or dogs (we call them *domestic* animals). Vital's tower is empty twice over: it is hollowed out and empty. It has no electricity, no running water, and most certainly none of the abovementioned accessories to the *comforts of home*.

Marble Tower quintessentially embodies the distilled architectural structure that results from Vital's research into the minimal conditions of the

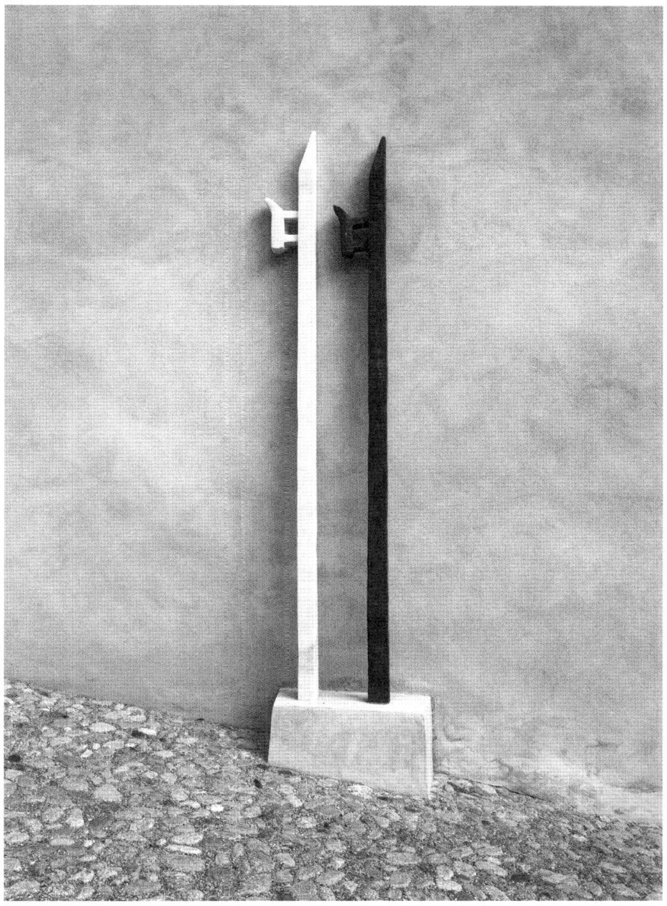

Arabia, 1985

3. Peter Handke, *The Innerworld of the Outerworld of the Innerworld*, trans. Michael Roloff (New York: Seabury Press, 1974), 103.
4. Bachelard, *The Poetics of Space*, 17.
5. Bachelard, 8.

habitat; the shape is simplified until it is bared and reduced to its essence. The consequence is definitive; nothing more can be subtracted. It then remains empty, liberated from the ballast of practical use.[6] This two-stage procedure is of considerable impact: practical, architectural space has been transformed into poetic, transcendental space.

Ten years before Vital created his miracle with Togni in Pietrasanta, his philosophical, conceptual interest in architecture and predilection for monumental sculptures were ignited during a trip to Niger.

NIGER

The most important item in Vital's luggage when he goes on journeys is his insatiable curiosity coupled with instinct and trust. In 1999, when he first traveled to the desert city of Agadez in Niger, he knew little about the country. A beautifully told story, an astonishing oddity, or even a simple visual impression can suffice to spark fascination or a visceral reaction. In the case of Niger, Vital had read about the Tuareg and the Peul nomads and, given his own restlessness, felt an affinity with these proud peoples whose habitat is simply wherever they pitch their tents and water their animals.

It was late at night when Vital arrived in Agadez. The next morning the Tuareg were there in front of his hotel offering their traditional jewelry for sale. Instead he asked them for land, found a piece, and purchased it before nightfall the same day. He drew maps and plans in the hot sand. Given his incredible speed and stunning ability to persuade, it is quite superfluous to inquire whether there were already workers available by evening to build Vital's first house, just as superfluous as asking a Tuareg if he can tell a good story. Of course they were already there.[7]

In close cooperation with local craftsmen, and sourcing the reddish clay earth of Niger, Vital built six sculptural structures in the decade that followed. Their singularity of purpose and utter lack of infrastructure thoroughly debunks the conventional distinction between sculpture and architecture as an obsolete formality. Three of them are functional, albeit rather idiosyncratically: *Mekafoni* (2001), *House Against Heat and*

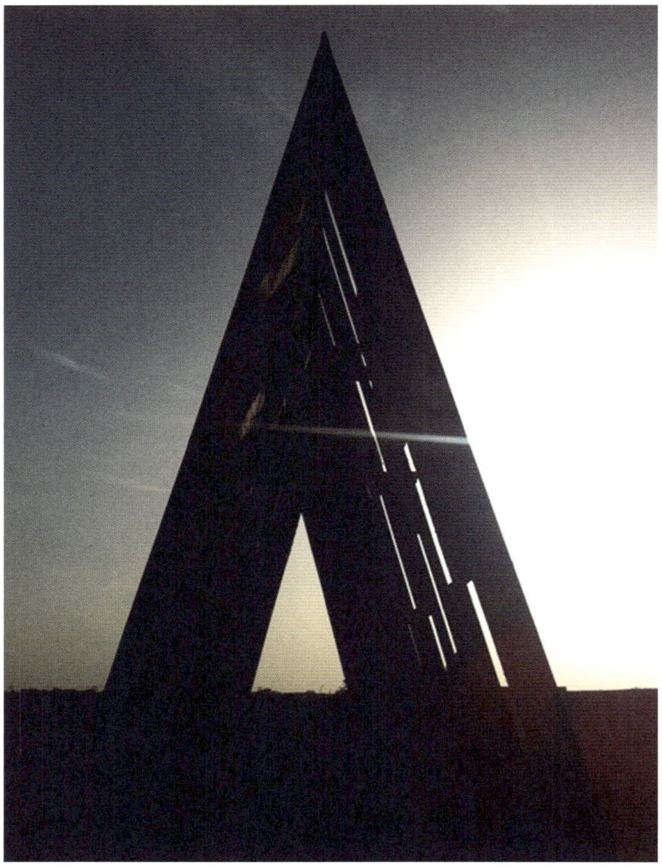

Mosque, 2013

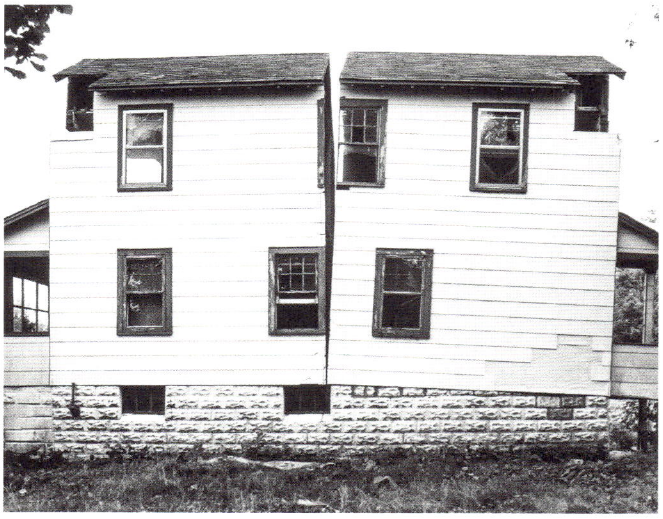

Gordon Matta-Clark, *Splitting*, 1974

6. Please note that in the case of *Marble Tower*, the unnecessary ballast was literally disposed of: the block of marble started out weighing 50 tons and weighed not even a fourth of that at the end.
7. The Tuareg say, "fast is good"—an interesting statement for people who live a rather quiet life. But mental speed is as inherently characteristic as elegance.

Sandstorms (2006), and *Mosque* (2013 [p. 18]). One of them is the product of pure necessity and nonetheless sculpture: *Makaranta* (2003). Two others are purely transcendental in purpose: *House to Watch the Sunset* (2005) and *House to Watch the Night Skies* (2006).

The first building Vital completed in Agadez was *Mekafoni* [pp. 120–25]: the title is a Hausa word and means "house with horns." As a matter of fact, it is not the Tuareg or the Peuls, but rather the Hausa who are the master builders in Niger. *Mekafoni* comprises a main building of three stories and a house with seven rooms, one for every day of the week. Each of the main building's three stories is conceptualized to accommodate a specific activity: the ground floor is for socializing, the second floor is for sleeping, and the top floor is for looking at the cityscape. In the seven-room house, the rooms are laid out in a line and incrementally decrease in size as if to reinforce the niggling feeling of losing time that insinuates itself as the week progresses. The complex is built of clay and embellished with the elegantly curved antlers of local zebu cattle.[8]

Having completed this dream city for his friends and possible visitors, Vital decided to build *Makaranta* [pp. 126–31], a Koranic school for the children in Agadez, many of whom have no access to formal education because the city has neither the money nor the infrastructure required. Conceived as a pyramid with four stepped sides and a passage through the middle, the structure is based on the idea of having children go on school instead of to school. The teacher stands in the hot sand in front of the pyramid and walks once all around the school in the course of a day as the children move from one side to the next so that they can always sit in the shade.[9]

In purely formal terms, *Makaranta* is an elegant, geometrically defined sculpture whose shape is reminiscent of the temples built, for example, by advanced civilizations in South America.[10] Once the structure is activated by practical use, however, something exceptional happens: the crowd of excited children turns it into a kinetic sculpture.[11] For a moment, *Makaranta*, stoic and sublime, is transformed into a stage for a pulsating present.

In addition to his projects in Agadez, Vital built three monumental sculptures in an oasis outside of Niger's desert city. Bachelard once said, "A dreamer is unable to believe that the work is finished when the walls are built."[12]

House Against Heat and Sandstorms [pp. 144–45], conic and spiral in shape, serves, as the title says, to hide from heat and sandstorms. Drawing on the shape of a seashell, Vital designed a hideaway that meets our deep-seated need for protection. Like a nest, the shell is a primal image related to notions of refuge and emergence.[13] Interestingly, in the imagination, to go in and to go out are never symmetrical images. And indeed, when we face the daylight again after having crept into Vital's house, when we emerge step by step out of the tranquil interior, we are like naked mollusks perceiving the world for the first time.

While *House Against Heat and Sandstorms* sharpens perception through temporary deprivation, *House to Watch the Night Skies* [pp. 148–49] turns the tables, treating us to an experience of the sublime through a kind of sensual overflow. The sculpture is simple in shape, similar to the wooden neck rests used by Peul nomads: it rises up slender and squared, the top slightly curved. But since Vital's sculpture is enlarged some 20 times in comparison to the neck rests, we have to access it by climbing up a narrow ladder in order to lie down the length of it on our backs. The imminent danger of falling off on one

8. Vital used the horns of zebu cattle to embellish *Mekafoni* because he could not understand why they are the only part of the slaughtered animal not used.
9. I am not a psychoanalyst but I suspect that Vital's traumatic school years may have influenced the design of this schoolhouse. In *Makaranta*, Vital exploited his artistic license and inverted the hierarchy: the children sit comfortably raised above the teacher. Who is doing the grading?
10. The pyramid shape, the stepped sides, and orientation according to the position of the sun show clear parallels with Maya, Inca, and Aztec temples.
11. In contrast to Vital's friends who never came to reside in the dream city conceived for them, probably because the region is too poor, dangerous, dry, or hot for them, the children came in droves, exceeding all expectations—and their interest has not abated. Vital is now working on two more schools for the children of Agadez. These will be shaped like seashells. See pp. 152–53.
12. Bachelard, *The Poetics of Space*, 115.
13. Bachelard, 109.

side or the other requires extreme concentration. As Vital likes to say, "Danger wakes you up."[14] With our senses sharpened by adrenaline, we are utterly awed by the night skies. Nowhere else on Earth are they as extraordinary as in the Sahara: with no light pollution, in total darkness, the Milky Way stretches out overhead like a portal above the desert. With the firmament for its terrace, *House to Watch the Night Skies* brings the heavens within reach, conquering distance like a telescope.

There is something extraordinary about the way *House to Watch the Night Skies* makes us feel at the mercy of the universe. Ordinarily, the house is an instrument with which to confront the cosmos. It helps us to say: "I will be an inhabitant of the world, despite the world."[15] *House to Watch the Night Skies* and many of the other towering buildings devised by Vital take a diametrically opposed stand: they are not interested in permitting us to inhabit the universe. Instead, they are the buildings of a poet who permits the universe to come and inhabit them.

House to Watch the Sunset [pp. 138—39, 249] is perhaps the key to Vital's cosmic, poetic architecture. The building, over forty feet high, has three stories, each unconnected and separately accessed via an outdoor staircase. In Niger, Vital had it constructed in reddish clay. Shortly after finishing this modernist and yet archaic structure, he declared that *House to Watch the Sunset* would become a global project: on each continent, a structure would be built for the sole purpose of contemplating the sunset. While the materials of the building would always be site-specific, the form and dimensions would be the same on every continent.[16]

Vital once told me that his lack of knowledge gives him great freedom. He has always been interested in architecture and particularly admires thinkers and makers—like Frederick Kiesler and Gordon Matta-Clark [p. 18]—whose independent output defies conventional architectural categories. But he never studied architecture and instead chose to pursue a career as an artist. Artists have much more freedom and, for Vital, working with clients who want a house with 230-volt lamps would most certainly be unbearable.

Given Vital's long-term interest in architecture, however, his lack of formal education should not be written off as ignorance; rather, it is a kind of arduous surpassing of the limits of learning. Lescure pinpoints the issue: non-knowing is "the price that must be paid for an oeuvre to be, at all times, a sort of pure beginning, which makes its creation an exercise in freedom."[17] This is the freedom that enabled Vital to invent SCARCH (Sculpture-Architecture) in Niger. The buildings Vital subsumes under his neologism are formalistic and exist primarily to fill one single—usually poetic and transcendental—purpose, such as the contemplation of the sunset or the night sky. Crucial to his built structures are not the comforts of home or the way in which we might live in them, but rather the way in which they enable us to look at the world: Vital conceives his monumental sculptures as windows to the world. His houses yearn to see; for them *having* is nothing but *seeing*. And when we are in them, gazing through their windows, crawling out of them, or lying on top of them holding our breath, then we are *seeing*. And seeing is believing.

CHILE

After a long time in Niger, where Vital has made deep, inspiring friendships, thanks, among other things, to a shared passion for storytelling,[18] he decided to build his next *House to Watch the Sunset* in South America. Finding the right location is vital (no pun intended) in many respects. To begin with, the name of a place will appeal to Vital; for instance, Timbuktu, Ulaanbaatar, or Flores. And it is important for the place to be in the countryside. In cities, the relationship between buildings

14. Not Vital in conversation with the author, 2017.
15. Bachelard, *The Poetics of Space*, 46–47.
16. For further reading on *House to Watch the Sunset*, see the following essays in this volume: Philip Jodidio, "Just Enough to Make the Sun Set: The Stories of Not Vital," pp. 68–77, Akhmed Haïdara, "Not Vital in Agadez," pp. 140–41, and Tilla Theus, "Poetry, Unique and Intense," pp. 244–49.
17. Lescure, *Lapicque*, 78.
18. In no other country has Vital met people who can tell stories so marvelously philosophical and surreal—and yet specifically concrete and expressive—that they can be adopted *telles quelles* to stand next to his own epic, surreal works, such as *11 asens da Sent* (1992).

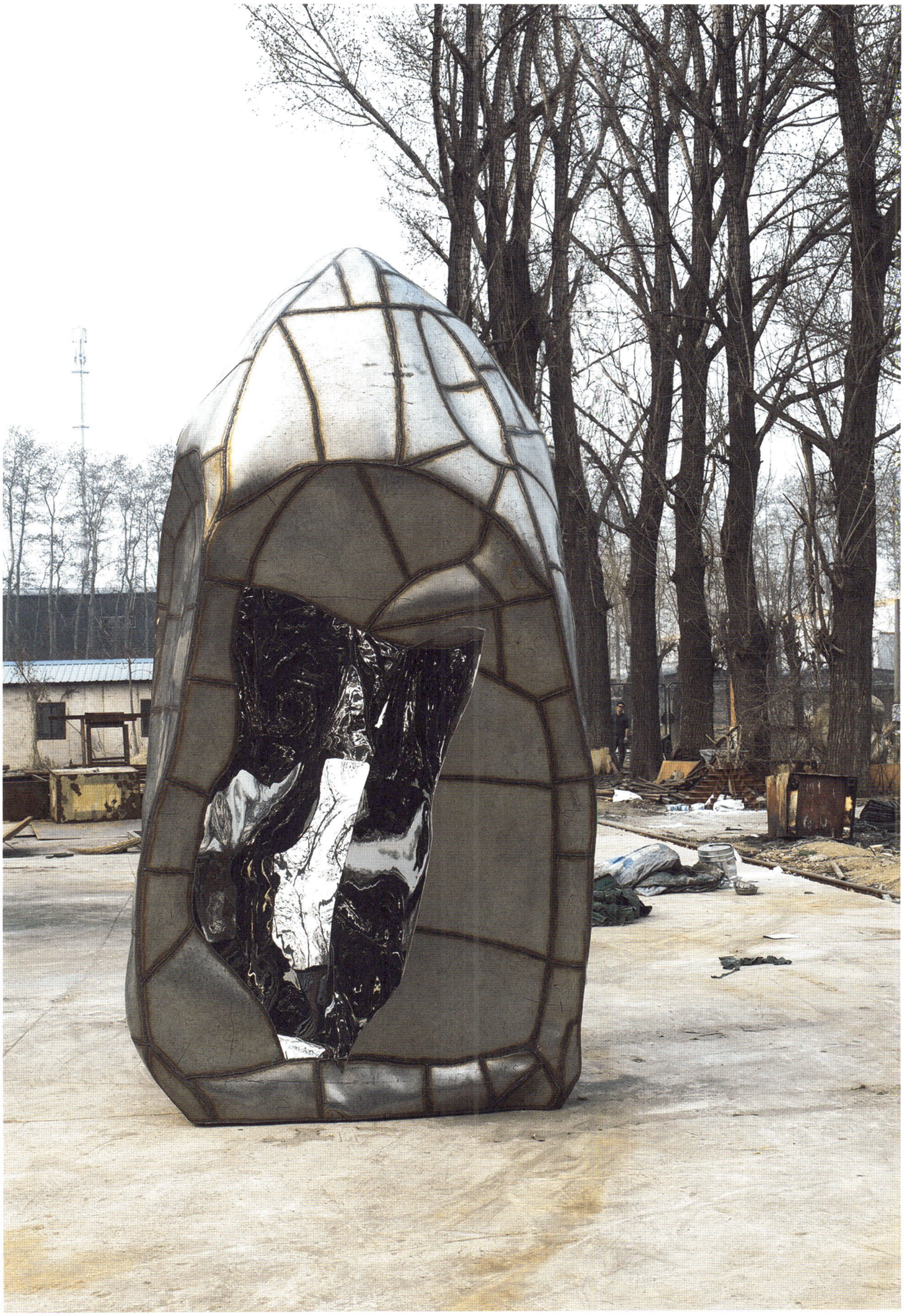

Date, 2016

and nature has become so artificial that one can no longer tell that a building is fundamentally a structure that rises out of the earth and into the sky. Moreover, most of the places that Vital *finds* are not widely known but usually very remote and in poorly accessible regions. Why? Because distant places spark the imagination.

Following this recipe, the sites that Vital has searched out over the past two decades contribute to making his SCARCH projects distant visions or even dream images. Our experience of them does not start when we set foot in them, but when we first hear about them and start building them in our imagination.

When Vital's former assistant, the Chilean architect Cristián Orellana Terrsy, told him in 2008 that an island of marble was for sale in the wild environs of Chilean Patagonia, Vital took immediate action. He traveled to Puerto Montt via Santiago, Chile, and from there spent hours driving on gravel roads to Lago General Carrera, one of the largest lakes in South America. The island he visited there is like a primeval mountain, its solid white marble rising up out of the immense lake, which mirrors the clear skies of Patagonia. Realizing that the island was too beautiful to build a house on it, he decided to transform it *into* a house.

Working with Orellana Terrsy and a group of local miners in the six years that followed, Vital succeeded in achieving the impossible: *NotOna* (2008–14 [pp. 160–73]), a space whose depth is comparable to our unconscious. Digging into the body of marble that constitutes the island, the group constructed a tunnel over 180 feet long. There, visitors come upon a cavelike sphere that allows a view of the lake, whose water appears in a big window at the lower end of the tunnel. Like a natural mirror, the water surface transfers the phenomena of the outside world to the inside space. Thus, as soon as the sun starts to set, the colors of the sky appear reflected on the water mirror, and the gradually diminishing light modulates the shadows within the space.

NotOna is a room that is defined by its relationship to the outside world. While we are in the belly or the uterus of the island, with the buried walls piled up behind us and behind them the entire dormant island, we perceive the phenomena of the outside world as if through a veil: only their essence succeeds in penetrating into the depths where, in solitary isolation, our thoughts are in harmony with the irrationality of the vastness, and our dreams are fathomless.[19]

Being inside *NotOna* is to go through a process of introspection. The effect is the opposite when looking at the island from the outside, where it seems stoic and withdrawn: the only evidence of Vital's artistic intervention is a white cube containing the residue of the marble that he excavated, and white marble paths winding like slender snakes around the island. With only one pale light from the window of the cave reaching the outside world at night, we are reminded of the light coming from a hermit's abode, which is symbolic of a man who keeps vigil: "all that glows sees."[20] This solitary light suggests reading *NotOna* as a one-eyed house; that makes it not only an underground house with cosmic roots, but also a house whose seeing eye has a direct path to the unconscious.[21]

INDONESIA

In 2013, Vital traveled to Flores, Indonesia, for the first time. The name of this island, which is located at the southern tip of Indonesia close to Timor-Leste, appealed to him. Vital decided to fly via Bali to Ende, the island's small airport. Naturally the name Ende appealed to him as well, since it made him feel as if he had reached the end of the world.

After reaching Moni, a village in the tropical forest not far from Mount Kelimutu—a mountain with three volcanic lakes that constantly change color—Vital decided to build his *House to Watch the 3 Volcanoes* (2017 [pp. 208–15]). Together with Tam, an inhabitant of Moni whose radiant white smile illuminates the night, he began to build a structure almost 43 feet tall and 75 feet long, conceived for the contemplation of Mount Kelimutu.

19. Bachelard, *The Poetics of Space*, 18: "When it comes to excavated grounds, our dreams have no limit."
20. Bachelard, 34.
21. Note that seeing is often mnemonic since it is based on pre-existing perceptions: in perception, the outer and inner are thus irreversibly linked.

House to Watch the 3 Volcanoes is perhaps the strangest work Vital has ever made: it complicates the dialectics of inside and outside to such an extent that we start to question the very skin we live in. The structure comprises two arms of increasing width, one of which stretches out on the ground in front while the other rises straight up into the sky. While the building's façade is of smooth, white concrete, its interior is clad in straw and bamboo, materials that in Flores are ordinarily used for the façades of buildings. When we walk into the structure through a back door, we enter a complex, surreal space: standing inside and looking up, we see cladding of brown straw reminiscent of a hirsute inner life. Once again, we feel as if we had been dropped into a kind of organism. When we look straight ahead, our gaze is channeled by horizontally arranged bamboo poles until it reaches the front door of the structure, which leads to the rampant green vegetation of the island. But if we climb the structure via the precariously suspended outdoor stairs, we walk up the white outside wall until we reach a small terrace that affords a view of Mount Kelimutu's three volcanic lakes.

Surreal and manifold, *House to Watch the 3 Volcanoes* confronts us with an inverted universe that subverts patterns of seeing and thinking: We need a key to unlock a door that leads inside, whereupon we find ourselves outside. Without a key, however, we can walk up the outside and reach the core of the house from which we can look outside.[23] To borrow Handke's expression, it is an "innerworld of the outerworld of the innerworld."[24]

In literature, the dialectics of inside and outside often serves as a metaphor for the debate on phenomena of internalization and externalization and questions of subjectivity. While the Austrian novelist Handke uses descriptions of the world outside to refer to his own inner consciousness, the French philosopher Gilles Deleuze complicates the distinction between inside and outside by introducing the notion of folding. Deleuze advances a critique of typical accounts of subjectivity: instead of presuming a simple differentiation between exteriority and interiority, a simple division between surface and depth, he proposes the concept of the fold to suggest that the inside is nothing more than a fold of the outside. To have, in this sense, is to fold that which is outside inside.[25]

Upon applying these philosophical insights to Vital's sculptural architecture, we realize that his work not only makes us see or recognize certain phenomena, it also enables us to absorb them into our consciousness so that they become part of our *selves*.

WINDOWS TO THE WORLD

While writing about Vital's SCARCH projects, I have often wondered whether I was merely describing or by now imagining. This question is eminently relevant to Vital's oeuvre as a whole, particularly in view of his ability to take familiar things that have settled down in memory and transform them into something miraculous that challenges the mind's eye. Take a look at *Date* (2016 [p. 21]): the fruit-shaped sculpture is almost 10 feet tall, the outside rough with traces of sculptural work but the inside shiny and smooth as a mirror. The resulting incongruence invites us to start imagining anew. Vital's SCARCH projects elicit a similar response. Often conceived for the contemplation of a natural phenomenon, they function as windows to the world. And when we step up to them, something strange happens: we are opened.[26]

In the course of his research into the minimal conditions of the habitat, Vital asks about the fundamental elements of architecture. What is a window? Can you enter a house if it has no doors? What makes a tower a tower? And what is the poetic essence of a house? His answers to these questions are as poetic as they are radical. In 2005, he titled a rock formation in the Sahara in Niger *The 10th House* [pp. 142–43]. Embraced by

23. Interestingly, *House to Watch the 3 Volcanoes* is among the few projects that are locked and require a key. Most of Vital's works are freely accessible. Even so, *House to Watch the 3 Volcanoes* is not private: the people of Moni can regularly climb the stairs to look at their volcano.
24. Handke, *The Innerworld of the Outerworld of the Innerworld*.
25. Gilles Deleuze and Jonathan Strauss, "The Fold," Yale French Studies, no. 80, 1991, 227–47.
26. Handke, *The Innerworld of the Outerworld of the Innerworld*, 41: "I go to the window and I am opened."

reddish desert boulders, it forms a cave that provides shade. And “shade, too, can be inhabited.”[27] In the Brazilian Amazon in 2016, Vital declared a small, overgrown refuge to be a *Cathedral* [pp. 202–03]. Nature is, after all, the oldest temple.

The carefully exploited freedom that underlies Vital’s poetic gestures applies to his drawings as well. They are both an outlet for emotions and a playground for experimentation. Vital often draws while traveling, but his destinations do not usually have paint supply stores so he purchases materials for his drawings at pharmacies and hardware shops, producing work that consists of whatever was available: tape, cotton swabs, silicone patches, and plastic bags [see pp. 27–67]. These astounding, often three-dimensional, drawings invariably make us see both the medium of drawing and the subject matter with fresh eyes: cotton gauze produces a *Hotel for Ardez* (2009 [p. 31]), *Synagogue for Tel Aviv* (2009 [p. 36]) consists of plastic straws and tape, and *Pavilion for NotOna Island* (2009 [p. 33]) and *2 Pavilions for Tarasp* (2018 [p. 49]) are made of dental floss and knee-highs, respectively.

The drawings are not necessarily preparatory sketches but rather parallel thought experiments, and although Vital’s built structures are less playful, they are equally subversive. Benefiting from his artistic license, Vital rebels against the traditional fullness of houses and reduces architectural forms or structures to essentials, as strikingly illustrated by *Marble Tower*. The moment he moves beyond the essence of form, as in *House to Watch the 3 Volcanoes*, he challenges us not only to question every single detail but also its implications. Why are certain materials used only for the outside and not for the interior? What about the dialectics of inside and outside and how does that relate to the dialectics of open and closed? Why is everything always getting locked and what is there outside that is not inside, and vice versa? Is living in an abode an act that excludes—that is directed against—nature?

To repeat, Vital’s SCARCH projects are not spaces of well-being, but rather spaces that produce a new reality of being. At times minimalist, at times archaic, at times utopian, most of Vital’s projects are conceived as poetic spaces for solitude and contemplation. When we visit them we are called upon to activate and approach perception in a variety of ways, ranging from introspection to extrospection. It makes sense for Vital to enlist the house as a means of communicating his message. After all, the image of the house flows in both directions: “they are in us, as much as we are in them.”[28]

Translated by Catherine Schelbert

27. Bachelard, *The Poetics of Space*, 132.
28. Bachelard, 37.

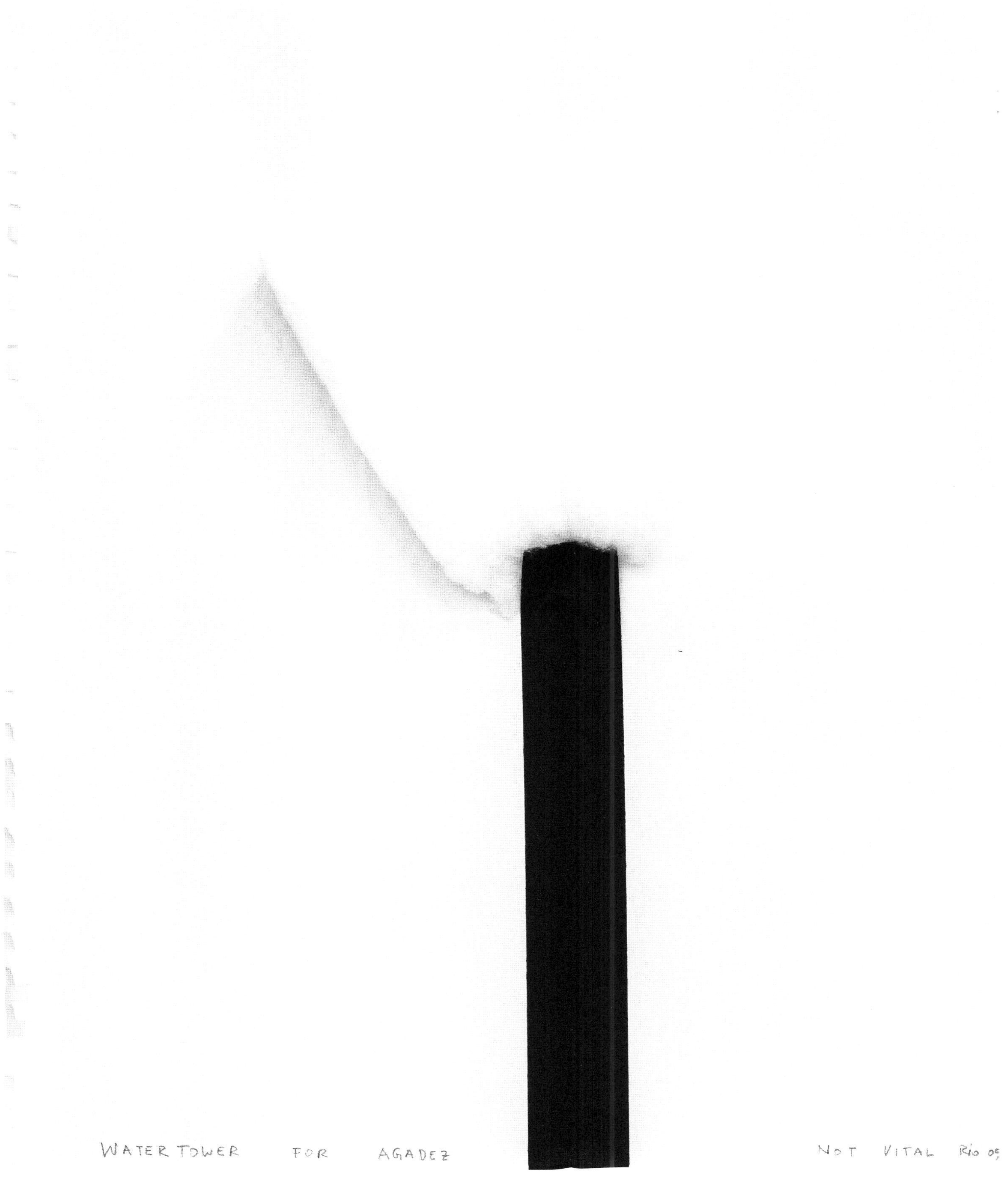

 Water Tower for Agadez, 2004

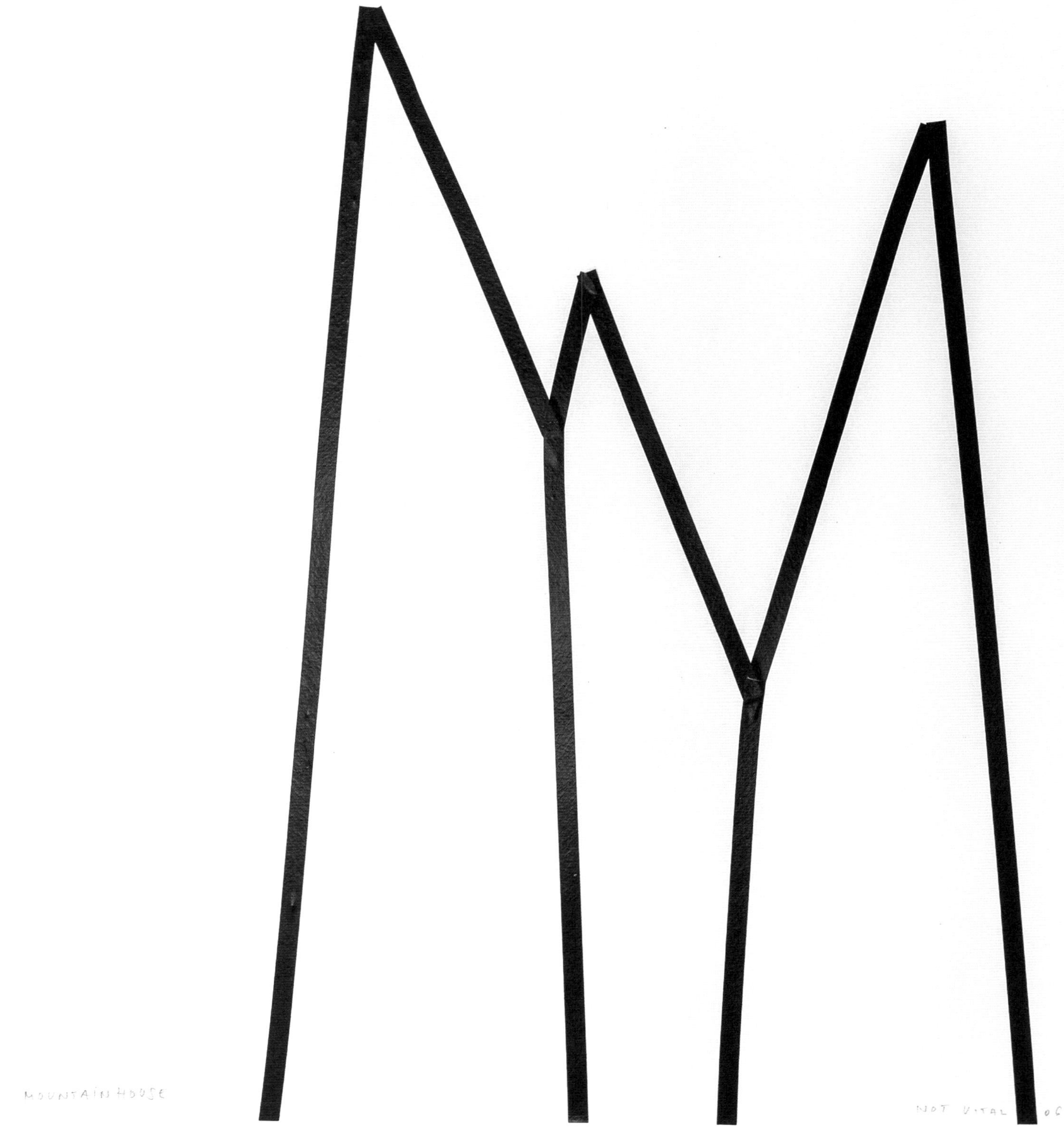

Mountain House, 2006

Hotel for Ardez, 2009

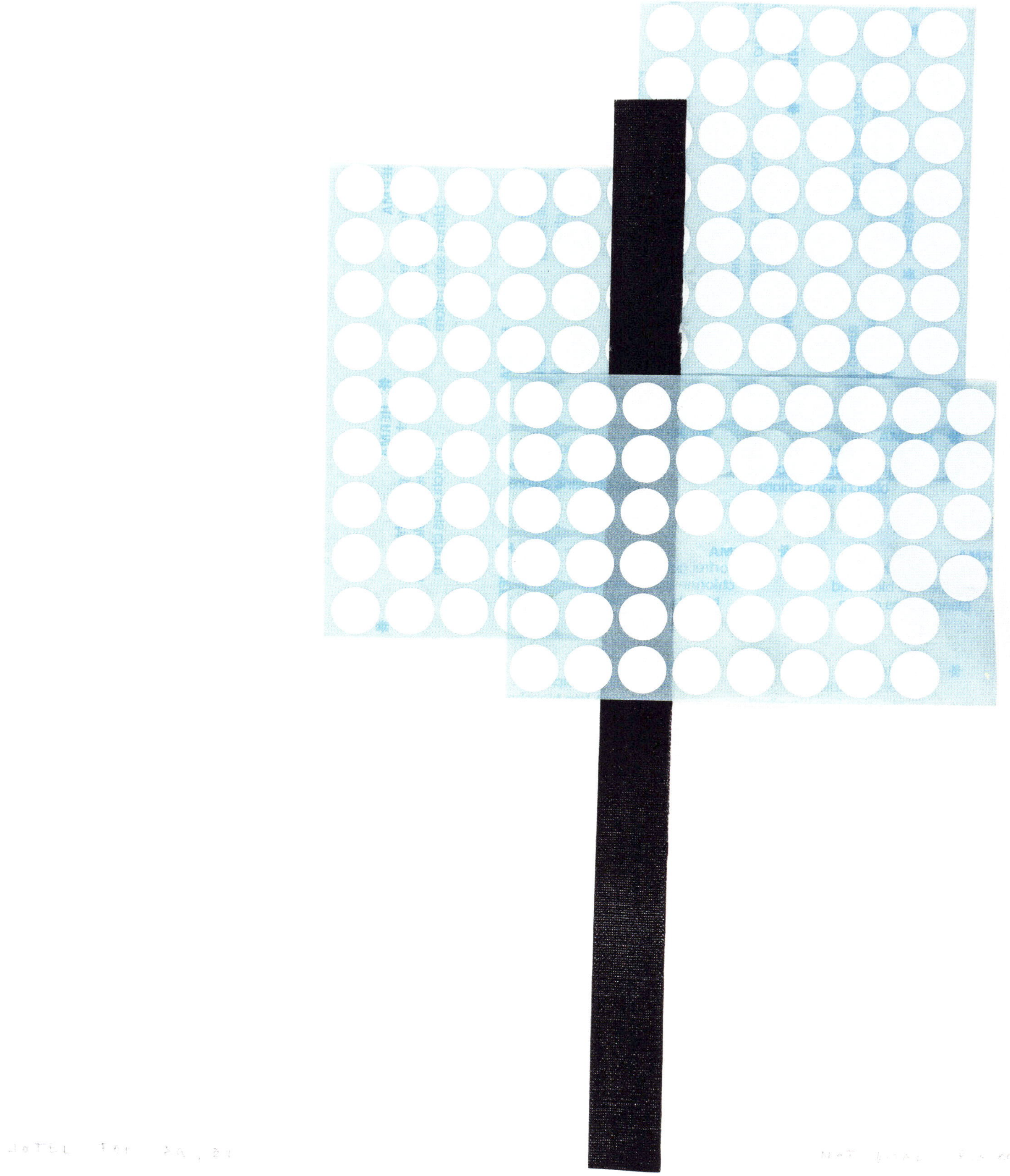

Hotel for Aa, ZH, 2009

Pavilion for NotOna Island, 2009

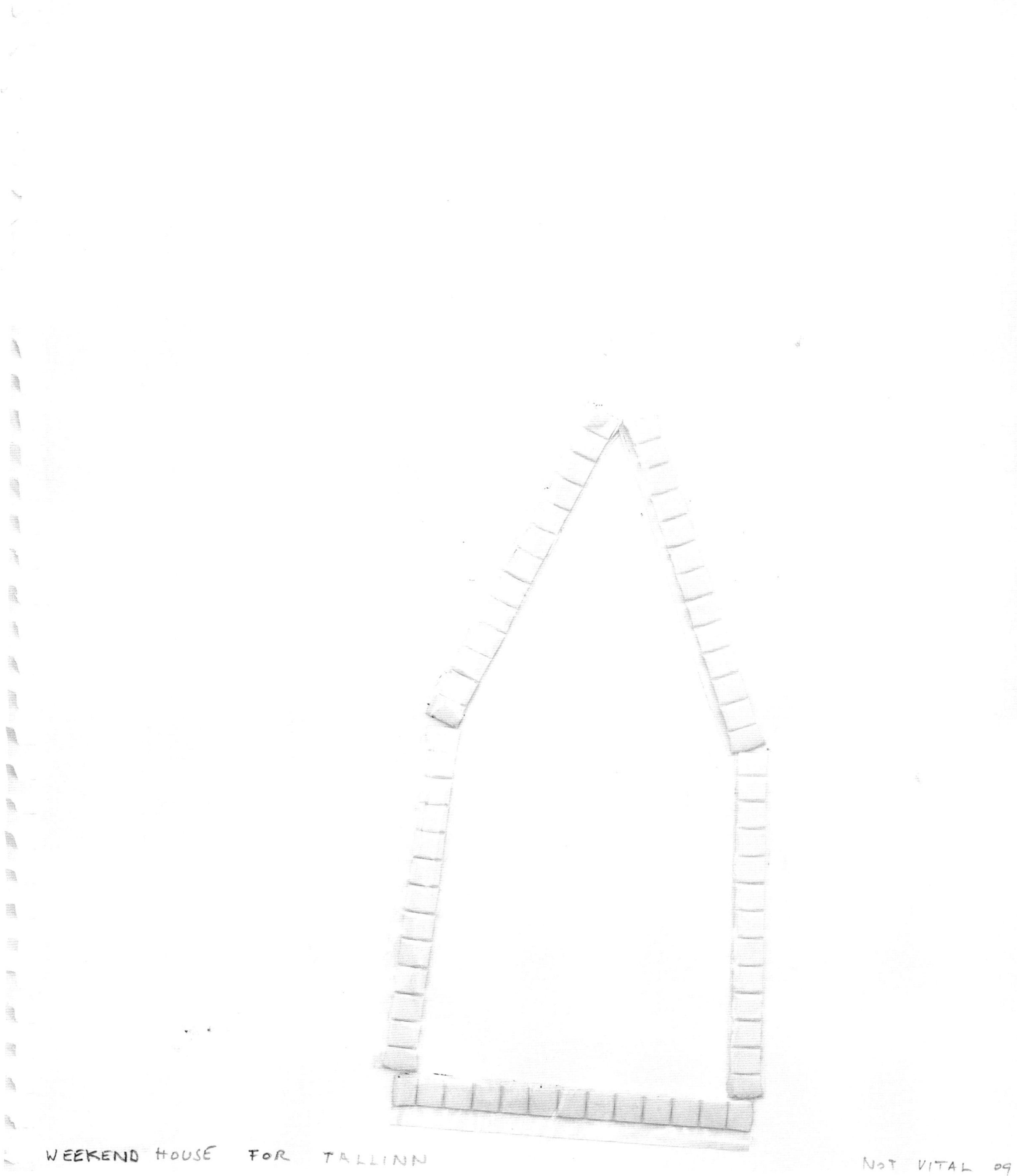

Weekend House for Tallinn, 2009

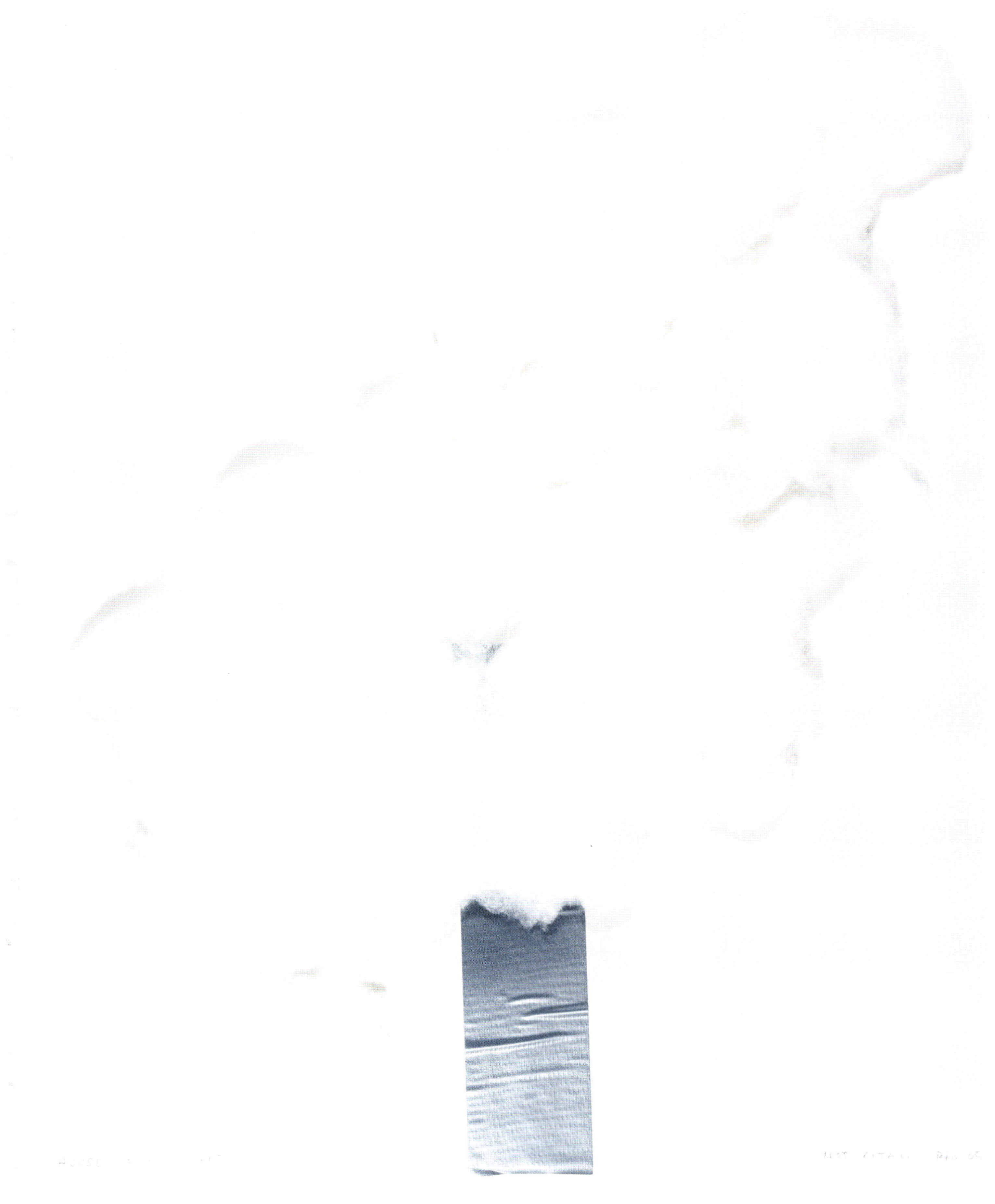

House for Sent, 2009

Synagogue for Tel Aviv, 2009

Entrance + Exit to the Tunnel at NotOna, 2010

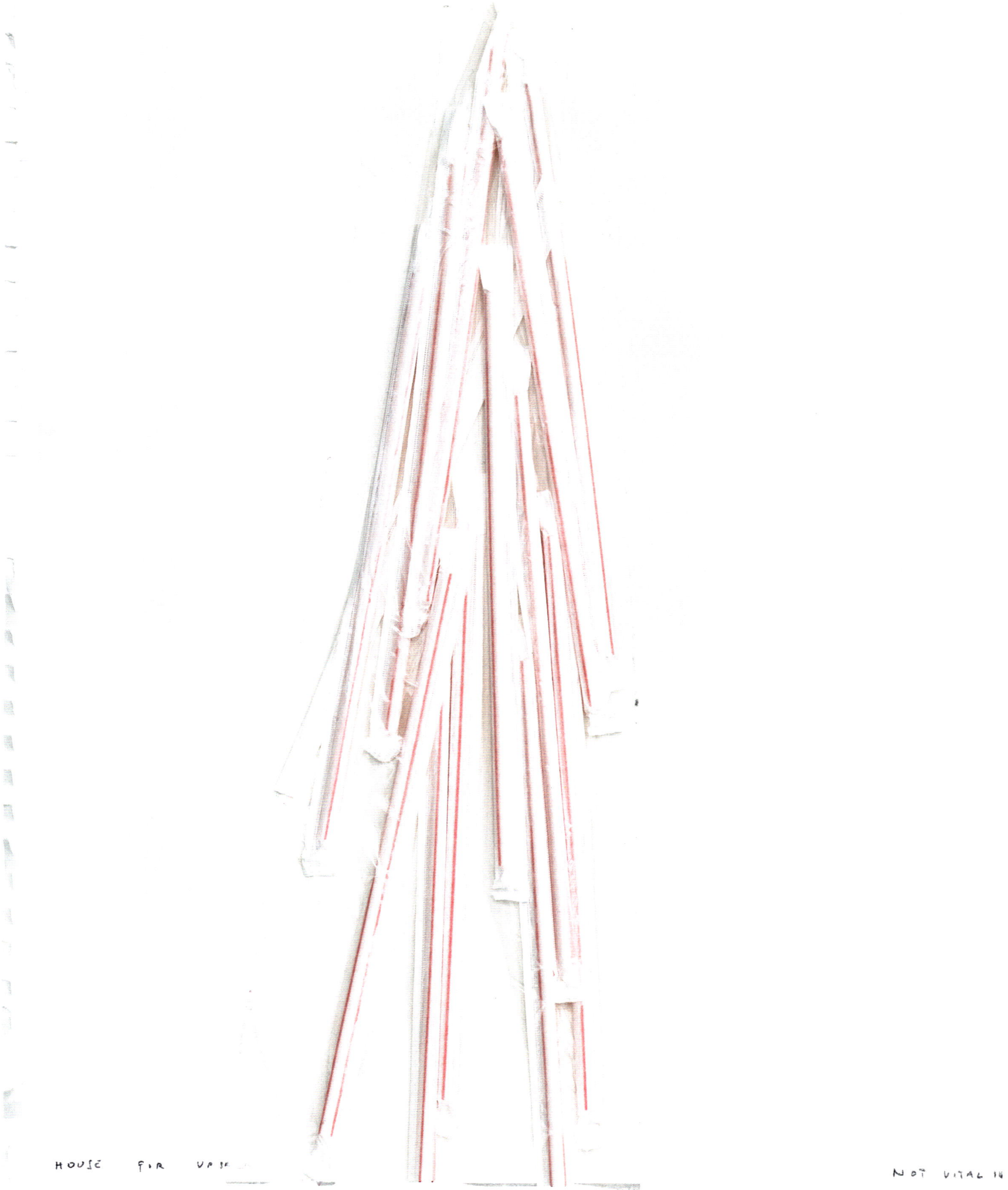

House for Upsala, 2010

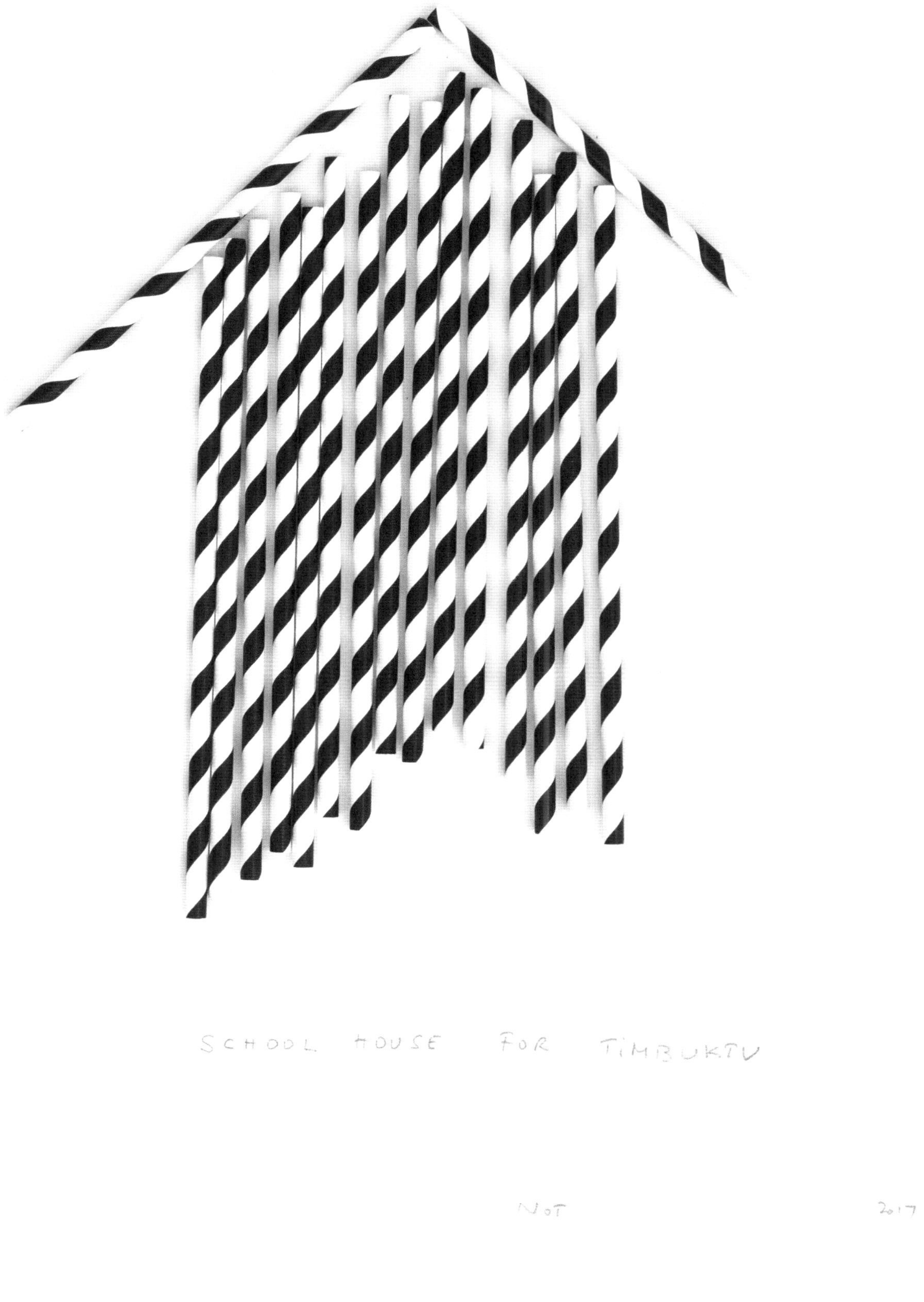

School House for Timbuktu, 2017

 Tower, 2017

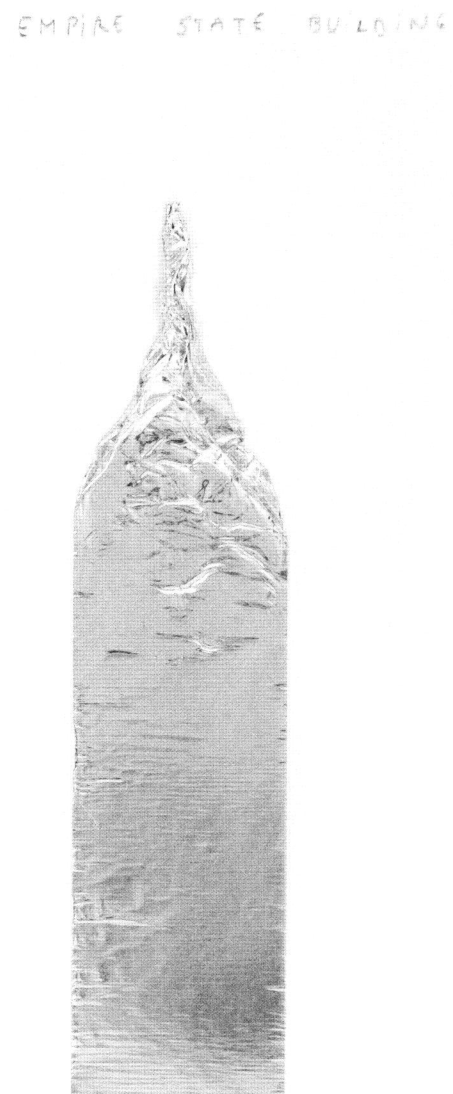

Empire State Building, 2017

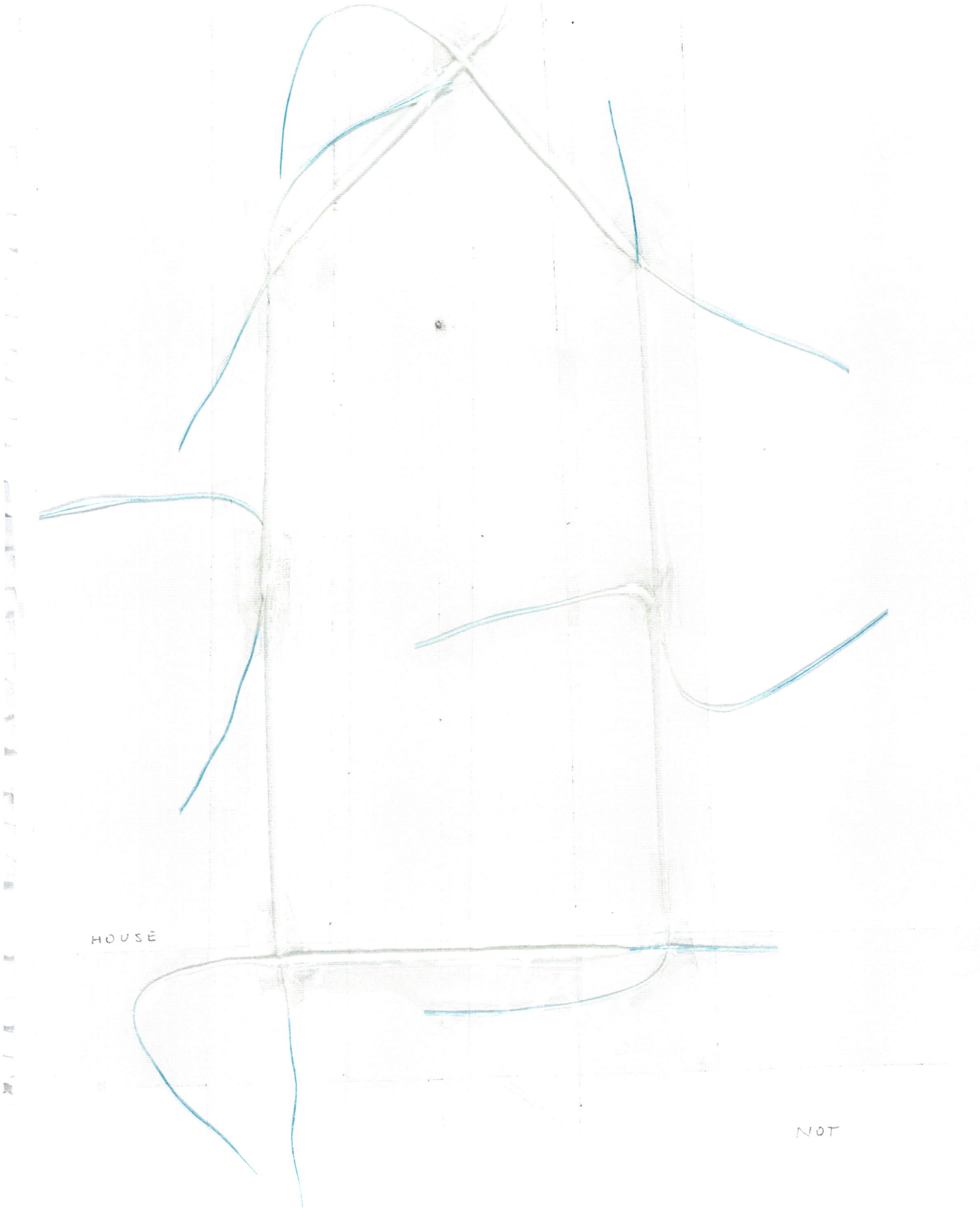

House, 2017

 Tower, 2017

Islands in Tonga, 2018

 Davos, 2018

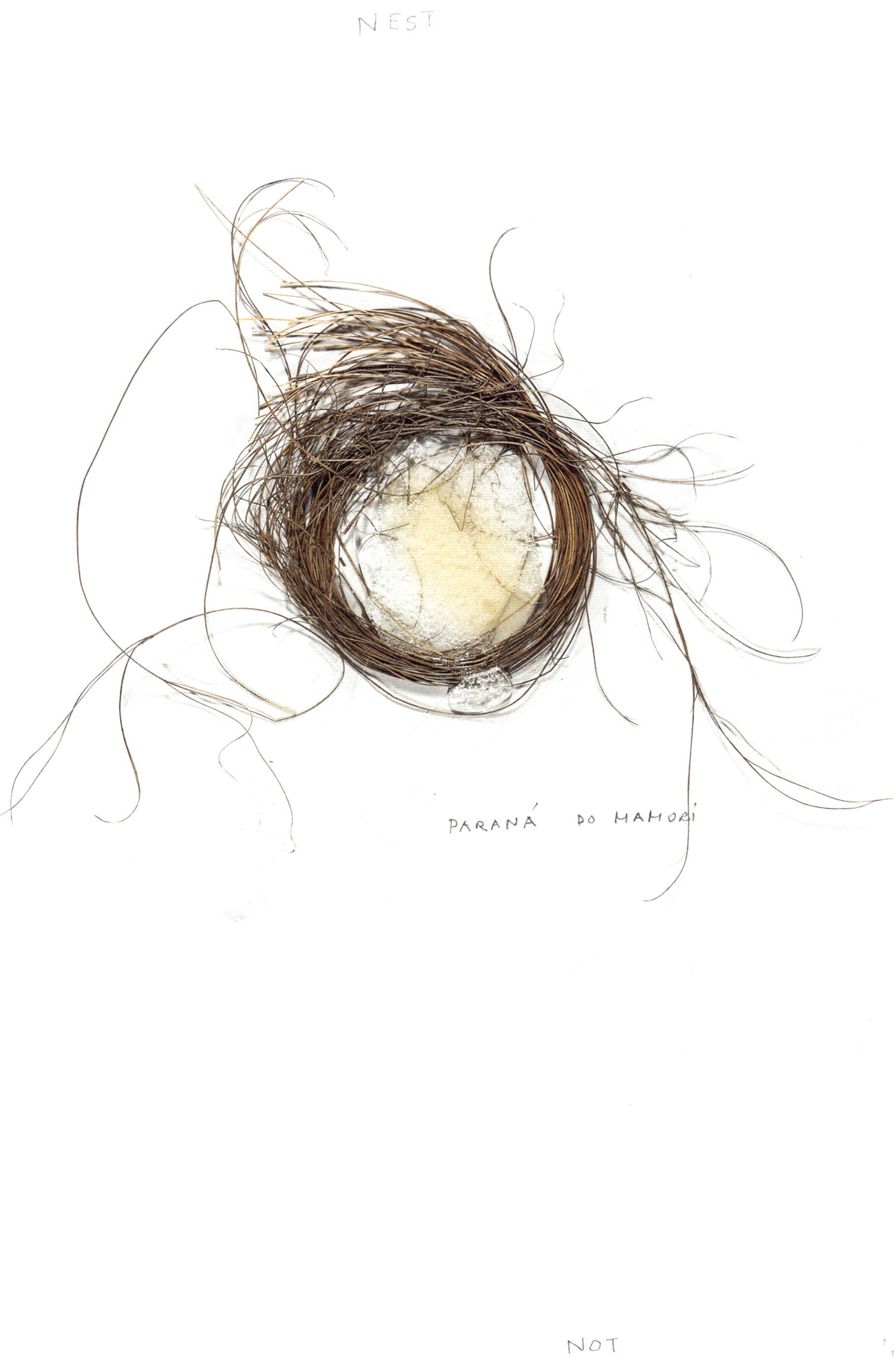

Nest, 2018

 Landing, 2018

Cabana, 2018

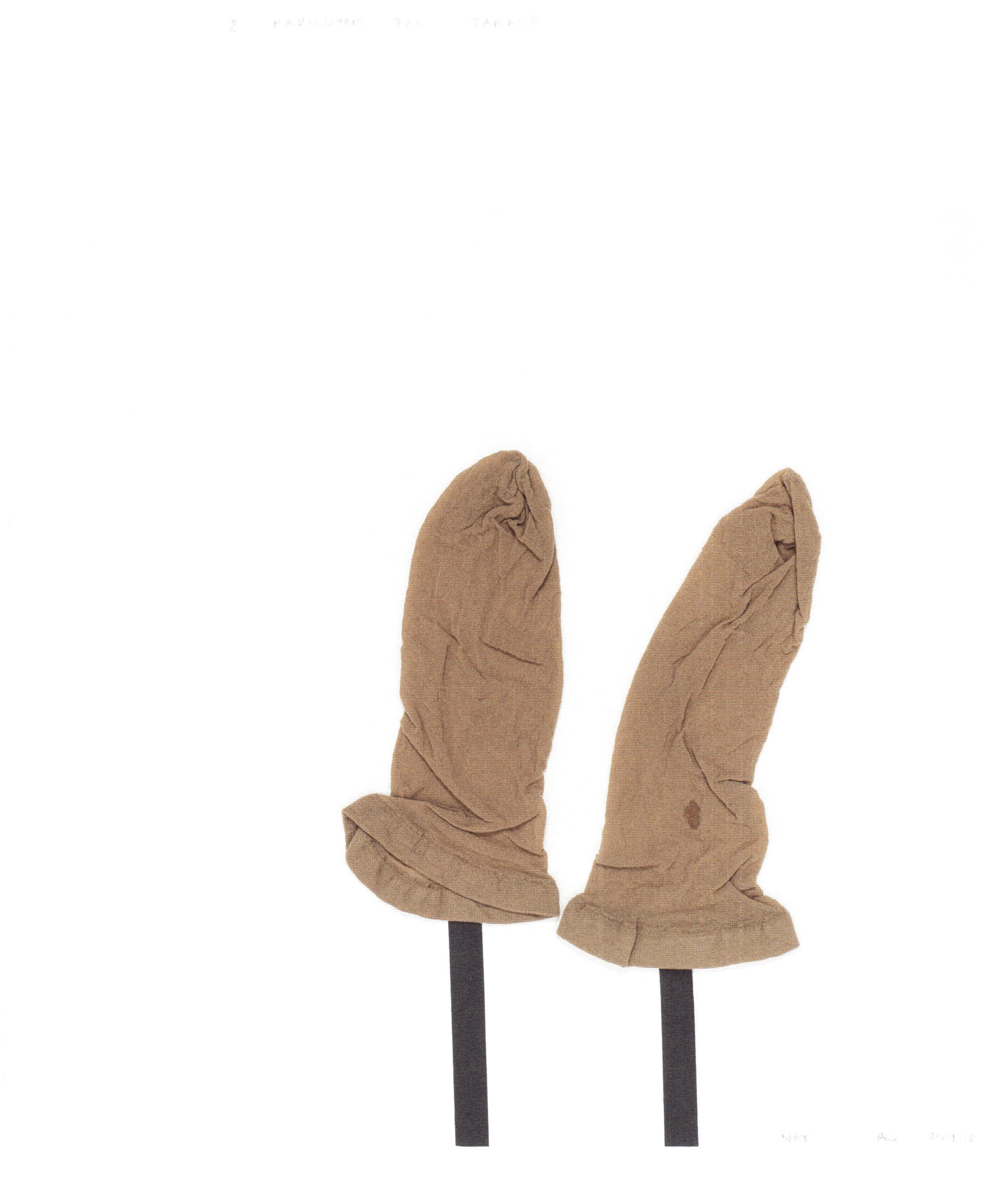

 2 Pavilions for Tarasp, 2018

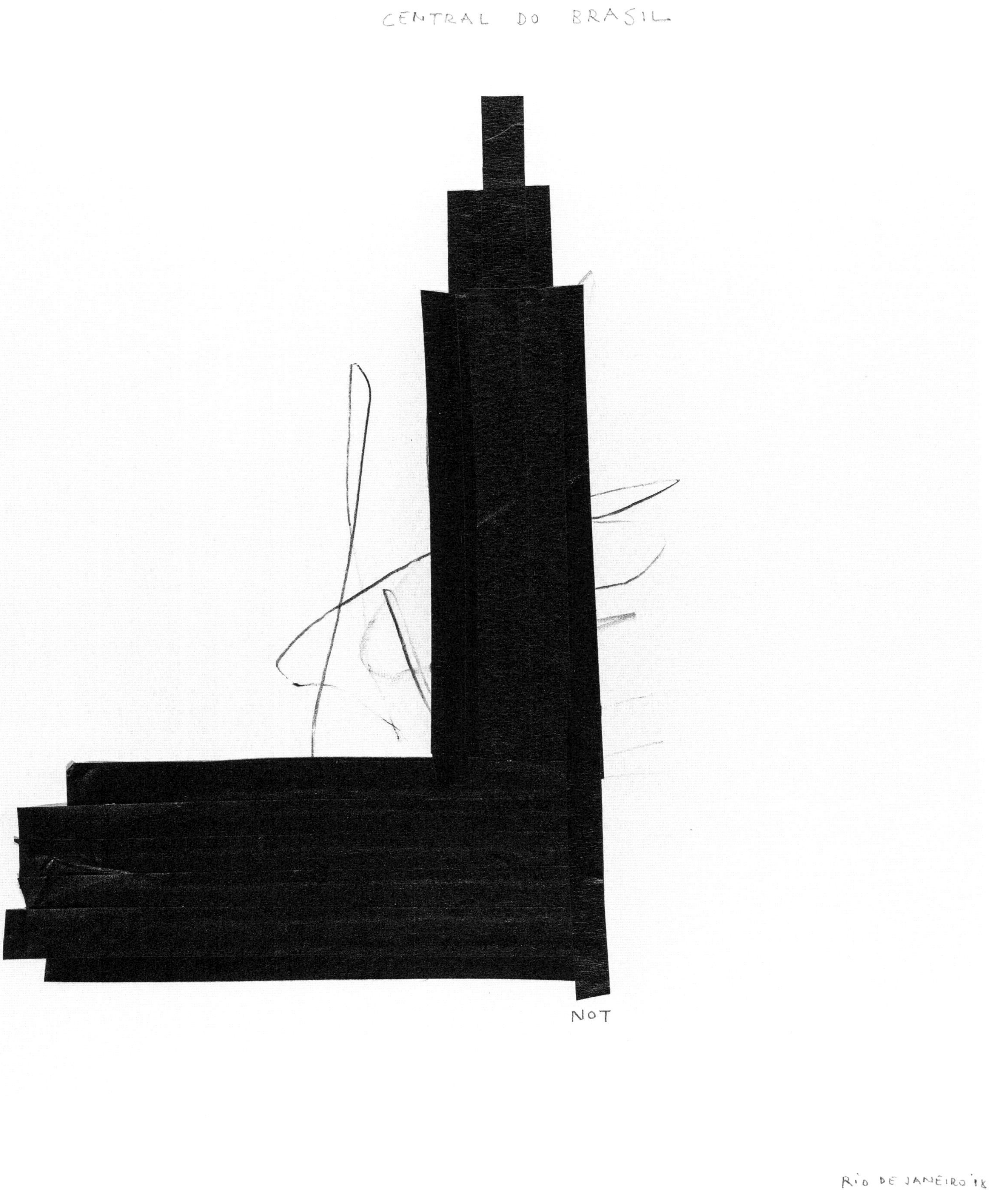

Central do Brasil, 2018

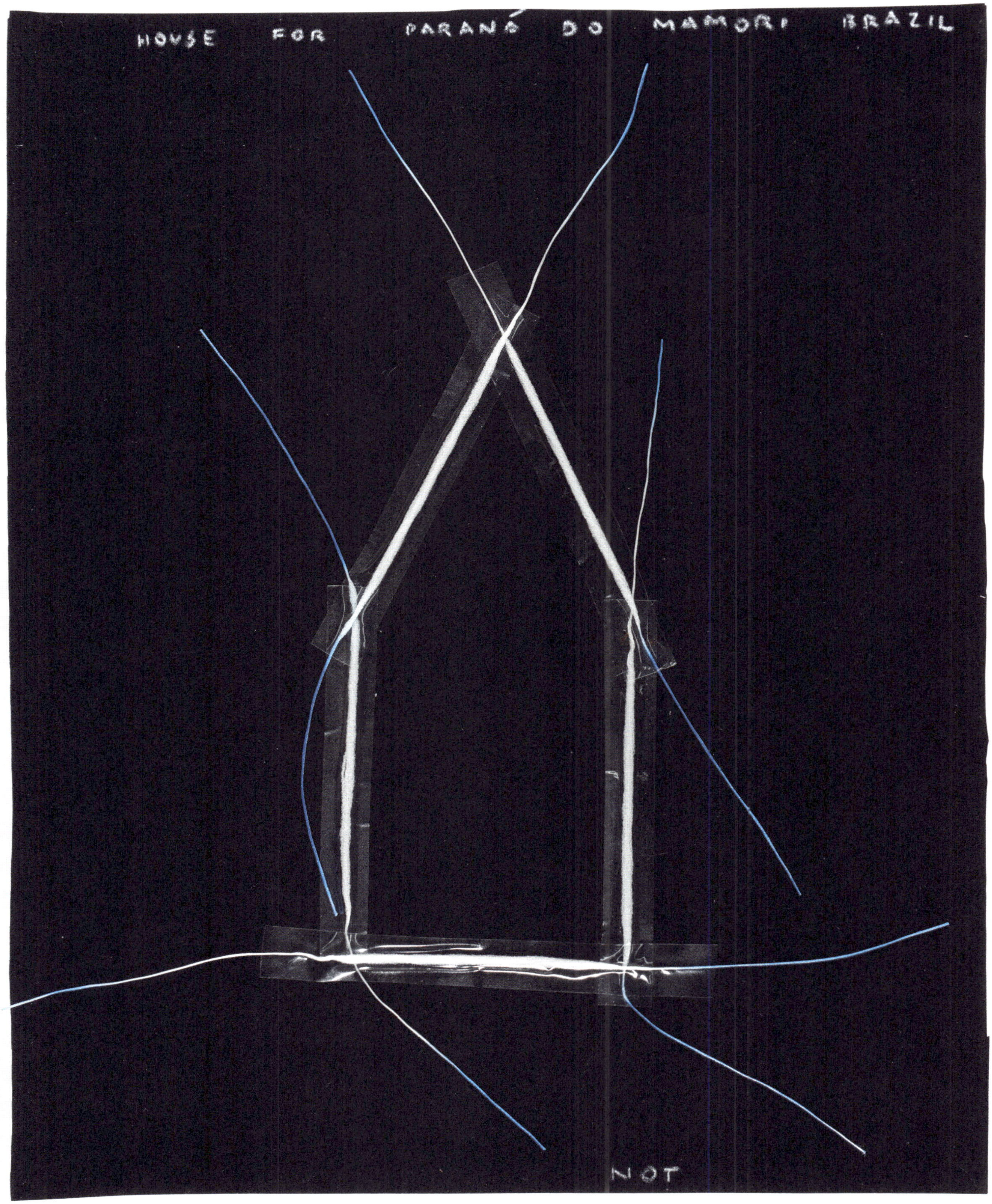

 House for Paraná do Mamori, 2018

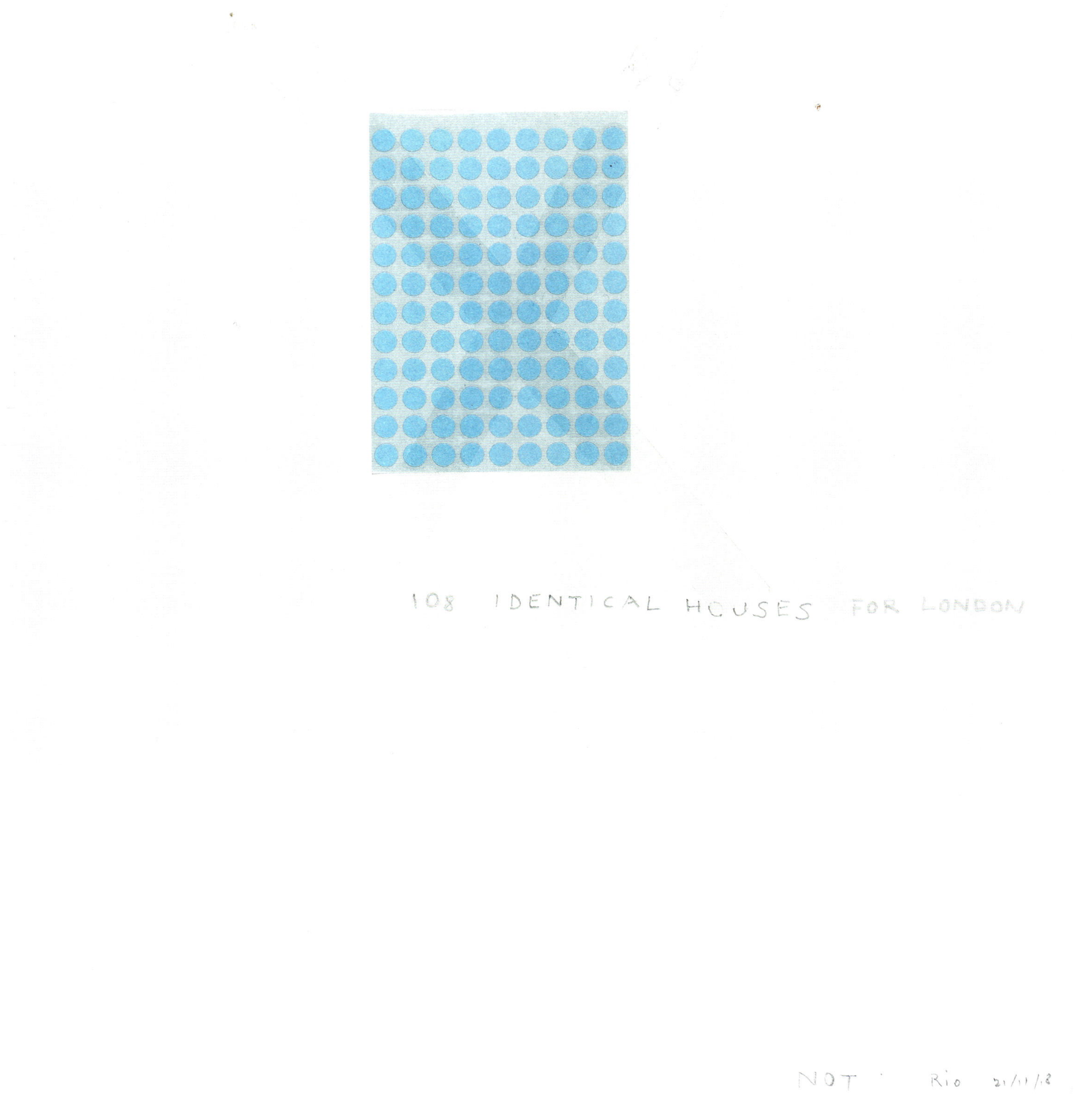

108 Identical Houses for London, 2018

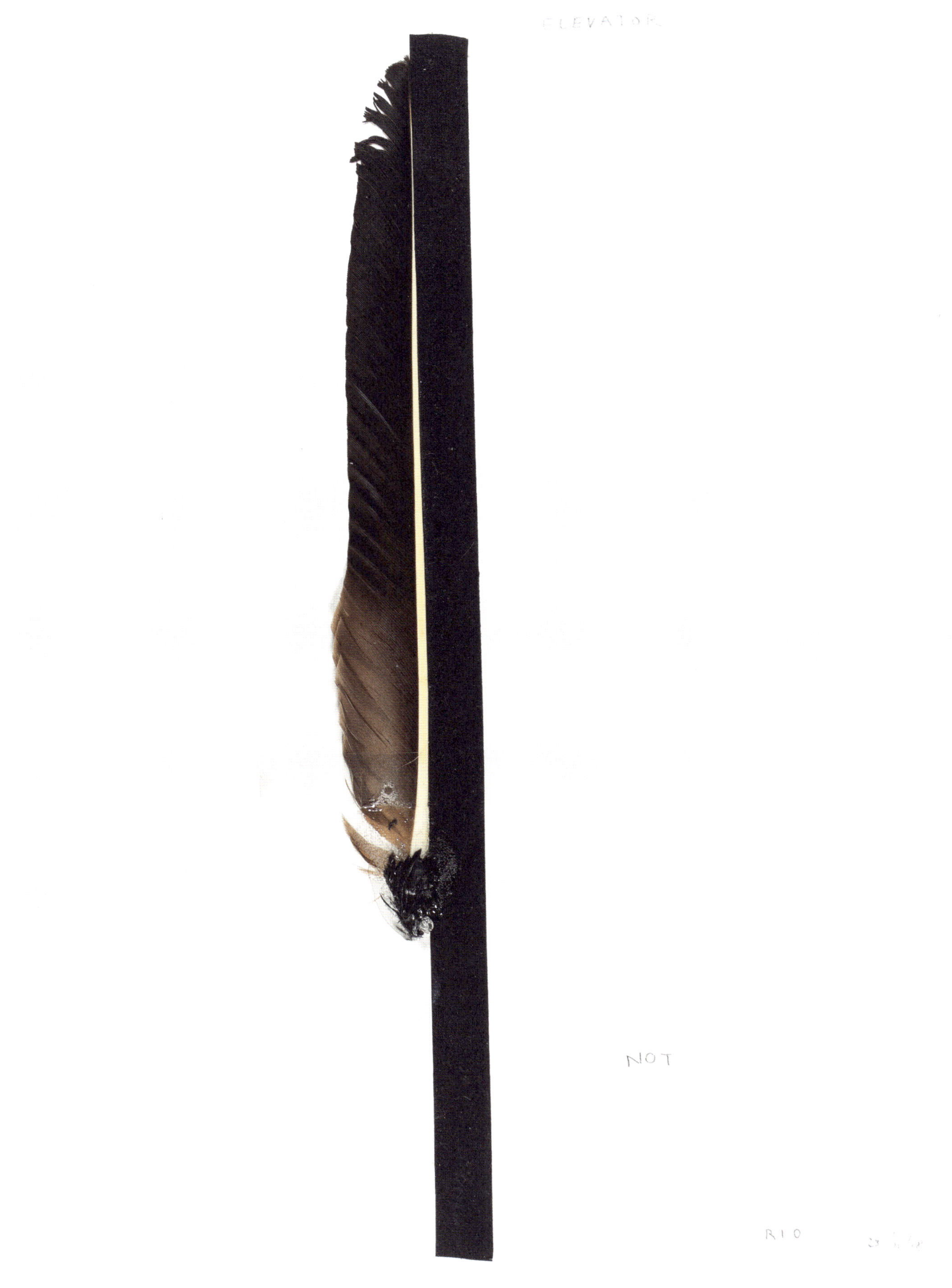

Elevator, 2018

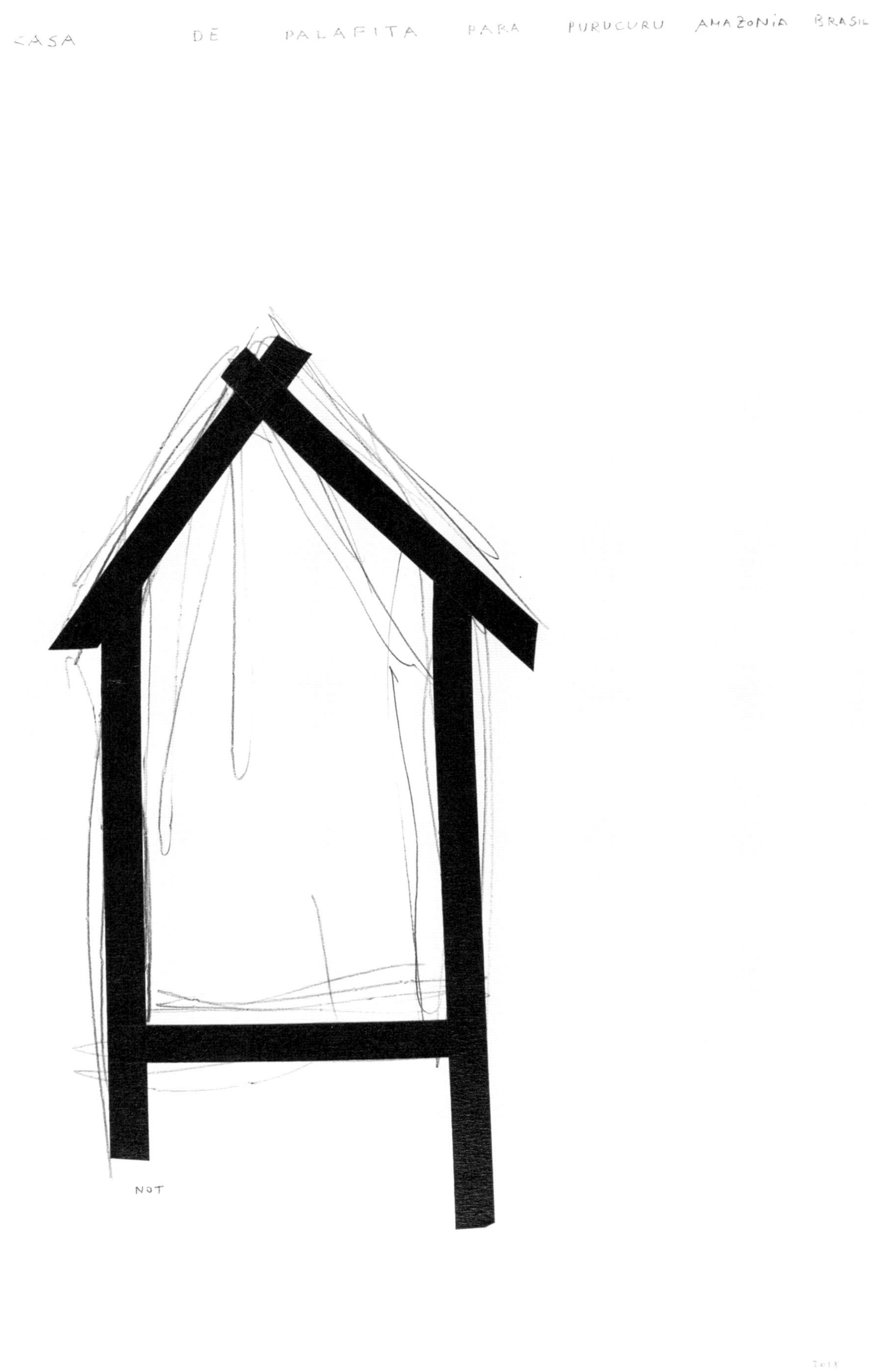

Casa de palafita para Purucuru Amazonia Brasil, 2018

 Centro do Rio, 2018

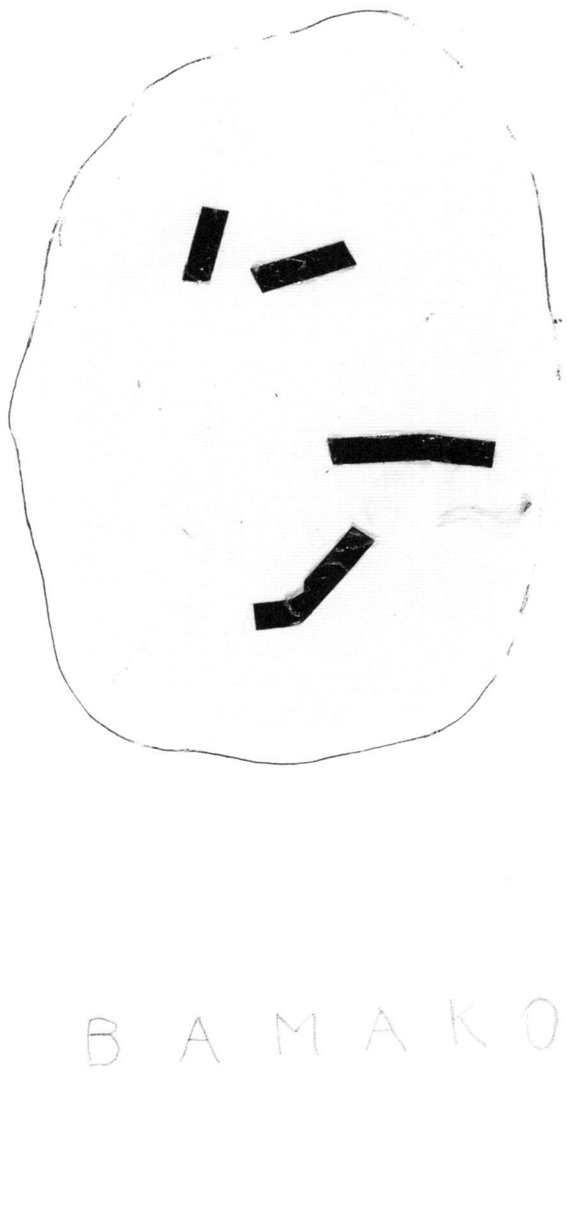

Bamako, 2018

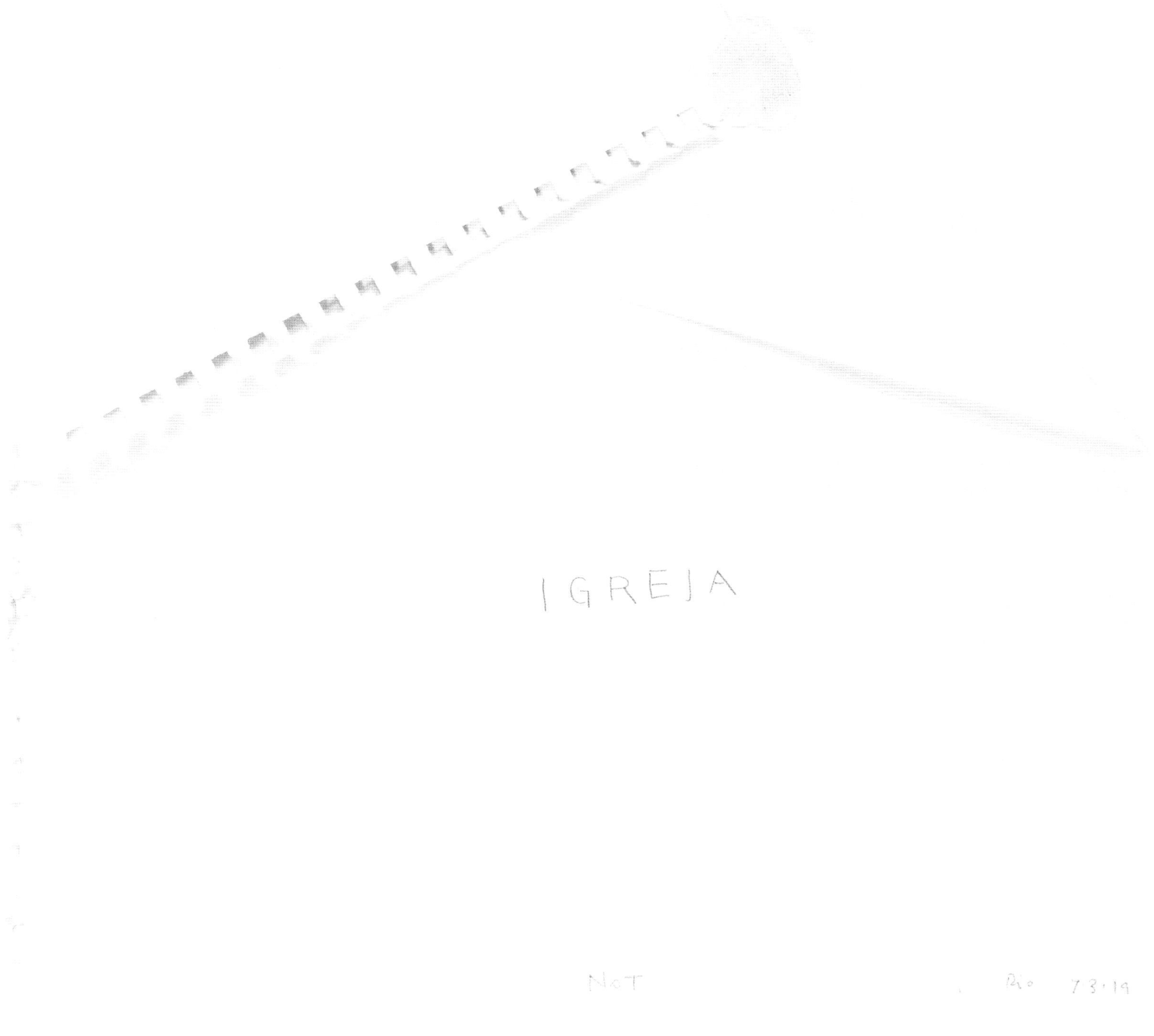

Igreja, 2019

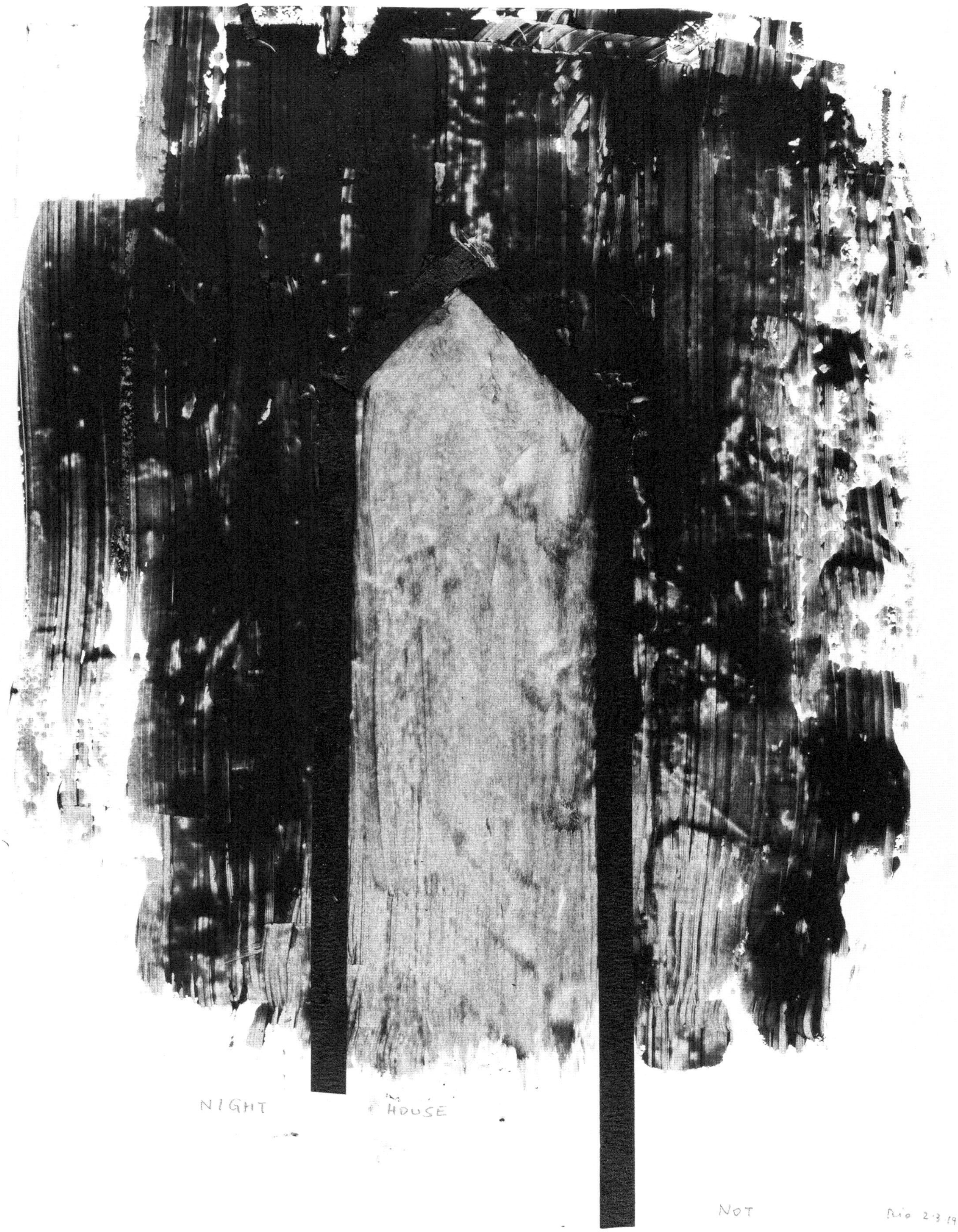

Night House, 2019

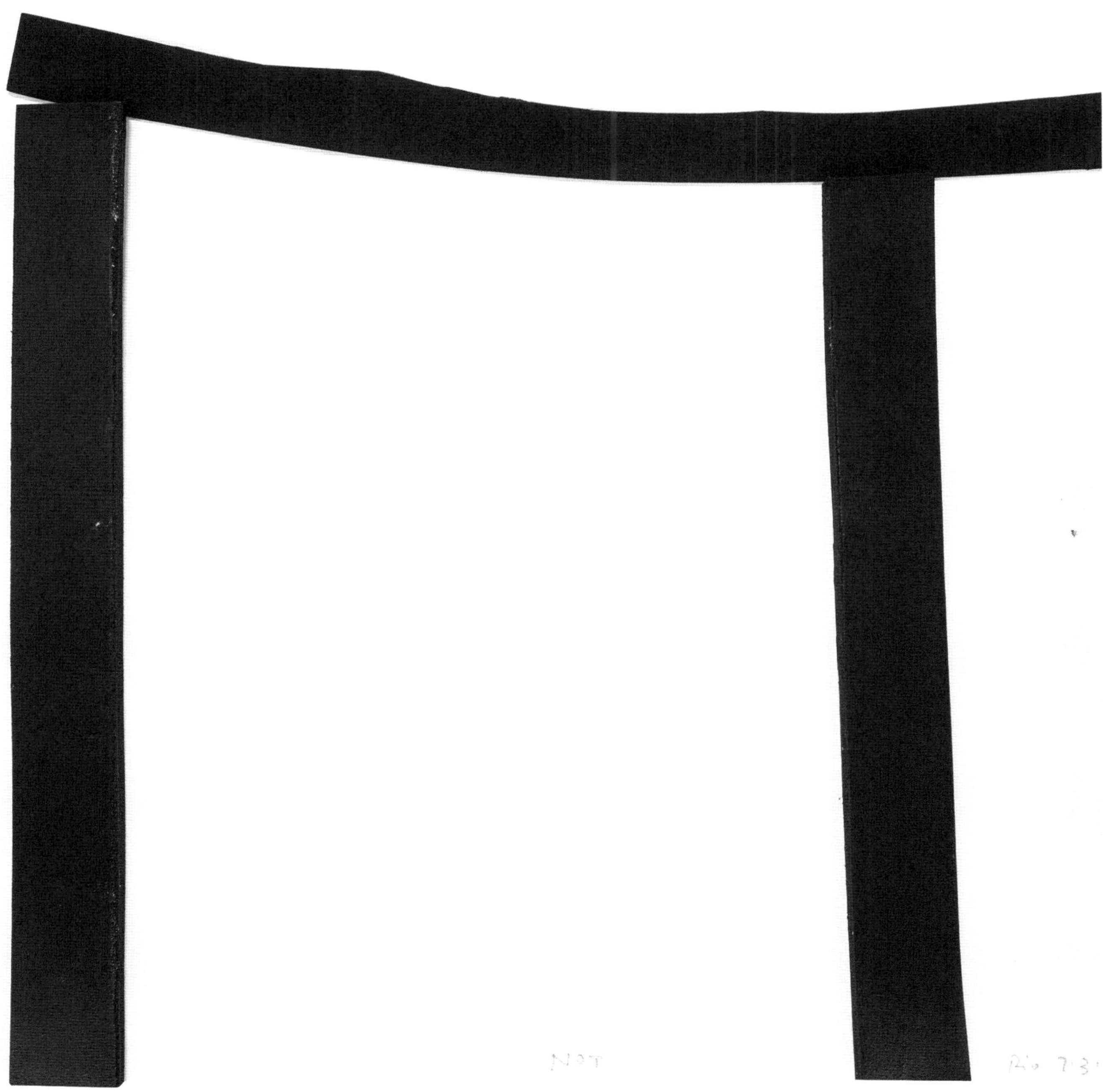

Bridge, 2019

Light Pole, 2019

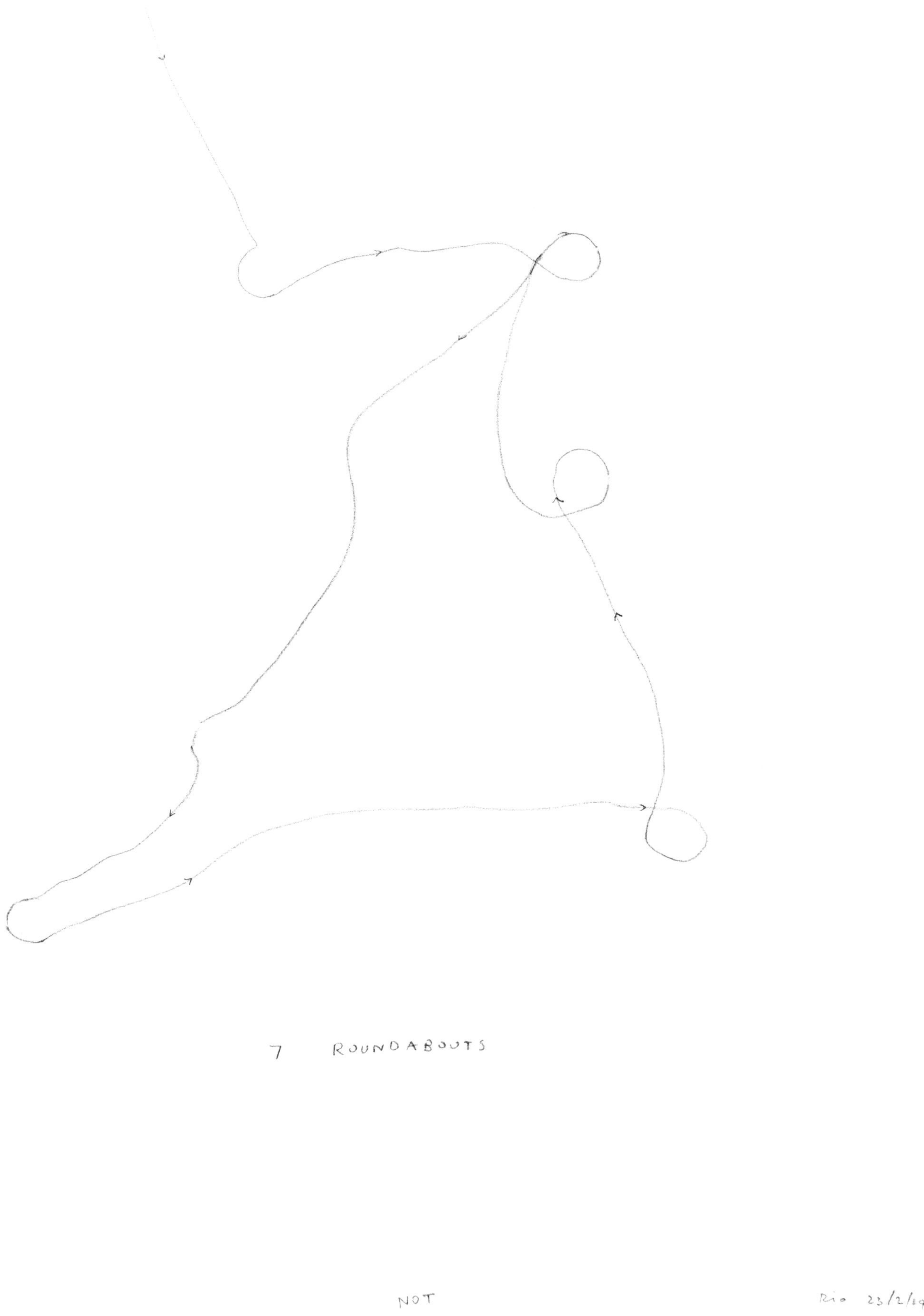

7 Roundabouts, 2019

Belo Horizonte, 2019

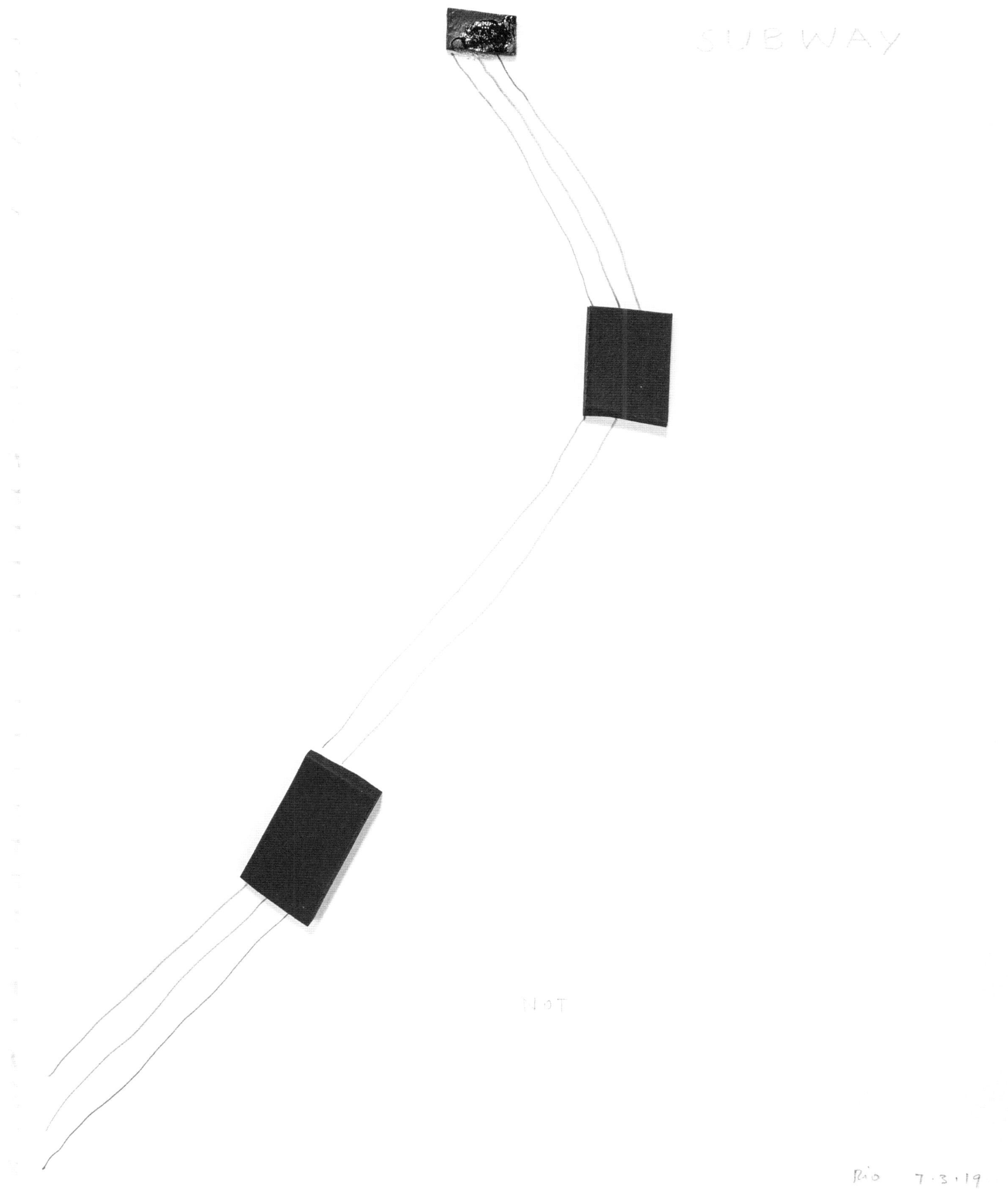

 Subway, 2019

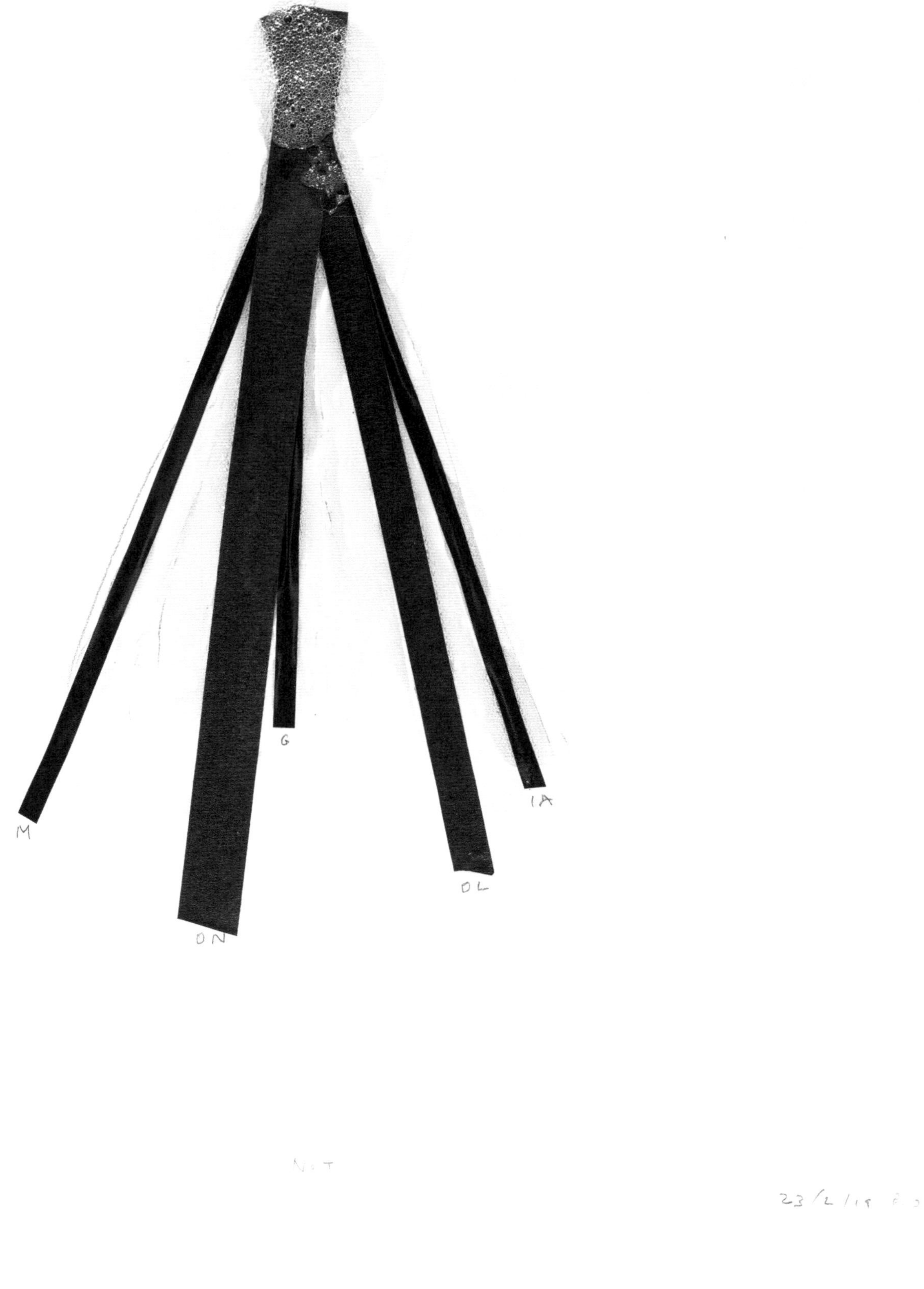

Mongolia, 2019

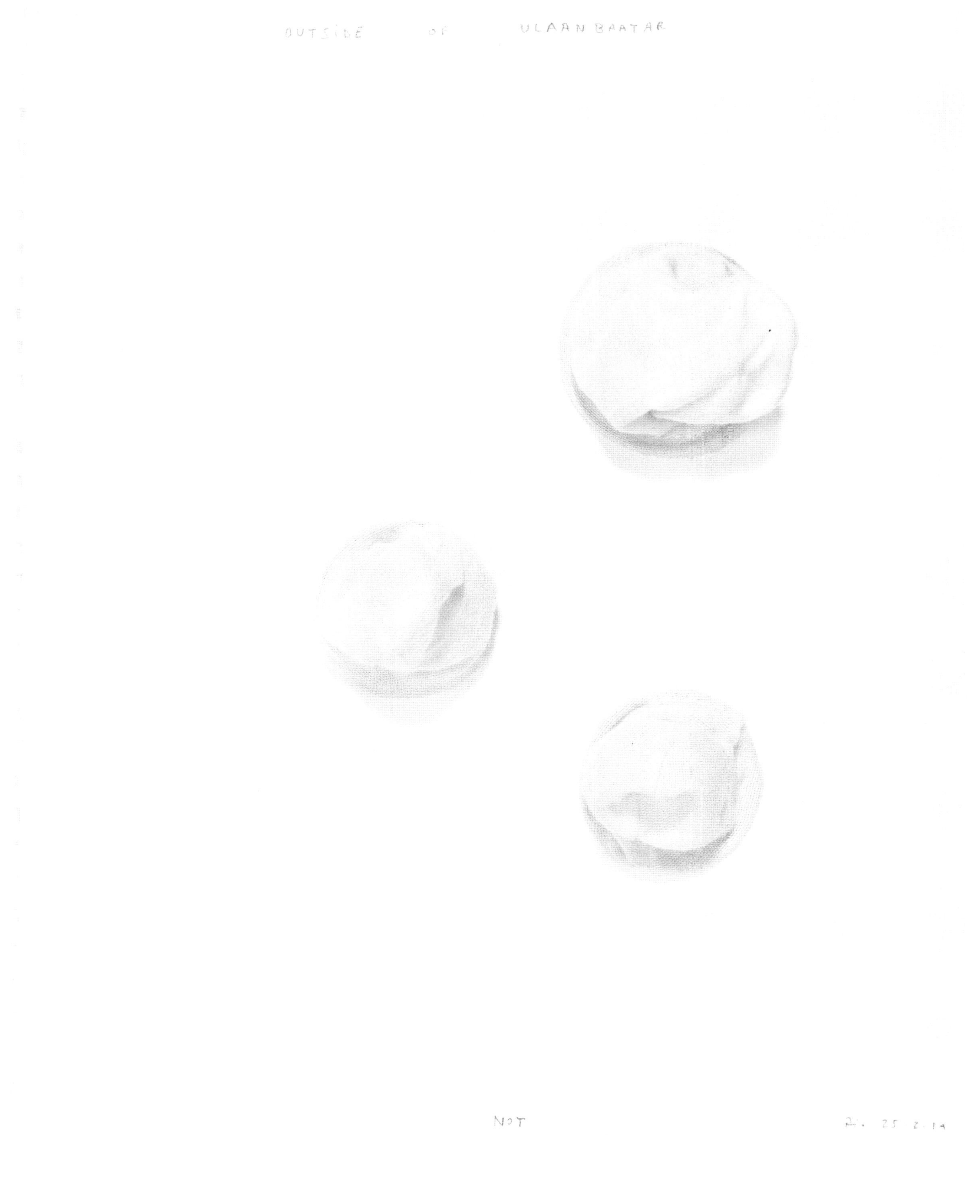

Outside of Ulaanbaatar, 2019

Earthquake, 2019

Just Enough to Make the Sun Set: The Stories of Not Vital

Philip Jodidio

Where is the boundary between art and architecture? Or is there one at all? Many artists and architects have explored this issue over time. Once, especially before the advent of modernity, the arts came together in the cathedrals and palaces of Europe, but also in temples across the world from Japan to Mesoamerica. Sculpture and often painting were an integral part of places of worship, tombs, and princely residences and, until the Renaissance, their authors were frequently anonymous. Great artists of the Renaissance such as Michelangelo designed buildings and spaces even as they painted or sculpted. John Ruskin wrote, "No person who is not a great sculptor or painter can be an architect. If he is not a sculptor or painter, he can only be a builder." Still, some of the great works of architecture that integrate the other arts are the product of many minds and hands working in harmony. In historical terms it is in fact the absence of this symbiosis that is new. As recently as the Vienna Secession and Bauhaus, the search for the Gesamtkunstwerk, the total work of art, proceeded apace. But then, did not many barriers between the arts dissolve, even as architecture claimed its independence from "decoration" and art left the museum to fuse more and more with the living world? The concept that art can fundamentally be an idea even more than it is an artifact can be traced to the work of Marcel Duchamp (anti-art) and the Dadaists.

WHY NOT?

While artists have actively explored the greater world beyond museum walls, architects have often been bound by laws and the need to assure function and safety, restrictions not imposed on sculptors or painters. Influential contemporary architects such as Frank Gehry, one of the most sculptural figures of his profession, have verbalized their frustration at these limits and explained their reaction. In his acceptance of the 1989 Pritzker Prize, Gehry said, "My artist friends, people like Jasper Johns, Bob Rauschenberg, Ed Kienholz, Claes Oldenburg, were working with very inexpensive materials—broken wood and paper—and they were making beauty. These were not superficial details, they were direct; it raised the question of what was beautiful. I chose to use the craft available, and to work with the craftsmen and make a virtue out of their limitations."[1] From another side of the creative world, another American, the sculptor Richard Serra, has stated that "the difference between art and architecture is that architecture serves a purpose."[2] Many architects admit in a guarded way that they would be pleased if their buildings could be considered to be works of art, but few have dared to break the bonds that tie them to the "real" world of increasing safety regulations, functional rules, and the various laws imposed on architecture. What if an artist decided that building was one legitimate form of expression, one way of making art? And what if that artist made structures that are freed from the usual constraints of architecture, simply because they are works of art? Why not?

THAT IS THE REASON

Not Vital was born in 1948 in the village of Sent in the Lower Engadine region of the canton of Graubünden, which today has a population of about 900 people. Nurtured by the isolated beauty of this village and its cultural traditions, he developed an interest in art in part through the Swiss art historian Max Huggler, who had a home in Sent. Vital studied in Paris in 1968–69 at the brand-new Centre universitaire expérimental de Vincennes, a left-leaning institution dedicated to the contemporary world, whose philosophy department was directed by Michel Foucault. Vital began to create sculptures in the 1980s. He emerged as a kind of prince from this mountain village, speaking Romansh, German, French, and English, open to the world. A prince not in any hereditary sense, but because he acquired the ability to grasp and develop his art on the basis of his origins but with no limits. His is a nobility of the spirit. The work of Vital can be described as protean, ranging from sculpture to drawing and

1. Frank O. Gehry, "1989 Laureate Ceremony Acceptance Speech," May 18, 1989, Todai-ji Temple, Nara, Japan, https://www.pritzkerprize.com/sites/default/files/inline-files/Frank_Gehry_Acceptance_Speech_1989.pdf.
2. Richard Serra, in conversation with the author, September 23, 1999, New York.

well on to the larger dimensions of architecture. The key to understanding his architectural work is surely to see all of these forms of creativity as being part of a continuous, very personal oeuvre. Nor is it necessary to speculate about the roots of Vital's architecture. When asked why he has embarked on the construction of a series of *Houses to Watch the Sunset* in numerous fairly remote locations around the world, he says, playing on his own first name,

> The most precise answer is not why. I was born in the village of Sent and for five months during the summer vacation, there was little to do. Vacations were so long that we forgot how to read and had to start all over again the following year. During this time, everyone was building huts and places to hide. For a child, it was phenomenal. There was no TV; it was extraordinary to be in nature, to be able to build a hut or a treehouse and to spend the night there. We were only 16 people in my class, but there were perhaps four groups and each built their own hideaway, which had to be a secret. It had to be hidden. I think building these habitats might have been the most important thing I did as a child.[3]

Vital's response to this question is in fact quite typical of his reasoning and a clue to his fundamentally open spirit. The artist says he has been diagnosed with ADD (Attention Deficit Disorder), which in fact means that for him, what may appear to be a straightforward question opens a multitude of thoughts and responses. It can be noted that this very thought process corresponds in a logical way to the variety of his projects and works.

Continuing from his description of childhood treehouses, Vital further develops his thoughts about architecture:

> When you grow up you don't build treehouses or huts anymore. You build a real house, and for that you have to get a loan, you have to get permissions, and all of this tends to kill the passion. In 1999, I went to Agadez, in Niger. Although I knew very little about this place, I knew this was where I should be. The day after my arrival, I bought a piece of land that was offered to me by Tuaregs and started to build. In Agadez, and everywhere else I have built, I have never sought nor needed permission. As for the remote places I am attracted to, I think of Nietzsche, who said if you love something or someone, it is often a place or a person that is far away. It becomes a myth. If you tell someone you have a place in Patagonia, that is already great. If you have an island in Patagonia, wow. And then if you have a house inside an island in Patagonia, then you almost don't need to show photographs. As a story, it is already enough, very much like the Little Prince on another planet. Rather than doing something in New York City, I prefer to do it somewhere that few people know about.

DESSINE-MOI UN MOUTON . . .

References to *The Little Prince* (*Le Petit Prince*, Antoine de Saint-Exupéry, 1943) and to Friedrich Nietzsche are revealing and coherent with the work of the artist. One of the abiding messages of *The Little Prince* is that everyone has a child within them, but that few remember the dreams of youth. The narrator of Saint-Exupéry's story, an aviator like the author, crashes in the Sahara, where he meets a little prince who lives on an asteroid "not much larger than a house."[4] Later, visiting the site of this crash, the narrator concludes,

> It is, for me, the most beautiful and saddest landscape in the world. . . . It is here where the little prince appeared on Earth, and then disappeared.
>
> Look carefully at this landscape to be sure you recognize it, if you travel one day to Africa, in the desert. And, if you manage to go through it, I beg you, don't rush, wait a bit just underneath the star! If, then, a child comes to you, if he laughs, if he has golden

3. Not Vital in conversation with the author, Sent, Switzerland, August 11, 2019. Other quotes from the artist in this text are from the same conversation unless otherwise noted.
4. Antoine de Saint-Exupéry, *The Little Prince* (n.p.: Classica Libris, 2019), chap. 4, Kindle edition.

> hair, if he does not answer your questions, you will guess who he is. So be nice! Do not make me so sad: write to me quick telling he came back . . .[5]

Imagine the artist travelling to Agadez and to Aladab in the Niger, which are indeed in the Sahara, and choosing to build precisely here between 2000 and 2007 not only his first *House to Watch the Sunset* (2005 [pp. 138—39, 249]) but also a "complex for living" titled *Mekafoni* (2001 [pp. 120–25]), a school called *Makaranta* (2003 [pp. 126–31]), a *House to Watch the Night Skies* (2006 [pp. 148–49]), and a *House Against Heat and Sandstorms* (2006 [pp. 144–45]). With the exception of the school, these houses have in common a sense for what might be called primal or primordial forms, somehow reminiscent of ancient buildings yet imbued with an undeniable modernity—as is very much the case of the *Houses to Watch the Sunset*.

Vital explains with candor, "the first *House to Watch the Sunset* in Aladab was imagined in about twelve minutes. I knew the building would have to be higher than the palm trees. It had to be a tower. Without measuring anything, I knew how it had to be. The building's stairs are not only for people to climb up, but also serve to stabilize the structure." It was in this informal way that the artist imagined a structure that has been built anew in Brazil in the Amazon at Paraná do Mamori (2016) and most recently in Tarasp (2018), near Sent. New iterations of *House to Watch the Sunset* will be built in Mongolia and in Vava'u, Tonga, an aluminum version slated first to be exhibited under the dome of Palladio's San Giorgio Maggiore in Venice in 2020.

Although his work is extremely varied, Vital appears to seek a certain continuity in his architectural designs. Asked why the different versions of *House to Watch the Sunset* are so similar despite their distant locations, he says (perhaps with a smile),

> Not why. There has to be a thread, especially if you go all around the world. If I have Alzheimer's one day and I want to visit my houses, they are all the same. The *Houses to Watch the Sunset* are so easy to build. Architecture is related to sculpture because in both cases you go around a form and see it from all sides. It is what it is, in a way. Painting is completely different, you make one more brush stroke, and you have a different painting.

Even in his description of his own method, Vital sometimes appears to be self-contradictory. "One of the reasons I am an artist and that I don't sell mineral water is that it gives me the opportunity *not* to be repetitive. But maybe I need a bit of repetition so that my SCARCH projects can be a coherent group of works." Vital has coined a term, SCARCH, to describe his own unusual fusion of sculpture and architecture on a global scale. "A structure is both architecture and sculpture. In my mind there is not so much of a difference between the two," he explains.

Asked what he thinks about Serra's affirmation about the difference between sculpture and architecture, Vital says, "In a way I disagree. To me, it is less black and white. When we build a house, we are used to the idea that it is meant to be lived in in a conventional sense. My houses have no water, no heat, no electricity. The purpose of these houses is often transcendental. An exception is the school in the Niger, which indeed does fulfill an important purpose—in this project, which is situated in one of the poorest countries in the world, sculpture, architecture, and a social purpose are combined."

Not only are the different iterations of *House to Watch the Sunset* very similar to each other, they are the product of a kind of mathematical progression. "I like numbers and numerology," says the artist. The numbers though are less an attempt to create order than to engender a kind of natural harmonic that can resonate from one remote place on the planet to another. These buildings are of course built to stand, to remain, but their proportions, inspired by the original location in Africa, are stated by Vital with a disconcerting simplicity and logic: "tower 13 × 3.40 × 3.40 m / 3 outside stairs / 1 with 13 / 1 with 26 / 1 with 39 steps / each 1 is 25 × 25 cm + / 45

5. Saint-Exupéry, *The Little Prince*, chap. 27.

degrees / the 1st floor has 1 door / the 2nd 1 door + 1 window / the 3rd 1 door + 2 windows / the 4th 1 door + 3 windows / 4 rooms 3 × 3 × 3 m / + 1 bed + 1 table + 1 chair / no water or electricity / just enough / to make the sun set."[6]

The architectural process of Vital is actually more complex and varied than can be perceived through these examples. He has, for instance, recently completed another structure that shares some of the characteristics of the *Houses to Watch the Sunset* but is different. On the island of Flores in eastern Indonesia, his *House to Watch the 3 Volcanoes* (2017) has 39 black, steel steps running up its white exterior façade and an interior clad in local bamboo and straw [pp. 208–15].

I HAVE NO CONSTRAINTS

This kind of mathematical progression is surely more a study of proportions (as in sculpture) than it is a scientific development of an architectural scheme. "Architecture can be scientific and therefore require precision," says Vital, "but I don't feel this burden. As an artist, I have fewer constraints. I think more about Nietzsche than I think about Buckminster Fuller." Citing a philosopher rather than an artist in contrast to the noted architect and engineer Fuller, Vital also further sketches the contours of his interest in building. It is the idea, the thought behind a structure that counts; it is the emergence of the idea that takes a form that can at once be sculptural and architectural.

"How many times can you watch the sun set?" Vital asks. "The only purpose of this project is to watch the sunset and that might not even be the purpose." Then, is this a spiritual quest, a place to dream, or, even more radical and interesting, basically a story? "It is spiritual but it is more than that," states Vital. "It is not practical, and that gives you room for all the rest. I don't need an elevator or a fire escape, so everything changes. I use no insulation. It is spiritual, poetic, or James Bond. These houses have no doors and no keys. We all want stories. Everything is about a story." The relentless practicality and cost consciousness of contemporary architecture is cast aside intentionally by Vital to leave "room for all the rest."

100 ARCHITECTS

In 2016, Vital created a series of 100 abstract sculptures whose proportions are based on the dates of birth of a selected group of significant architects through history [pp. 73, 78—81]. His method confirms his interest in mathematical progressions but also underlines his abiding and profound interest in architecture, even if he rejects the practical (or bureaucratic) aspects of the art of building. With forms dictated by the dates of birth of the architects, these "portraits" depict figures as different as Ludwig Mies van der Rohe (b. 27 March 1886) and Leon Battista Alberti (b. 14 February 1404). Though often recalling a standing person, the works are the result of a strict mathematical model that converts a date of birth into an abstract form. In a way this series represents an inversion of his creation of works of "architecture" that are also sculpture. Here the masters of architecture are made into sculptures that are in no way figurative, even if their dimensions are a reflection of precise dates of birth. The very substance of the history of architecture is sublimated into sculptural form—again the idea is unexpected and radical, and yet is based on an interpreted form of basic reality. Even the word abstraction may be subverted by the numerological method of the artist—there is something fundamental about any person's date of birth, something incontrovertible about Vital's mathematical approach.

RETURN TO THE GARDEN

Near the western entrance to his native village, Vital has created a sculpture park on a spectacular, steeply sloped site. Here he has placed numerous works that have a bearing on his own story and his interest in architecture. One of the first structures visitors encounter is *Chamonna spanada* (*Board House*), built in 2004 with his brother Duri Vital, the architect [pp. 74, 102—03]. Though it assumes the form of a hut, this tumultuous assemblage of scrap wood would appear above all to be a reminiscence of the childhood refuges described by the artist. This is in many

6. Not Vital, "House to Watch the Sunset," pp. 242—43 in this volume.

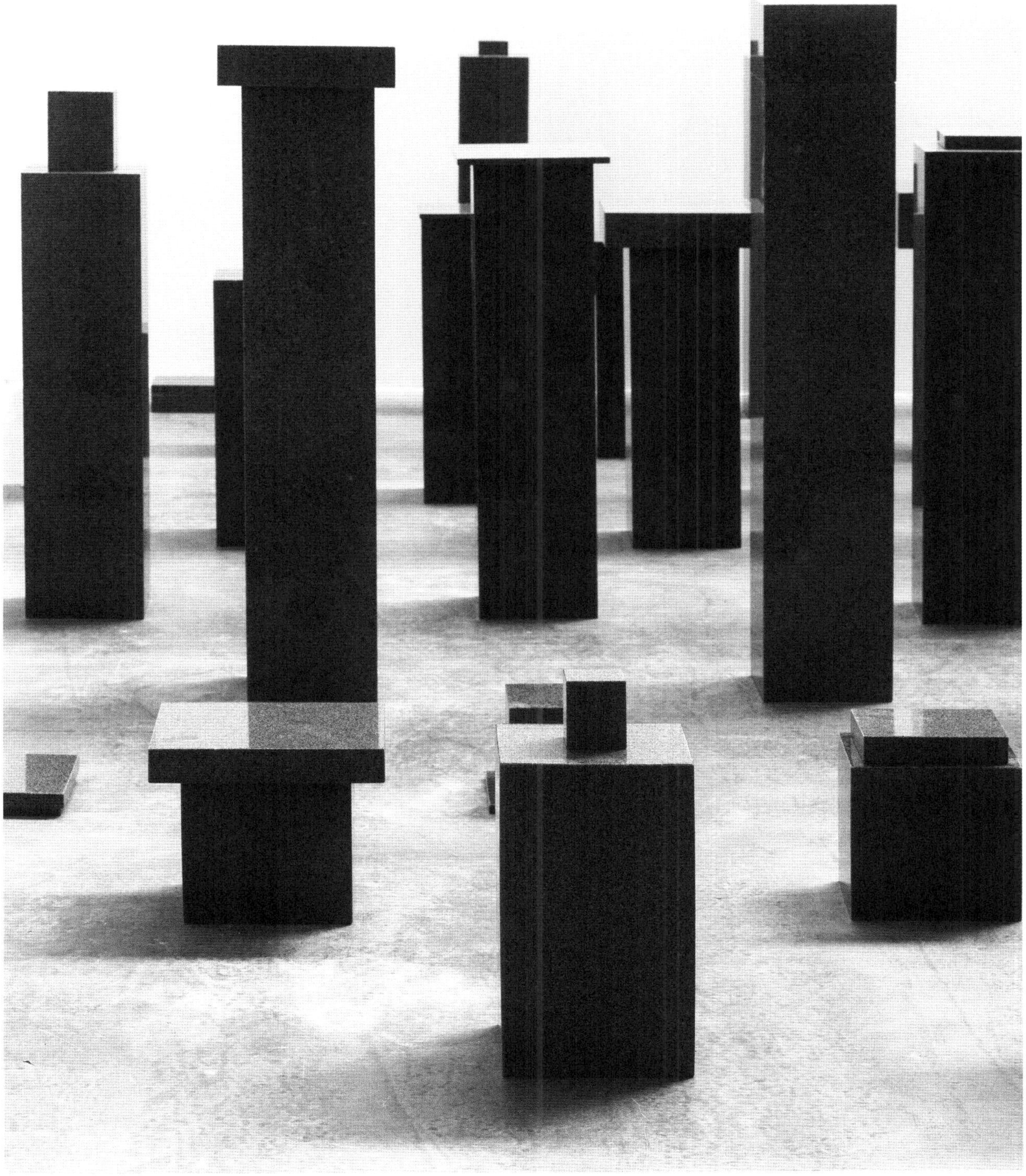

100 Architects, 2016

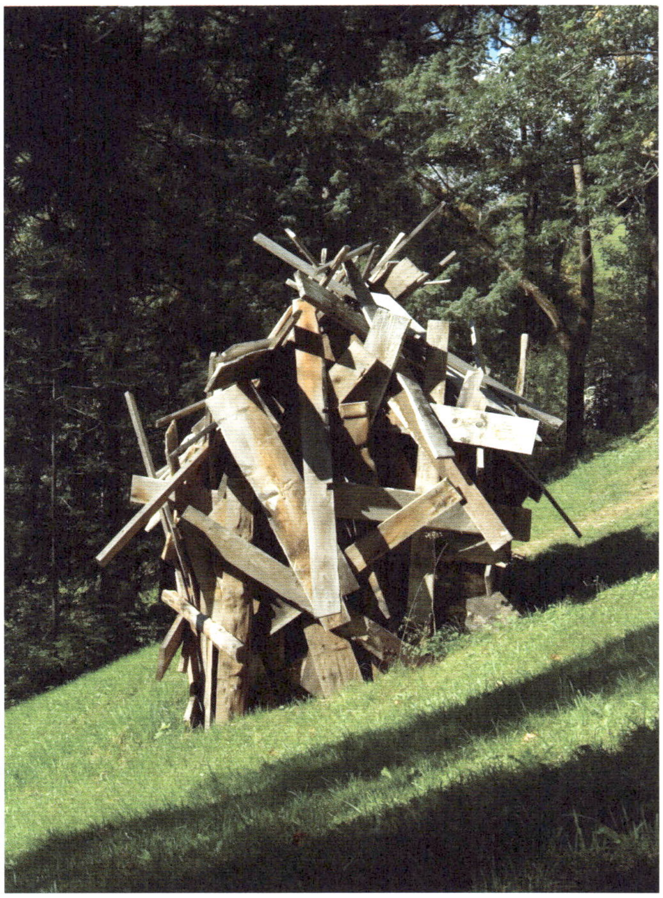

Chamonna spanada, 2004

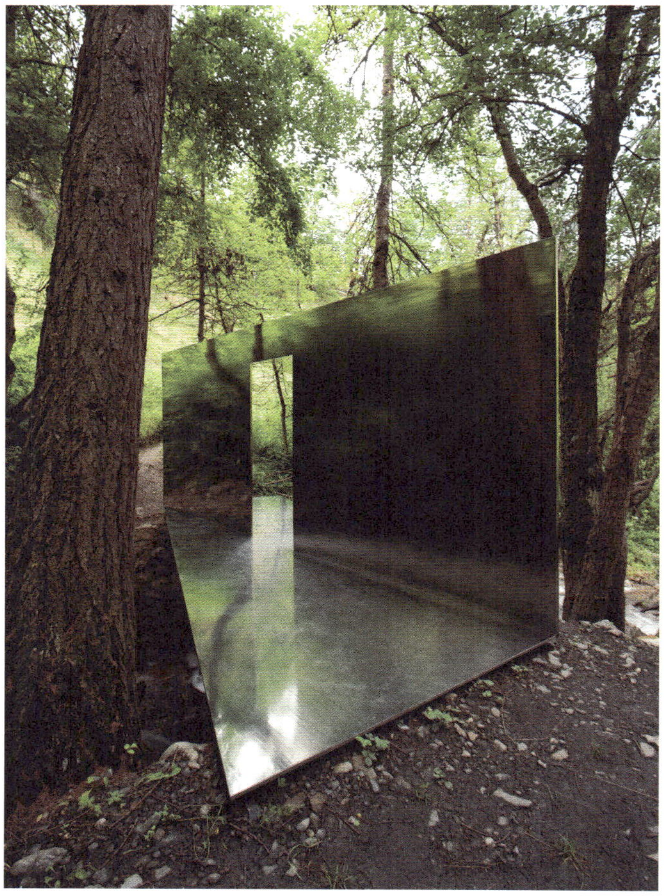

Bridge, 2008

ways a reference to his beginnings in art; a chaotic appearance yields a work that is at once sculptural and architectural. Another piece of note is the *JOSÜJO* (*Disappearing House*, 2007), which highlights an additional aspect of Vital's work, his capacity to combine unusual ideas with a certain sense of humor or social commentary [pp. 106–09]. In its closed position, the *Disappearing House* is completely invisible but, with a touch of a button, a patch of the grassy hillside progressively rises up to reveal a simple white block form with openings, which does recall a small house. Walking in the park, Vital explains, "Many people come to the Engadine and build houses because nature is exceptionally beautiful here, but their houses remain closed most of the year because they only come for a few weeks of vacation at most. The houses that these people like are often inspired by local architecture, but they are poor copies, they are empty. My idea would be that when you cross the pass, you just push a button and let your house out. And while you are gone, the house disappears underground."

Further down the slope in the sculpture park, another work that calls on engineering occupies a stunning location against the backdrop of the forest and more distant mountains. *Palc* (*Stage*, 2011) is a Corten steel platform that consists of a stairway and a flat "stage" with no barriers, a pure 3.7-meter cantilever, seemingly hovering in the landscape [pp. 116–17]. This work is clearly architectural in nature, but it is daring and minimalist in its detailing and design. A kind of minimalism often pervades the architectural works of Vital, but so too does a sense of risk. Standing on this platform one is taken with a kind of vertigo induced by the mountains, the slope, and the cantilever. Here we are near the edge, or perhaps closer to an artistic expression that is visceral, profound, challenging. The *Stage* itself can accommodate any number of performances, imposing no order except that of the risk of a (the?) fall.

Another minimalist piece on the grounds of the park is the six-meter, stainless steel *Bridge* (2008 [pp. 74, 110—11]), which crosses the Val da Muglins stream. Part of a series of seven bridges that the artist designed in a single night for a narrow canal in Venice, this work again has no protective barriers. A door in the middle of its polished central wall seems to make visitors quite literally disappear the instant they walk through it. This impression is difficult to describe but watching a person cross is a moment of magic. The lack of barriers suggests an idea of (relatively low) risk, but this polished steel presence in the forest is another work that fuses architecture and sculpture, in this case with the "purpose" of crossing the mountain stream.

Near the bottom of the wooded slope in the park, the artist leads the way to the *Chasa barcha / Chamonna süll'aua* (*House by the River*, 2002), one of the earliest works on the grounds [pp. 96–99]. A triangular hut built around existing trees, the house has place for at least two persons to lie and gaze through a window at the stream. "I built the house with my brother," explains Vital. "It is a kind of boat anchored in the hillside. It is like a child's treehouse. Everything could happen here." But this is not only a place of escape to dreams of childhood; another presence is sometimes felt. As Vital explains, the artist Francesco Clemente came to the hut and asked if he could stay alone inside for a time, saying that he felt something unnamed that he had only once experienced in a temple in Kyoto. Vital moves on quickly from this story to speak of the similarities between Japan and Switzerland, but the idea has been voiced. Some feel a spiritual presence in this place. Nor is it in the character of Vital to tell people what they should feel in one of his works. What is important is that they feel something—risk, amazement, reminiscence, inspiration, spirituality, or even rejection.

MASTER OF TARASP

The architectural presence of Vital, even in the region of Sent, has other dimensions, including his painting studio [pp. 234–37], built with his brother, which has an irregular, cavelike, gray gunite (sprayed concrete) exterior and a precise, light-filled white interior. The rough exterior of this building and its refined interior might be considered to be yet another metaphor for the creativity of the artist. Then too, a few kilometers away, is Tarasp Castle, established by the lords of Tarasp in the 11th century, now purchased by Vital, the once and future prince of Sent, as a place for exhibitions of contemporary art and the display of works by the artist.

TO GIVE BIRTH TO A DANCING STAR

Finally, the boundary between architecture and art is no longer (or not) the issue when viewing and thinking about the work of Vital. He says, "*Ars una est*. It is all one. While I don't like order, I do like the harmony." Even when an architectural work of Vital has an avowed purpose such as viewing the sunset, he admits that he is first attracted by the names of places . . . Patagonia, the Amazon, the Sahara. From Beijing to Rio de Janeiro, Vital straddles the globe, often in places that are not part of any itinerary but his own, on a unique path from Sent to worlds that spin in his mind and leave their trace in ink, in steel, or in concrete. Like the Little Prince, whose home Asteroid B 612 is "not much larger than a house," Vital appears where he might least be expected and leaves a message that is radical in its simplicity—that art (architecture?) originating in the dreams of childhood can touch the soul of a viewer who is able to see, who is able to look within. Nietzsche, who is often cited by Vital, found inspiration for his philosophical novel *Thus Spoke Zarathustra* (1883–85) in Sils Maria, a village in Upper Engadine, not far from Sent. In that work, the German philosopher wrote, "You must have chaos within you to give birth to a dancing star,"[7] words that might well define the process and multiple oeuvre of Vital. When he was asked by the *New York Times* where he would like to be buried, Vital responded, "Nowhere. But if they catch me, I'd like to be burned and put in different places. I would like a little bit here in the village, and some in Agadez, then in Rio a little bit, and then at the island in Patagonia. I would like to have my ashes travel the world."[8] Like Saint-Exupéry's Little Prince, Vital was born on a planet "the size of a house" and he has gone on to travel

7. Friedrich Nietzsche, *Also sprach Zarathustra*: "Man muss noch Chaos in sich haben, um einen tanzenden Stern gebären zu können."
8. Andrew O'Hagan, "Inside the Many Houses of Not Vital, Maker of Dreamscapes for Adults," *New York Times*, Style Magazine, October 18, 2013.

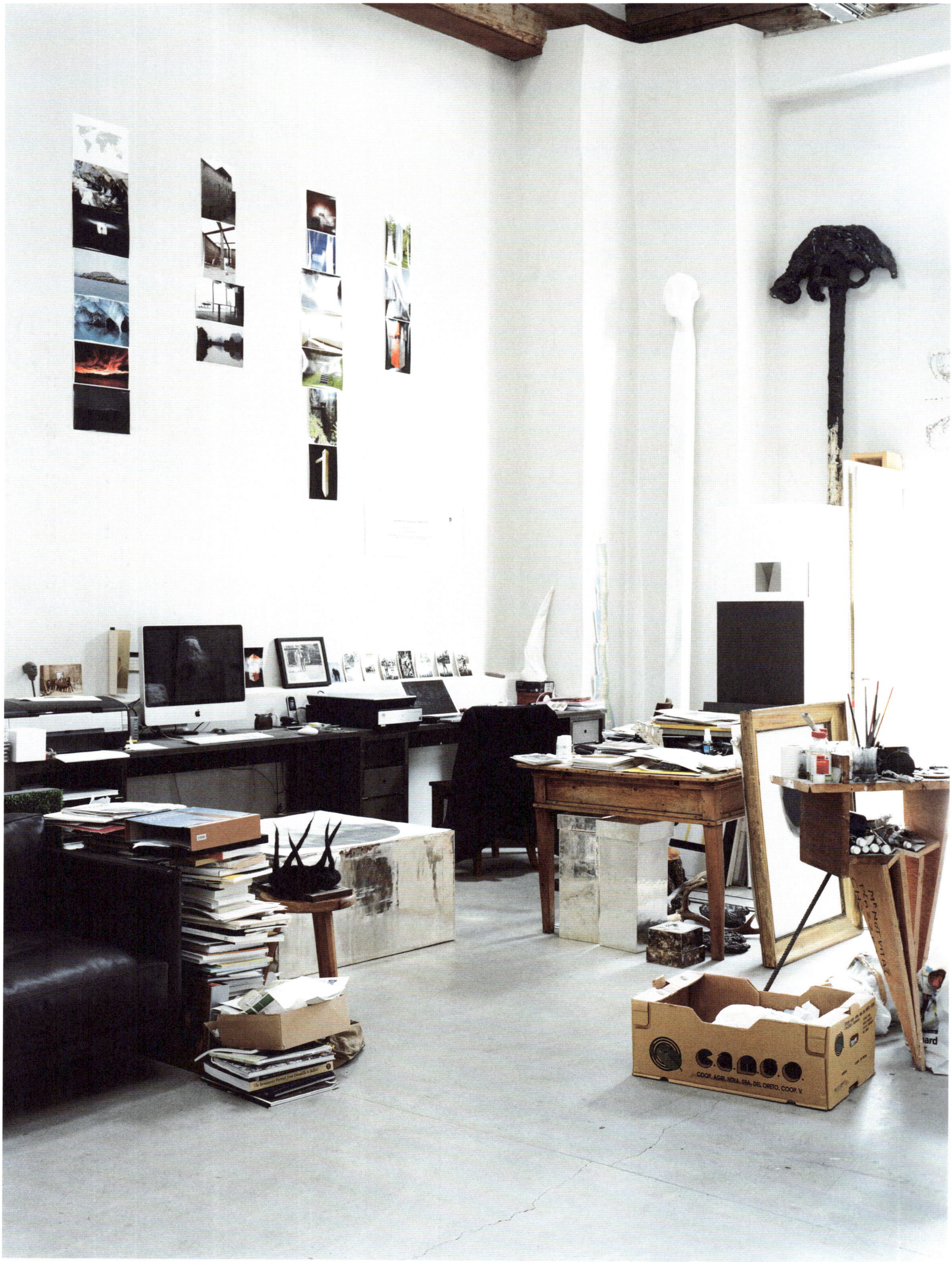

Not Vital's studio in Sent, Switzerland

the world and to build again and again, challenging the barriers of art, but also of architecture, creating a sculptural reality of his own, searching, as he says, for a friend who will, in the end, tell him that he has done nothing.

> Mais, bien sûr, nous qui comprenons la vie, nous nous moquons bien des numéros! J'aurais aimé commencer cette histoire à la façon des contes de fées. J'aurais aimé dire:
> "Il était une fois un petit prince qui habitait une planète à peine plus grande que lui, et qui avait besoin d'un ami . . ." Pour ceux qui comprennent la vie, ça aurait eu l'air beaucoup plus vrai.
> —Antoine de Saint-Exupéry, *Le Petit Prince*[9]

Millbrook, New York
September 21, 2019

9. Saint-Exupéry, *The Little Prince*, chap. 4: "But, of course, we, who understand life, we make fun of numbers! I would like to start this story like fairy tales. I would like to say: 'Once upon a time a little prince who lived on a planet not much bigger than him, and who needed a friend . . .' For those who understand life, it would have seemed much more real."

100 Architects
2016

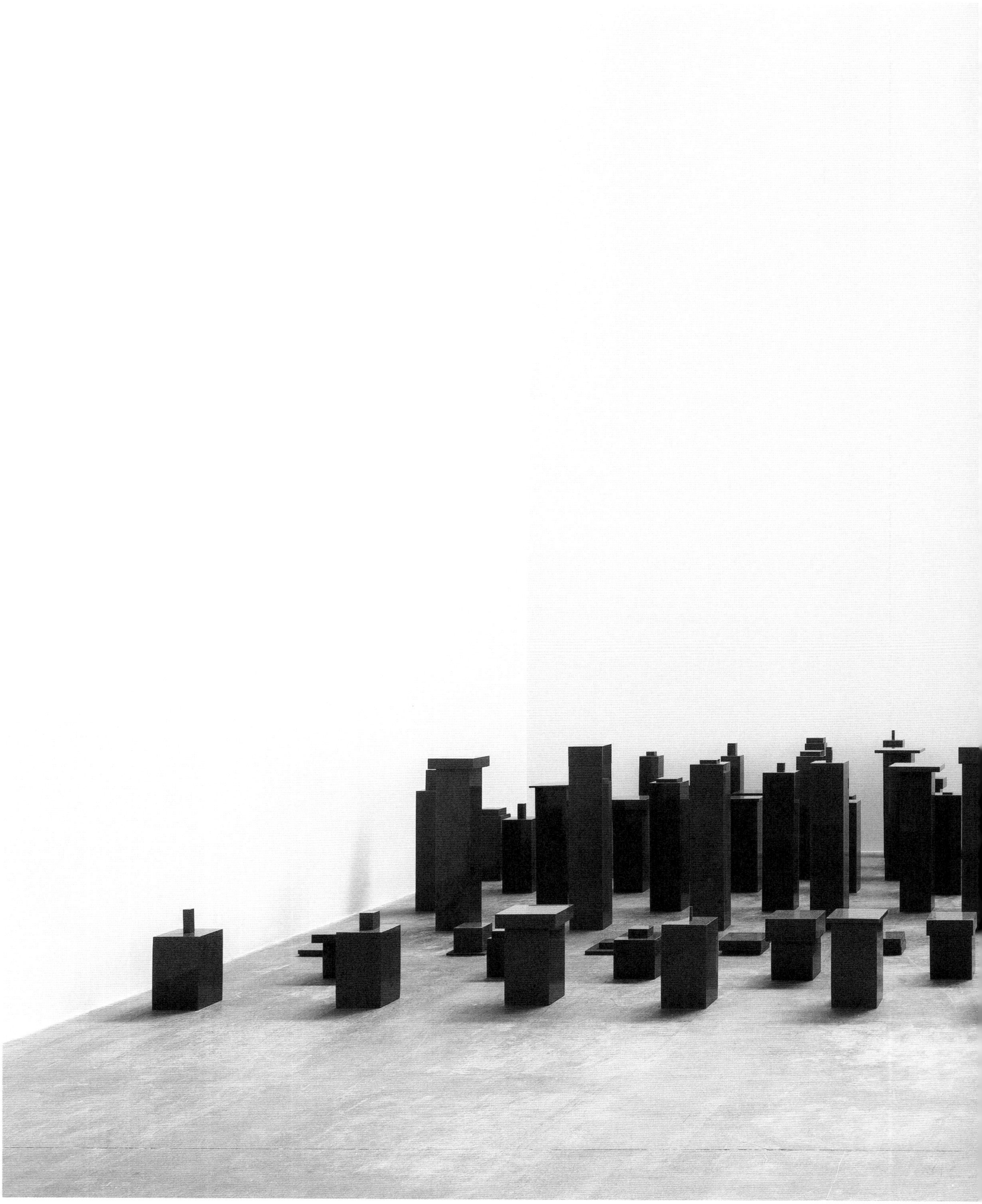

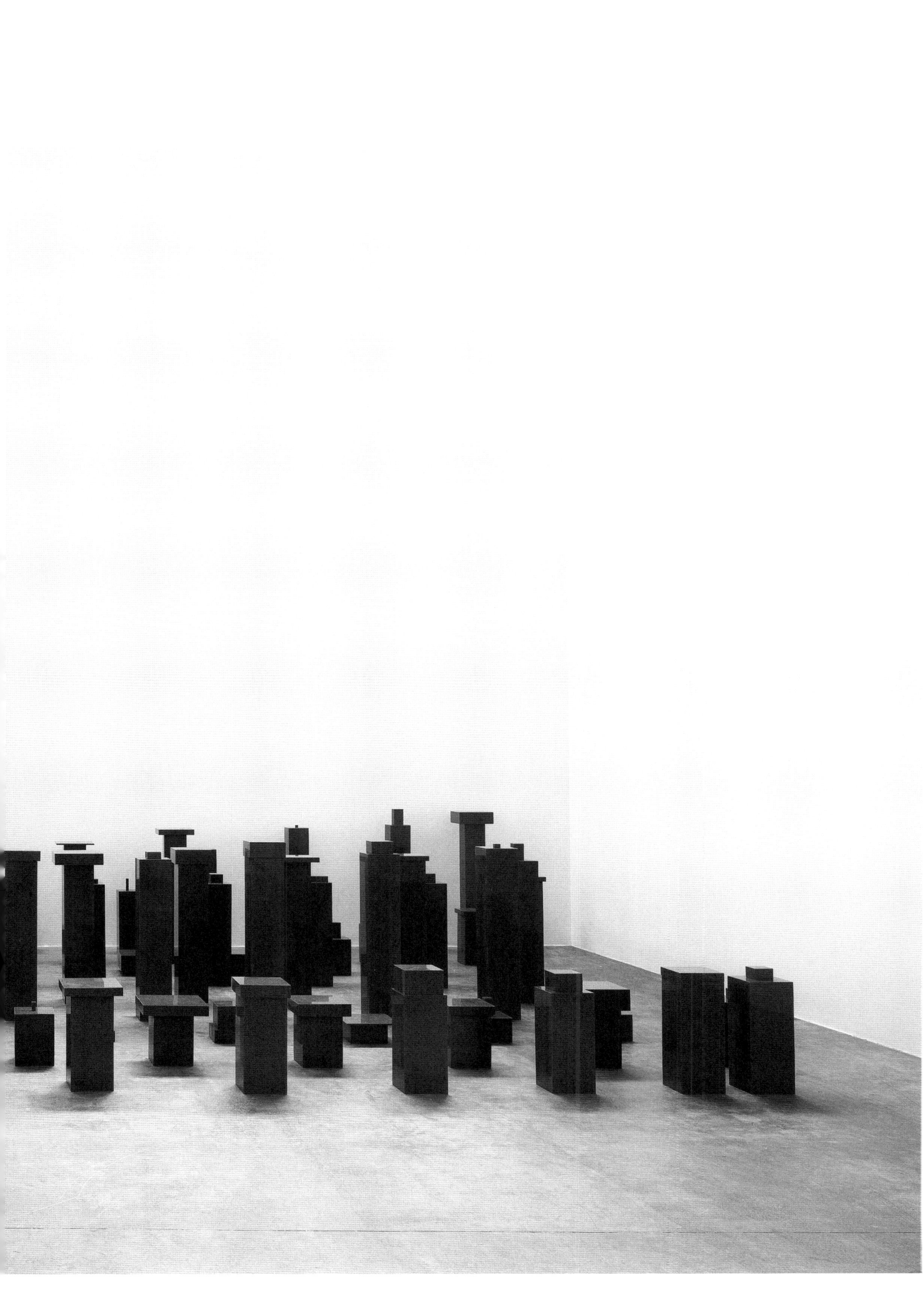

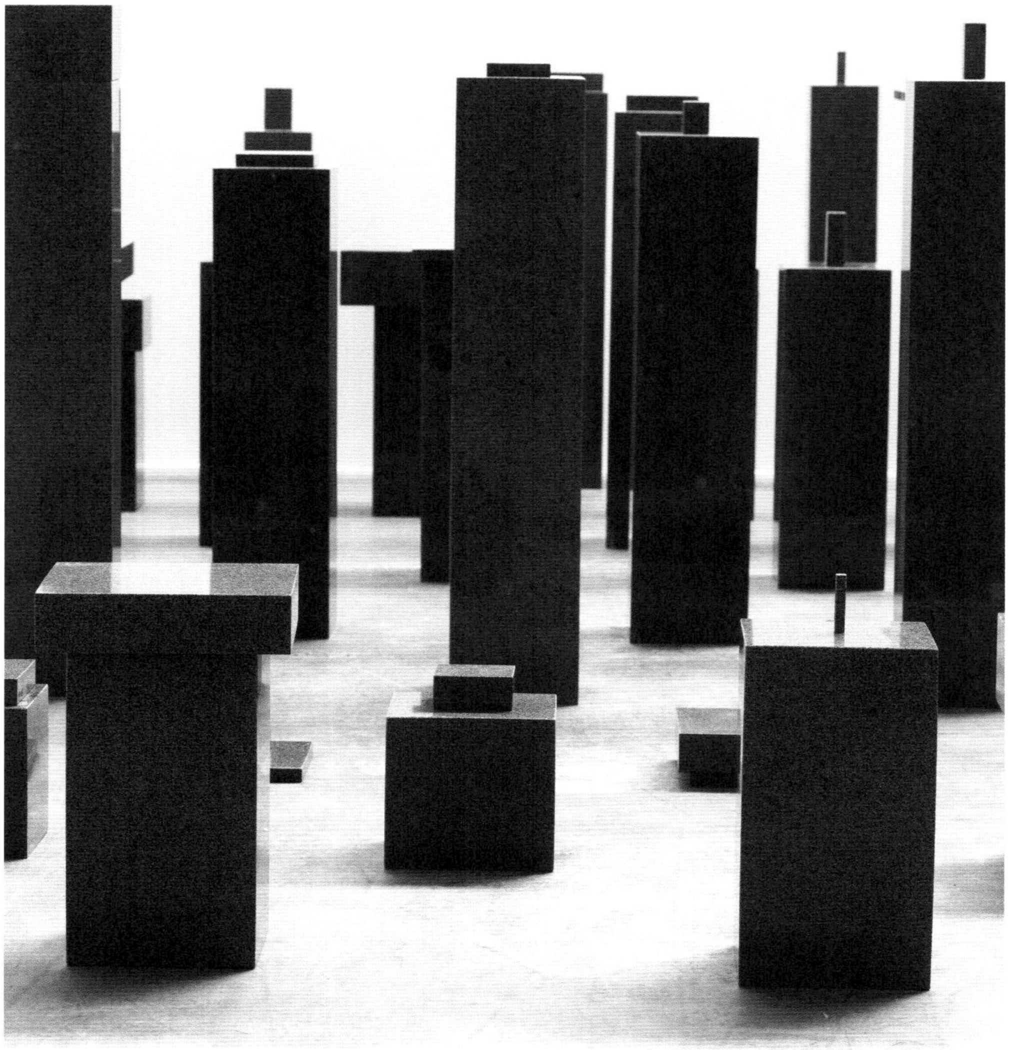

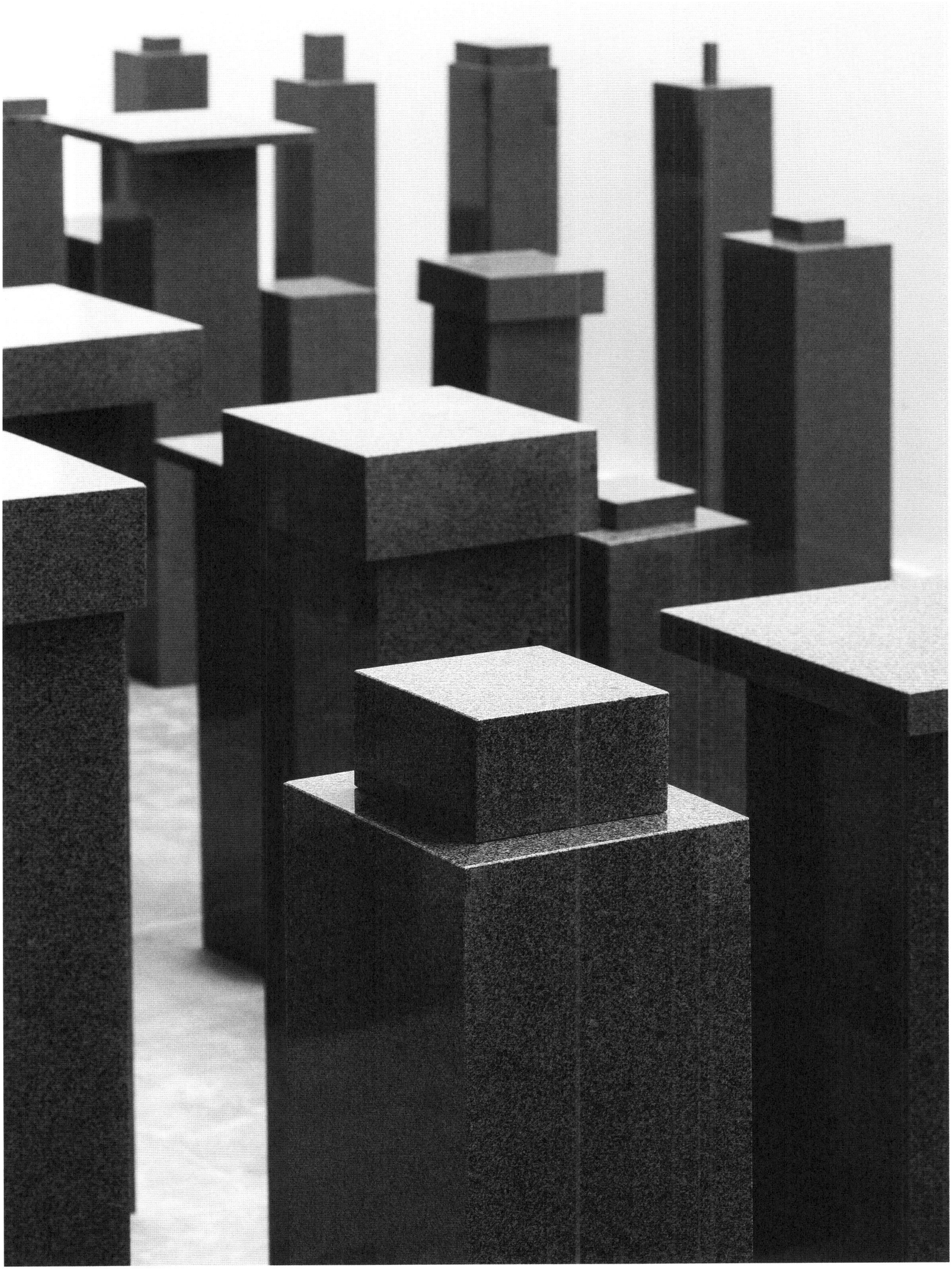

Switzerland

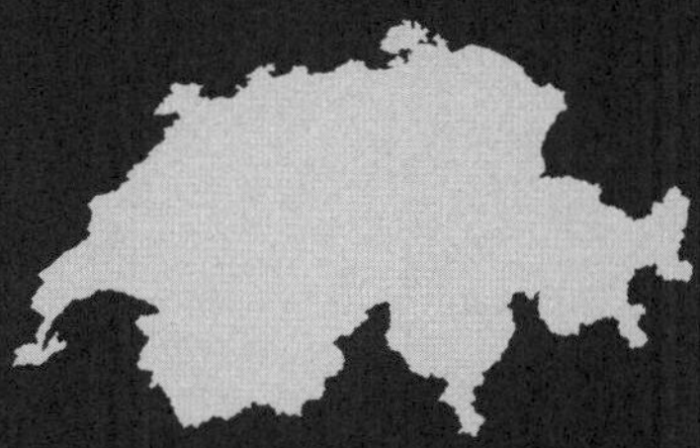

Handrail and Waterpipe
Parkin, Sent, Switzerland
2000

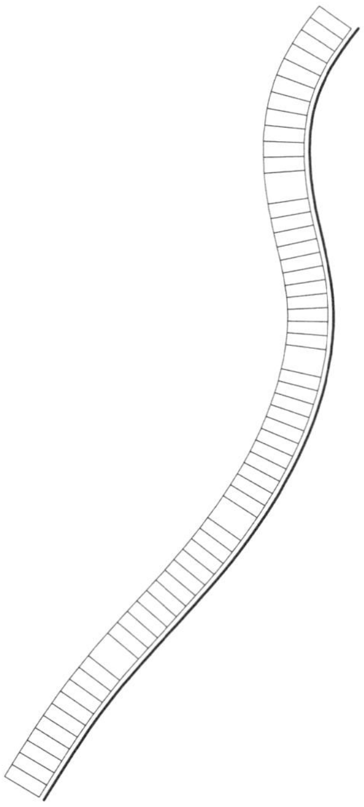

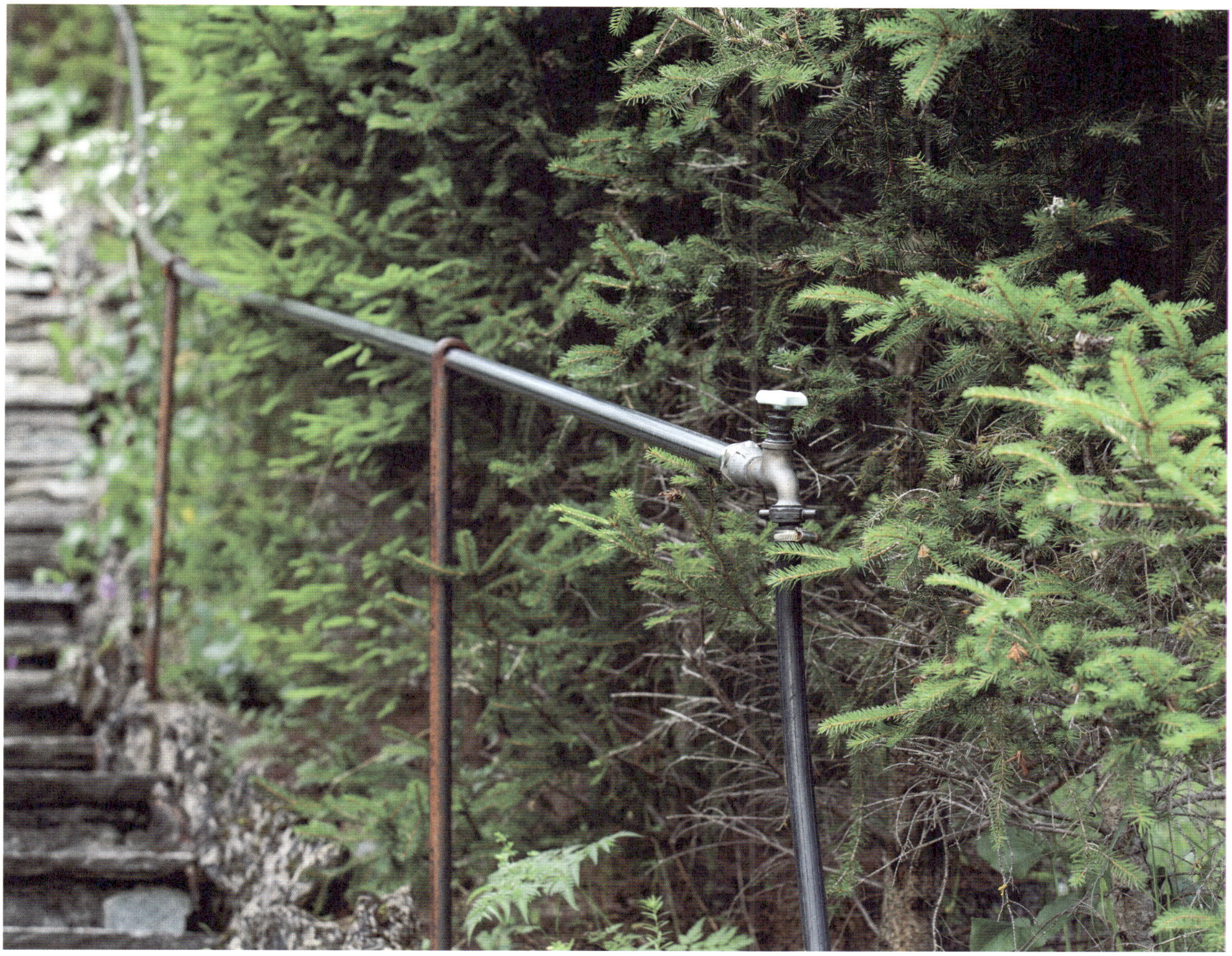

Punt dals asens
(Donkey Bridge)

Parkin, Sent, Switzerland
2001

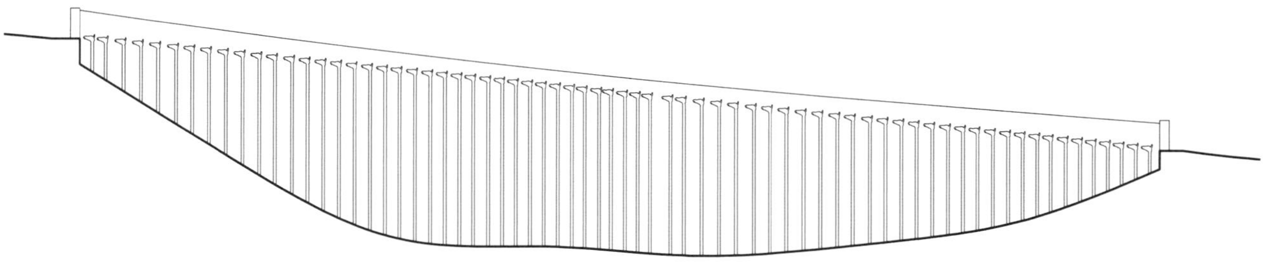

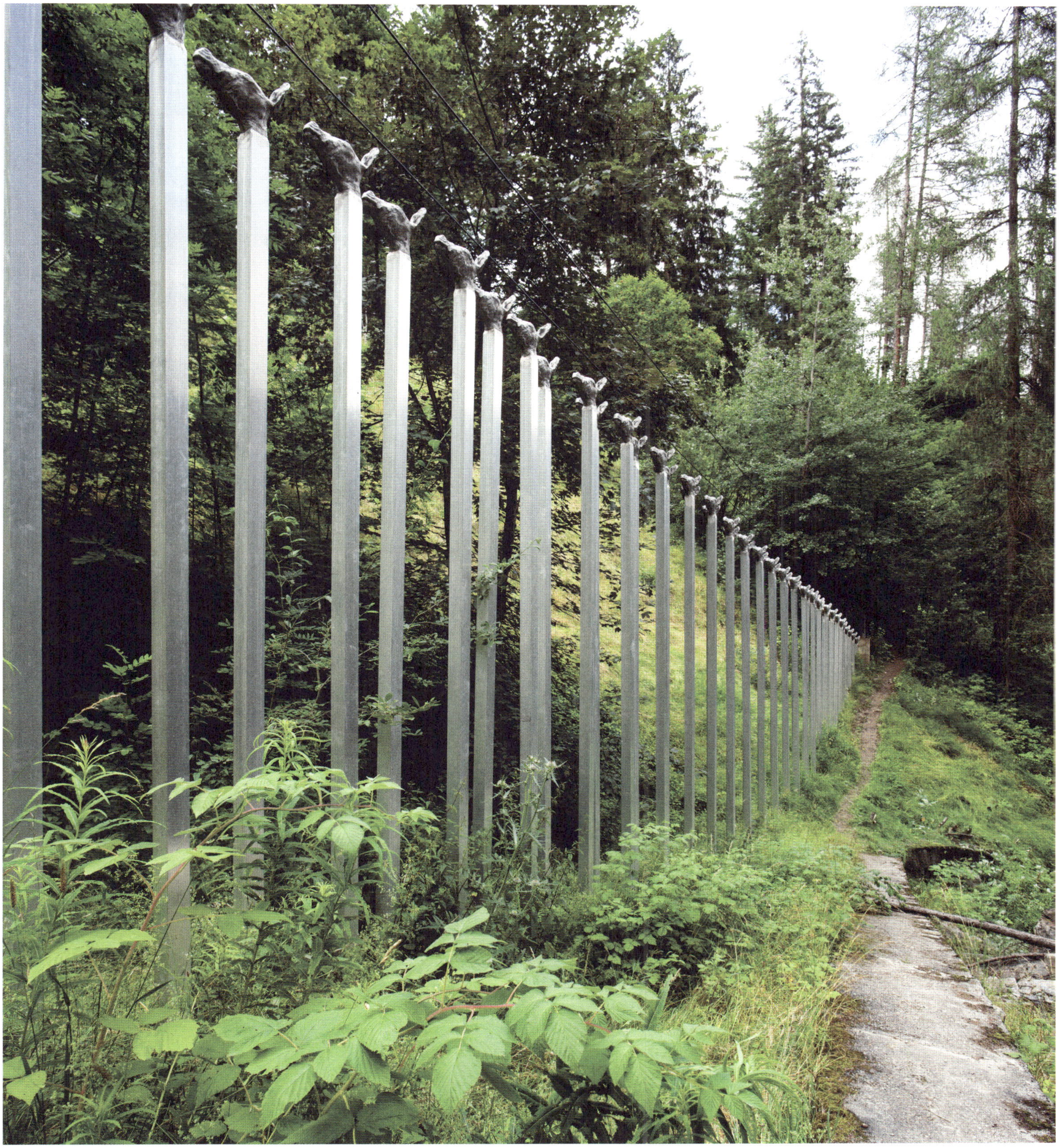

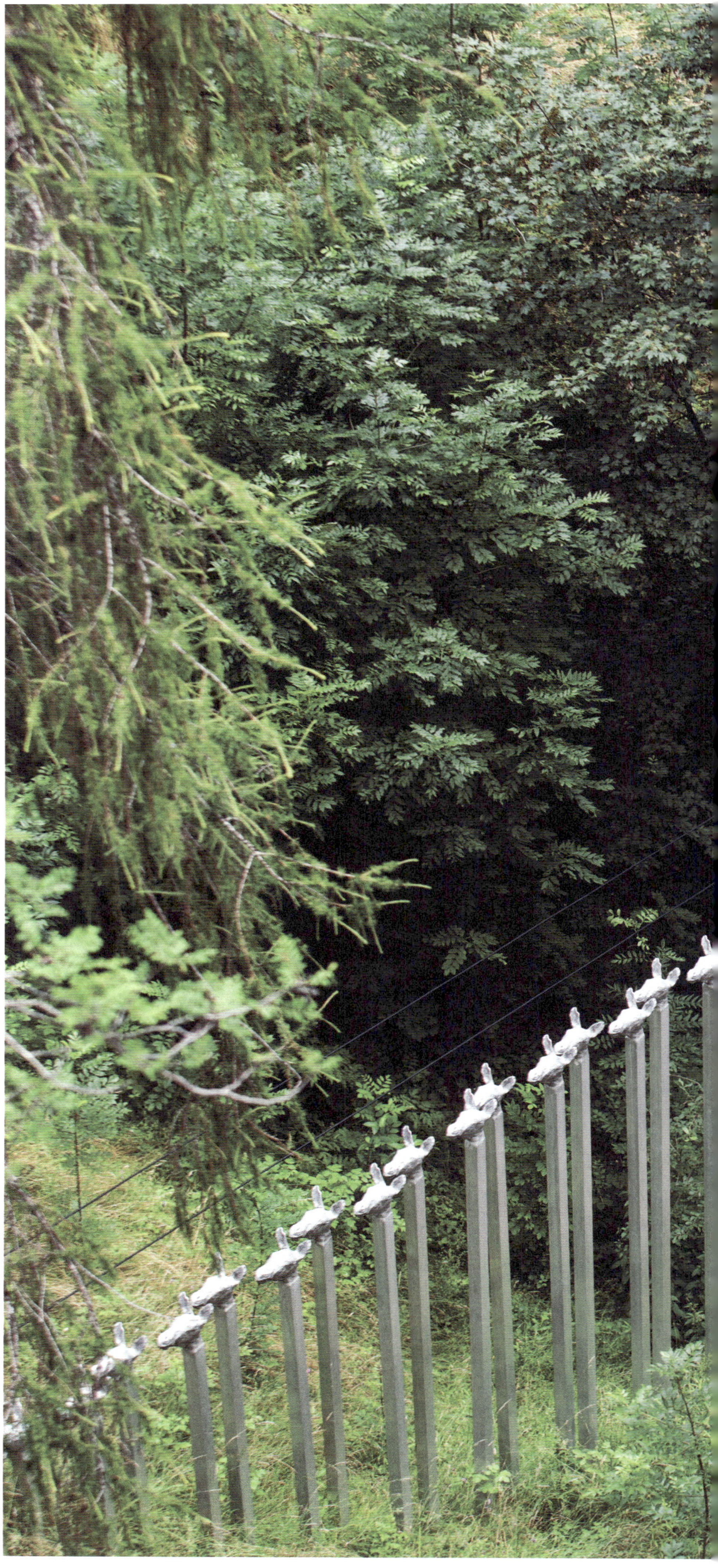

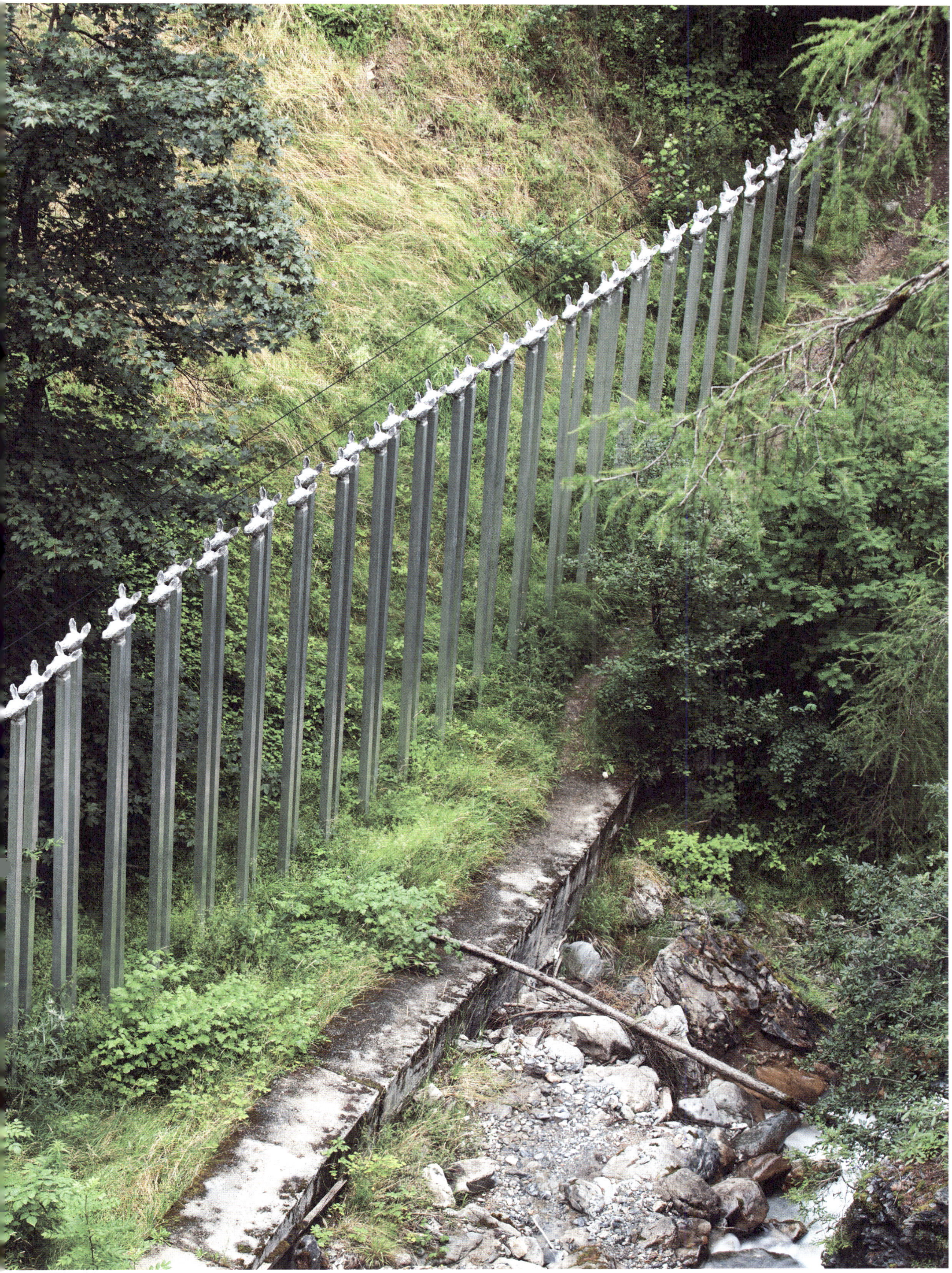

Tuor per ir pella bos-cha (Hair Tower)

Parkin, Sent, Switzerland
2001

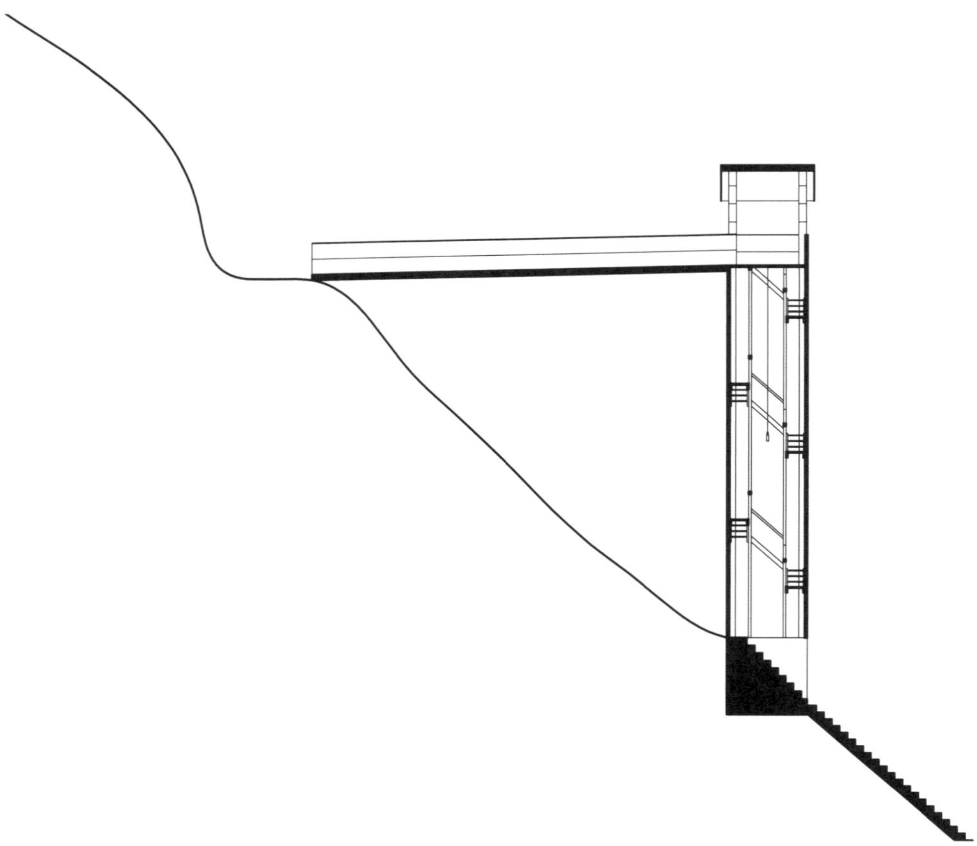

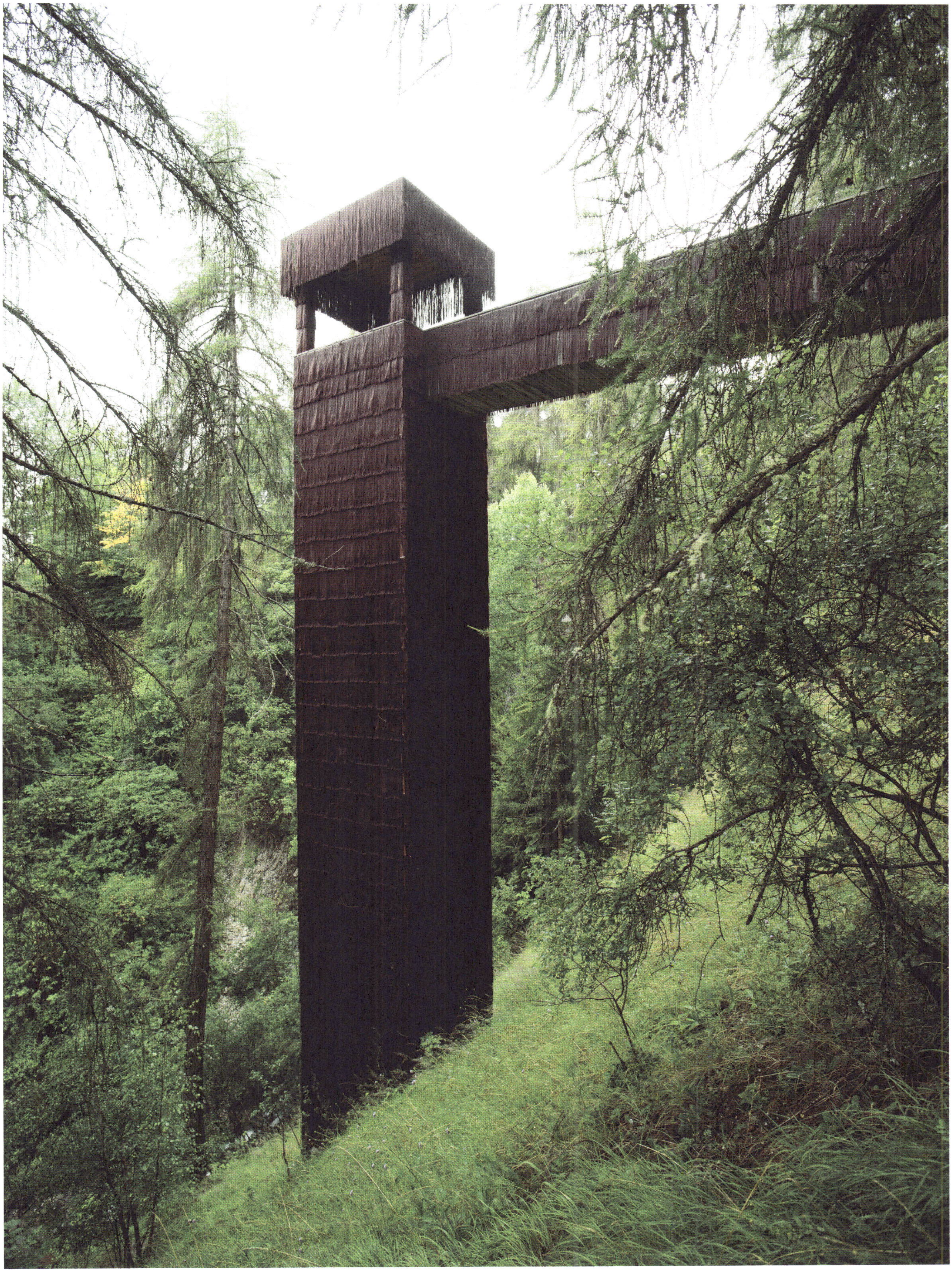

Chasa da glatsch (Glass House)

Parkin, Sent, Switzerland 2002

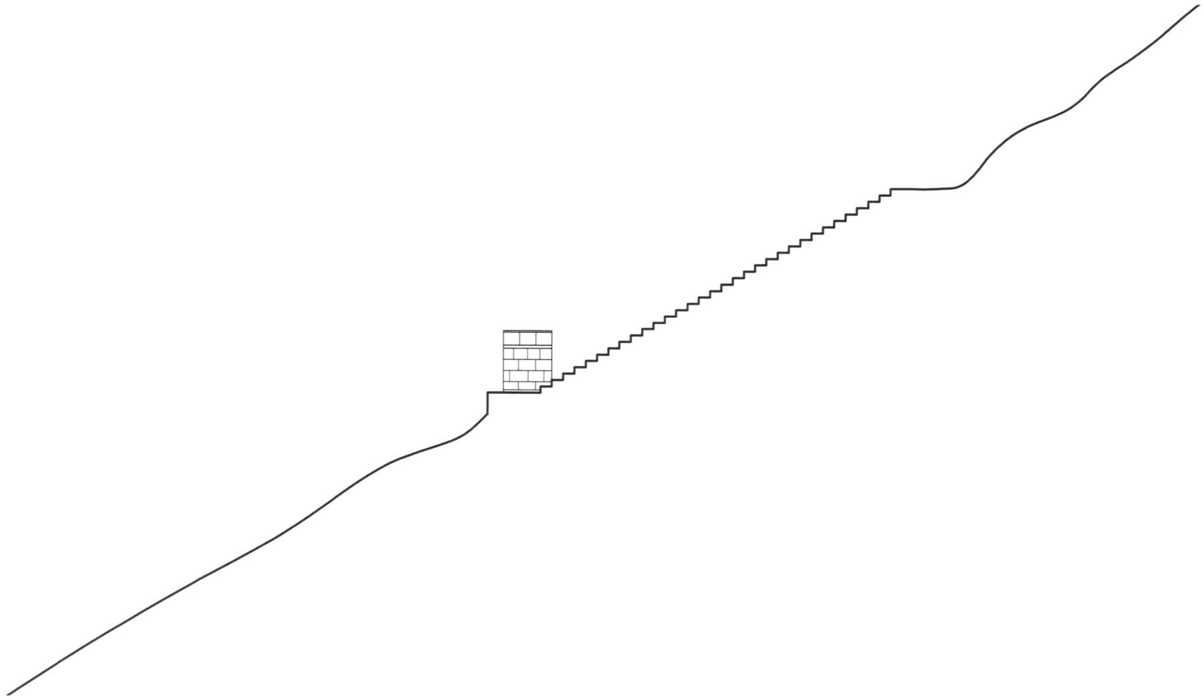

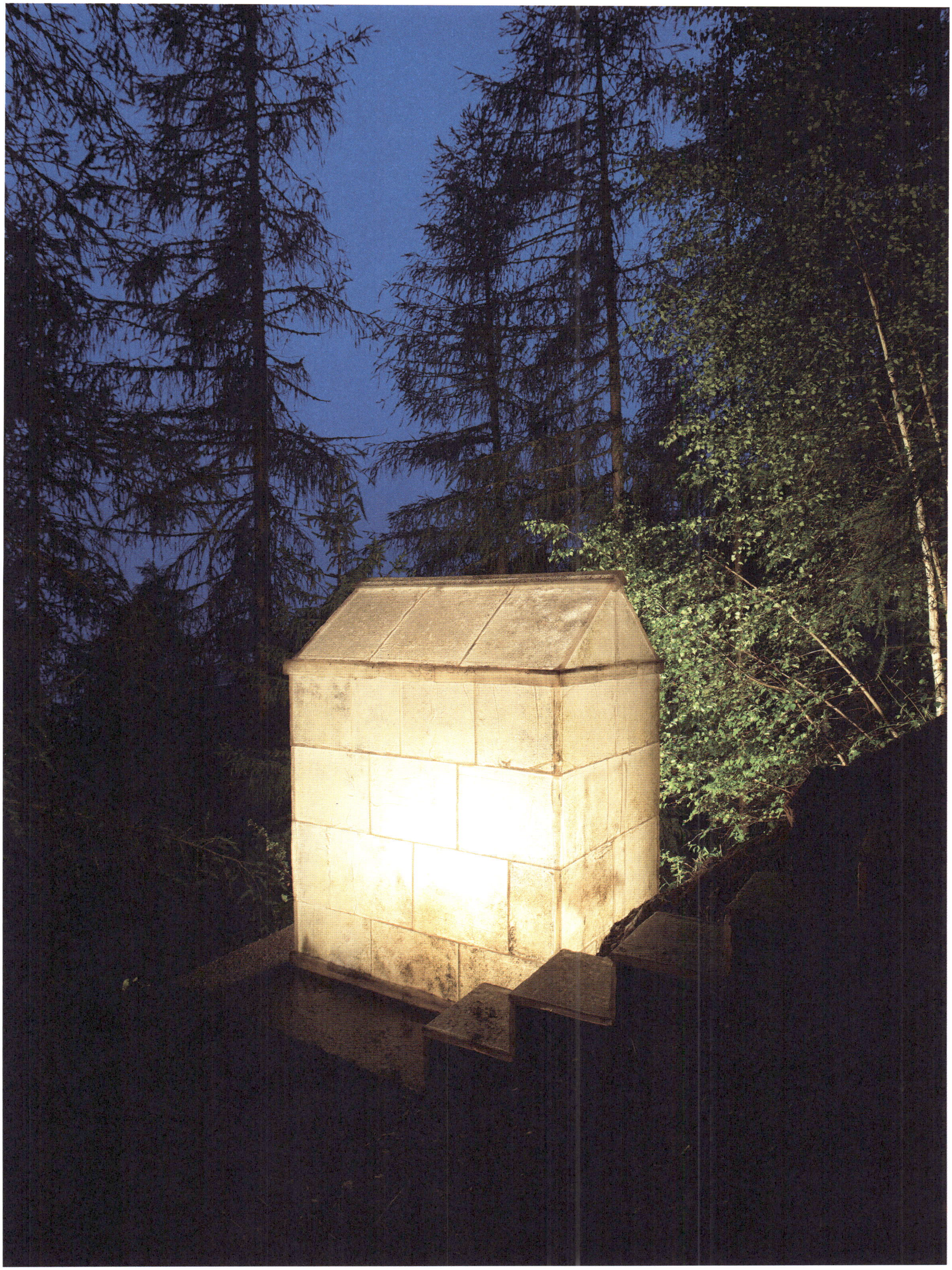

Chasa barcha / Chamonna süll'aua (House by the River)

Parkin, Sent, Switzerland 2002

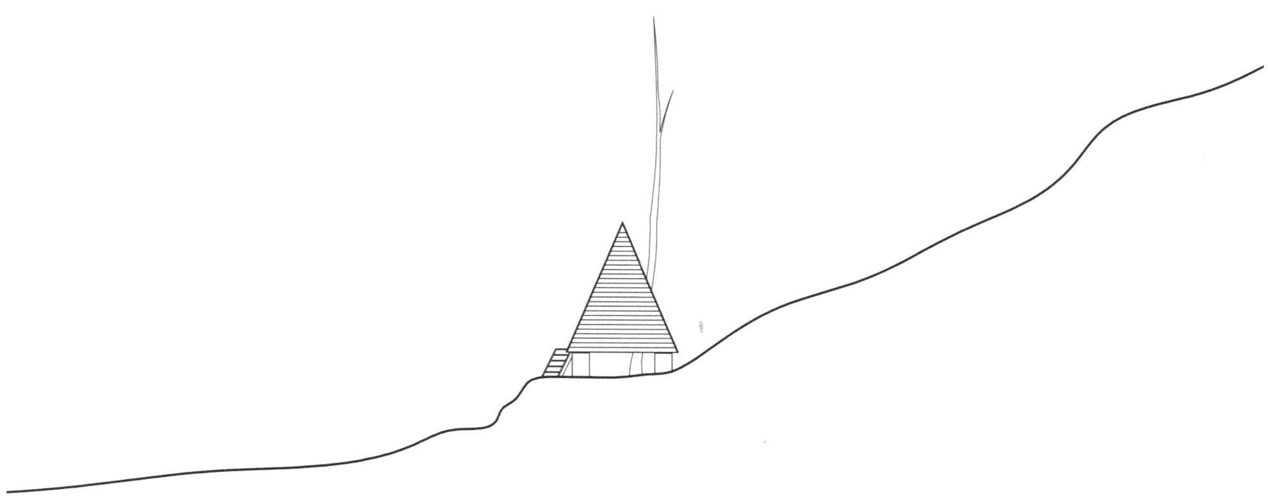

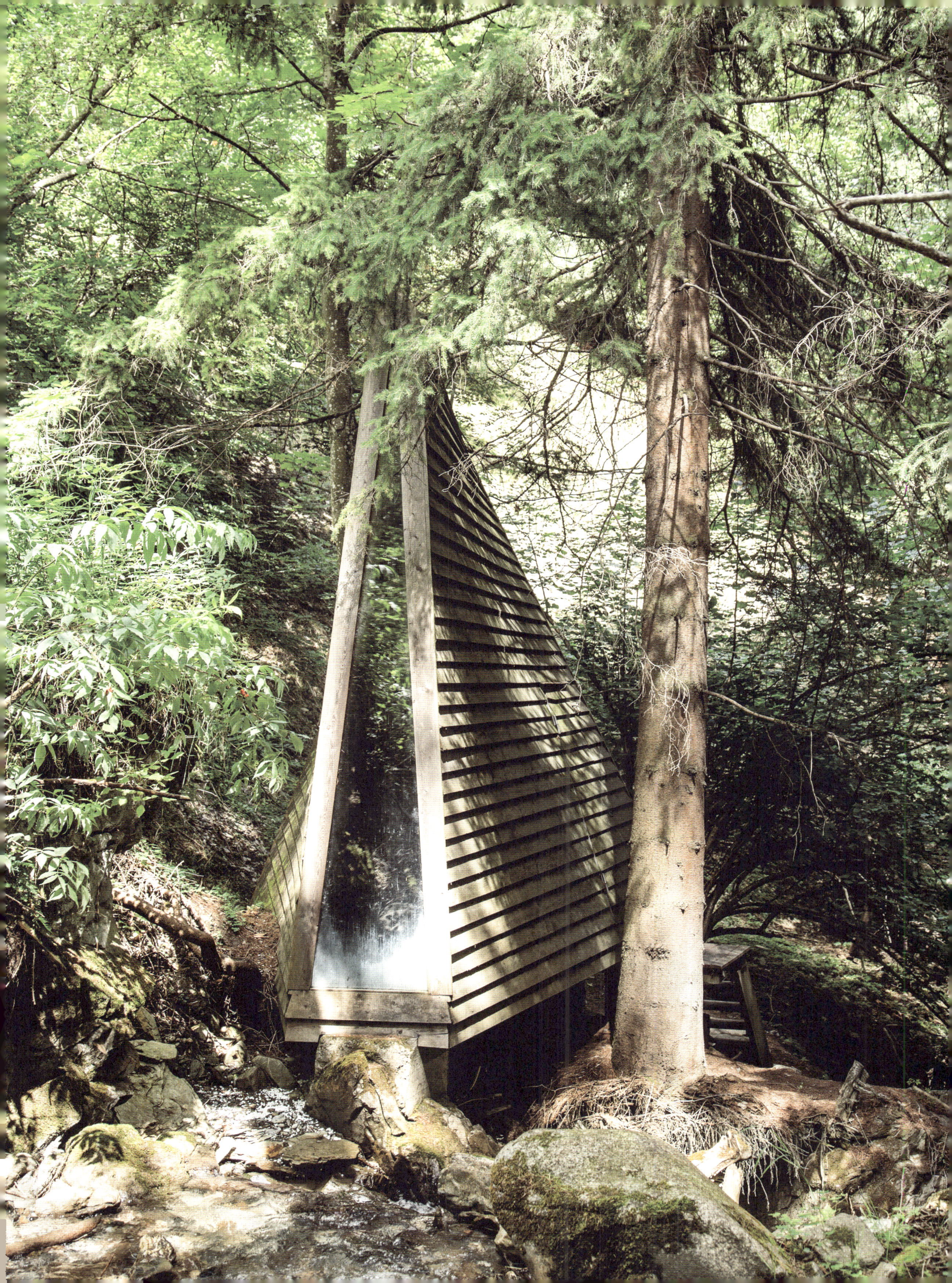

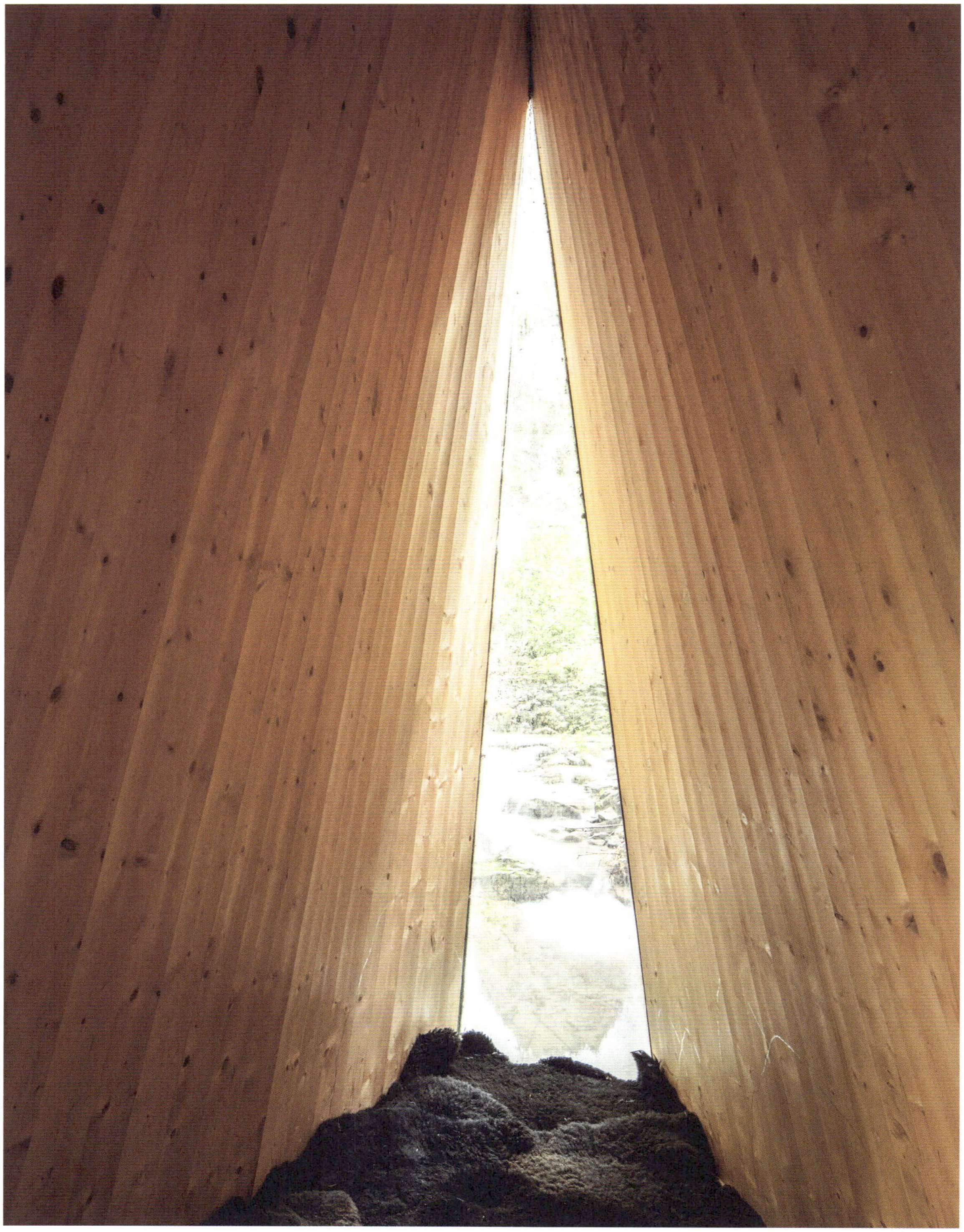

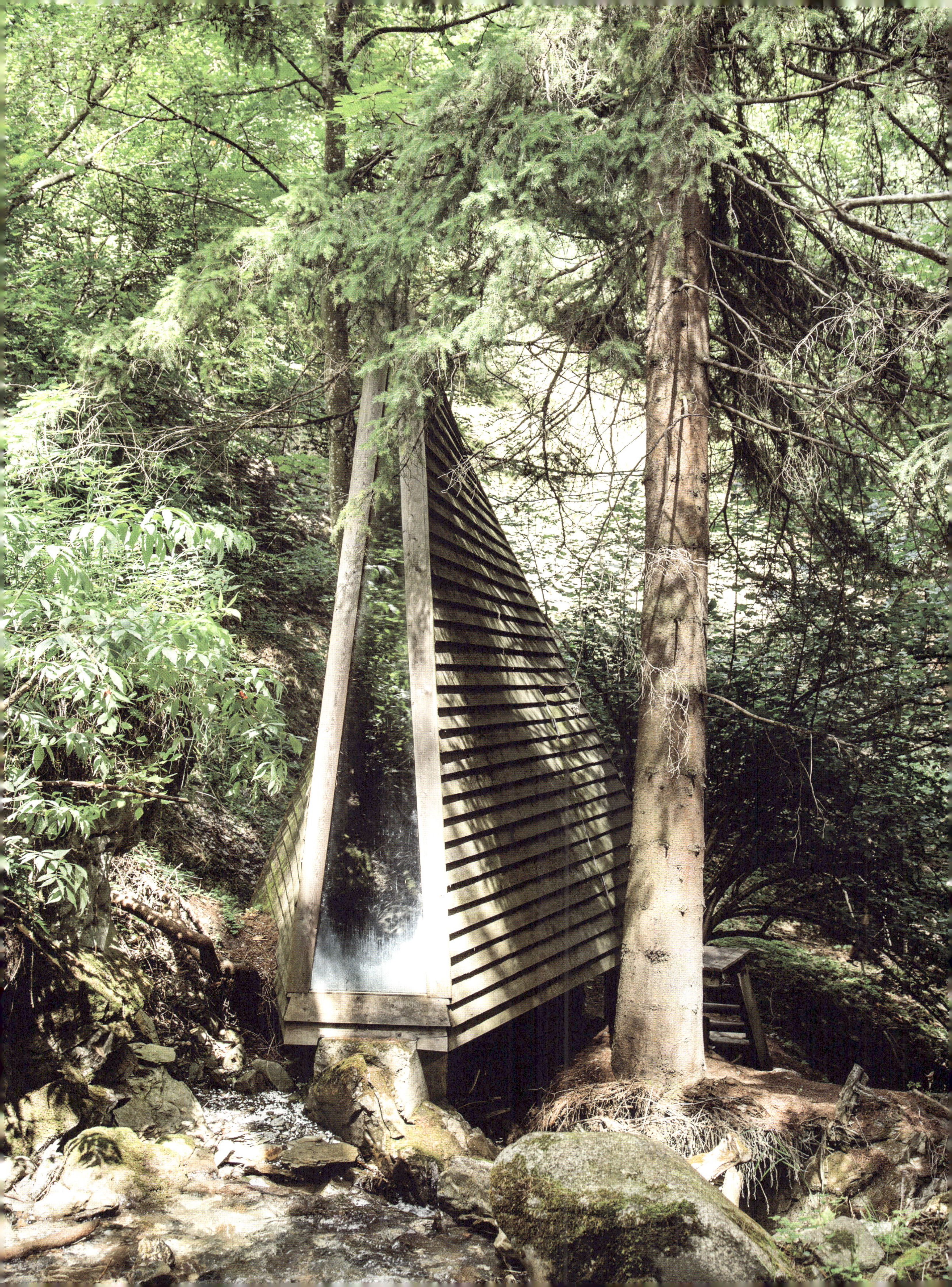

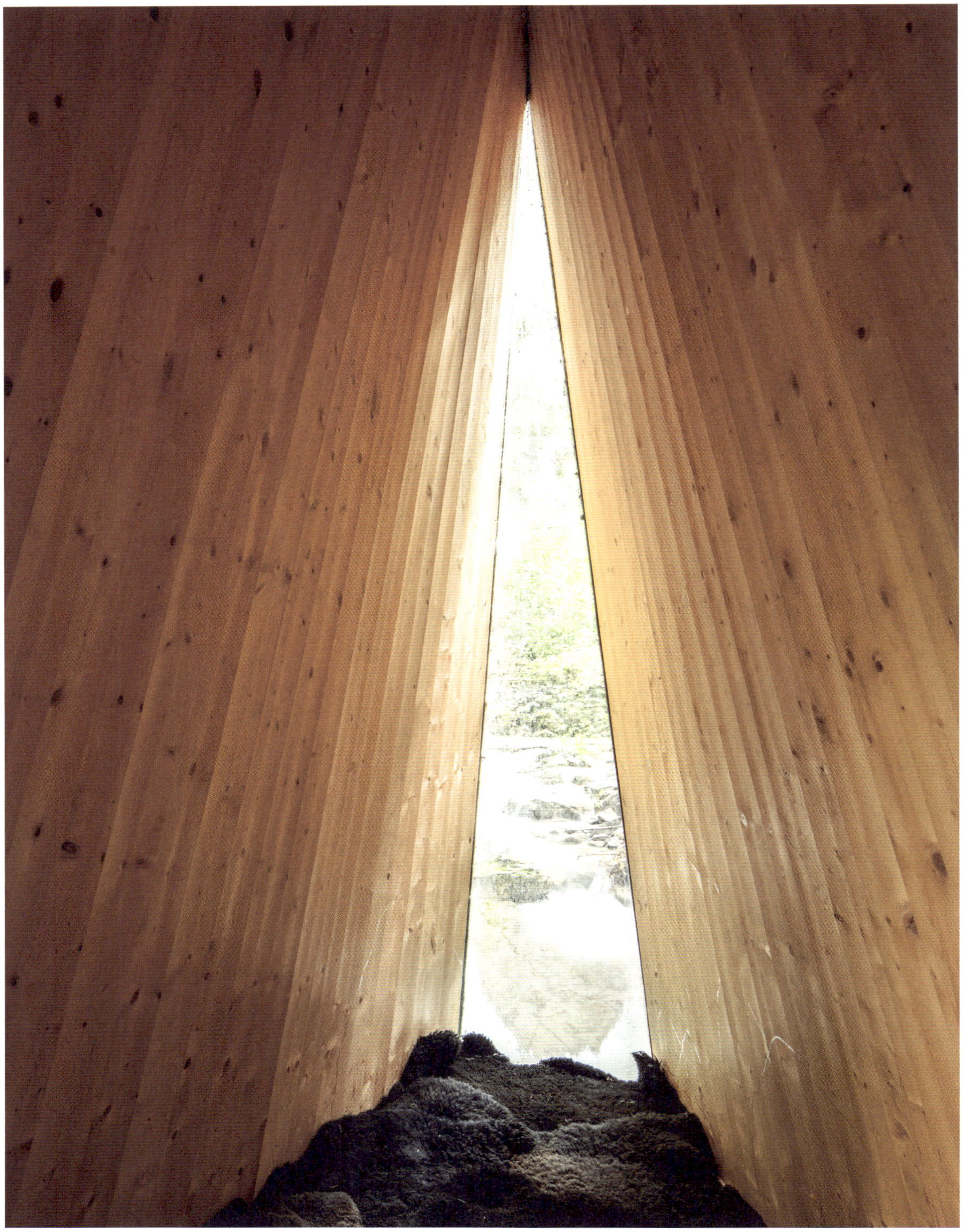

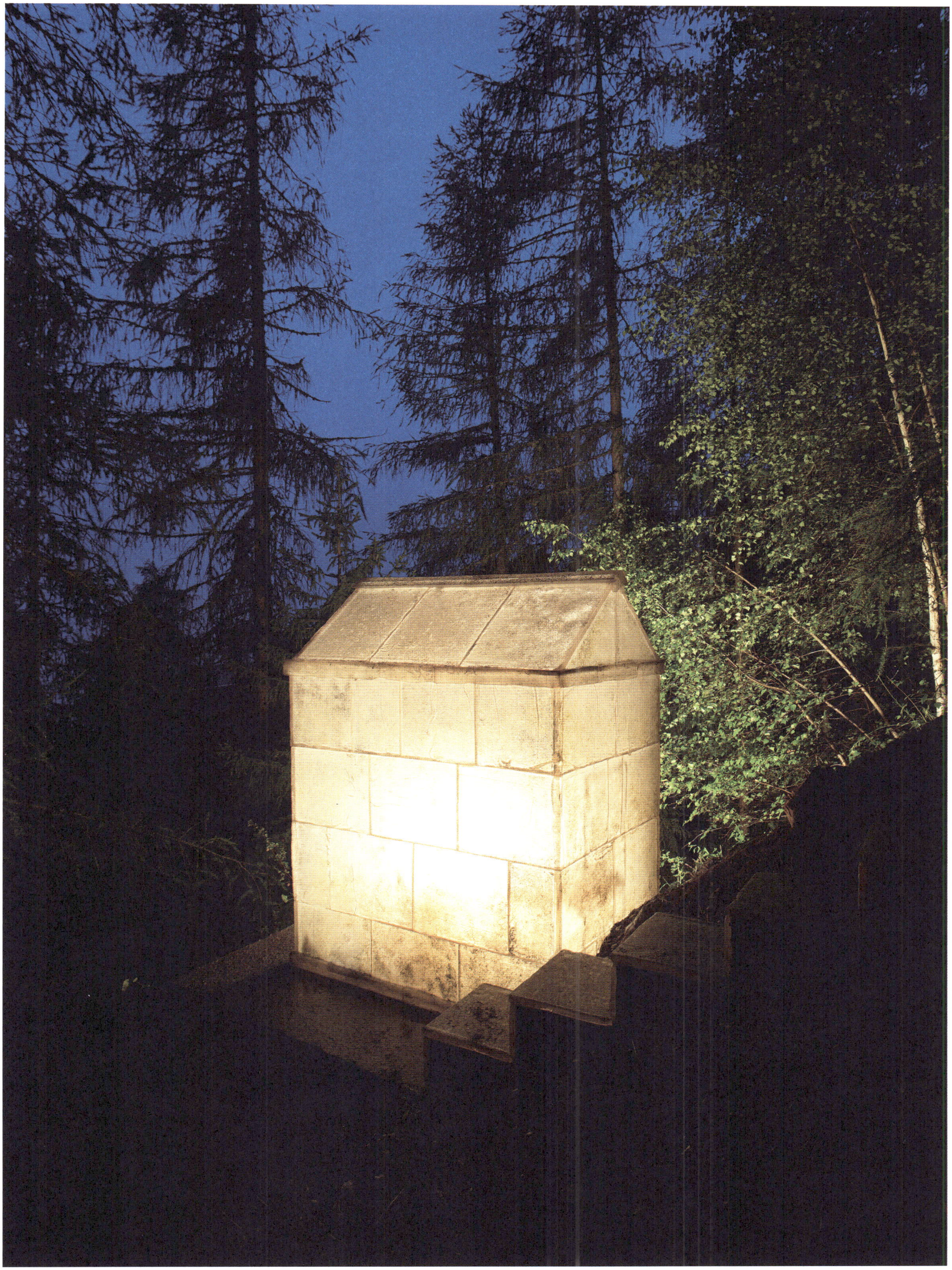

Chasa barcha / Chamonna süll'aua (House by the River)

Parkin, Sent, Switzerland
2002

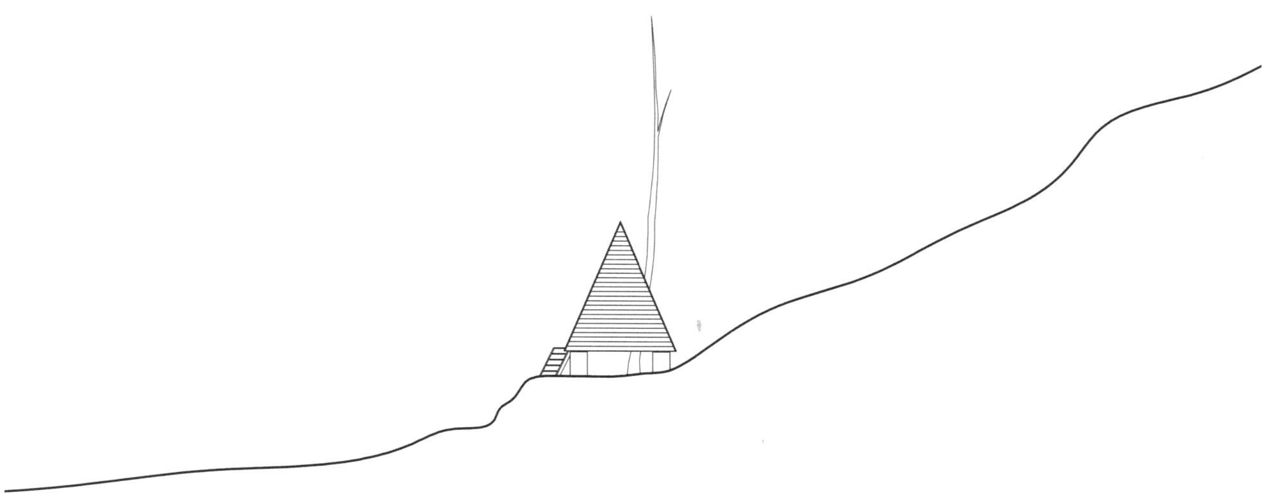

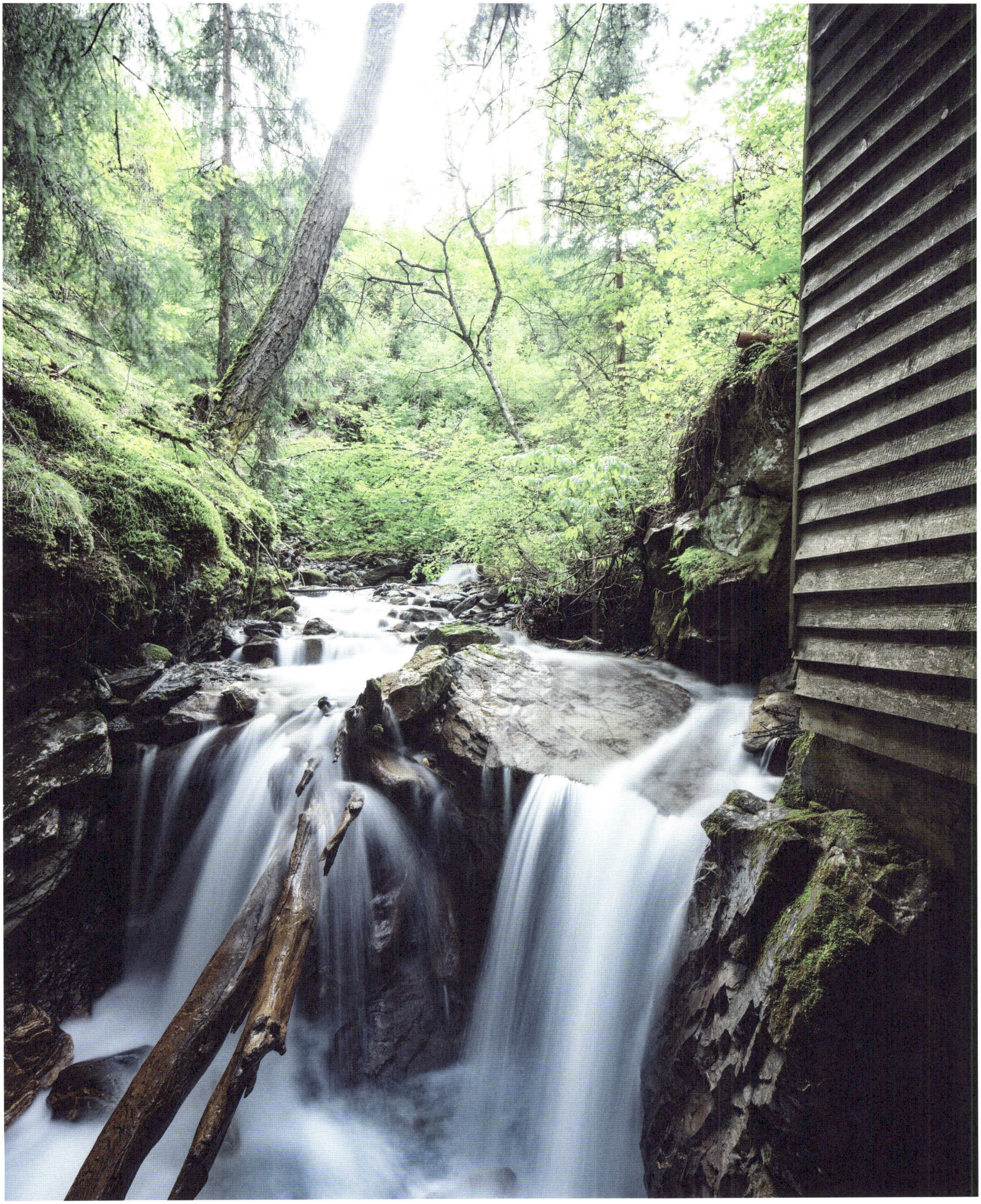

Tuor da silenzi
(Tower of Silence)
Parkin, Sent, Switzerland
2003

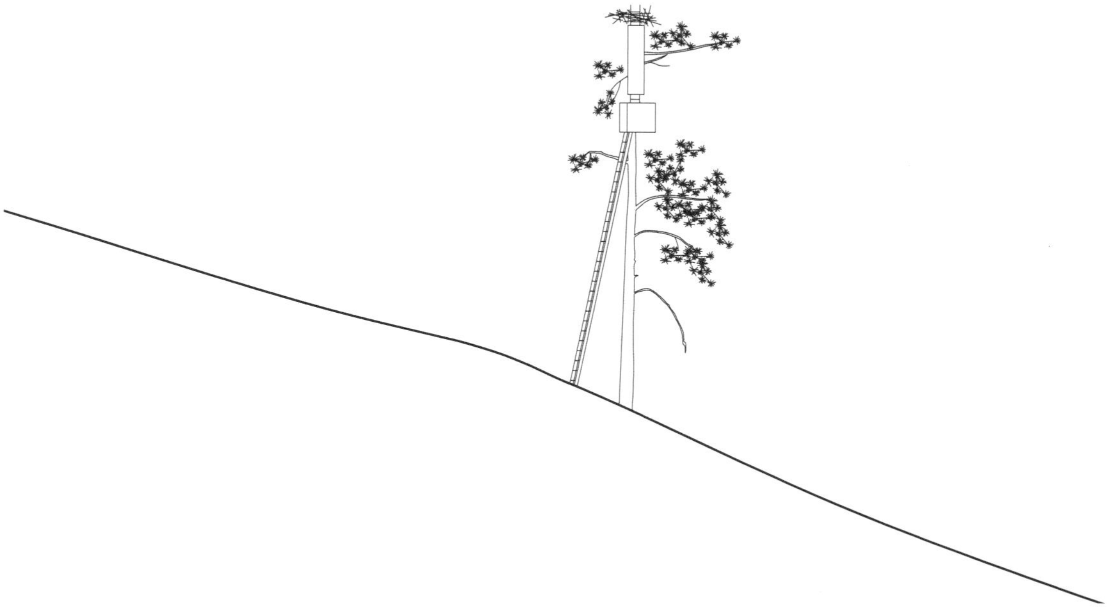

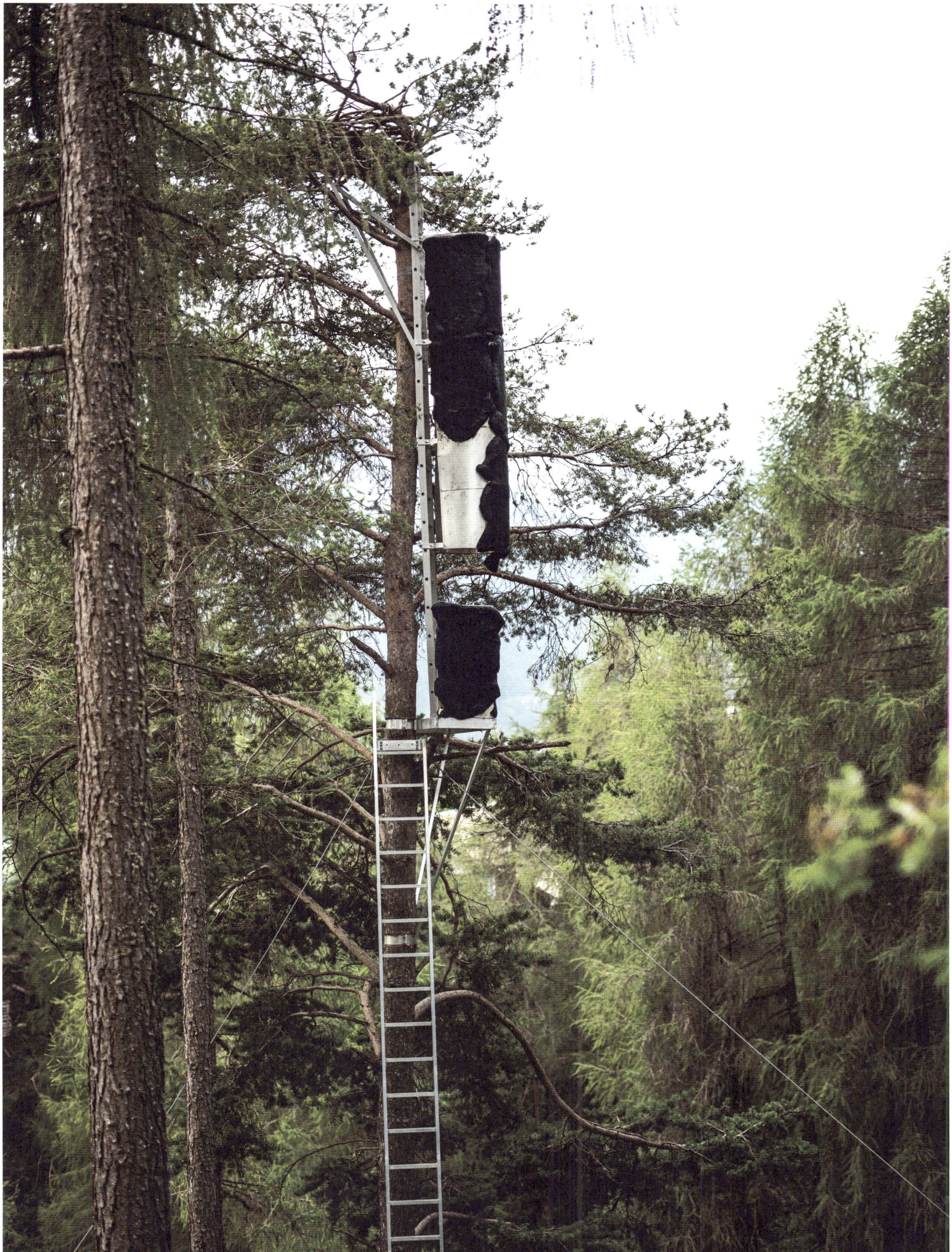

Chamonna spanada (Board House)

Parkin, Sent, Switzerland
2004

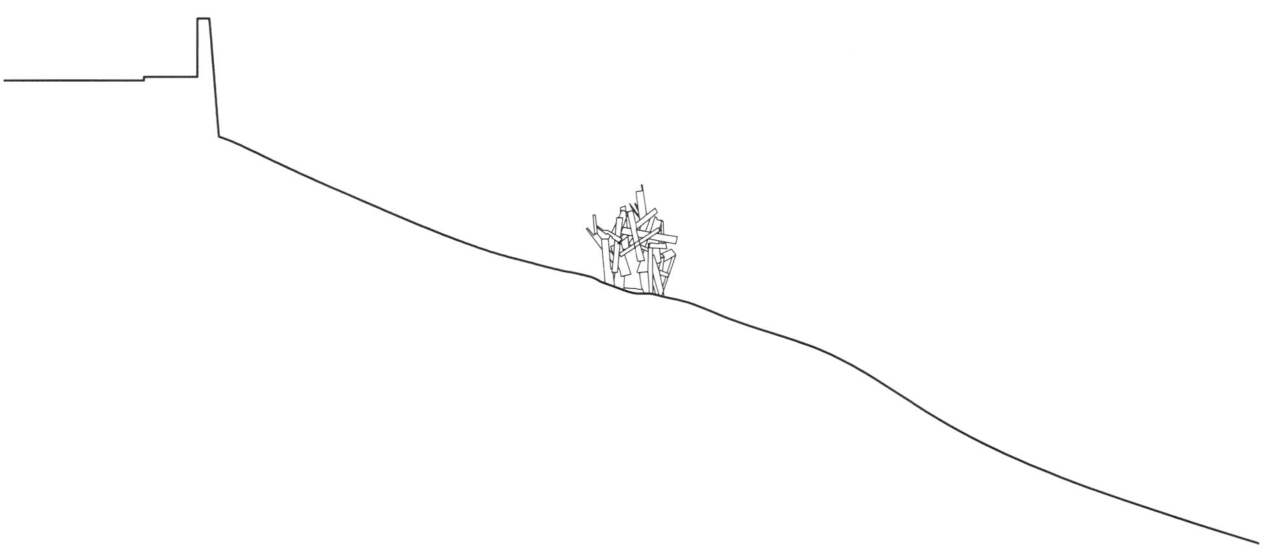

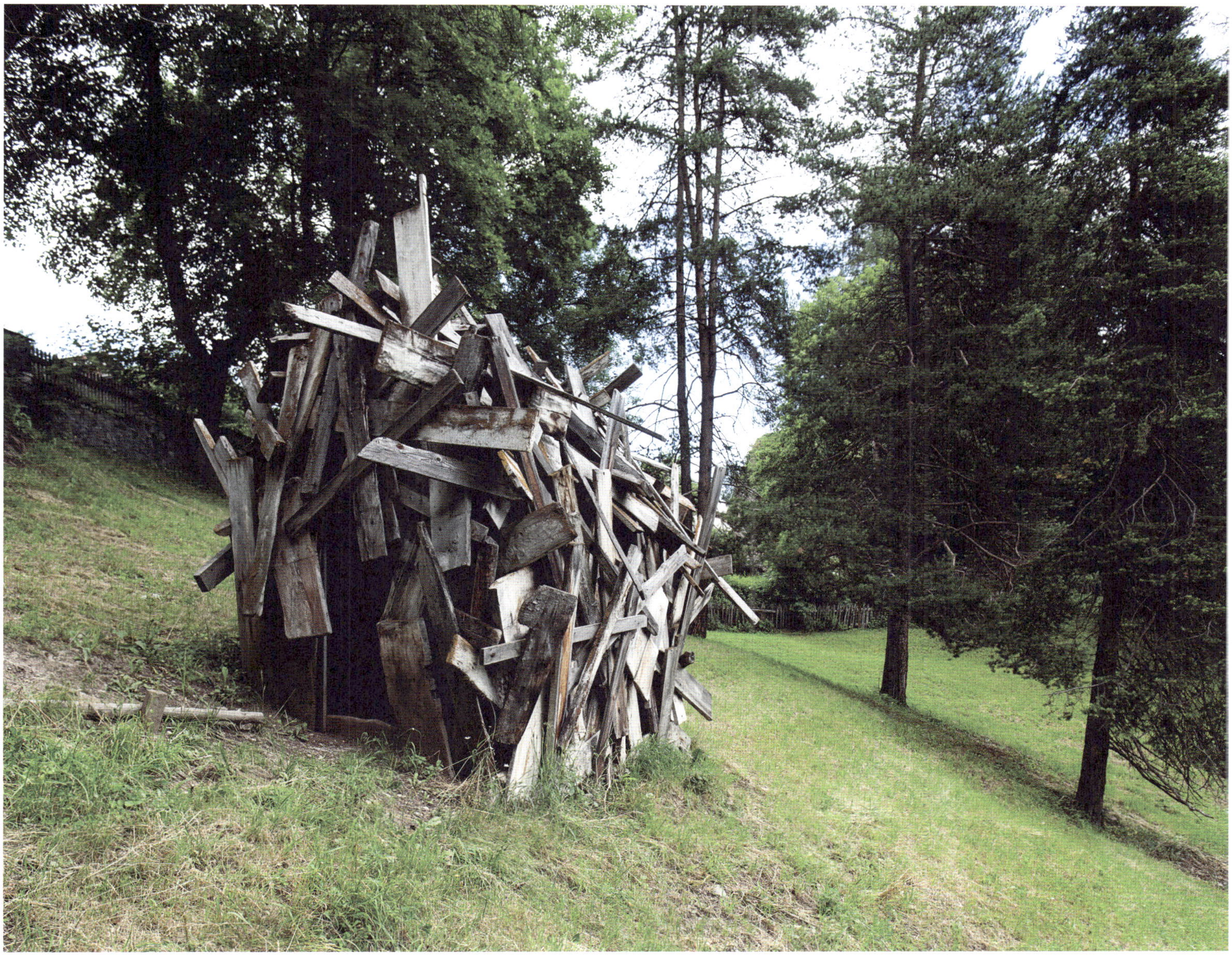

Biotop
Parkin, Sent, Switzerland
2007

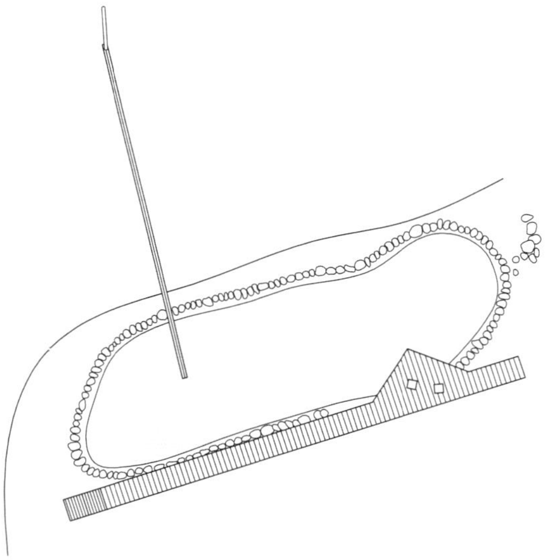

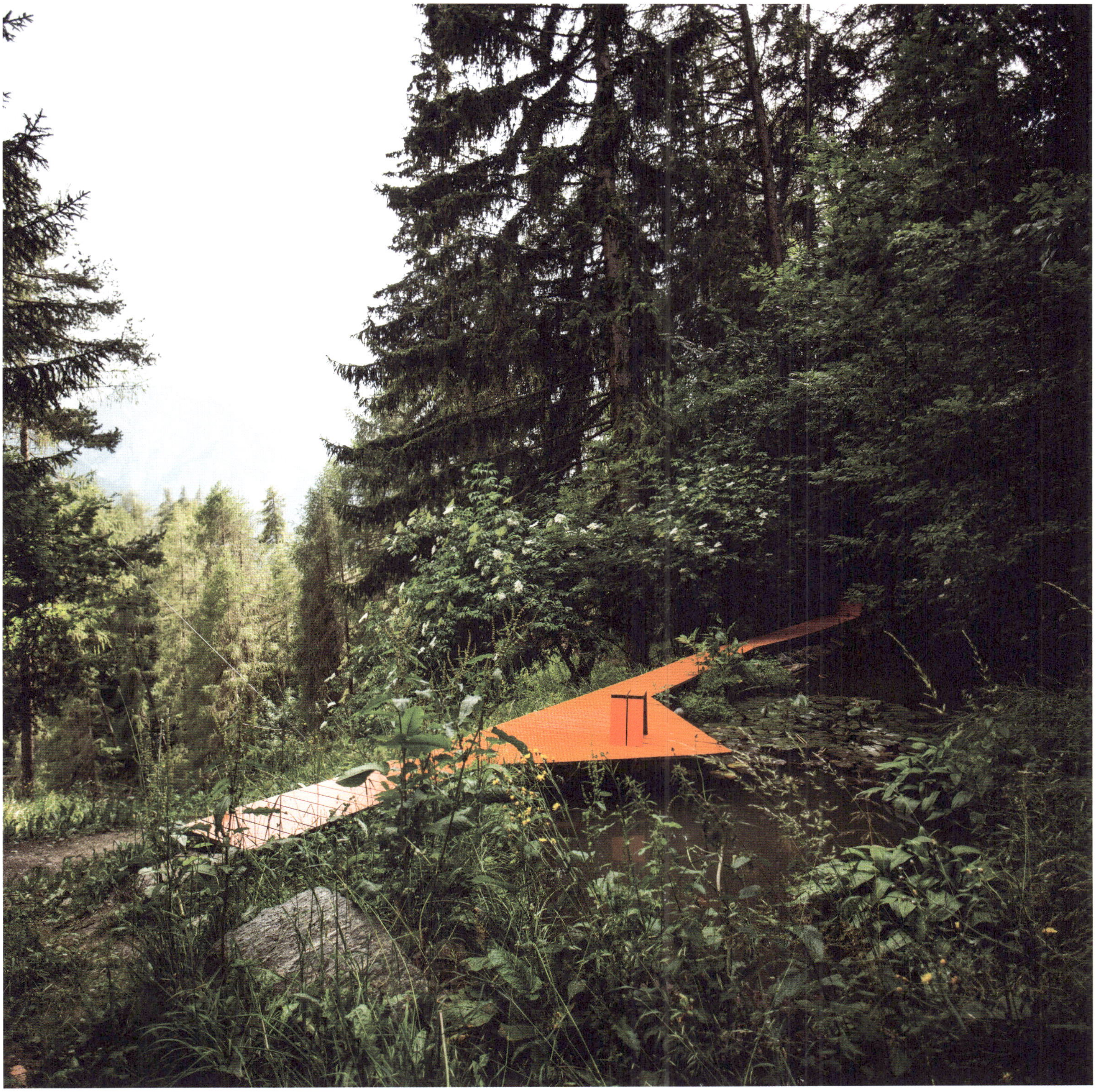

JOSÜJO
(Disappearing House)
Parkin, Sent, Switzerland
2007

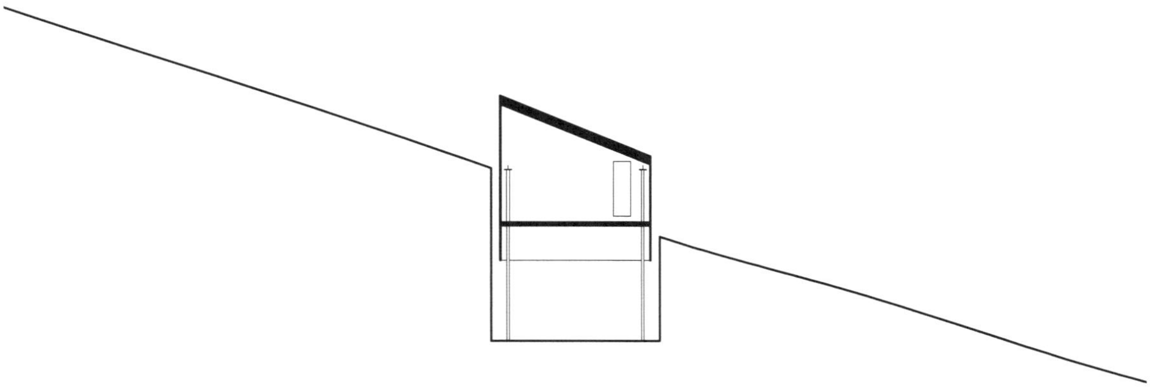

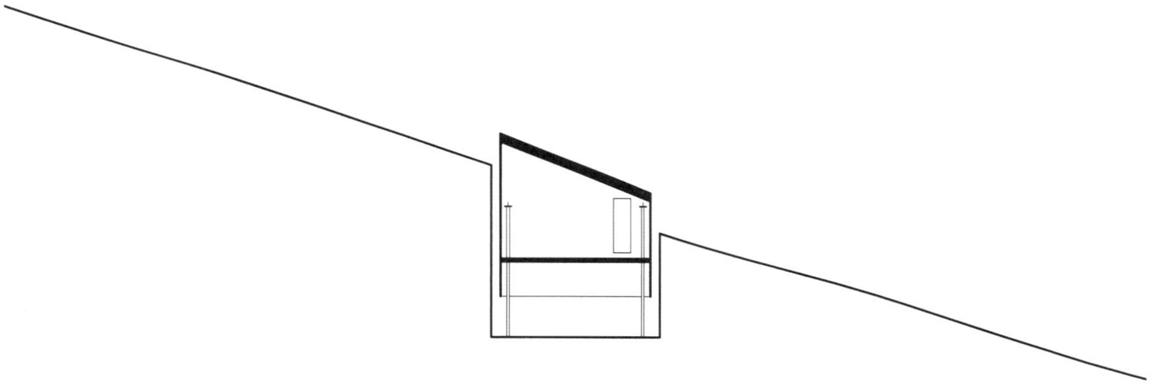

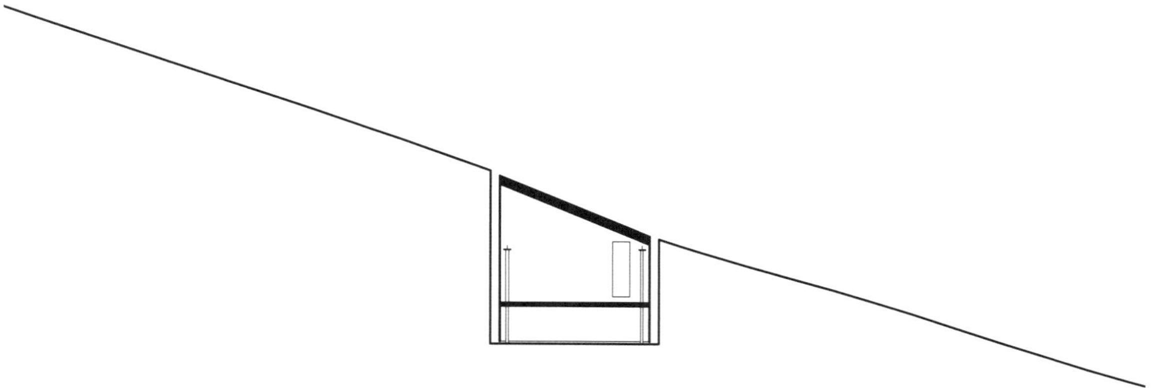

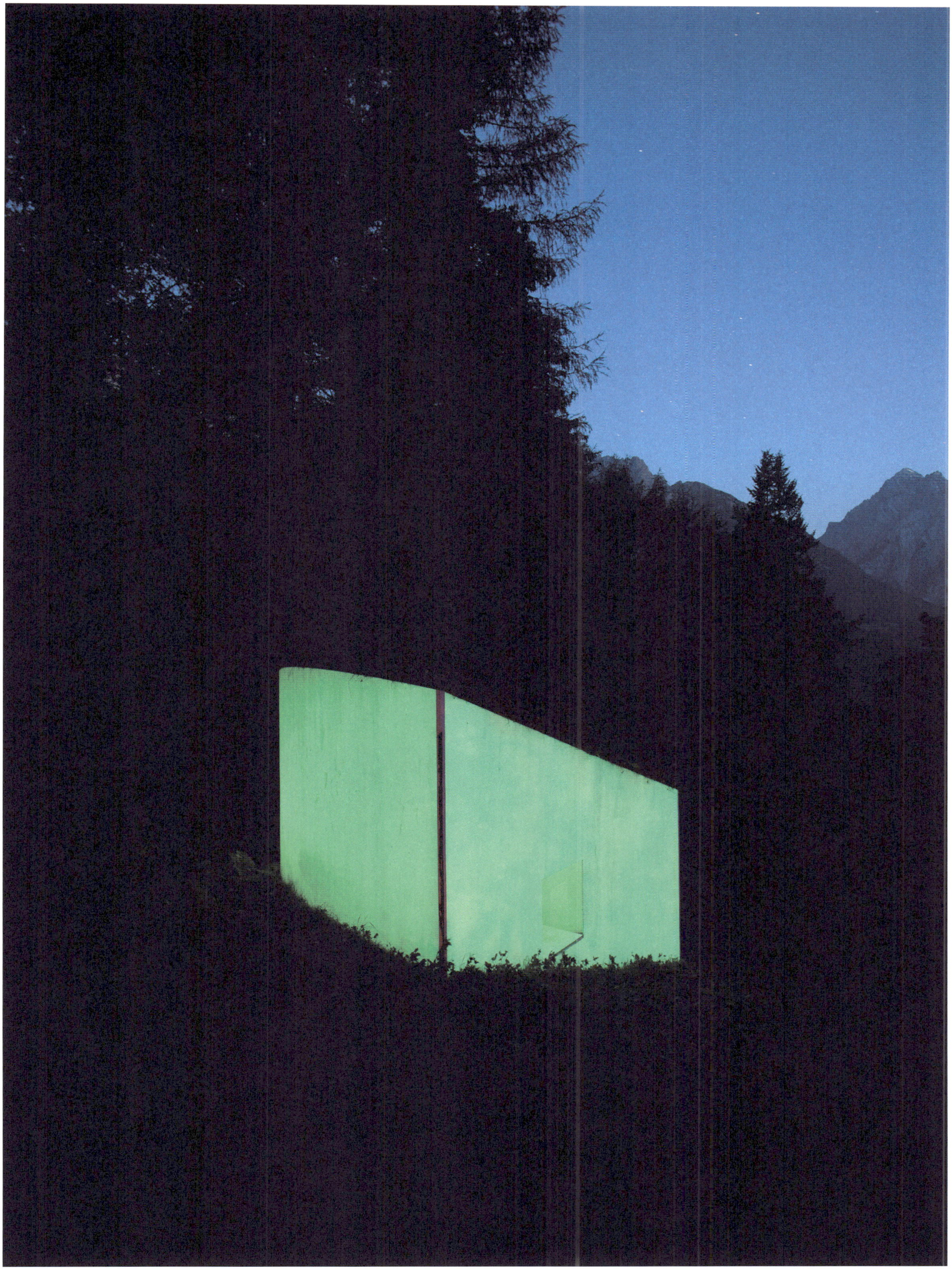

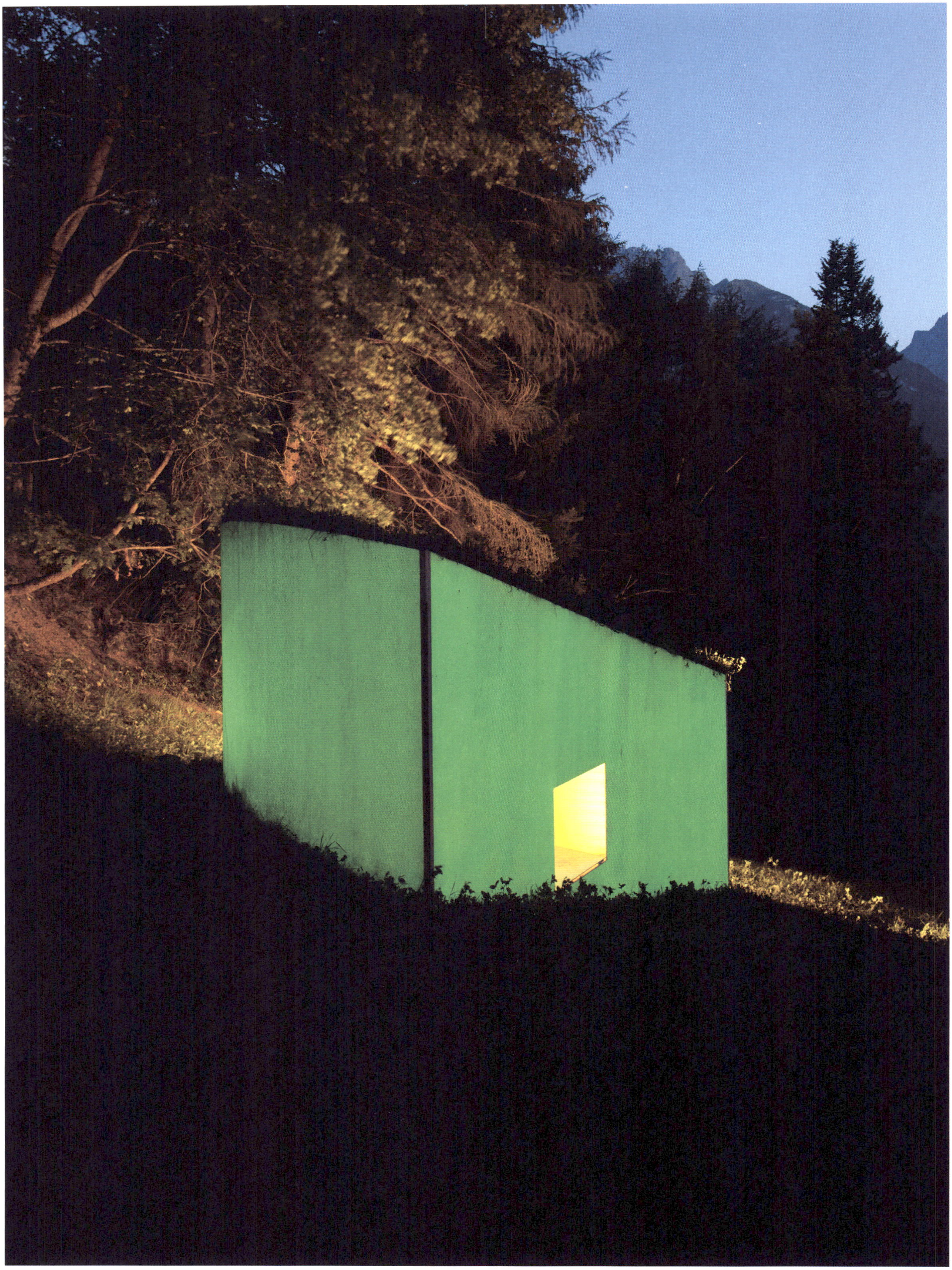

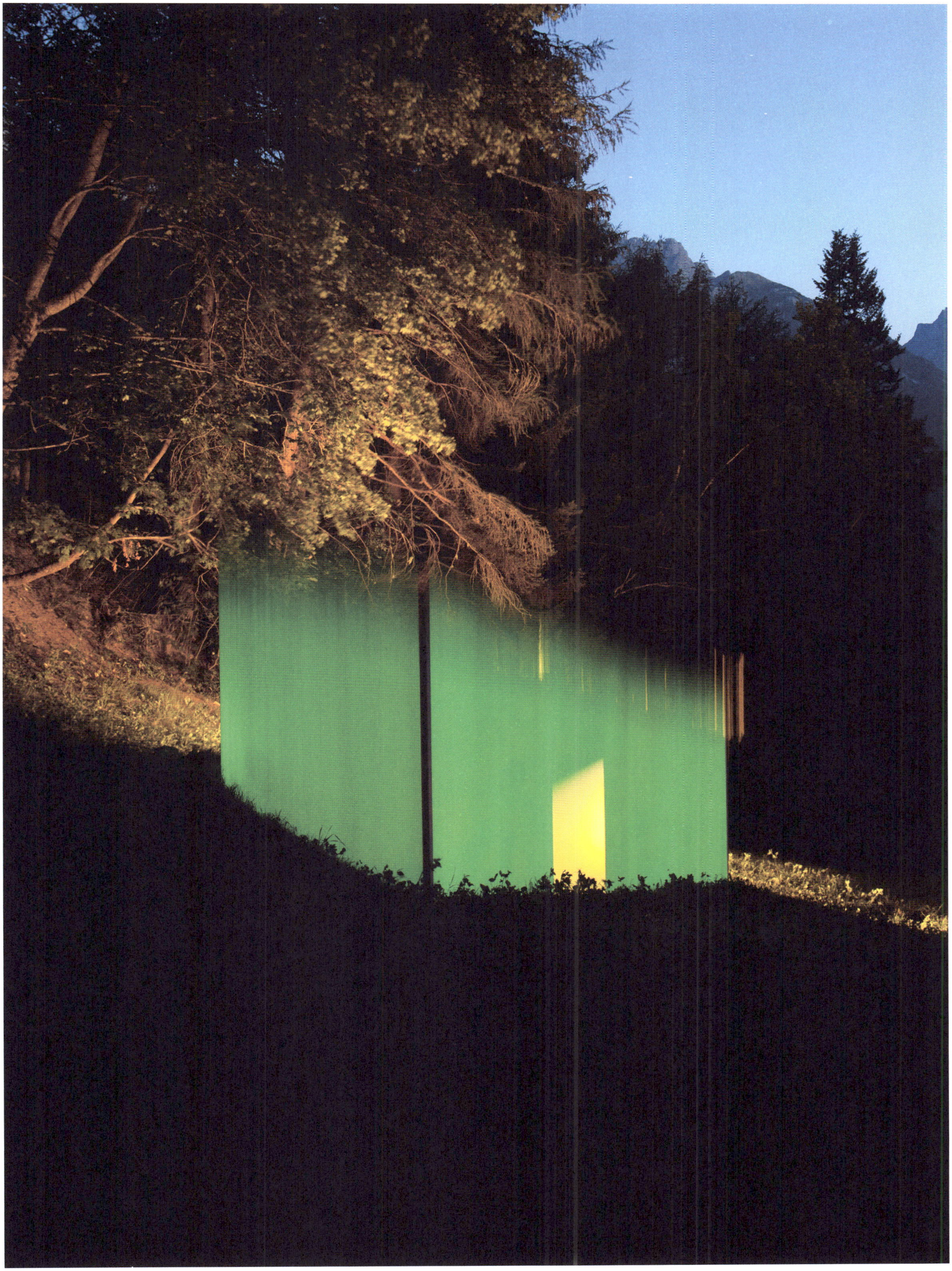

Bridge
Parkin, Sent, Switzerland
2008

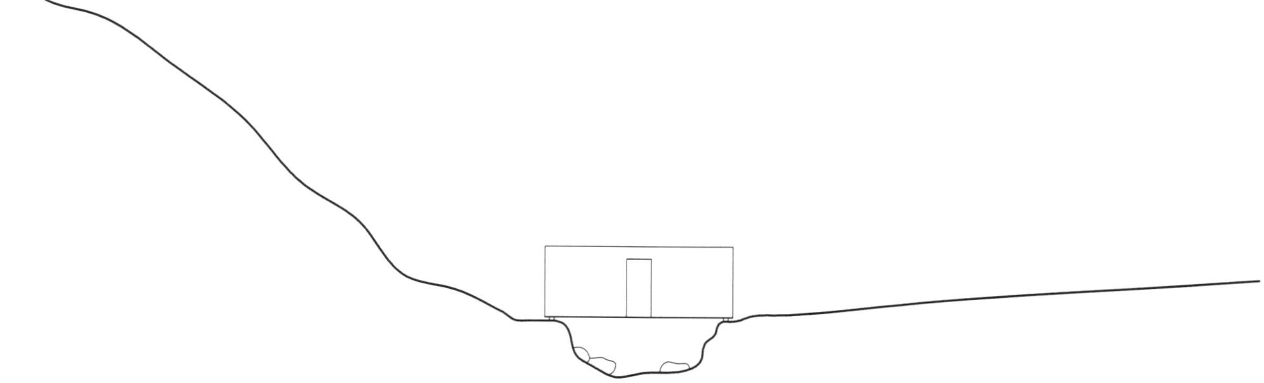

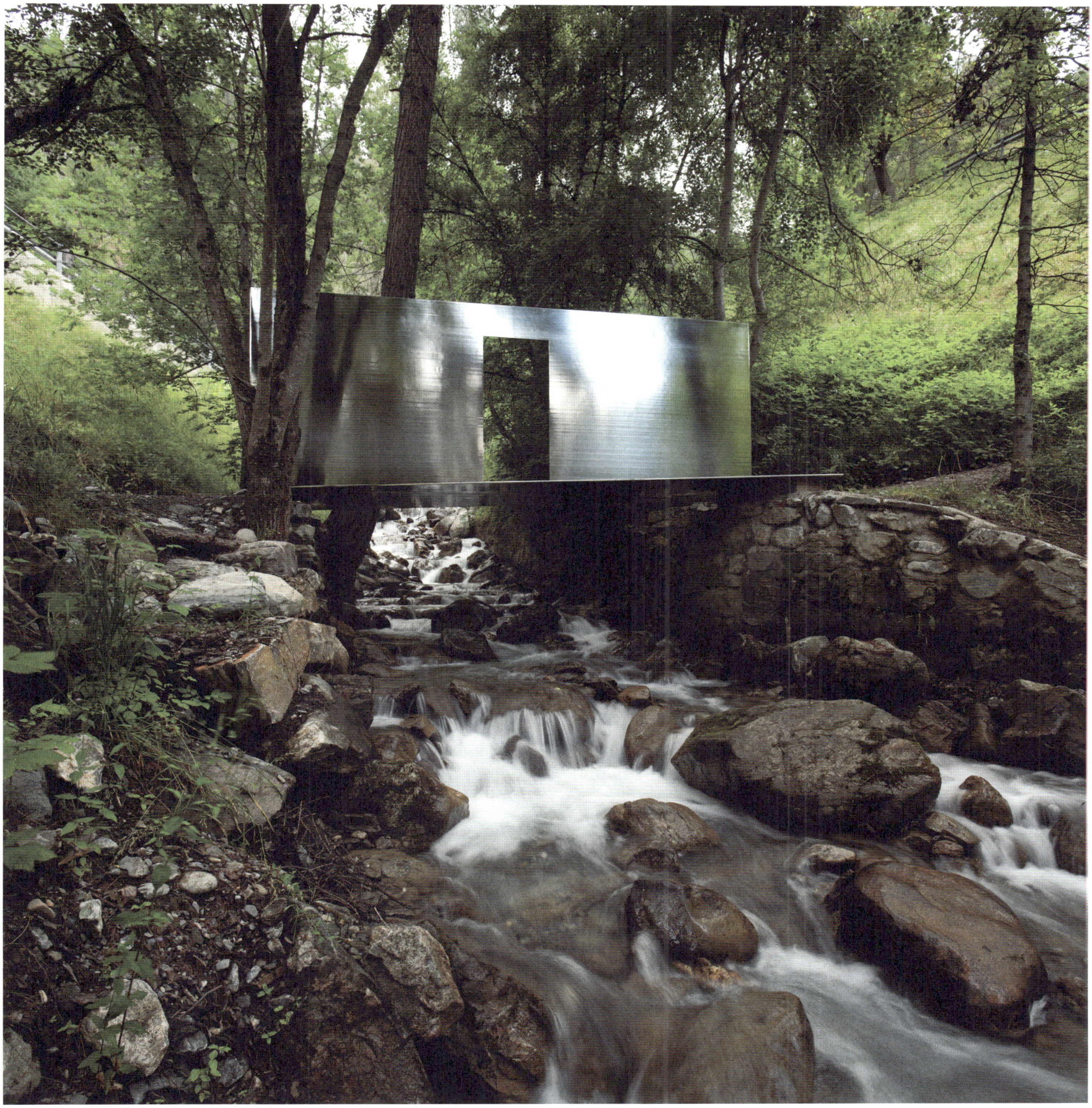

3 Brothers
2016

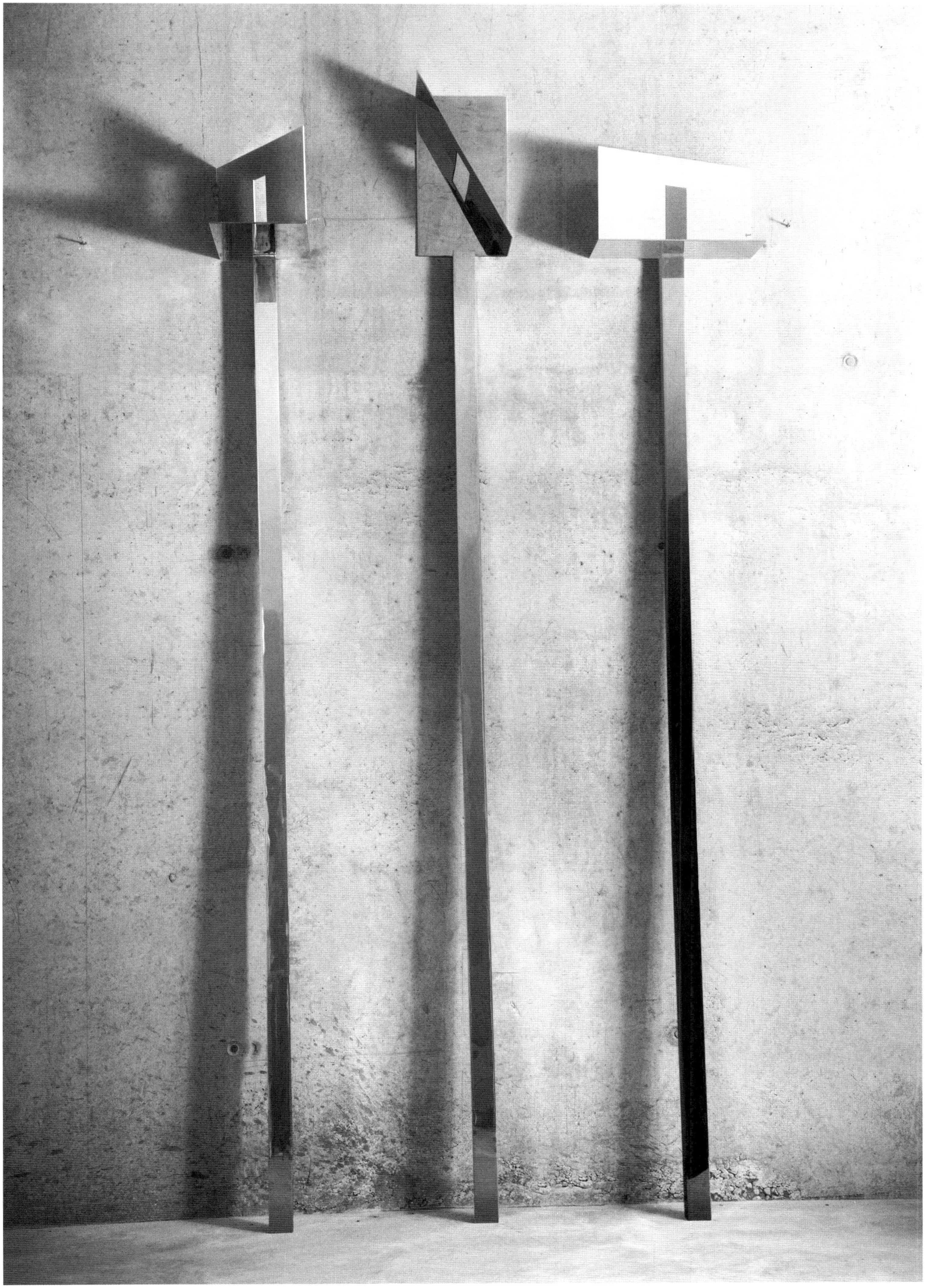

Bridge
2017

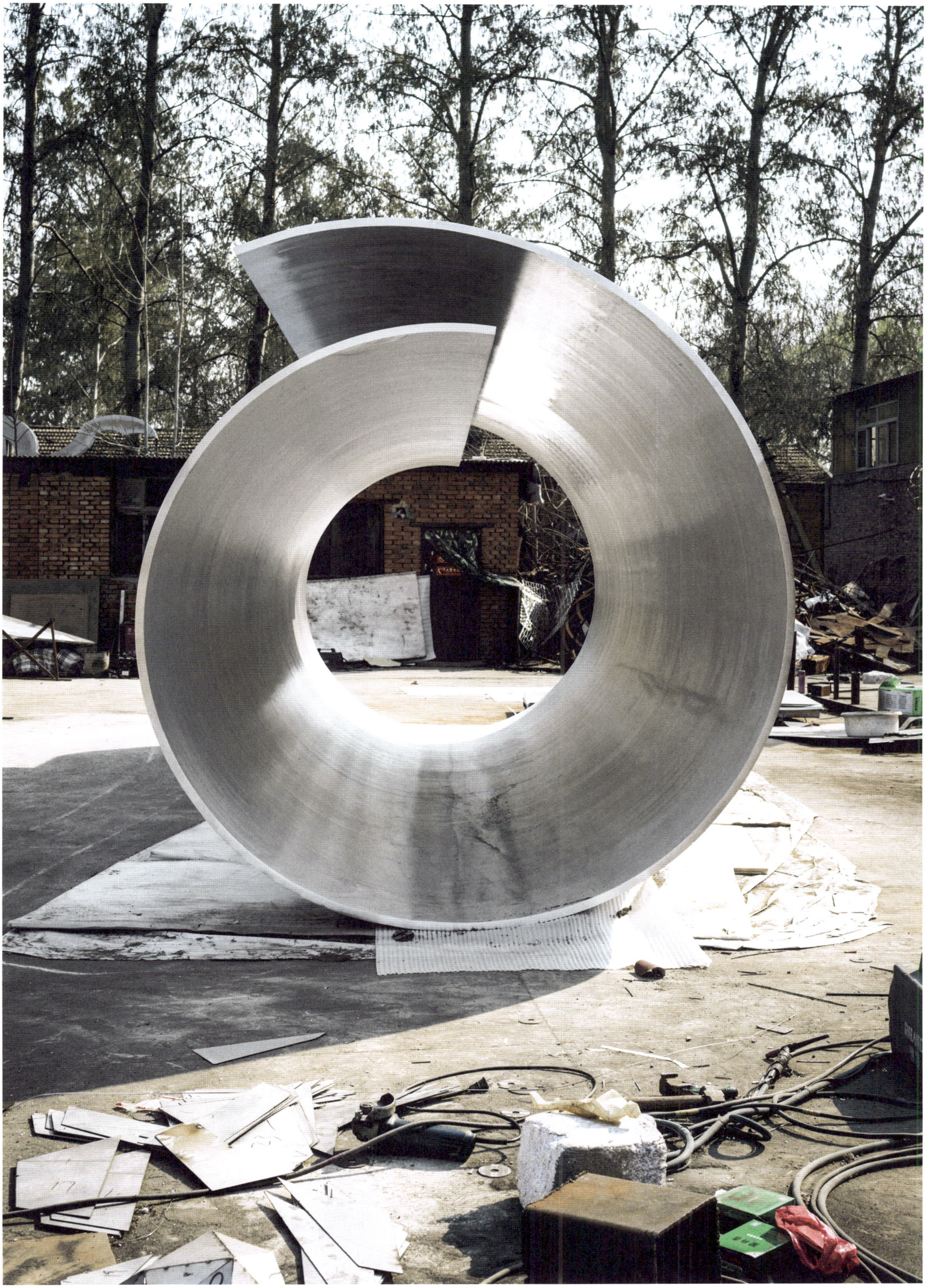

Palc
(Stage)
Parkin, Sent, Switzerland
2011

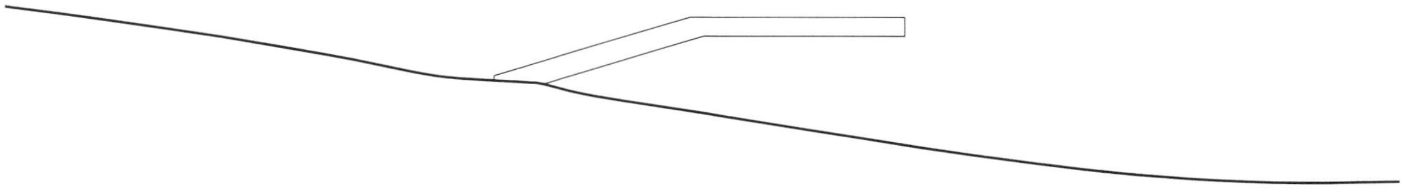

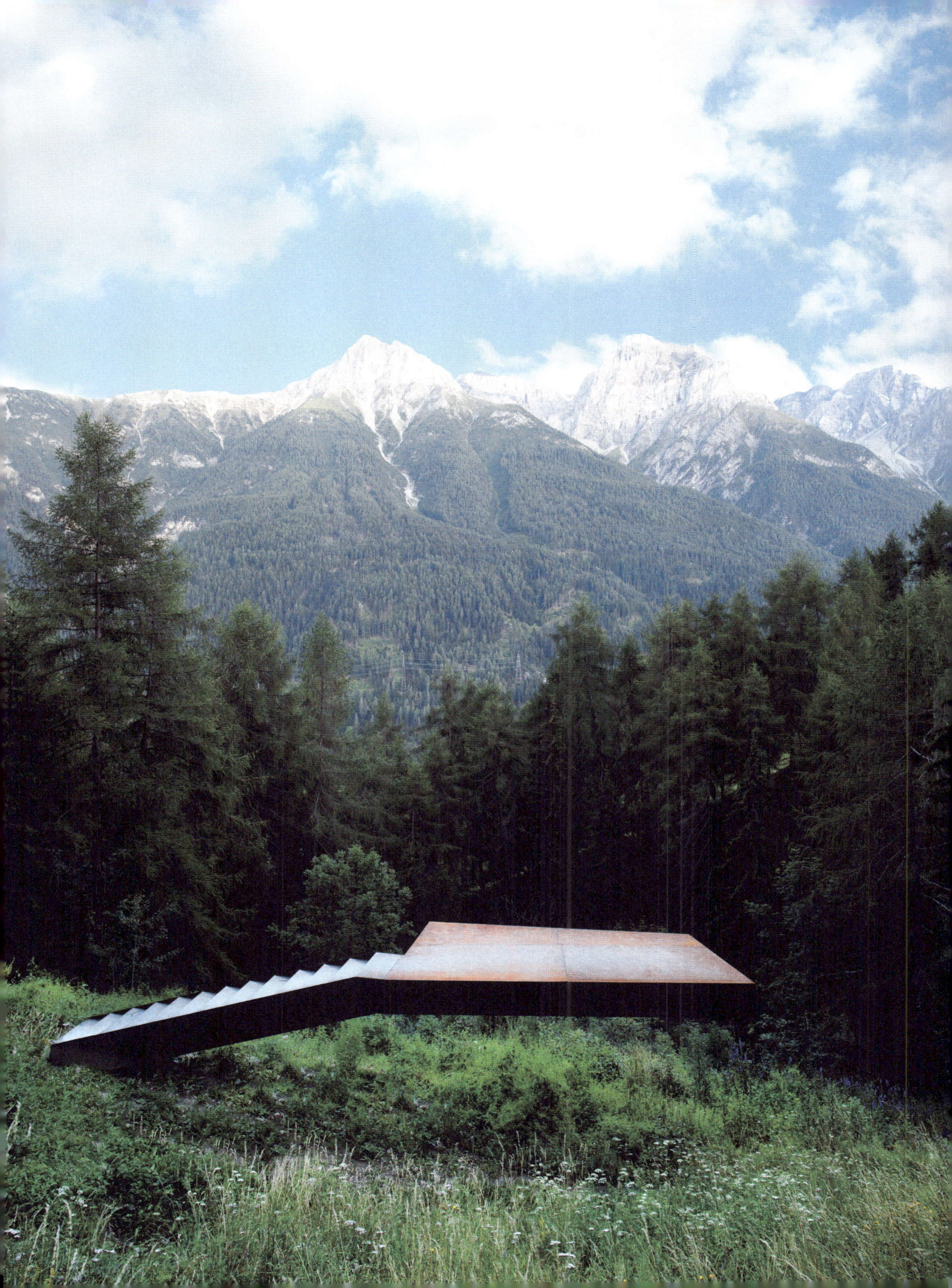

Niger

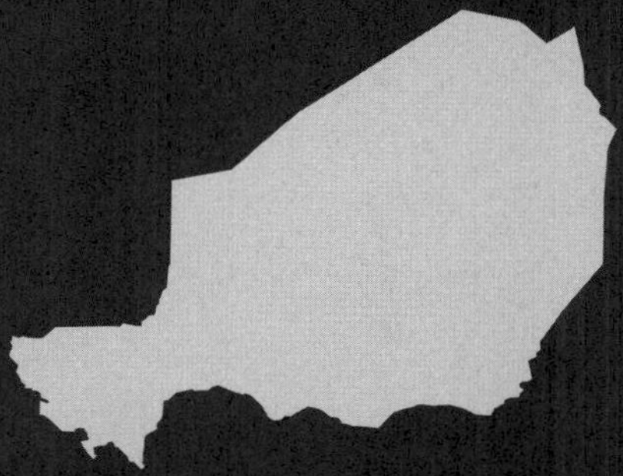

Mekafoni
Agadez, Niger
2001

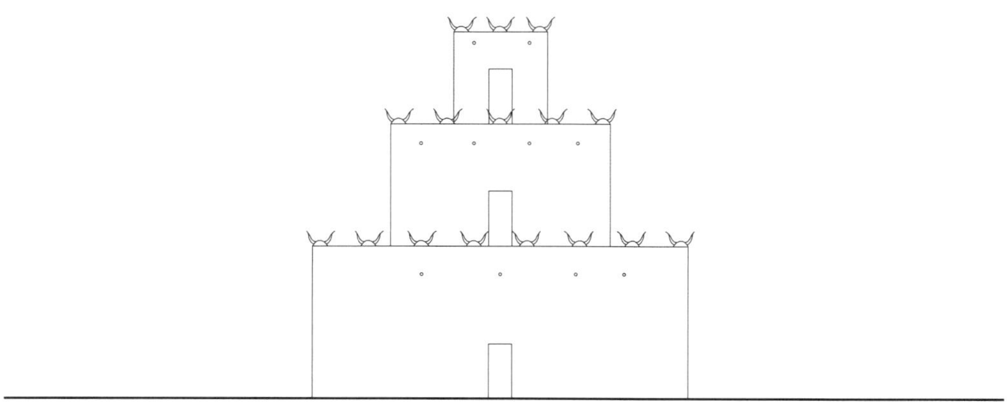

Opposite page: *Mekafoni* with *Camel* (2004) in the foreground

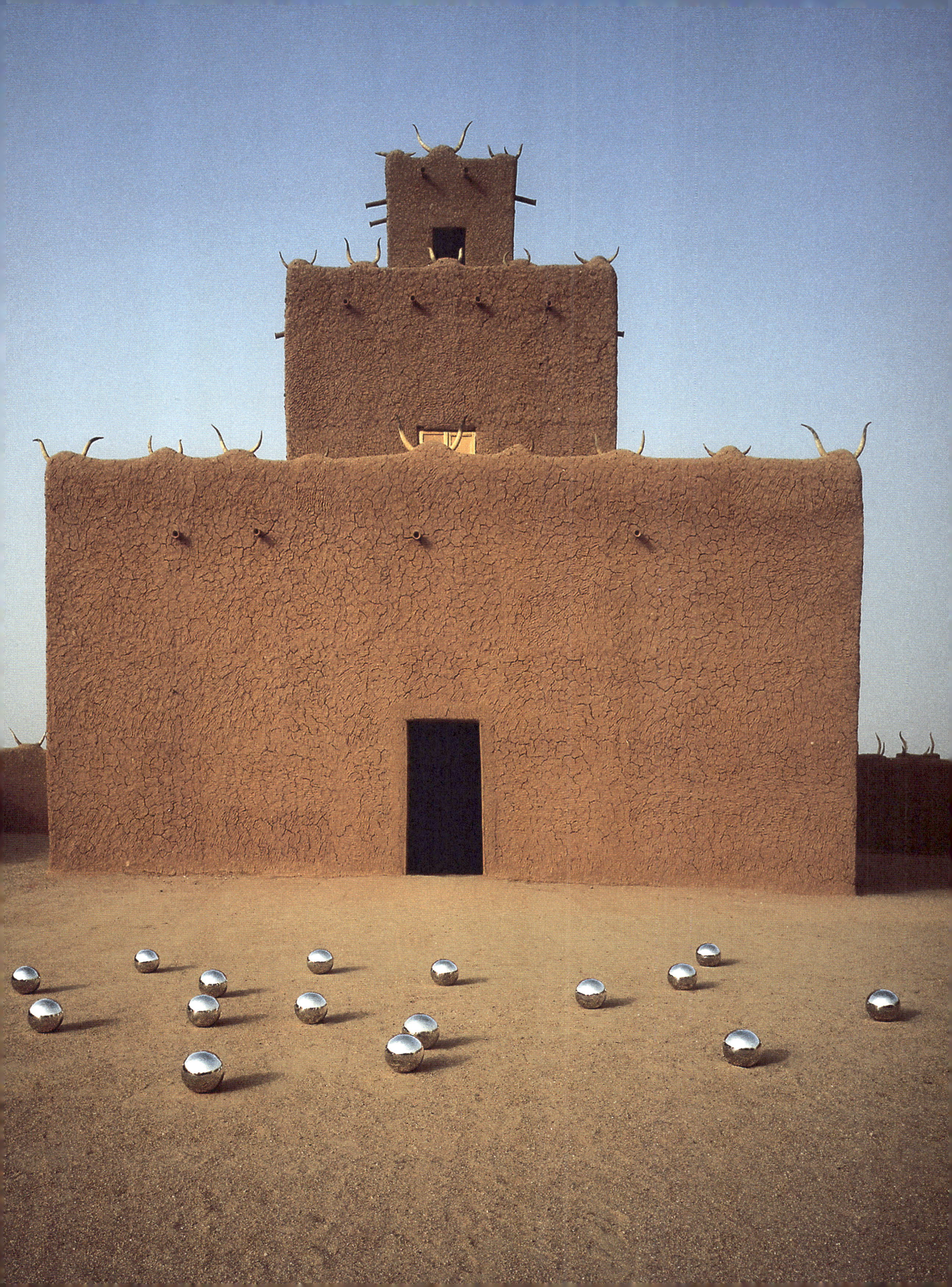

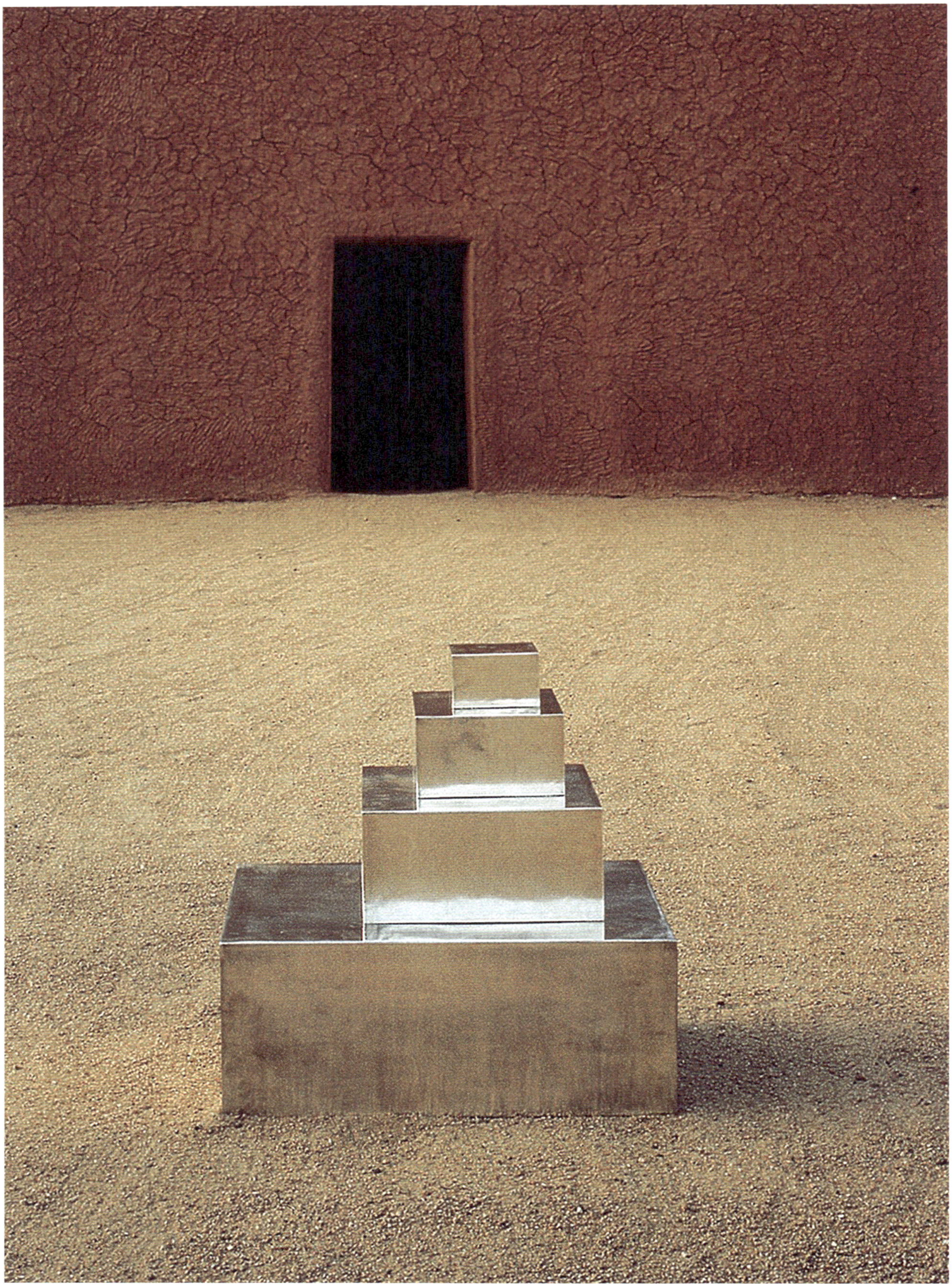

Foreground: *Bremer Stadtmusikanten* (*Musicians of Bremen*), 2004; background: *Mekafoni*
Opposite page: interior of *Mekafoni*

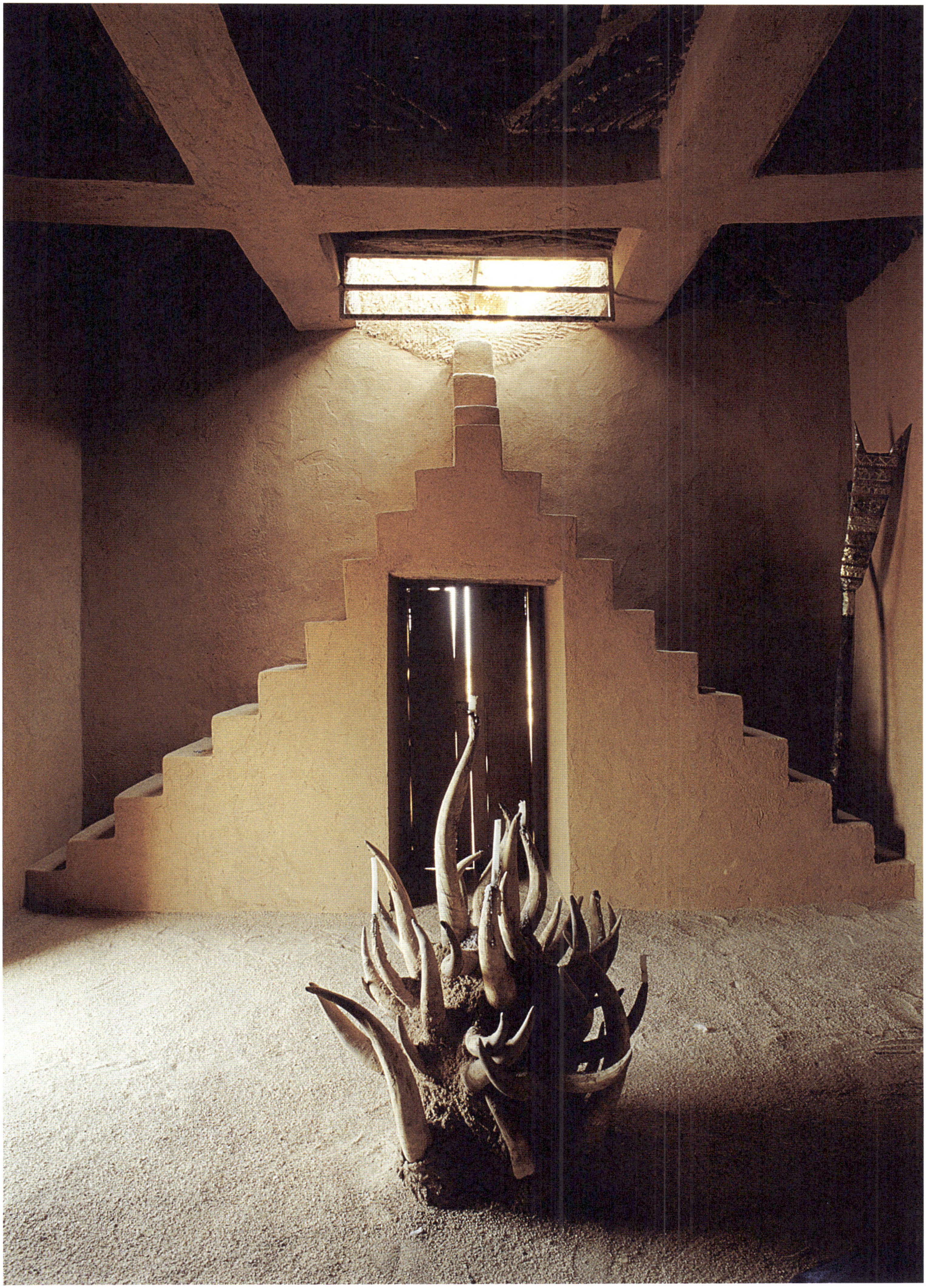

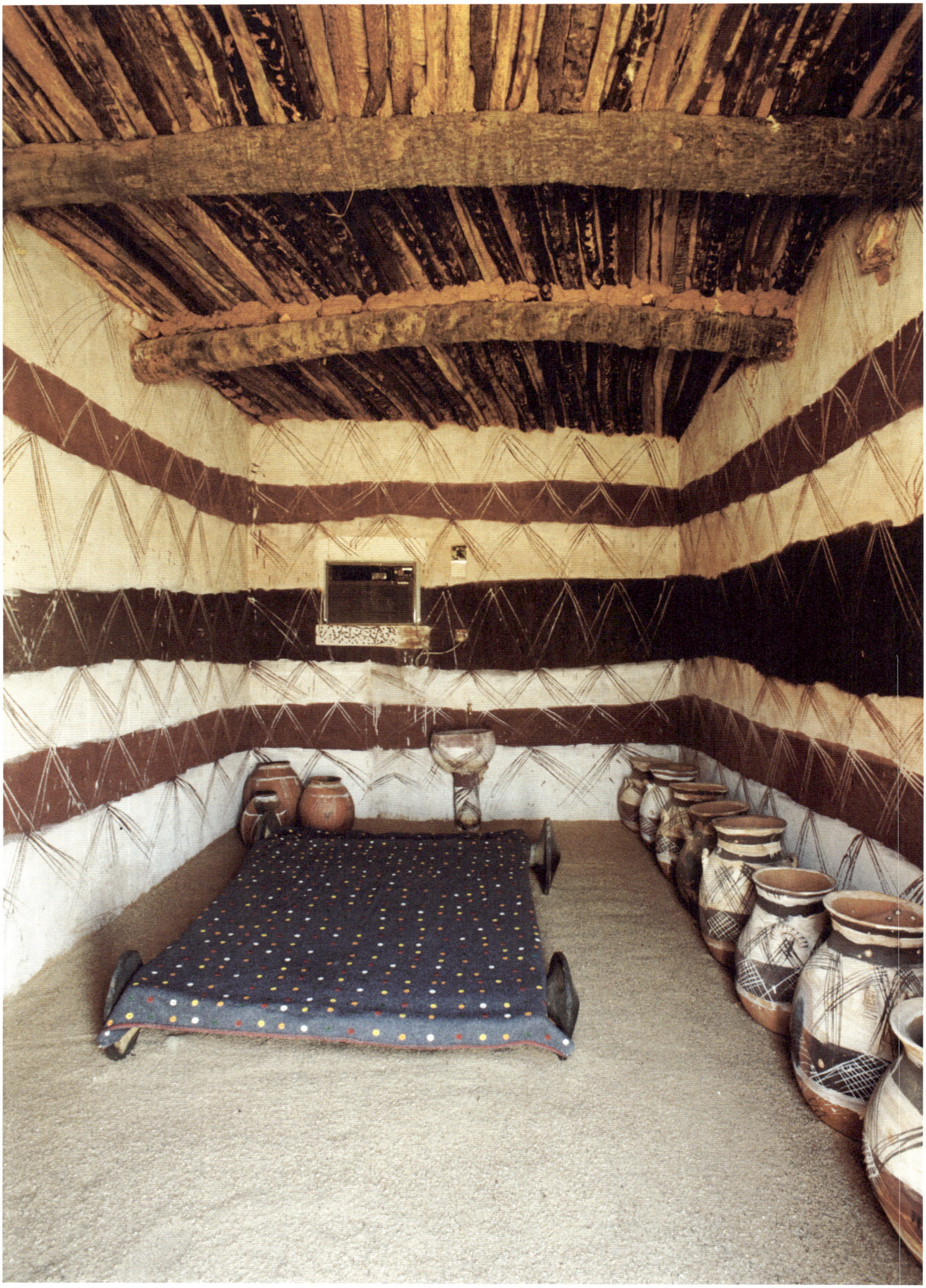

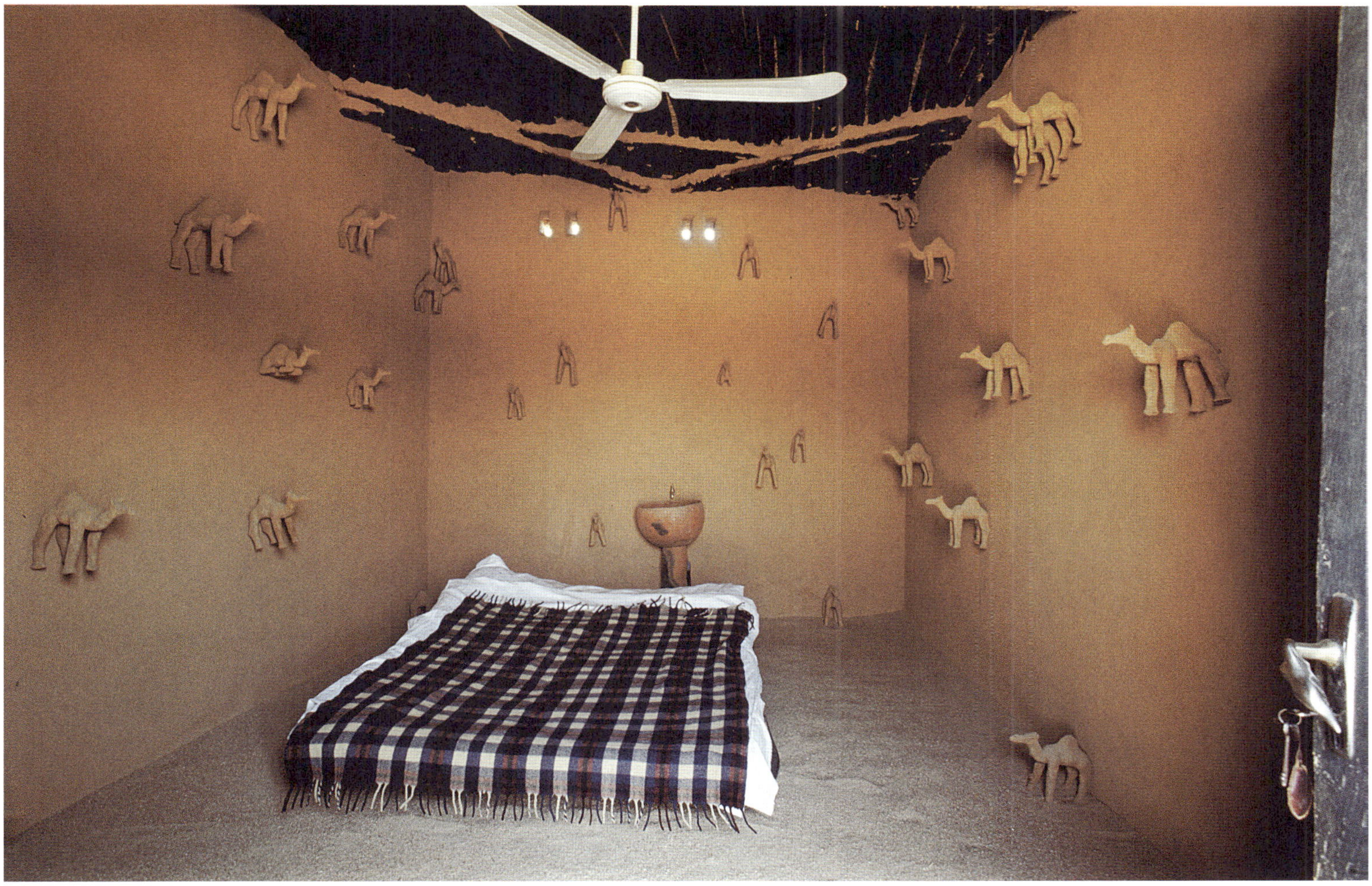

Interior views of *Mekafoni*

Makaranta
Agadez, Niger
2003

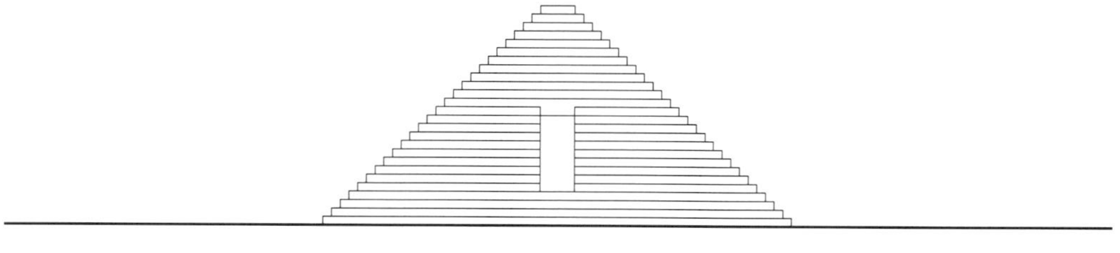

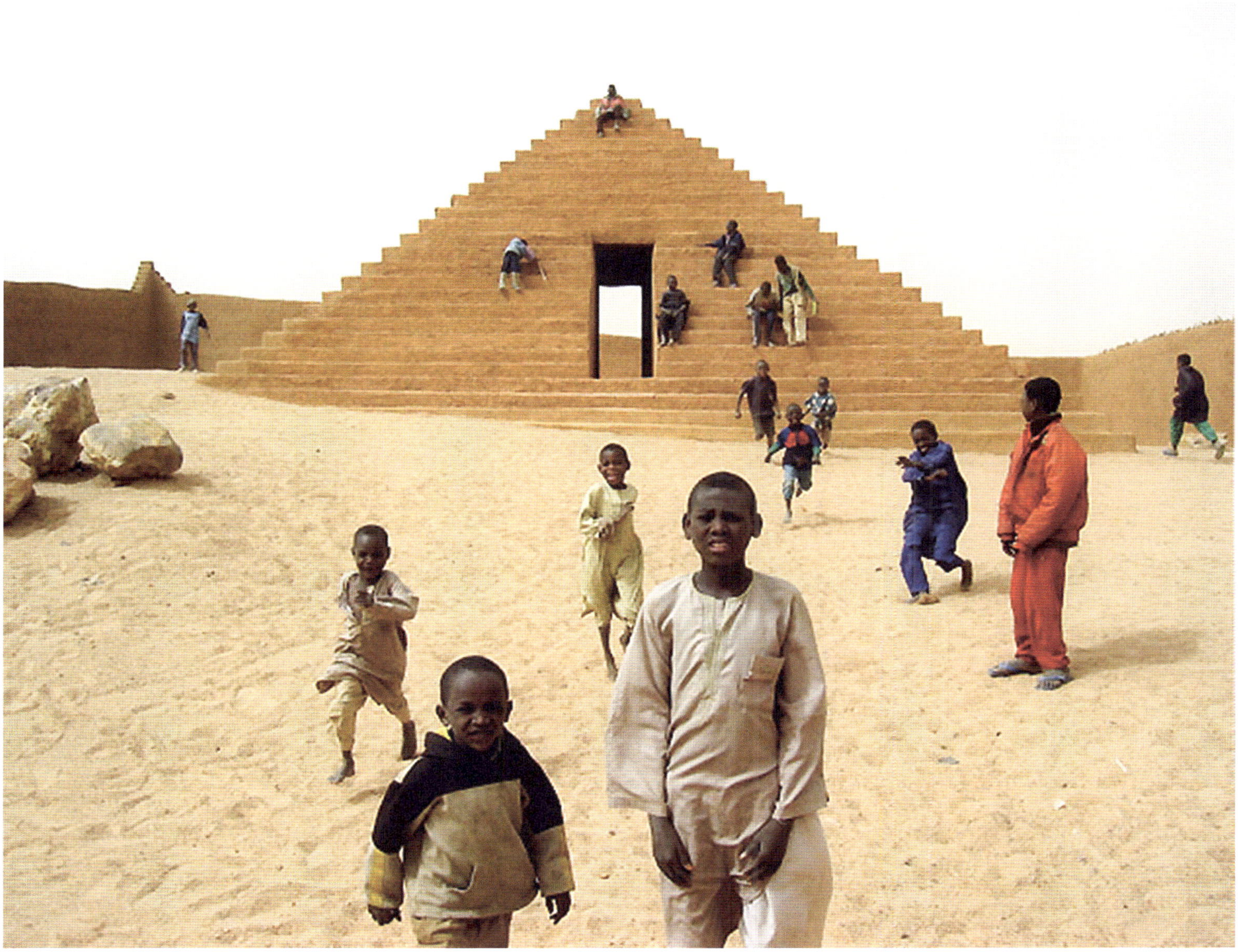

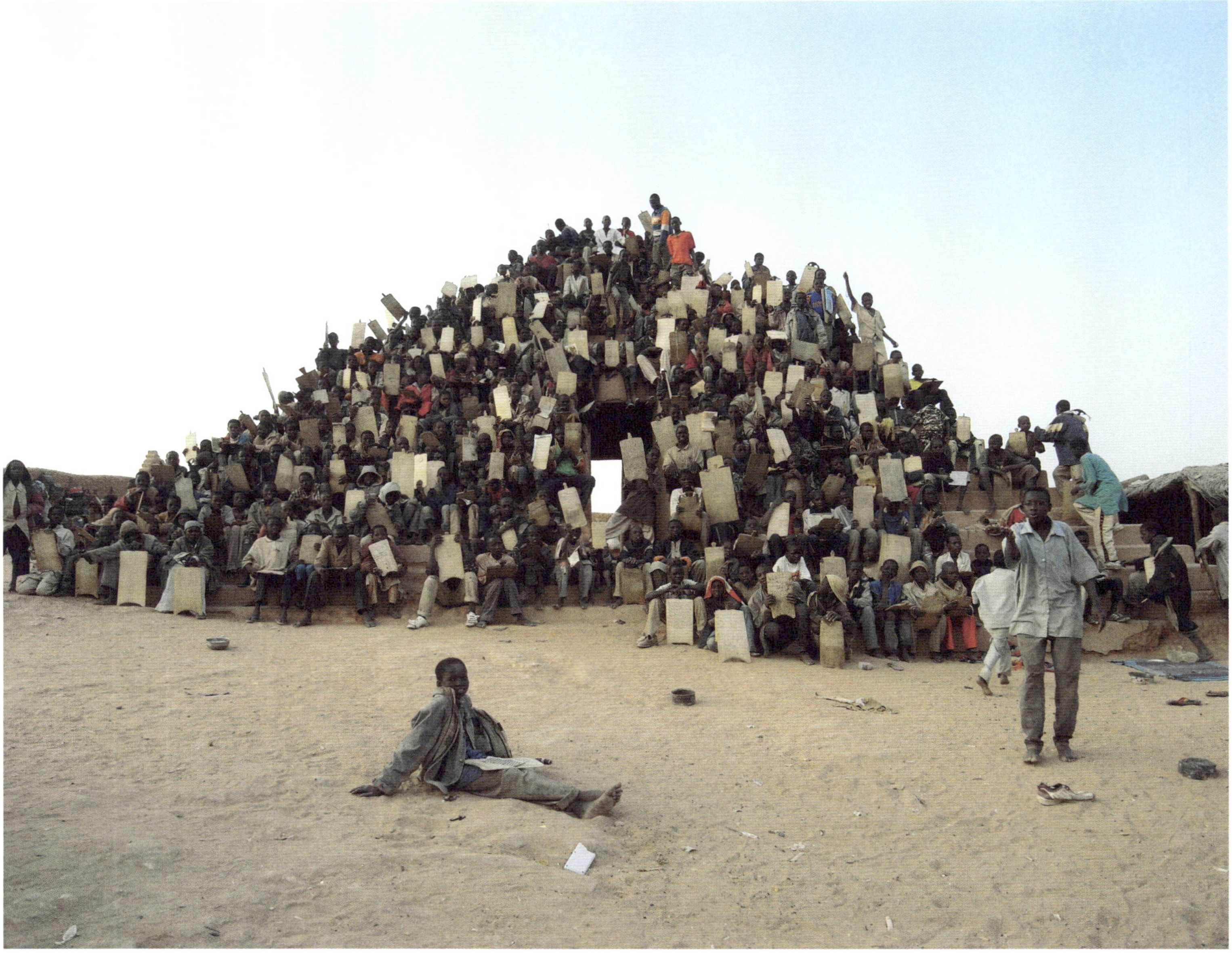

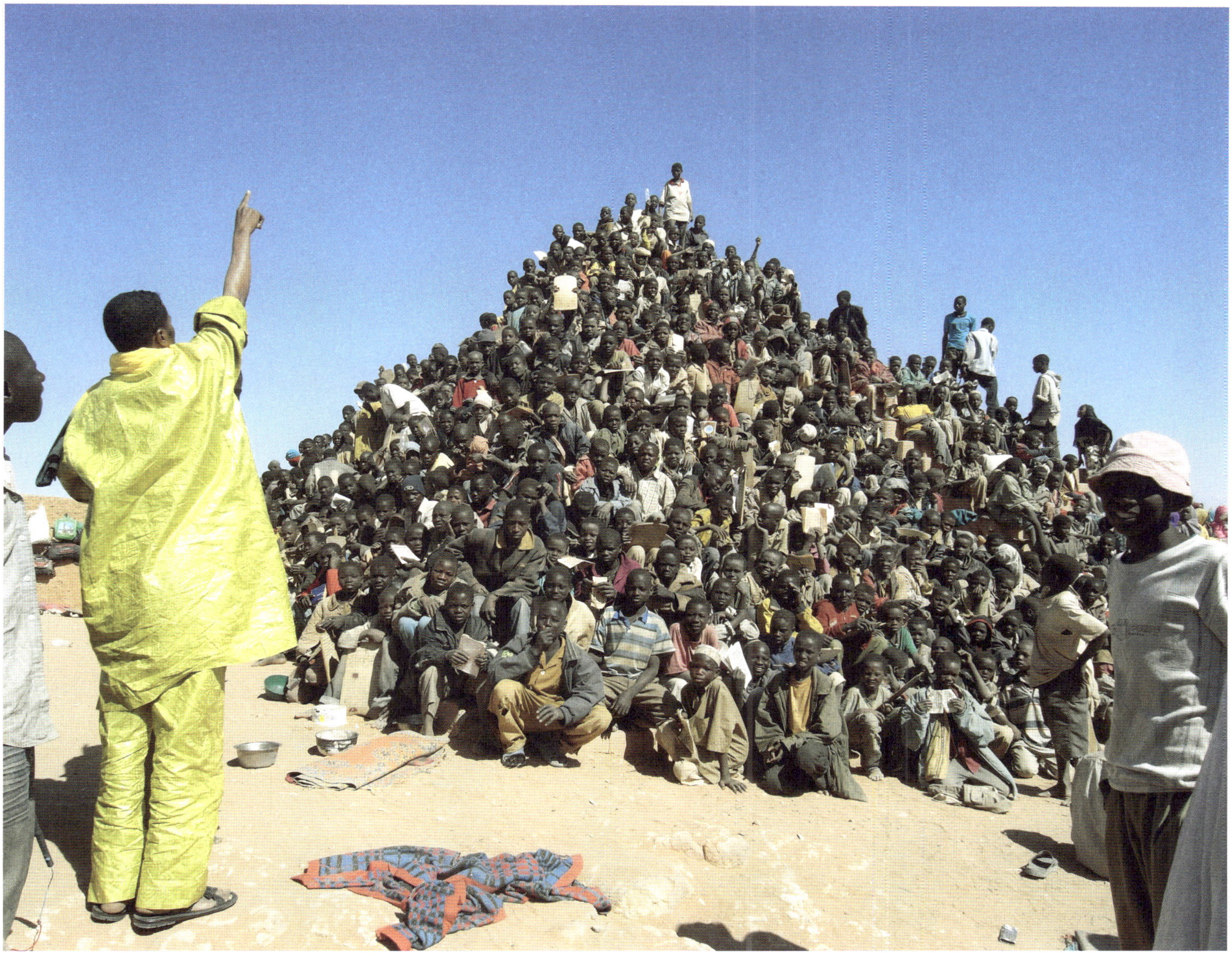

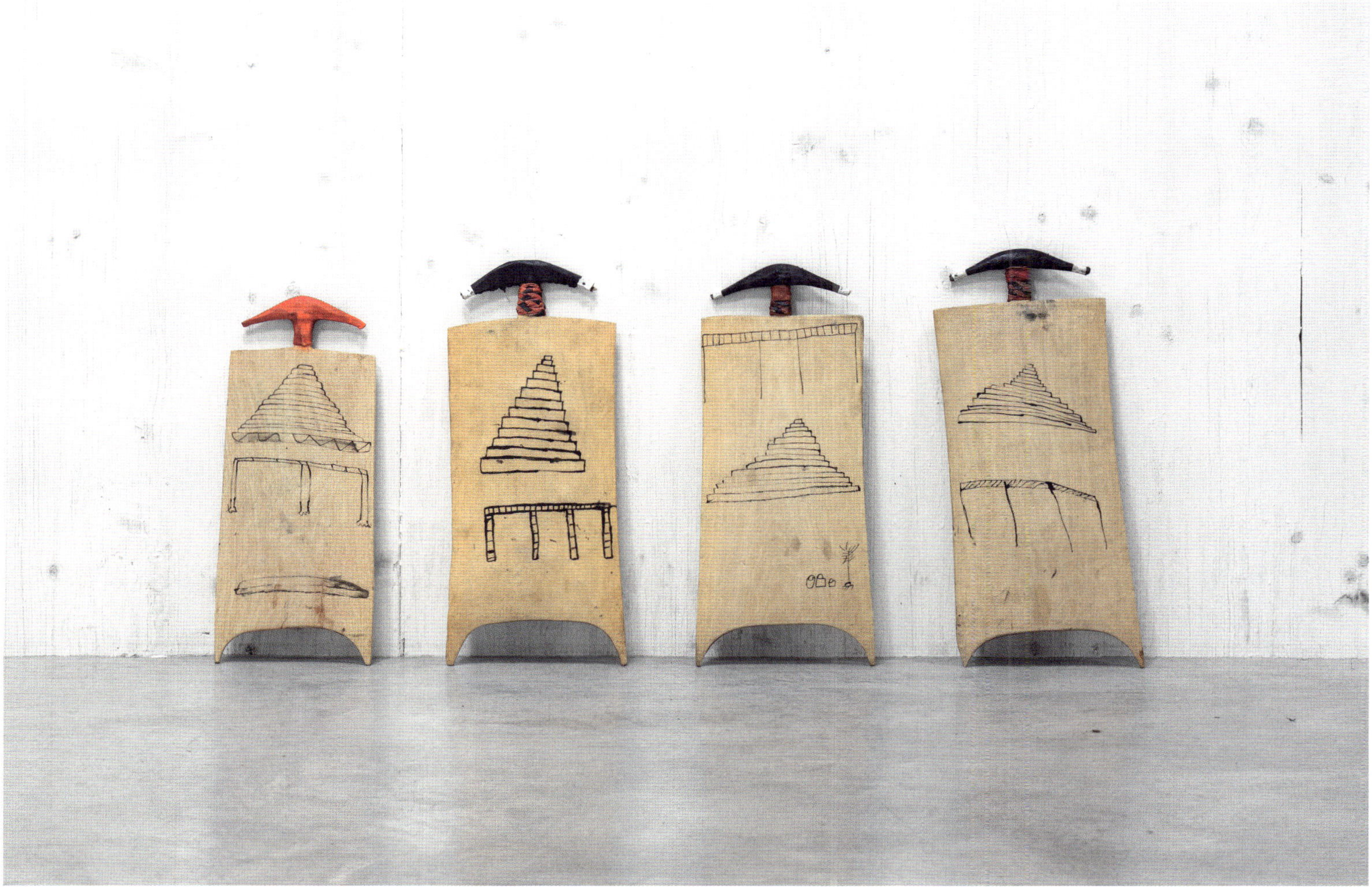

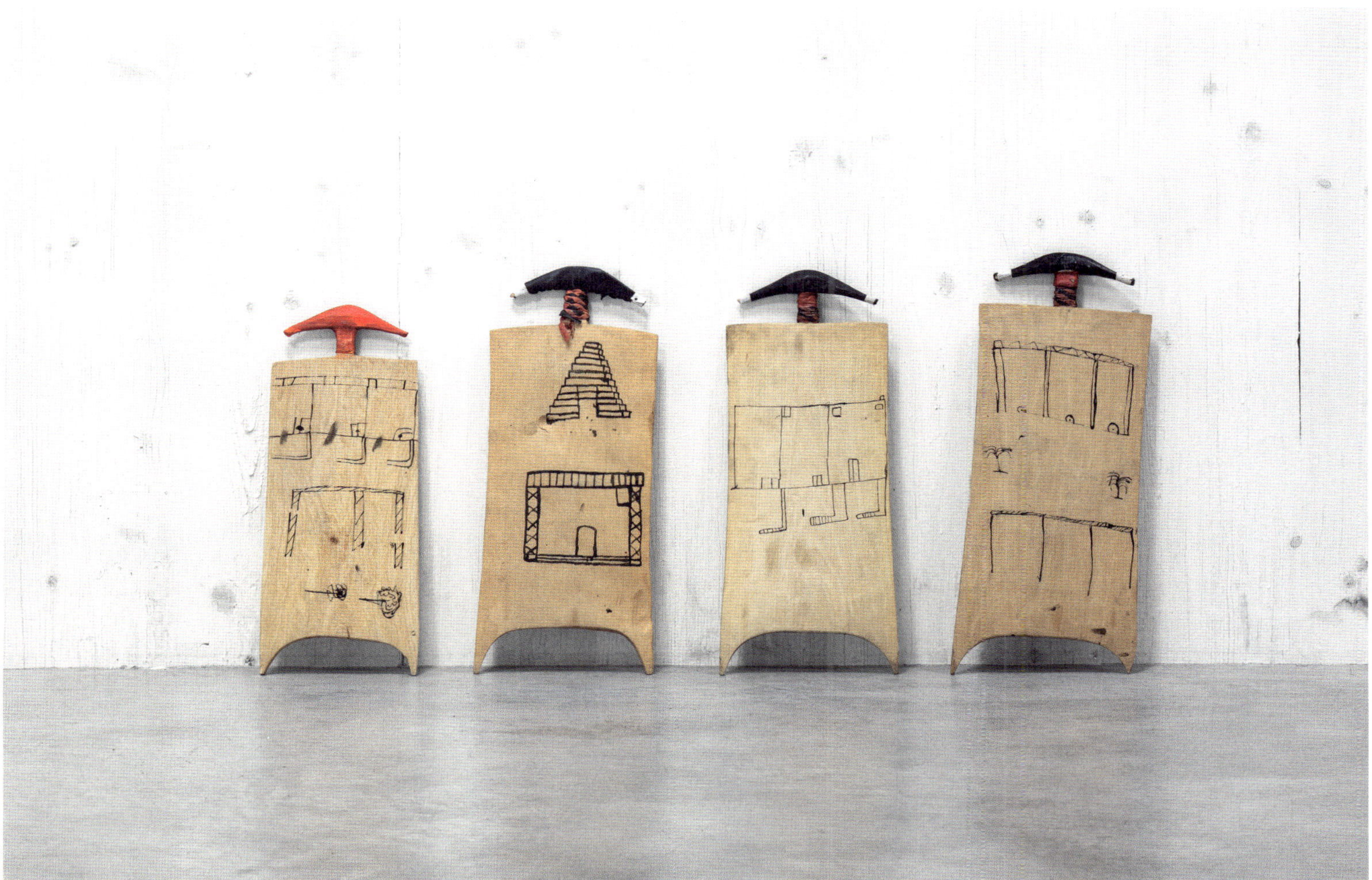

Drawings of *Makaranta* made by schoolchildren

Model for a Water Tower
2004

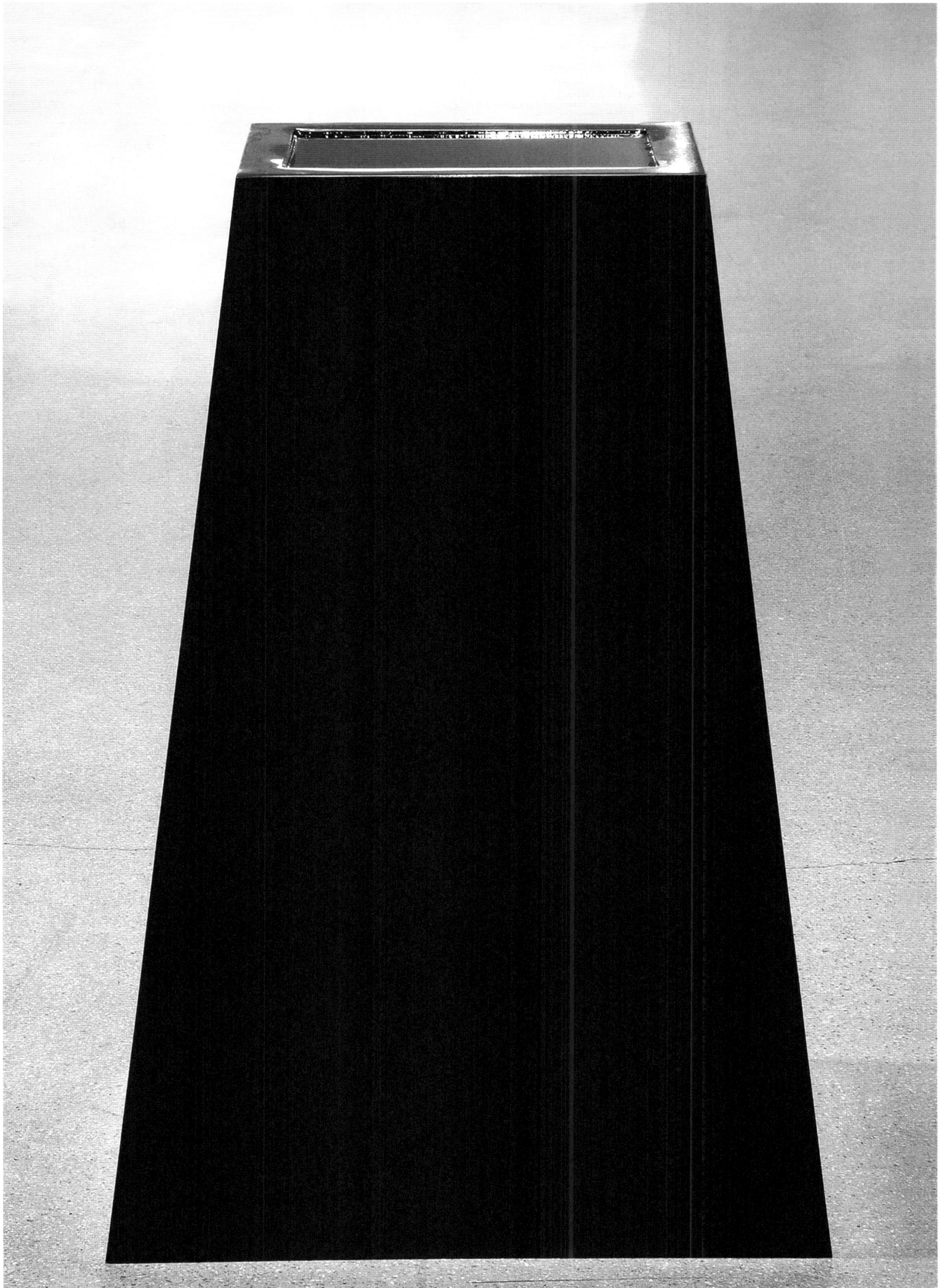

From Agadez to Aladab

Not Vital, Niger, 2005

1 late October afternoon, when I couldn't think of anything better to do than to watch the sunset once again, I flip-flopped north & crossed the Kouri River, which hadn't seen a drop of water in 10 years. There, I met Ukulla, who was coming from Azel, which means "branch" in Tamashek. He is a Tuareg, blue & a blacksmith. His watery eyes continuously scratched by the sand. He always carries 3 or 4 knives on him, since he is, after all, a blacksmith. Like most blacksmiths in African tribes, Ukulla belongs to a lower class, a lower caste, because he knows how to manipulate fire. As a blacksmith, he can allow his tongue free rein & doesn't have to adhere to the strict & proud rules of the other Tuaregs. It's always fun to talk to Ukulla, that is if he speaks at all. Likely, he had been at a celebration of some sort in Azel, slitting a couple of sheep throats. After uttering a few religious words, he moves his sharp, thin knife so elegantly & gracefully on their throats that it looks as if he's drawing a bow across the neck of a violin.

He is very economical about everything & sits quietly in front of you, like a blue sculpture. I have to be economical with my questions, too, even though I'd like to coax so much more from his eyes. Usually, he asks the same questions, as if he were not asking you anything at all.
"Et la fatigue?"
How can I still be tired from the voyage, if I arrived weeks ago?
"Ça va?"
He looks at you, no, he doesn't look at you at all, but through you, as if you were a piece of glass. His moist, intense eyes laugh & cry at the same time. Meanwhile, I'm wrenched into immense

depths as if I were high & I don't know how to escape from there. We talked about business, the same way men do in New York & night fell.

The sun sank as fast as Usain Bolt runs a lap. Night. The sunsets in the desert are as intense as a masturbation. Ukulla wore on his middle finger a ring with a silver sphere. "Culla" means "sphere" in Romansh. A *bijou Tuareg*, which I don't know how to describe. Never seen before. After ½ an hour, I asked him if he'd made the ring. The perfect sphere. He said "yes," & we both thought, who else?
Meanwhile, there were more stars in the sky than sky. The sky was an ocean of stars, upon which we kept sailing. Ukulla, unmoved, like a lapis lazuli stone. This sky is a waste of nature over the desert, which knows no waste itself. I asked Ukulla if he could forge a silver sphere as big as a melon.
"*Pas de problème*," he said, so proud that it seemed his beautiful teeth would burst out of his mouth. "No problem." That is a great friend, I thought & he thought the same. No room for doubt, if one wants to survive.

(With us, in the west, the word "problem" shows up in the 1st sentence, or the 3rd, at the latest, when someone is given a commission.) I have learned from my Tuareg friends to be sparing in my use of this word. Once I asked my wise friend Akhmed why in the Tamashek language, you seldom hear the word problem. He said: "Because we know it."

I wanted to know what to fill this sphere with, in order to make a sculpture. Neither stars nor sand nor Ukulla nor I would fit into it. His camel,

Koura, lay on the ground 12 meters away, as still as his master, ignoring the sky, grinding his ugly teeth & perhaps dreaming lustfully of an old camel or even a young 1 & I said, "We have to fill the sphere with a camel."
"*Pas de problème*," said Ukulla.
"But you have to make 12 spheres, so that the whole animal after being dried in the sun, will fit in."
A slight smile escaped his lips.
"*Comme ils sont bizarres ces blancs*," he must have thought, once again.
"*Jojo*," he said in Tamashek, which means the same in the Swiss-German dialect, or "yeah, yeah" in English. No more questions were asked while the sculpture was formed; every blacksmith in Agadez knew what was going to go into it. But if the spheres had remained empty, there would have been 1,000 questions and no valid answer. In our state of affluence, we are better prepared to deal with emptiness than a man from the desert.

The daily expeditions taken by the tribes when they go off seeking pasture are not what constitutes real life in the desert. Real life, as Saint-Exupéry says, is the game that is played on the side.

House to Watch the Sunset
Aladab, Niger
2005

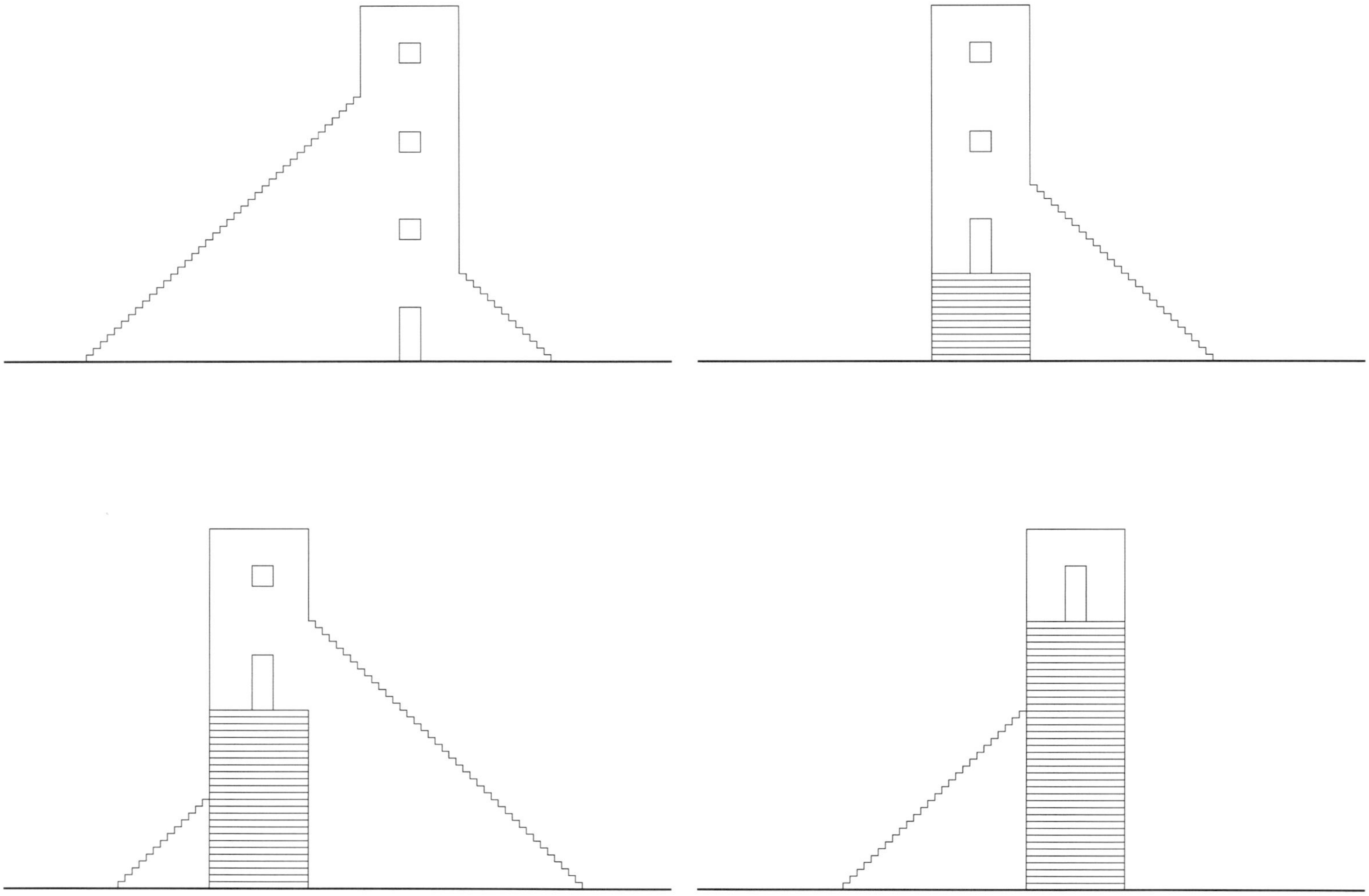

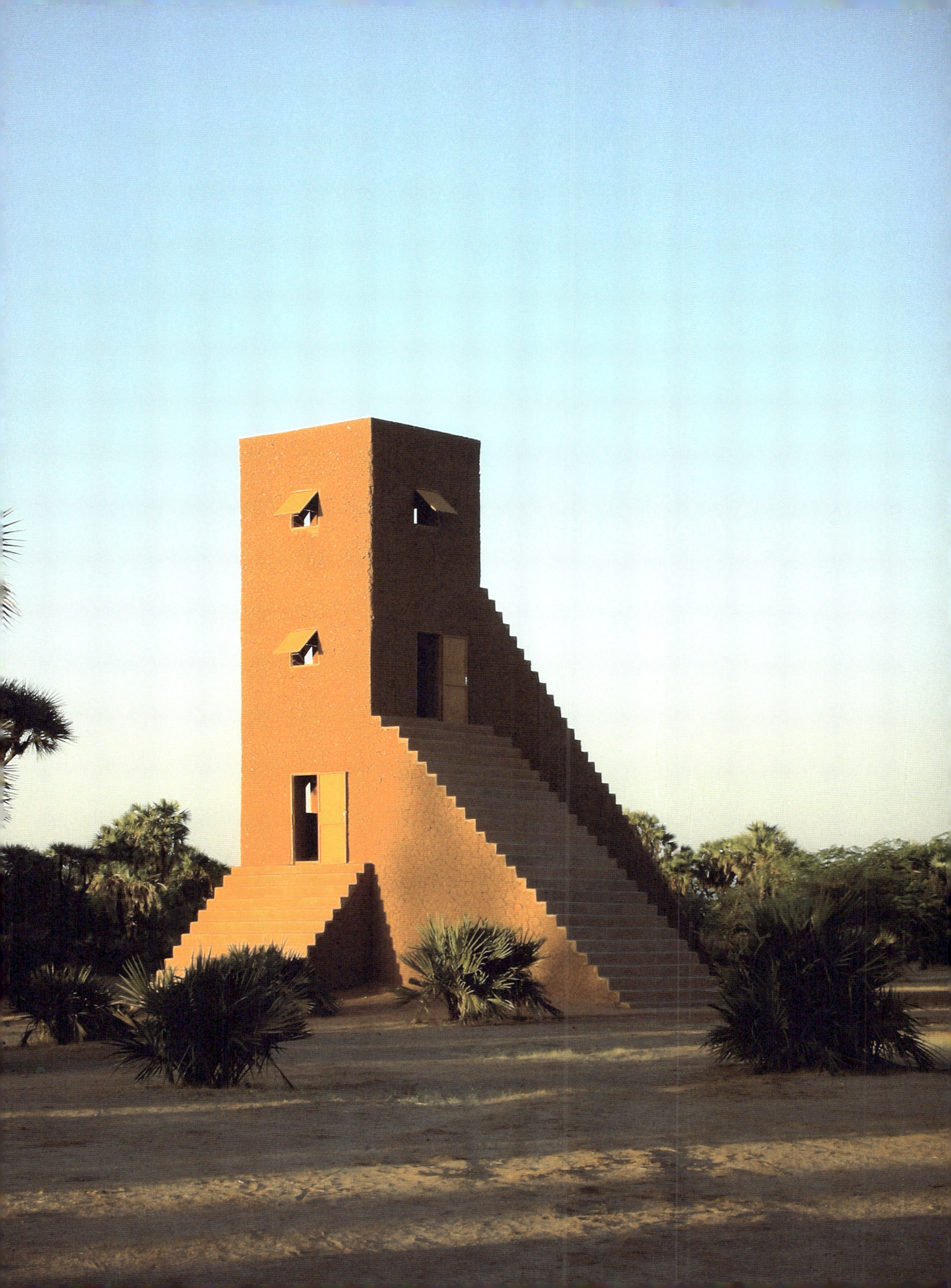

Not Vital in Agadez

Akhmed Haïdara

Like we say, what's done quickly deserves thanks! During an afternoon walk in the multicolored light of the setting sun, Not suddenly told me he was going to build something here in this garden on the banks of the Koti Telwa, the riverbed in the Alarcess oasis, where fences and tents had been put up to make my village of Aladab, which means "respect."

"What do you want to build then?" I asked him, and he answered, "A house."

"A house to live in?"

"No, a house to sit and watch this sunset you can't see anywhere else!"

Astounded, I just about managed to say, "Just for that?"

Not replied, "Yes, just for that."

My heart took a couple of minutes to check with my brain and come up with this plan that seemed so tremendous that I doubted it could be achieved; and I thought about the waste of bricks.

When the sun had gone down, we went back to the house, where the rest of the family lived, both of us alive with plain and boundless happiness.

On the way, we stopped to admire the clear, clean sky. Its millions of stars like pink and white flowers sown in a black desert were doing their best to light the lanes.

We got back to the house. My mother had just dished up a delicious dinner. My father, who had finished his evening prayers, invited us to eat; we sat in the space between the big shed where we chat in the evenings and my parents' bedroom. The mood was nice and pleasant. My mother asked us about our walk.

I said nothing, except that Not was thinking about building a house in the garden.

She said, "Why can't he live here with us?"

I answered, "No, he's not building it to live in!"

"What for then?"

"To look at the sunset."

I noticed that the spoons that were dipping into the dish of rice and meat sauce had stopped moving. I saw that my father and the two brothers who were allowed to eat with us, spoon in hand, were flabbergasted to hear that the house would even have three floors.

"What?" exclaimed my father. "I reckon Not has lost his goats," meaning that he was out of his mind. There was a slight smile on everyone's face. My brother Aboubakar, who was only five, spoke up to say that if Not really was out of his mind, he wouldn't have built the well for the village.

One fine morning I woke up and saw that house. It towered over the palm trees and other great trees in the gardens around. There it was, as though it had dropped out of the sky from nowhere. Then I realized that the dream had come true.

And all that to look at the sunset. And if the house should fall down after seeing the sun go to bed just once, it would still be rewarding. It would not only have been right to build it; it would stay in the minds of everyone who had been fortunate enough to see it. Because that's what it was about. It would have its place in the most heavenly of dreams come true.

What was this building for? Its only reason to exist was to watch and be seen. From the top, you could see very far; the horizon looked a bit curved, as though the earth might really be round. You could also see the Aïr Massif and the birds wheeling over. You could only see their backs, the way you maybe do from a plane.

The nights belong to the stars. The constellations they show are not drawn by hand. There are so many of them for such a young sky, which can offer you a star for every glass of tea. Till then I had always thought that dreams belonged to another world and only came true during the deepest sleeps. I never thought that such a dream could come true on earth and even less in my village of Aladab.

Not's house has three staircases, each one leading to a little square room with a window. They are like three dimensions that climb to heaven to beg for pardon.

The 10th House
Tigidit, Niger
2005

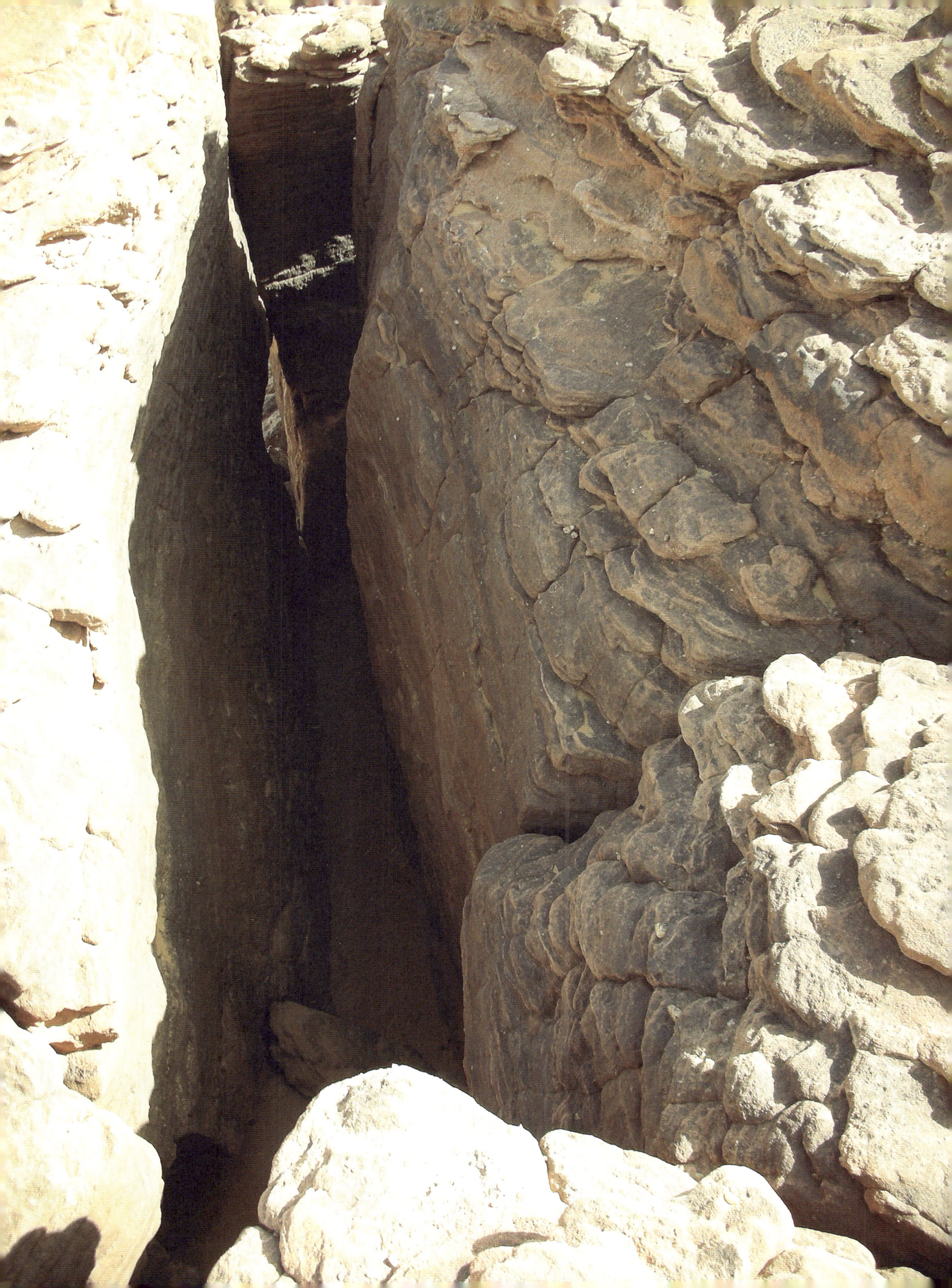

House Against Heat and Sandstorms
Aladab, Niger
2006

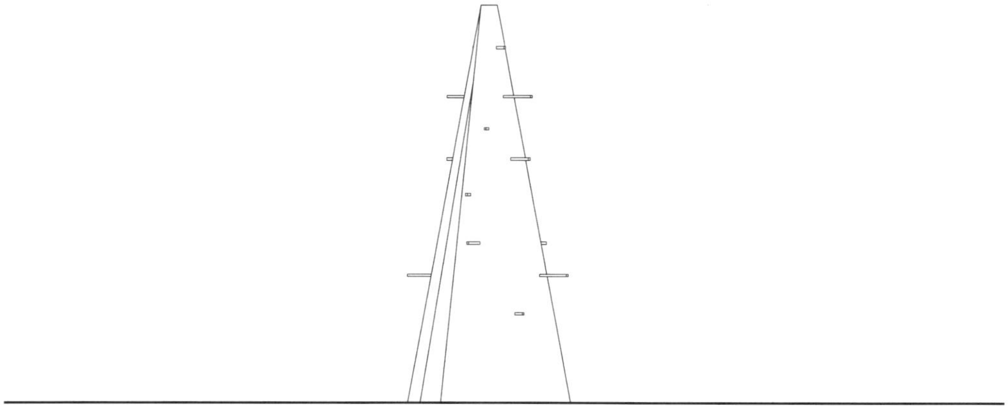

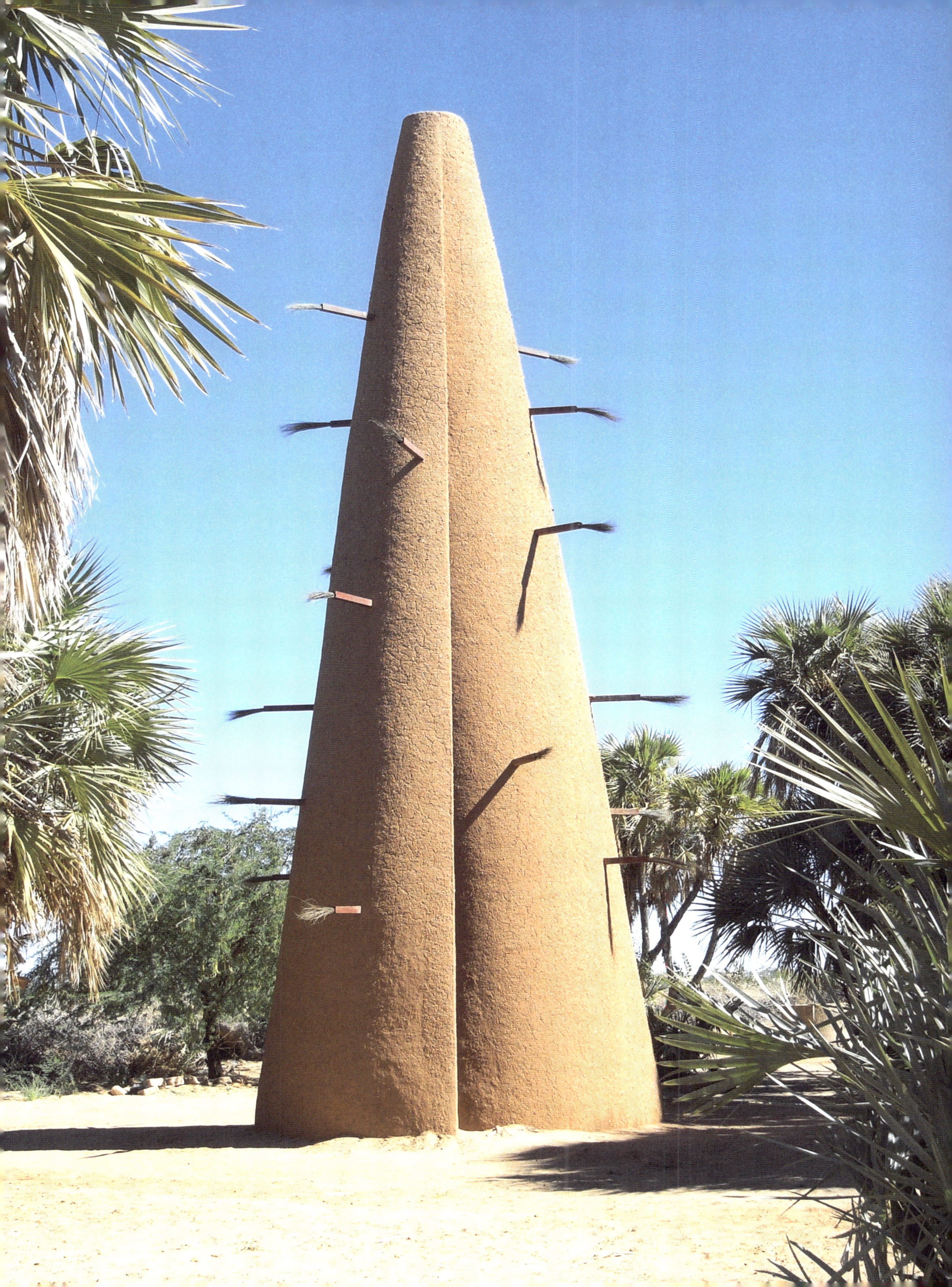

Sleeping House
2010

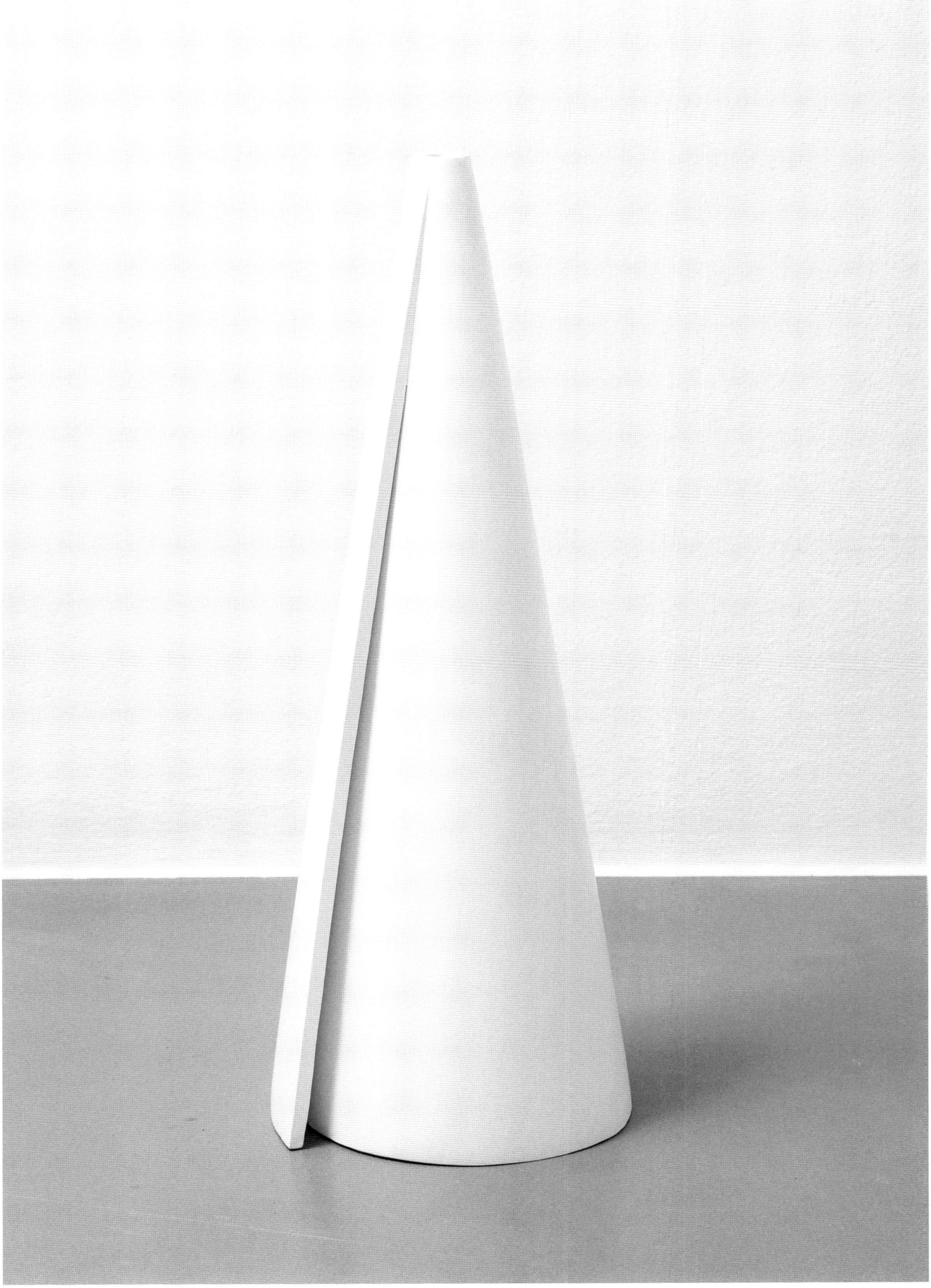

House to Watch the Night Skies

Aladab, Niger

2006

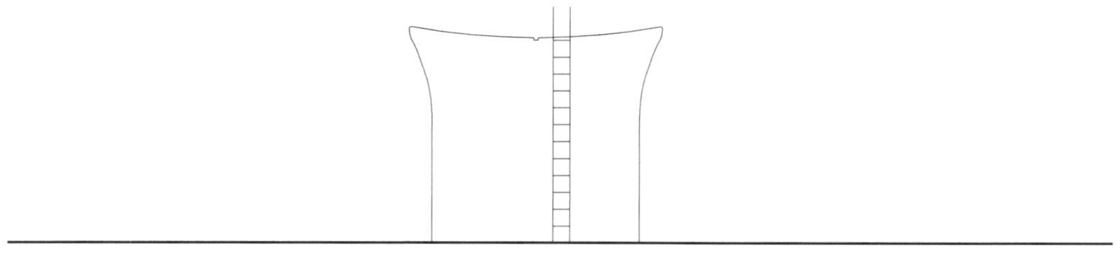

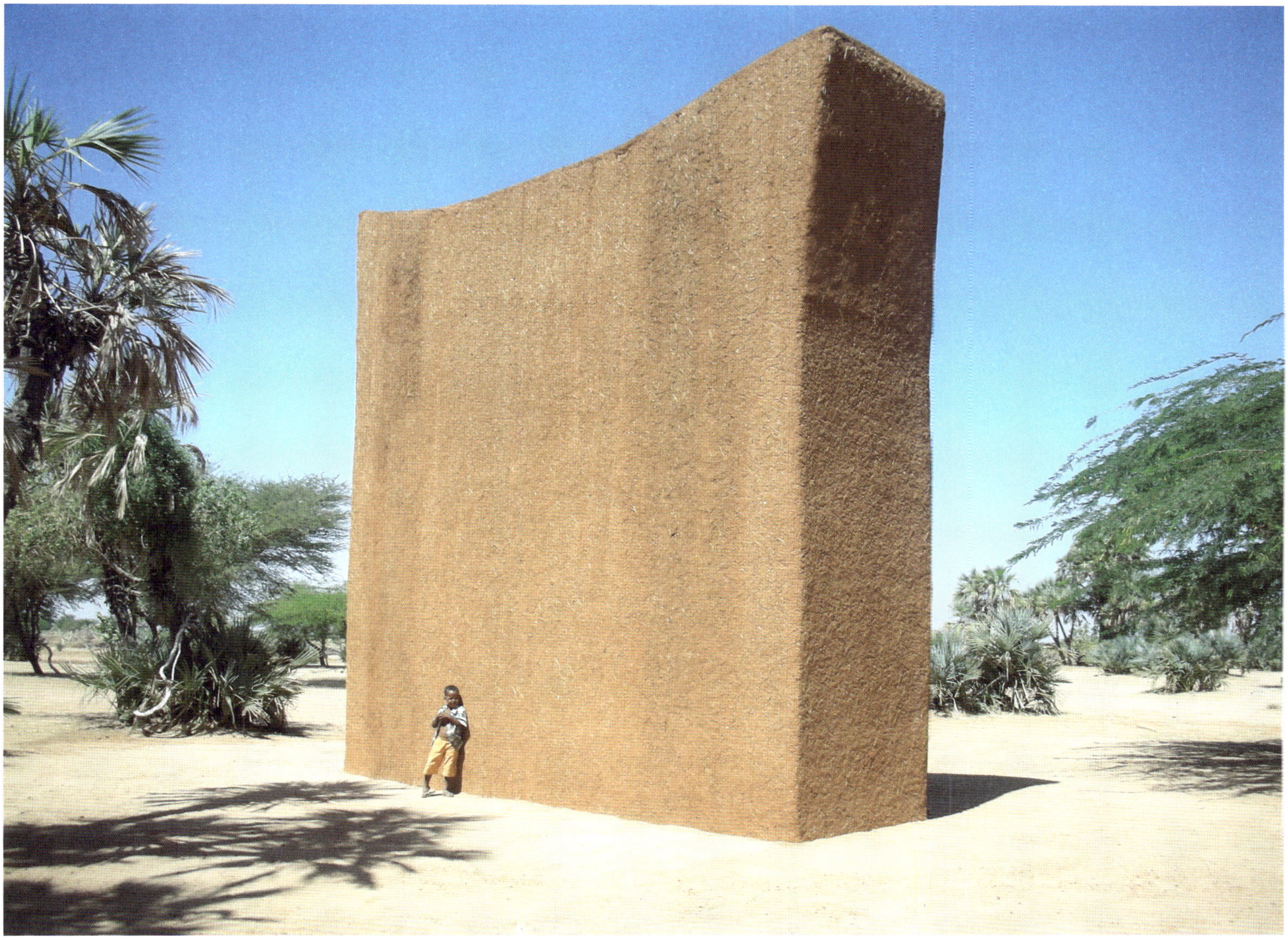

House for 8 Brothers
Alarsas, Niger
2006

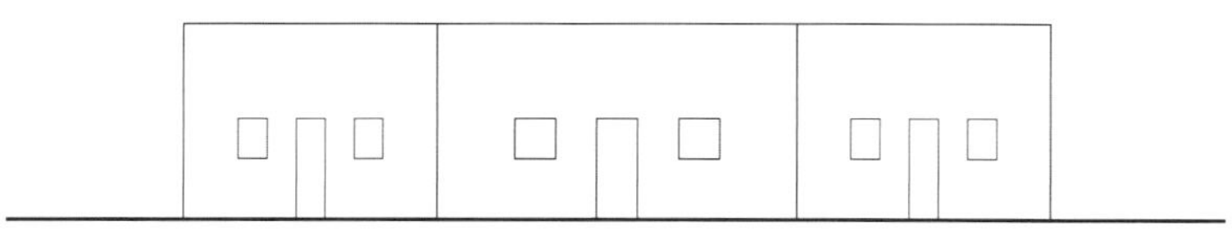

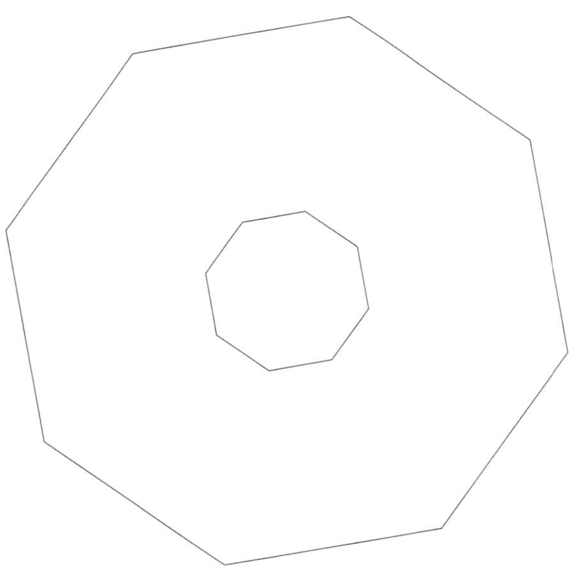

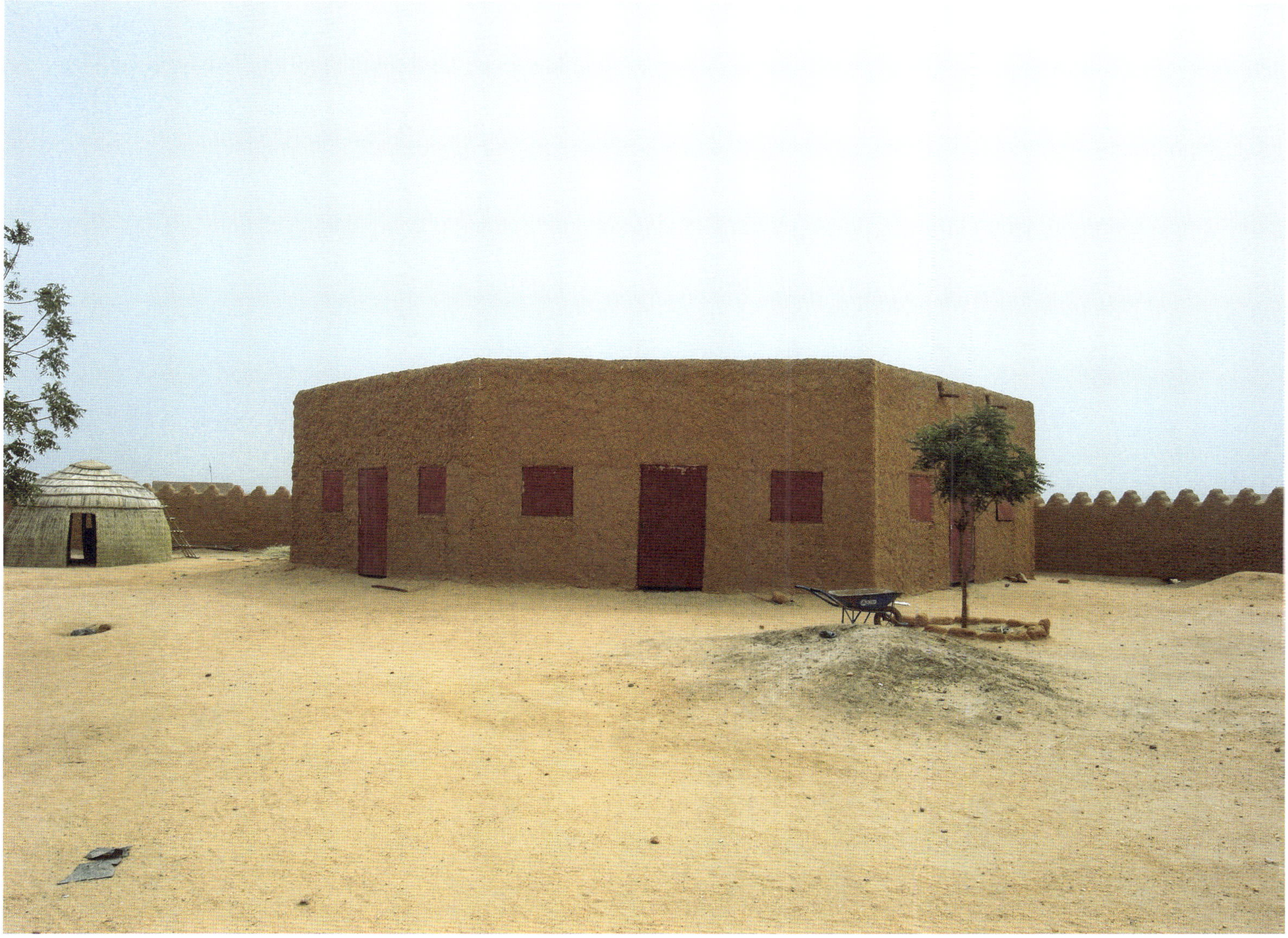

School for Agadez
2009

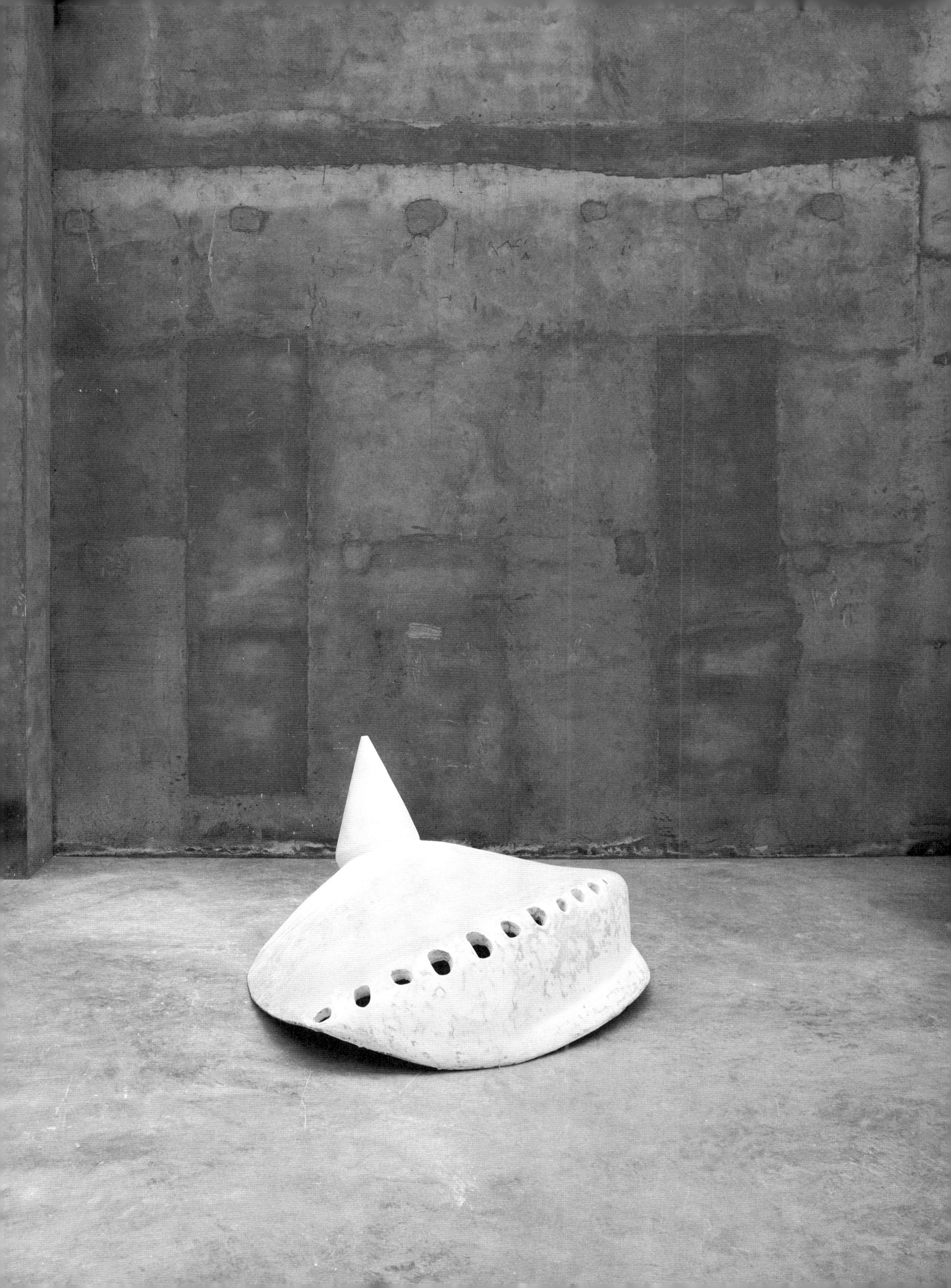

Minaret for Agadez
2009

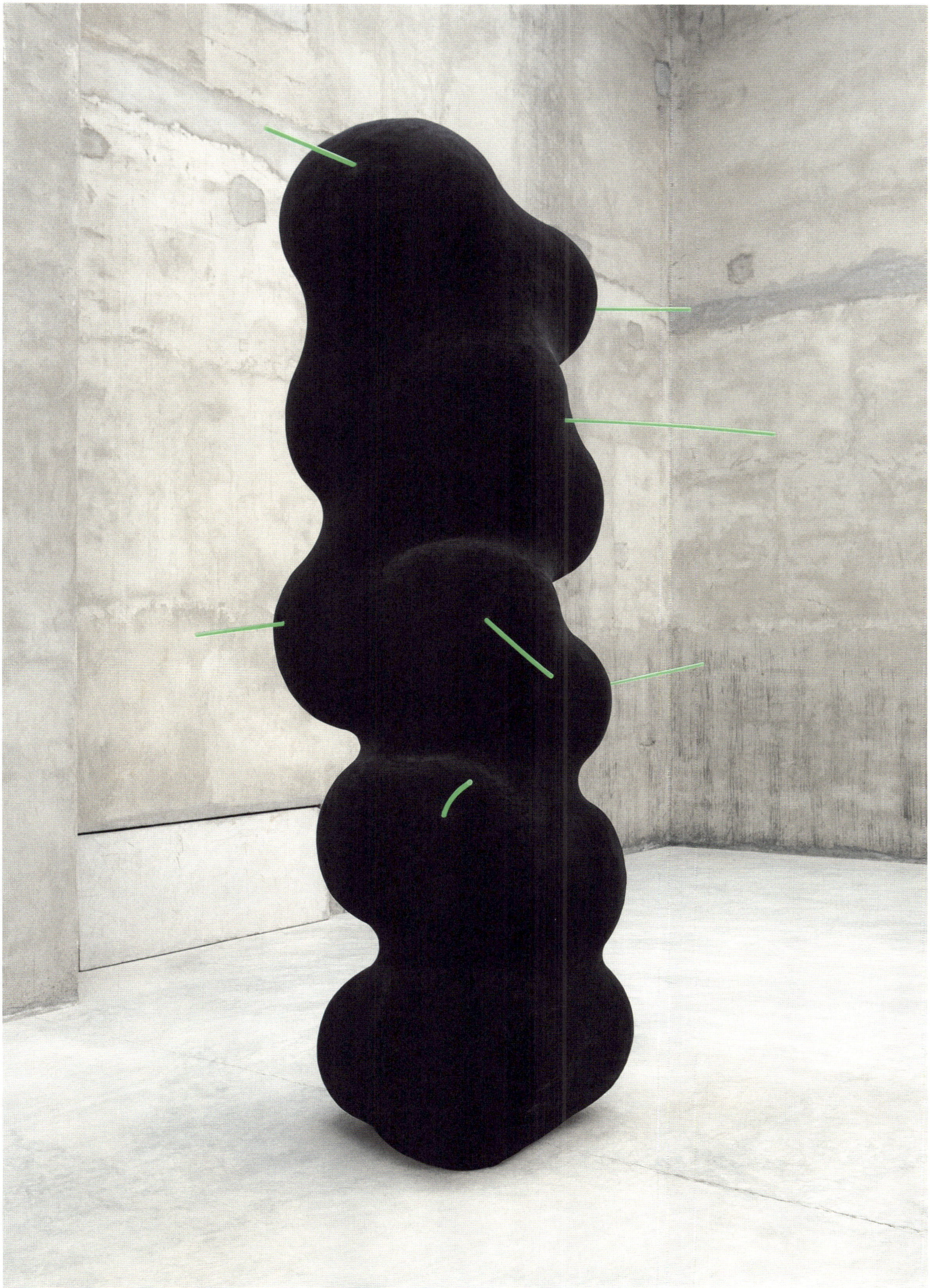

House to Watch the Sunset
2013

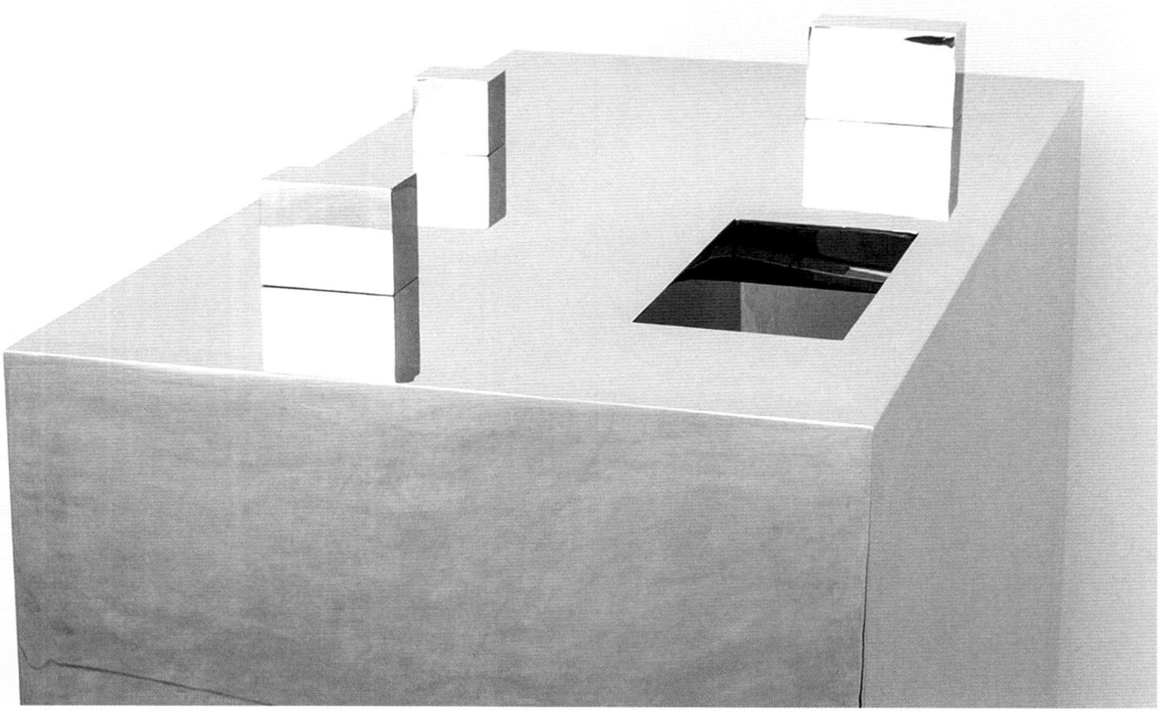

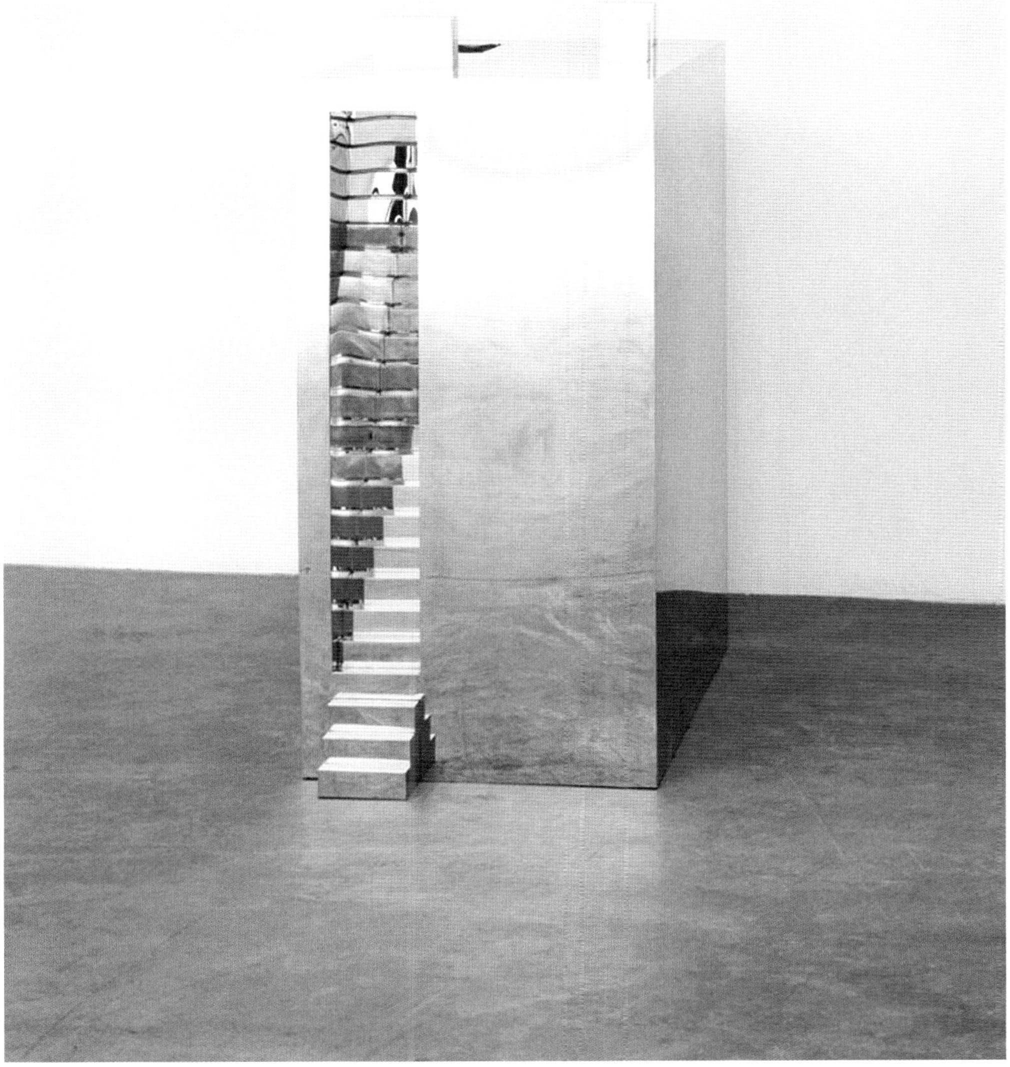

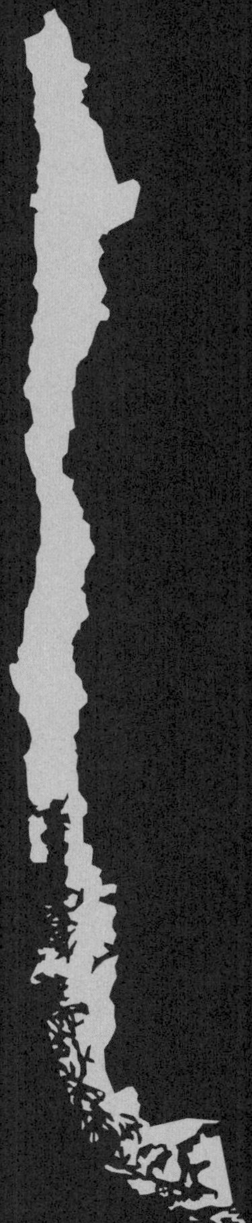

NotOna
General Carrera Lake, Patagonia, Chile
2008–14

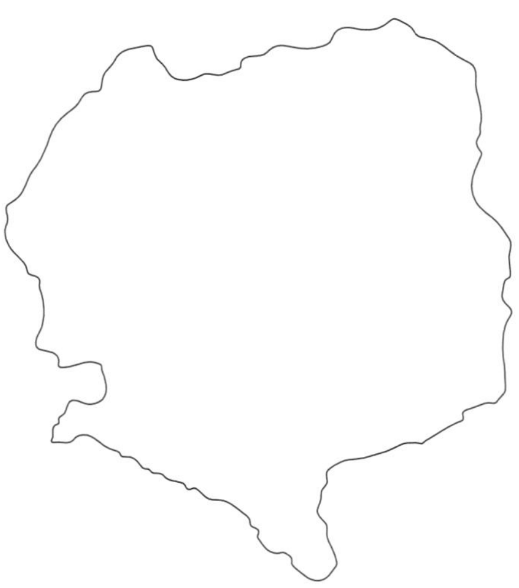

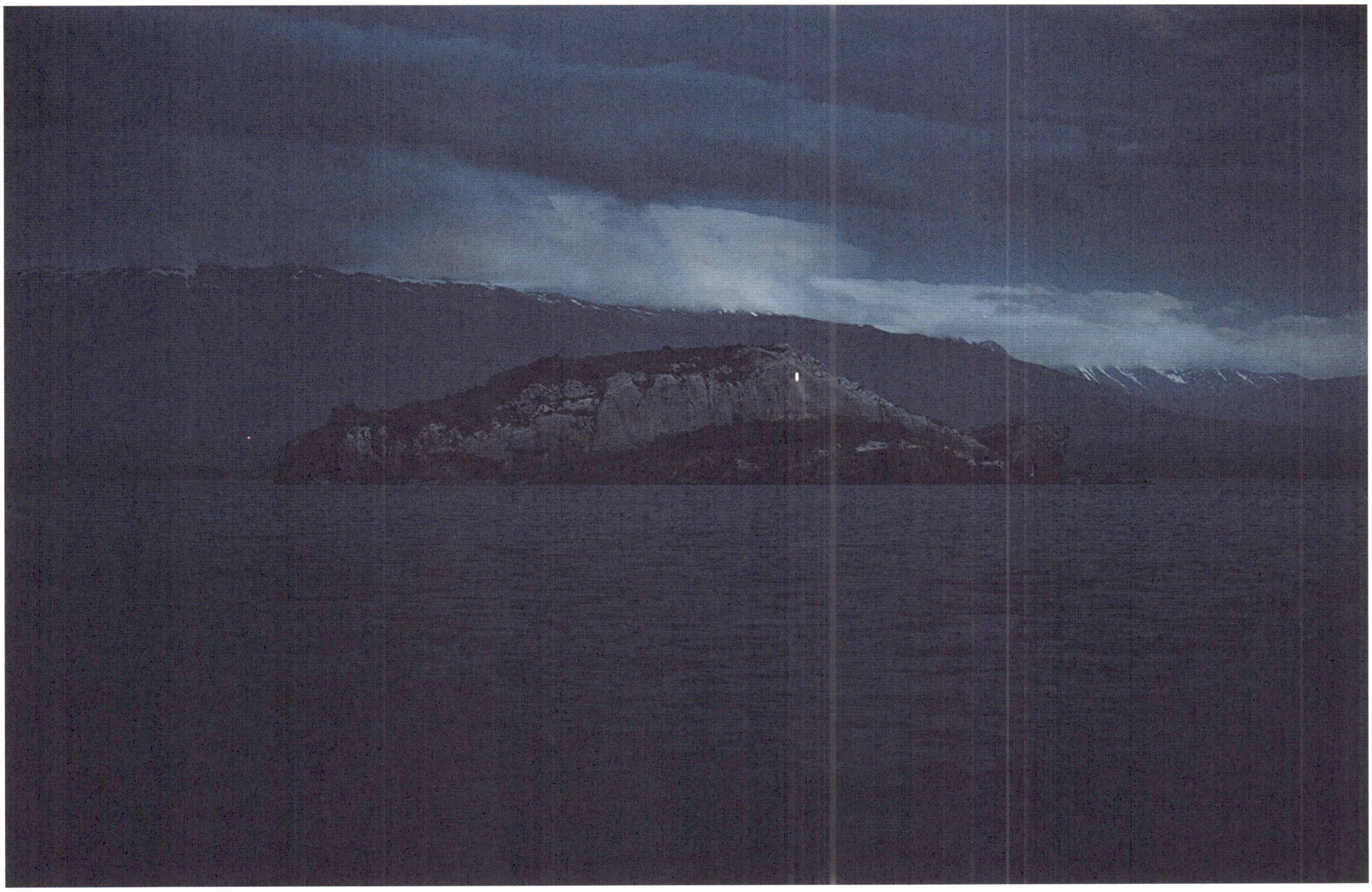

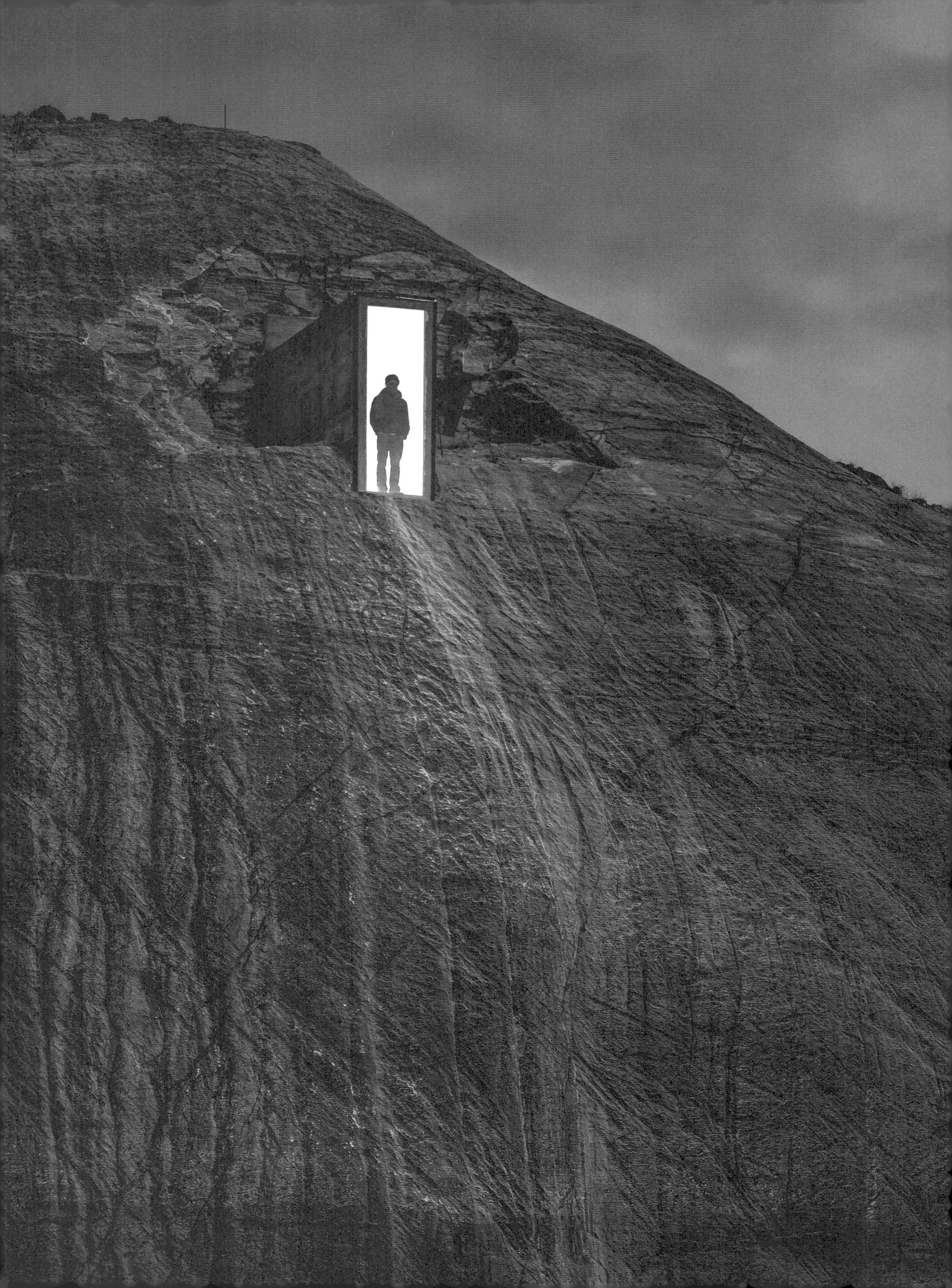

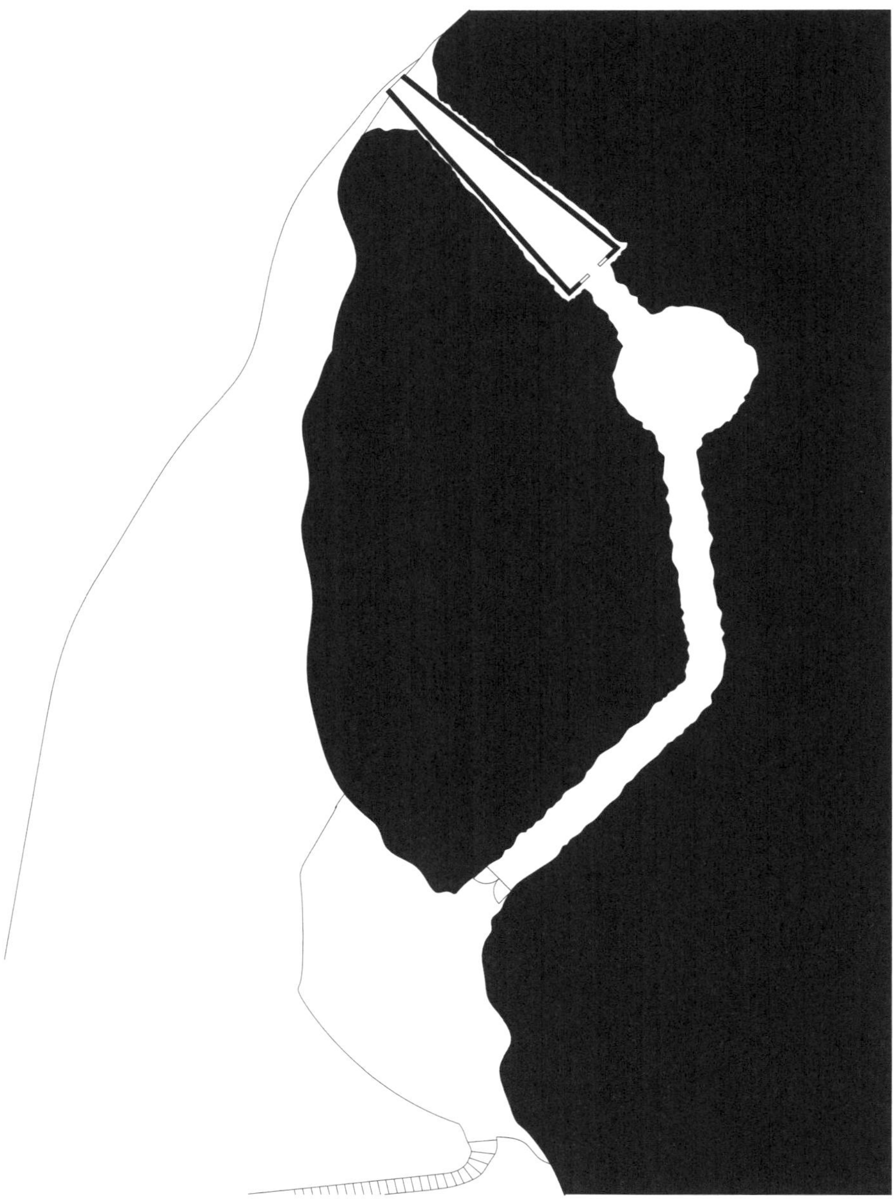

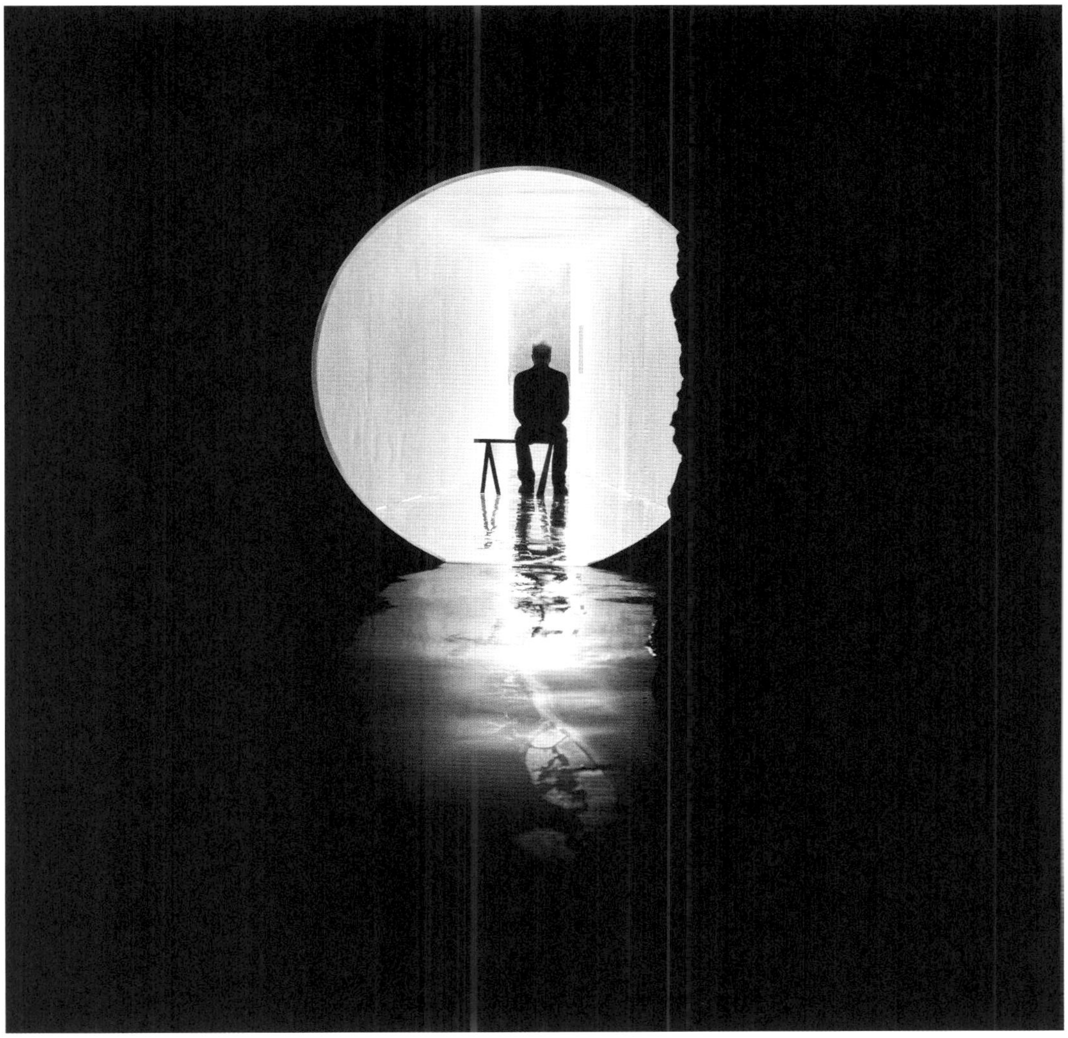

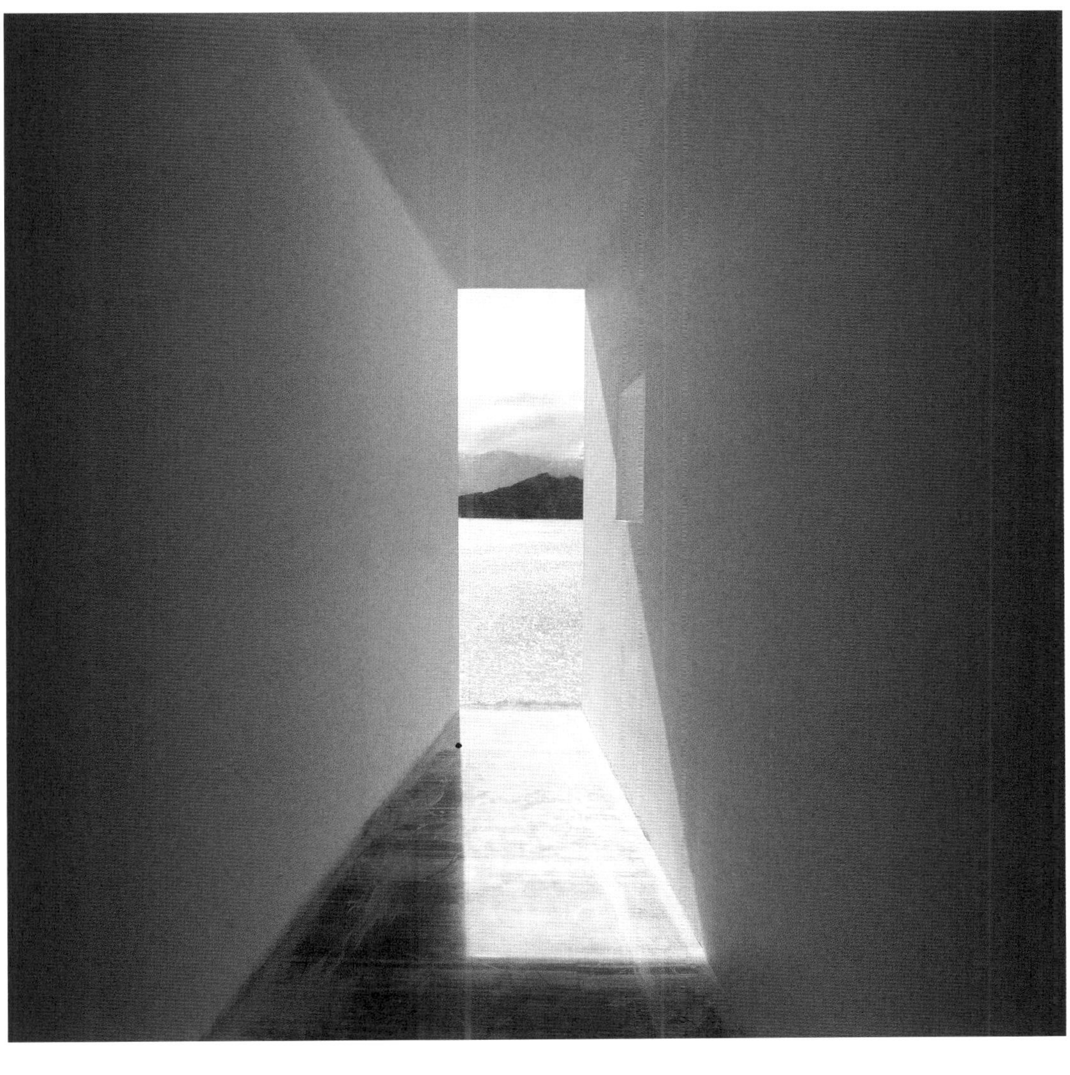

NotOna

Not Vital, Chile, 2014

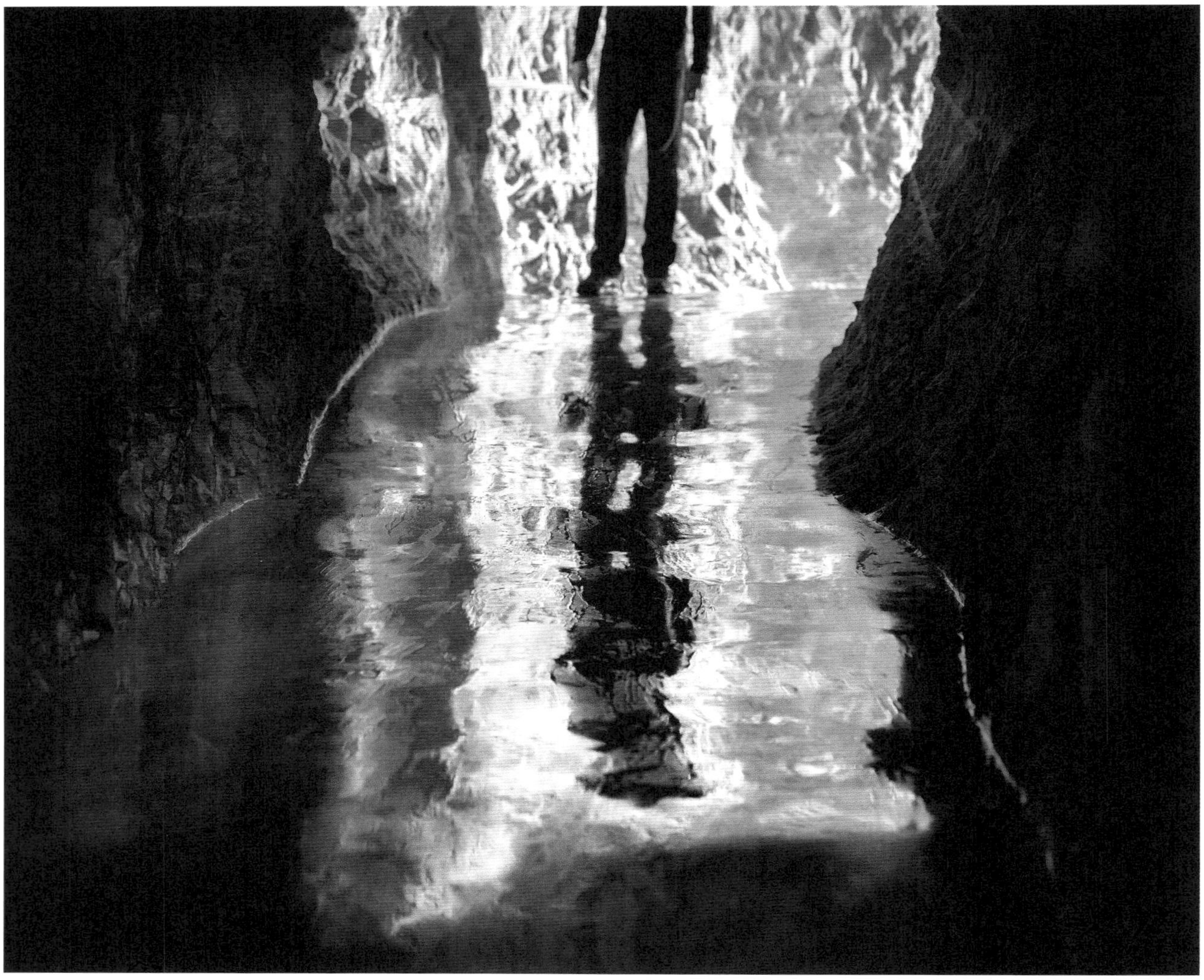

& suddenly everything surrounding you becomes precious on *NotOna*. The sunset, the rise of the sun & the moon & the setting of the moon in the early morning. You spend a lot of time chasing them, going from 1 side to the other of this island, which has its own shape & doesn't resemble any other.

The best is to be alone on *NotOna*. You have to become your own friend since no one is here with you. You start looking at your toes who just became your 10 best friends. You cannot get away from the heavy winds, the downpour & the branches of a tree that knocks on the house all night like there is no tomorrow. You go out in the dark to see the skies that pretend to be the most powerful source that you have ever seen—& they are. All of this, you see alone, like a child who is seeing a mouse for the first time. You stop talking, even opening your mouth becomes precious. Everything surrounding you is sparse. A lonely flower, a lonely bush, or a single arrayán tree form a new experience in your life, similar to the moment in which you took your 1st step, alone, like the 1st time you saw a waterfall, or like the 1st love. Objects that seemed so unimportant become vital & can suddenly save your life. Objects like a match, a knife, a cup, or a spoon. You store them safely. You pick up a piece of plastic or a piece of paper when you see them dancing around the island in the wind & you burn them. You don't want them to pollute *NotOna*. Your shoes are suddenly not only shoes but become like a friend who protects you while walking on a sharp rock & so does the wool of your sweater in the wind. & if it is too windy or too magnificent, I go to the house that is carved into the marble on the mountaintop.

You walk on a single 55-meter-long slab of white marble so smooth you can fall and break your tailbone. A castle in the ground without a king, or queen, or slave. I enter a world unseen before. You watch the sunset from the inside of the world & that's the reason why this tunnel was carved. No sound, no noise, no smell, or phone. The womb of the earth. Since childhood, I wanted to enter this world, to be inside the stone & to see the world from within. It seemed like the surface was not enough. Maybe that's why I wanted to be a sculptor, after all. A habitat where you see the stunning surroundings, the lake so blue it almost hurts your eyes & in the distance, the glacier of San Valentín, 55 kilometers long. The house is joining the outside world for good it seems. & I am there, inside, so small.

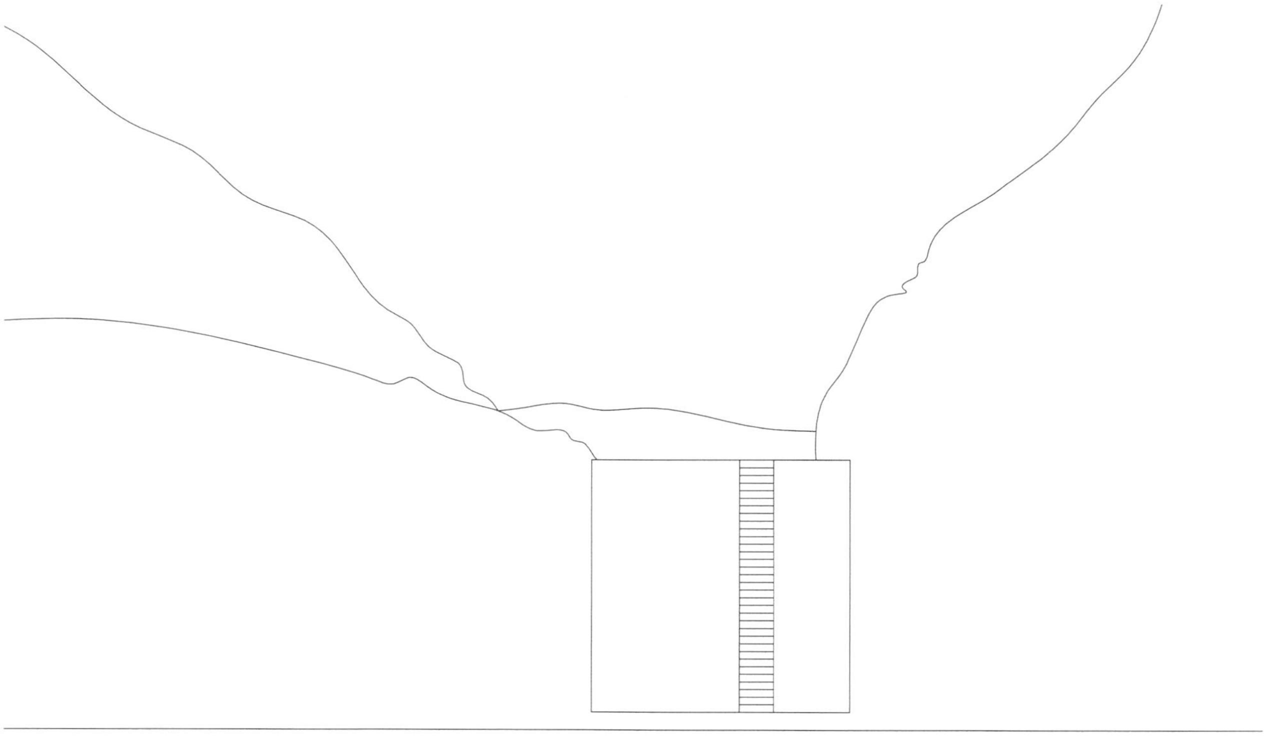

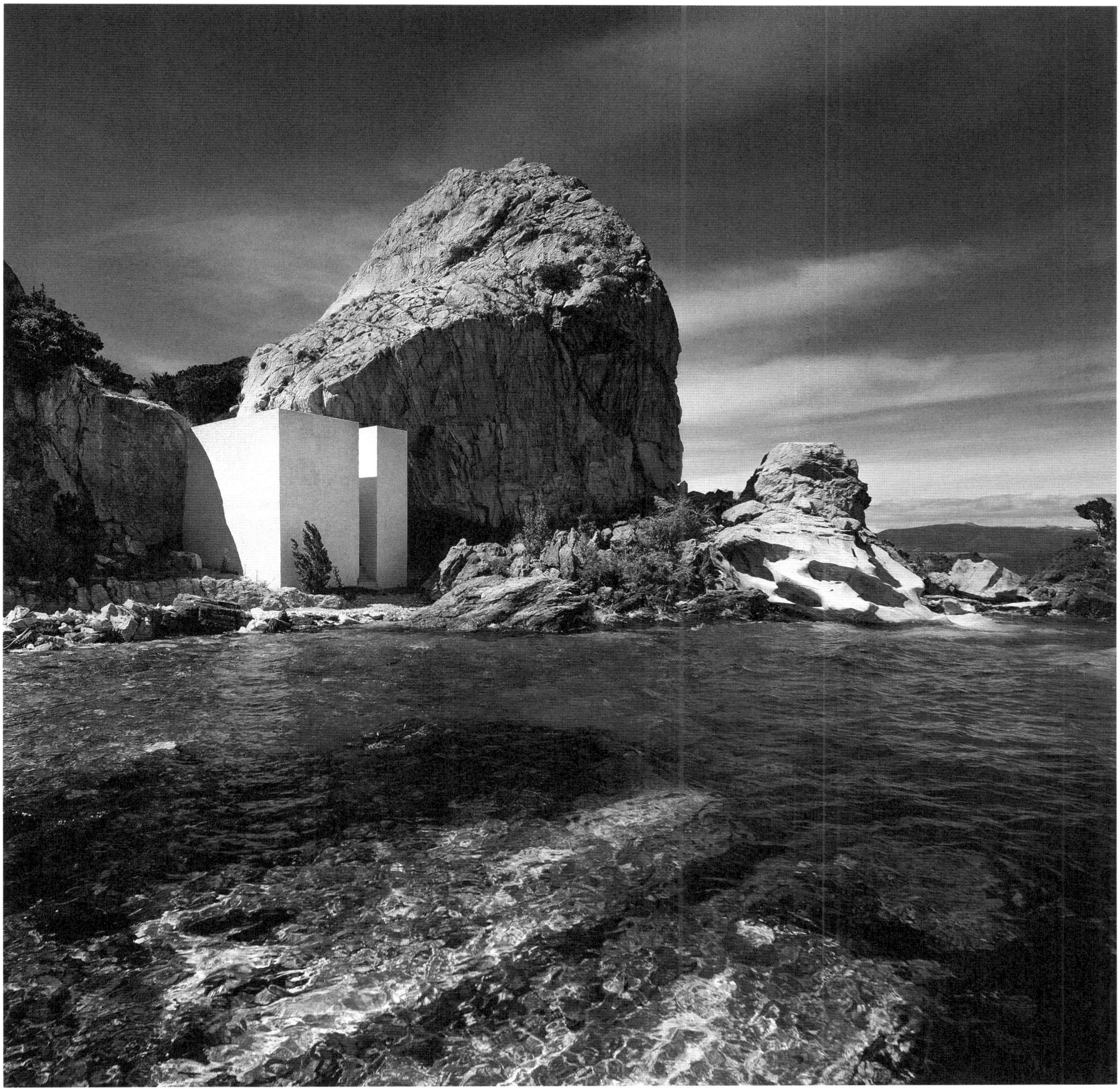

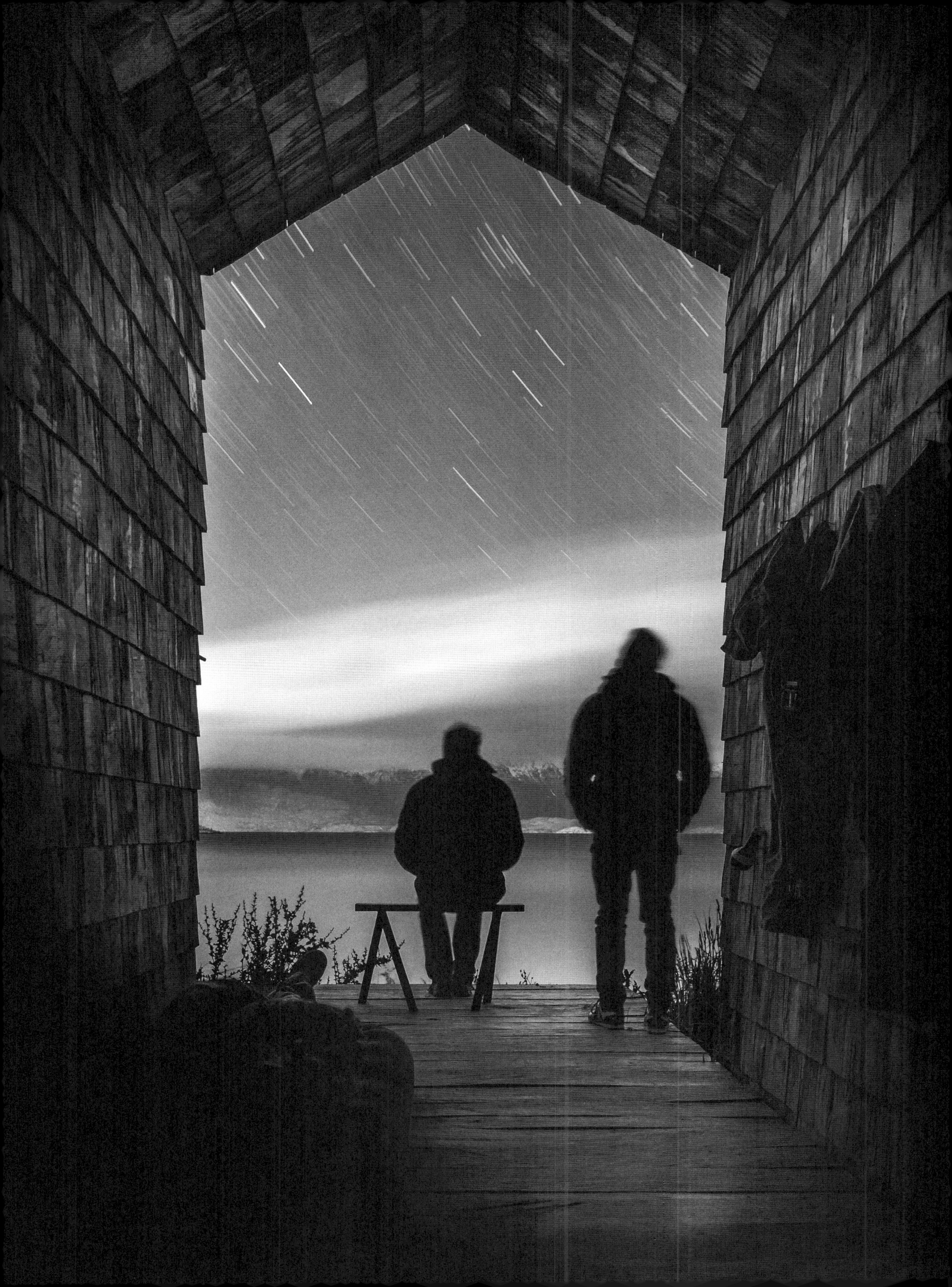

NotOna
2011

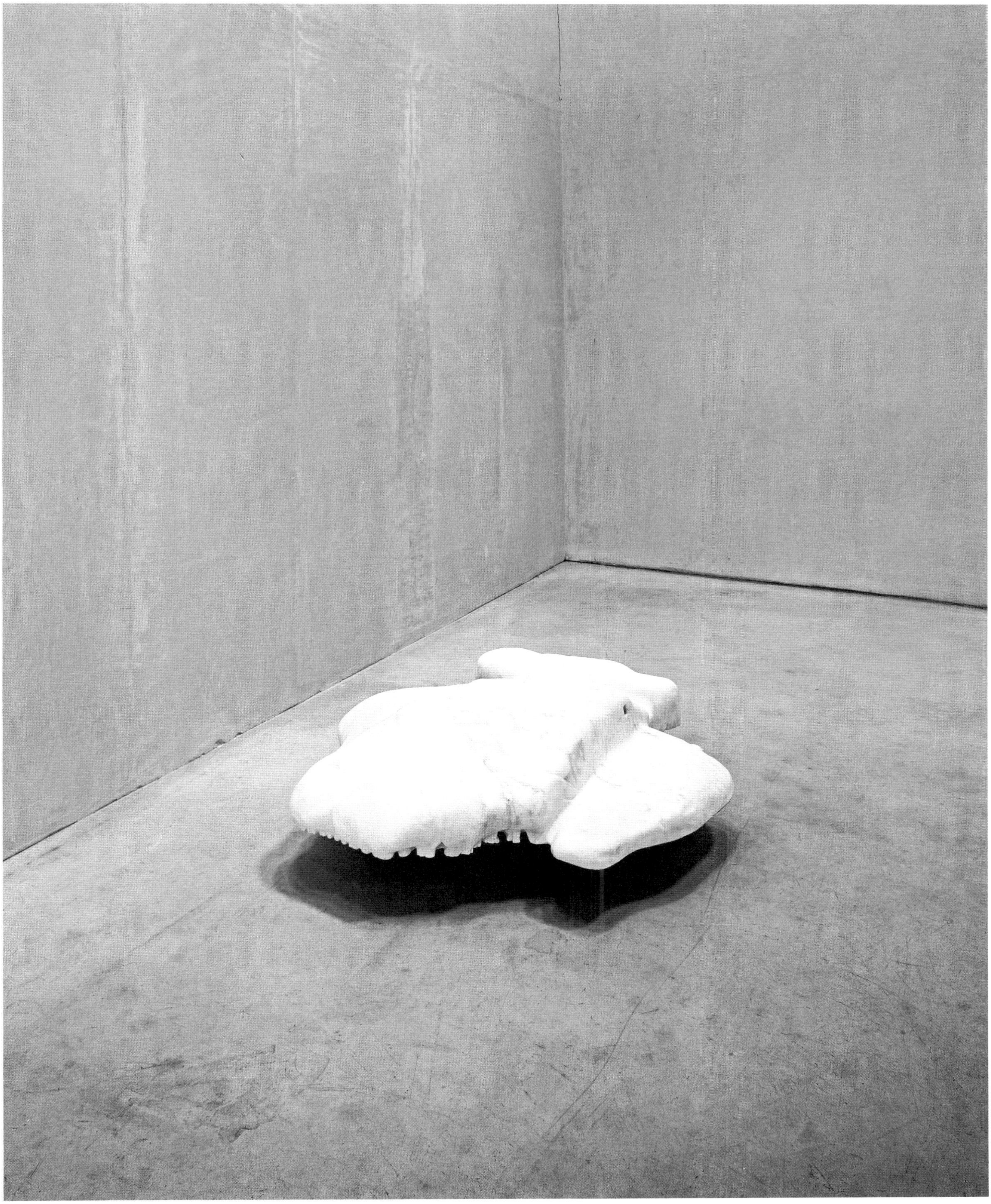

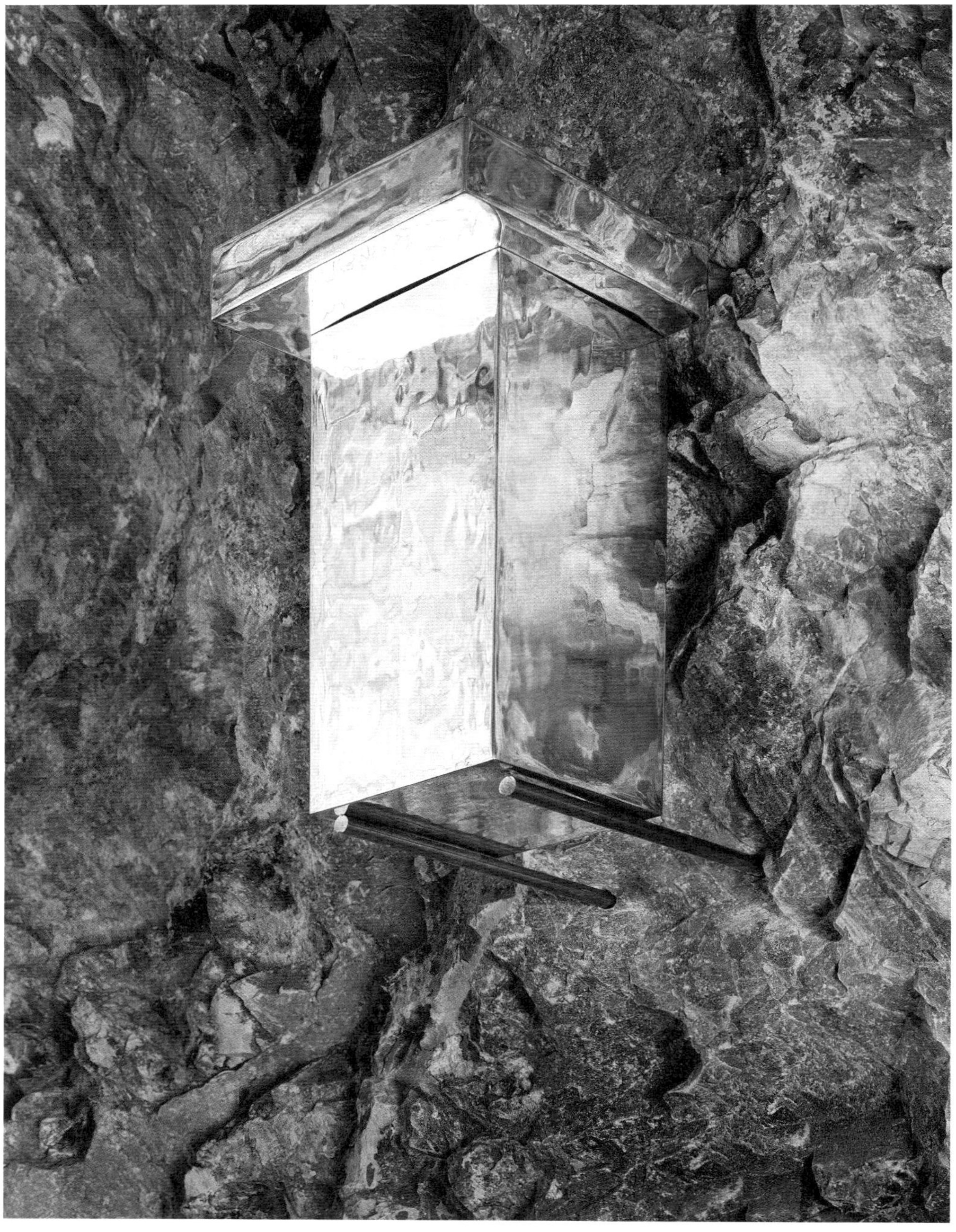

Gordon Matta-Clark (2014), installed at *NotOna*

I am often asked why I do what I do, why I build habitats all over the world. My most sincere & exact answer is that I don't know. "Assai sa chi sa che non sa" is an Italian proverb stating: "the 1 who knows that he doesn't know, knows enough." The equivalent in Chinese would be "woo way," or, "to do nothing." This may be the closest I can come to an answer. Certainly, it has to do with my interest in building. Since my childhood, I dug tunnels in the snow, built houses in the woods, or simply spent a whole afternoon in the shadow of a tree. But then, why didn't I study architecture? I don't know either. Probably I sensed that if I were to study architecture, I would become an architect whose main purpose would be to build houses for people he doesn't know. & this, most certainly, would not have satisfied me.

Now I am here, in the Chilean Patagonia, on *NotOna* island, alone. No one is around me. The only ones here are a condor & his chick. Their nest rests high up on a cliff. I am completely by myself. I didn't know how that feels until a few years ago, when I was here, alone, for 1 whole week. I still don't have a phone or a boat & hence no means to contact anyone in the nearby village of Puerto Sanchez, a tiny village I don't even see from my island.

With 1 of my best friends, I have often talked earnestly about moving to a remote cabin & living there with only 1 goat or 1 sheep. That may not only be a good idea, but even a justified 1, if you live in a palazzo in Venice, or in a castle in Switzerland. To try & do the opposite is often attractive. But in this case, it is more than just that: such a trajectory may indeed be a good solution for the future, considering that 1 day our planet will probably be completely overpopulated, overheated & computers will run our affairs.

When I say "eating architecture," I mean doing something as easy as eating food when you are hungry (if you have anything to eat), or sleeping when you are tired. When entering a tunnel that you dug in the snow, you see the color of ice & smell the snow, but, most importantly, you know how it feels in there.

The 1st thing I do when I get up on *NotOna*, after taking a piss, is make a fire. I am now able to light a fire with only 1 match. Such a skill is normal for most people on this earth, but it is not common for most Europeans or Americans, or most people living in big cities.

The next thing I do is get water from the lake & heat it to make tea. Then I make my bed, wash my face, eat an apple & prepare food. I am really lucky to have drinkable water in this lake, which is the 2nd biggest lake in South America. It could be just as polluted as the biggest 1, which is called Titicaca. Also, having enough food is not at all self-evident here. Last time I spent a week on the island, I ran out of food because I assumed that I could catch a fish, but I couldn't. Or maybe I simply forgot to buy enough food. Now, I have 4 apples, 5 avocados, 6 tomatoes, nuts, 6 eggs & some bread, all of which I haven't eaten yet. So, why do I say "eating architecture" & then talk about food? Because food & habitat are so closely linked. You are more aware of it when you live in a hut on a remote island than if you stay in a 5-star hotel.

As a kid, growing up in Switzerland, I didn't like to eat. I wouldn't eat for days, so my father would carve little houses & towers out of cheese & I would eat the houses & towers without even being aware that it was food. So, I was eating architecture. 1 of my first models for the tower in my park in Sent was made out of cheese. After all, this is the food we are most renowned for in Switzerland, together with chocolate.

I conceived *NotOna*, this habitat here in the Chilean Patagonia, as a place to watch the sunset. That was the whole purpose of doing this project. But now I don't know if that was truly the only purpose, because I seem to spend much more time looking at the color of the lake, which is like a blue emerald. But that doesn't matter, because the most important fact is that this house is not built in a conventional or Western way, with infrastructure for comfortable living. If I eat some of the food I have here on *NotOna* & then spend the night in my house, a house that is 55 meters long & dug out of white marble, then it feels like the house is digesting me.

Tower of Cheese
2012

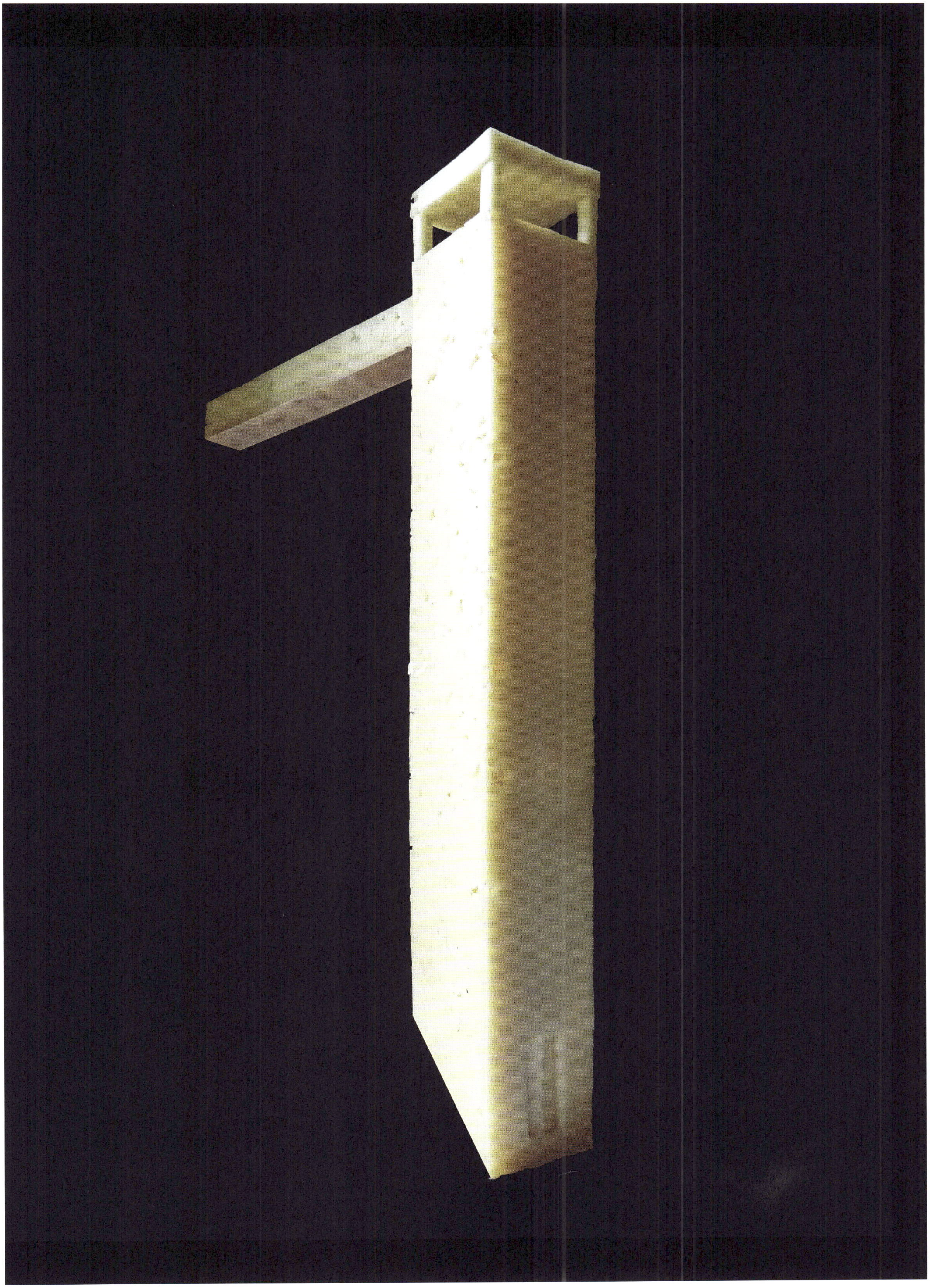

House for CS (Bread)

2013

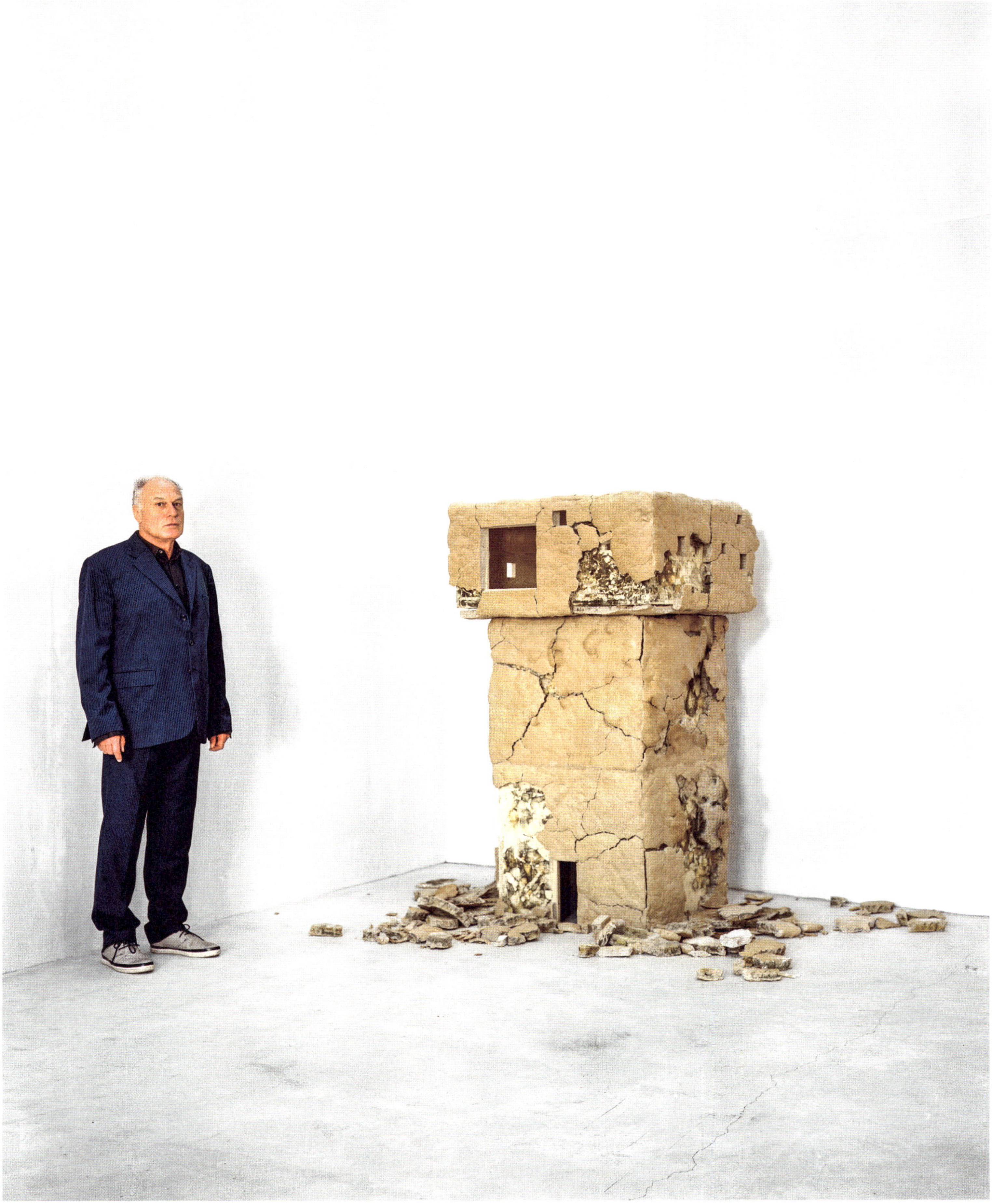

Belgium

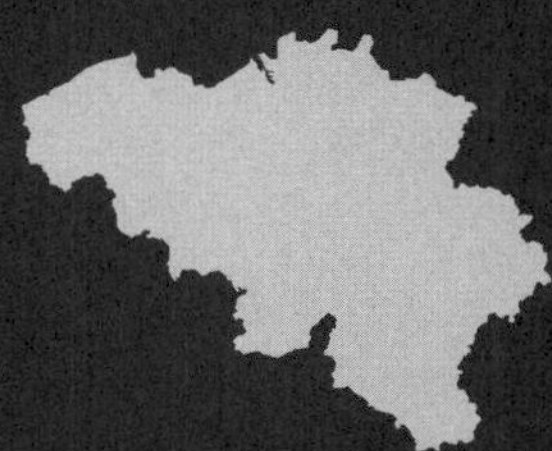

Marble Tower

Walloon Brabant, Belgium

2009

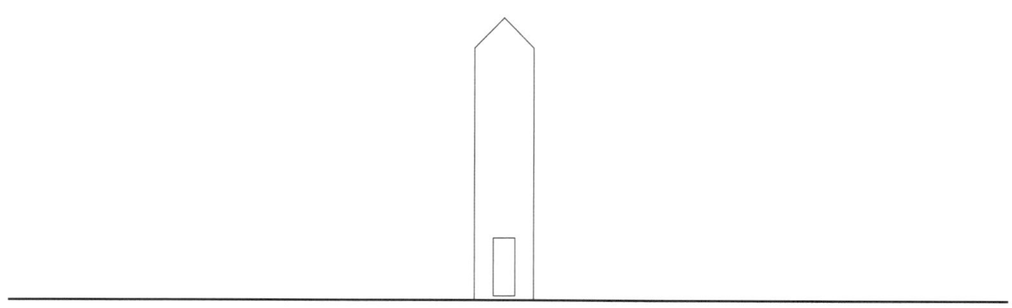

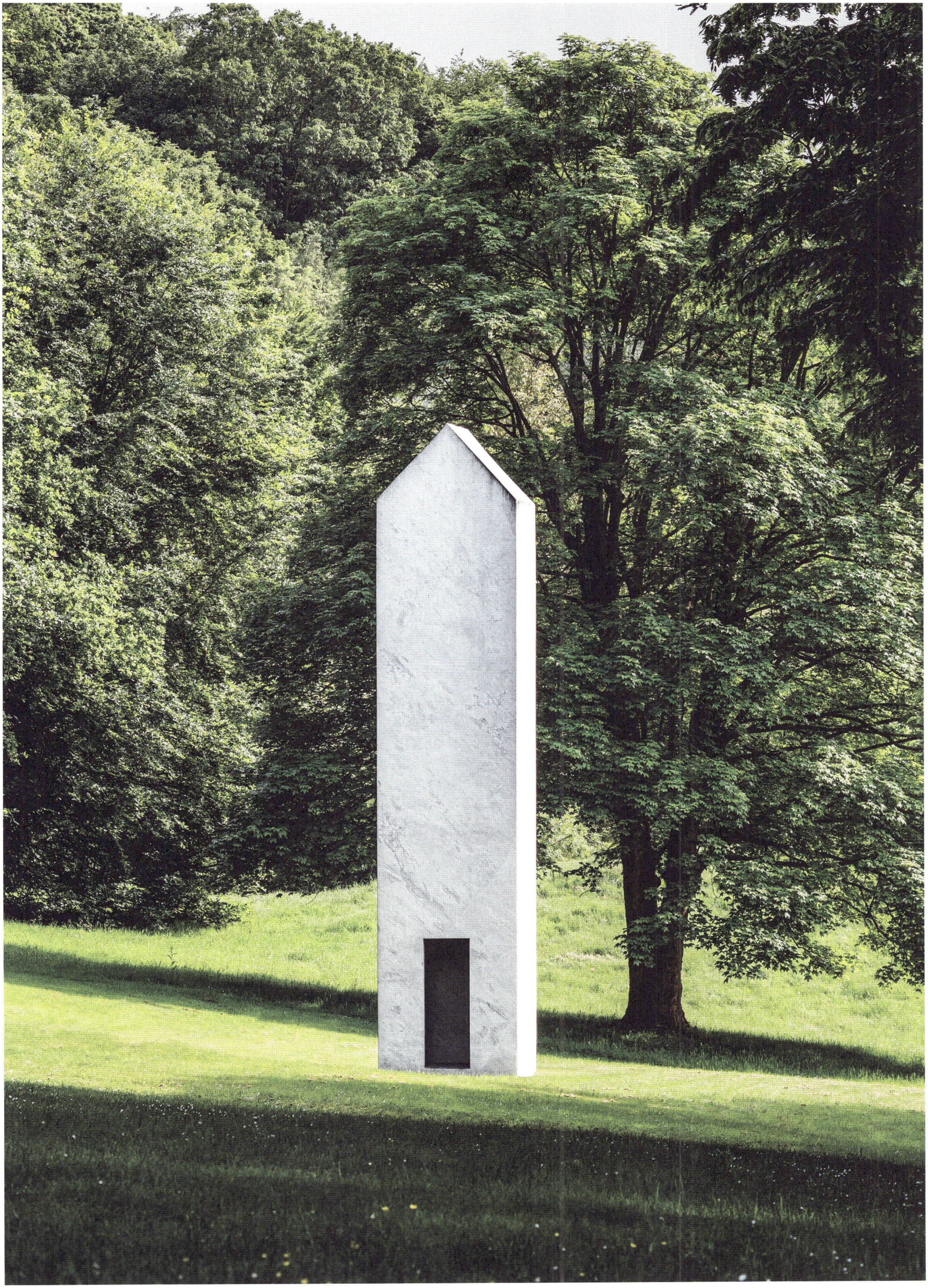

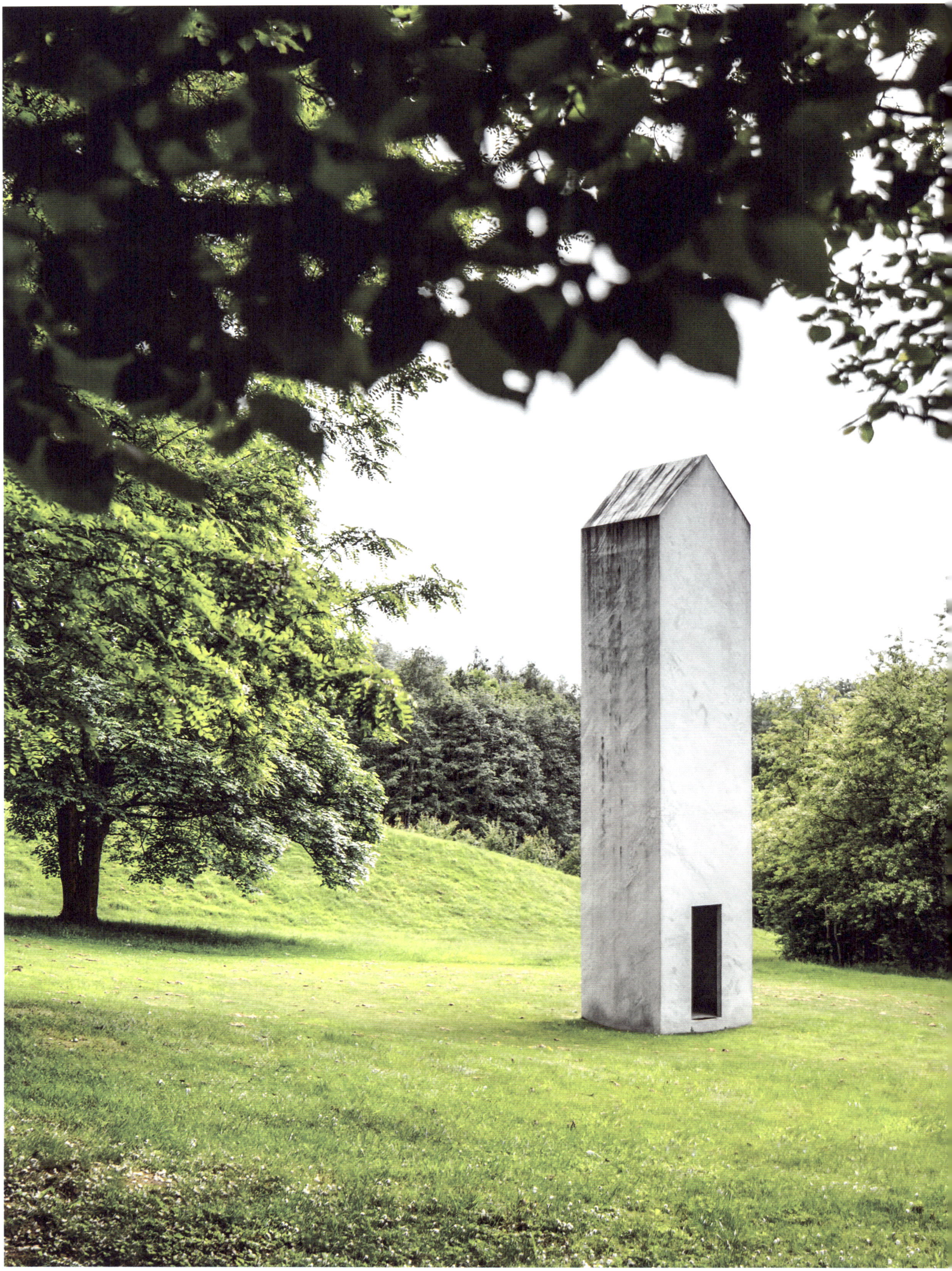

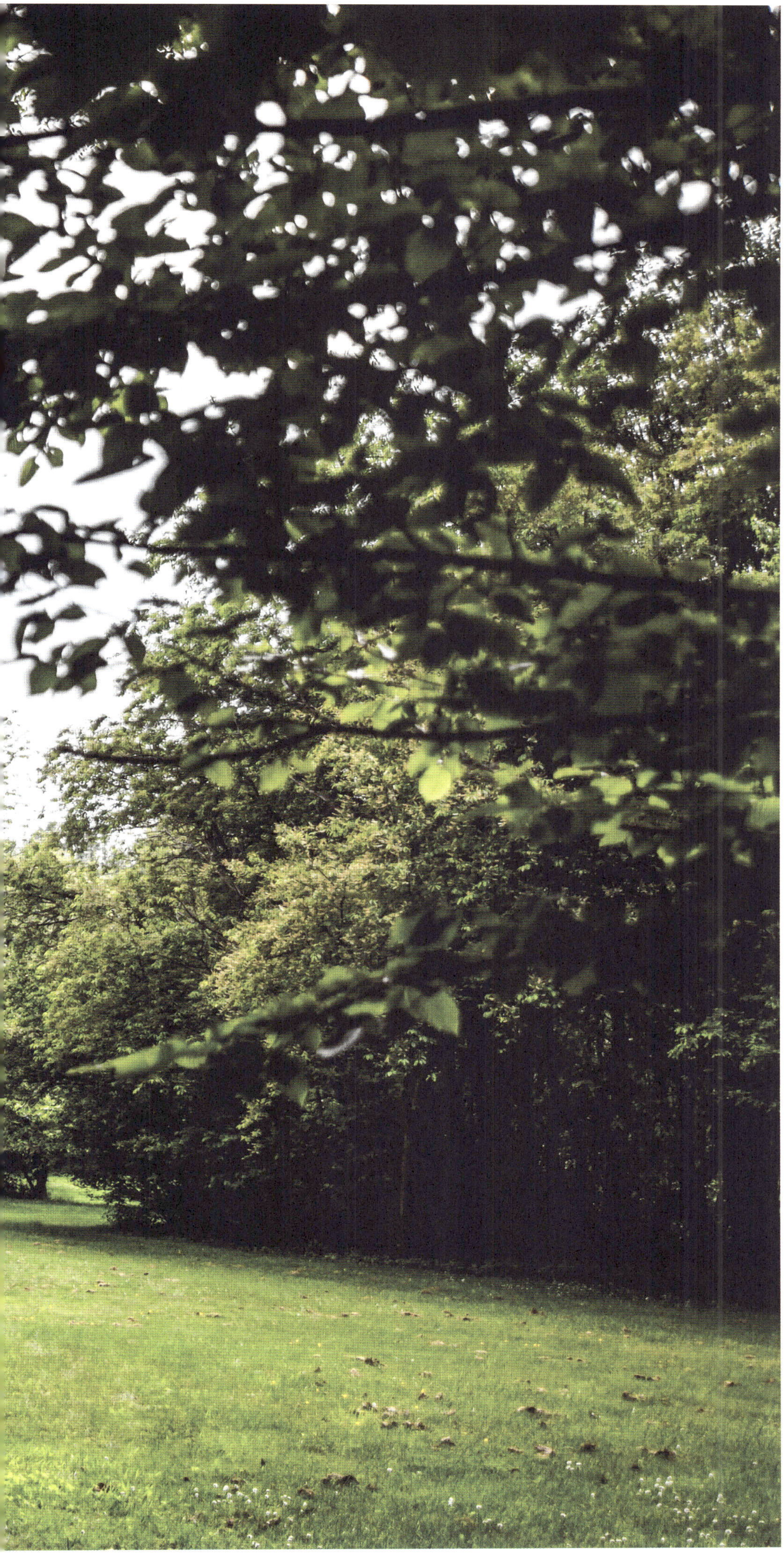

Brazil

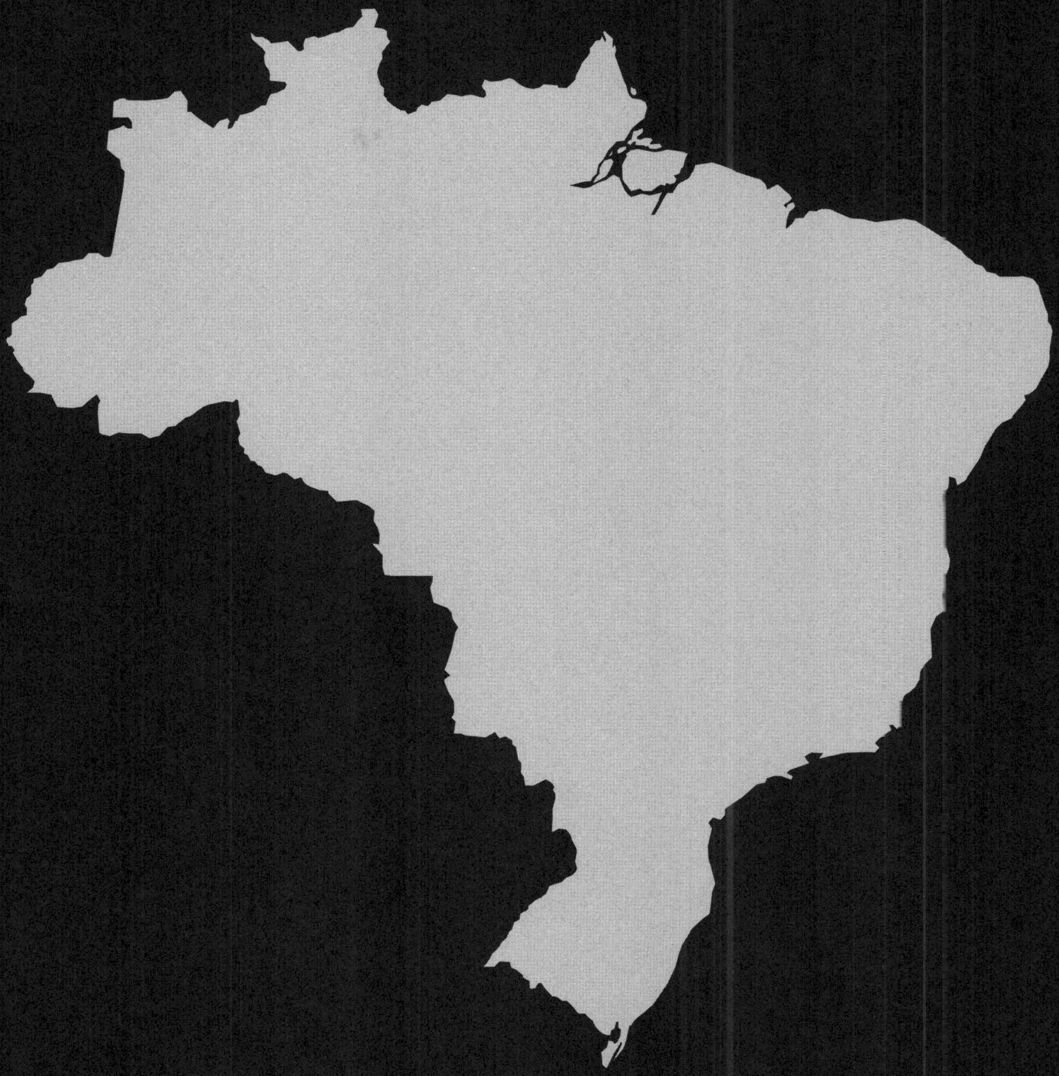

House to Watch the Sunset
Paraná do Mamori, Brazil
2016

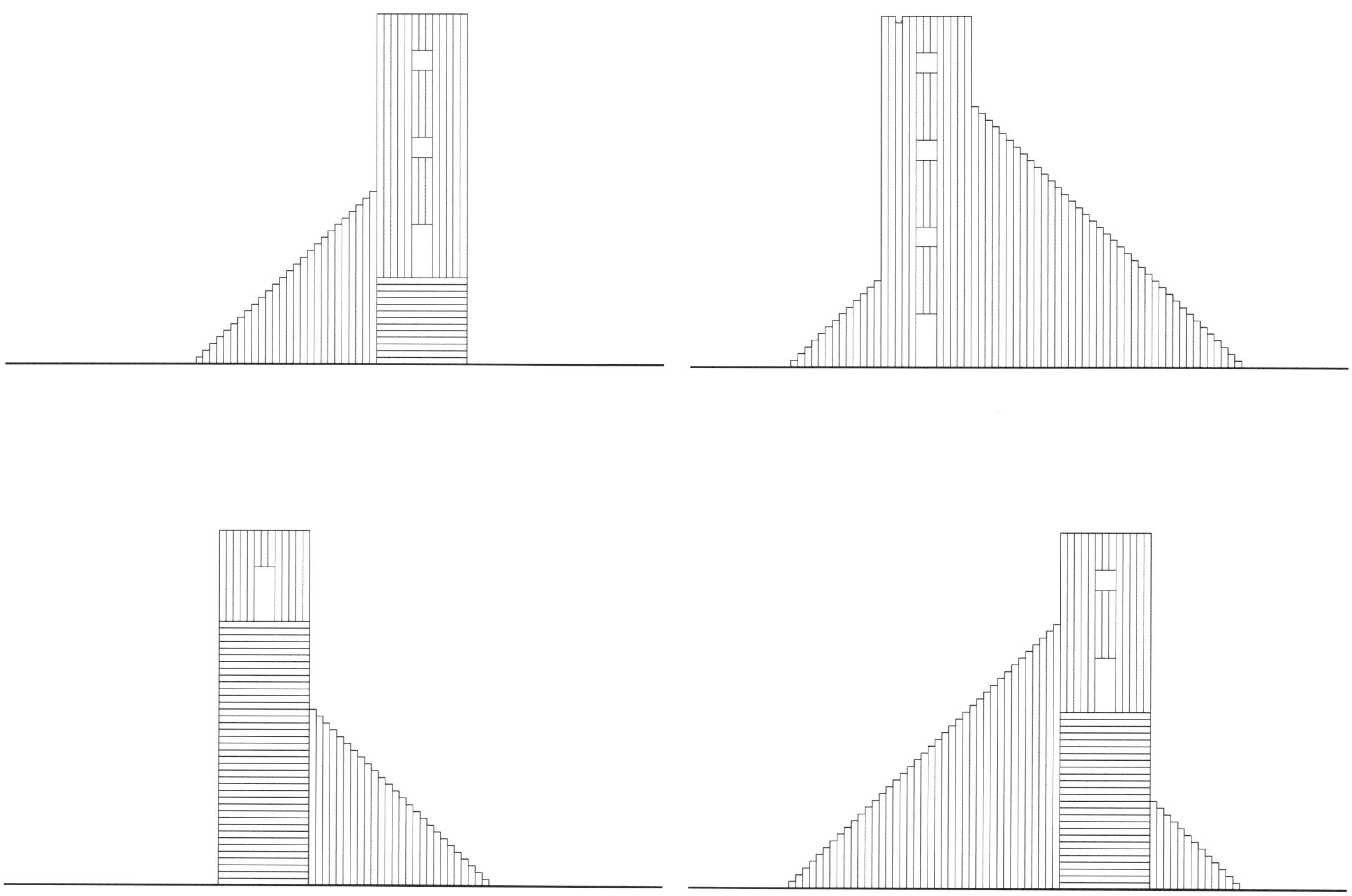

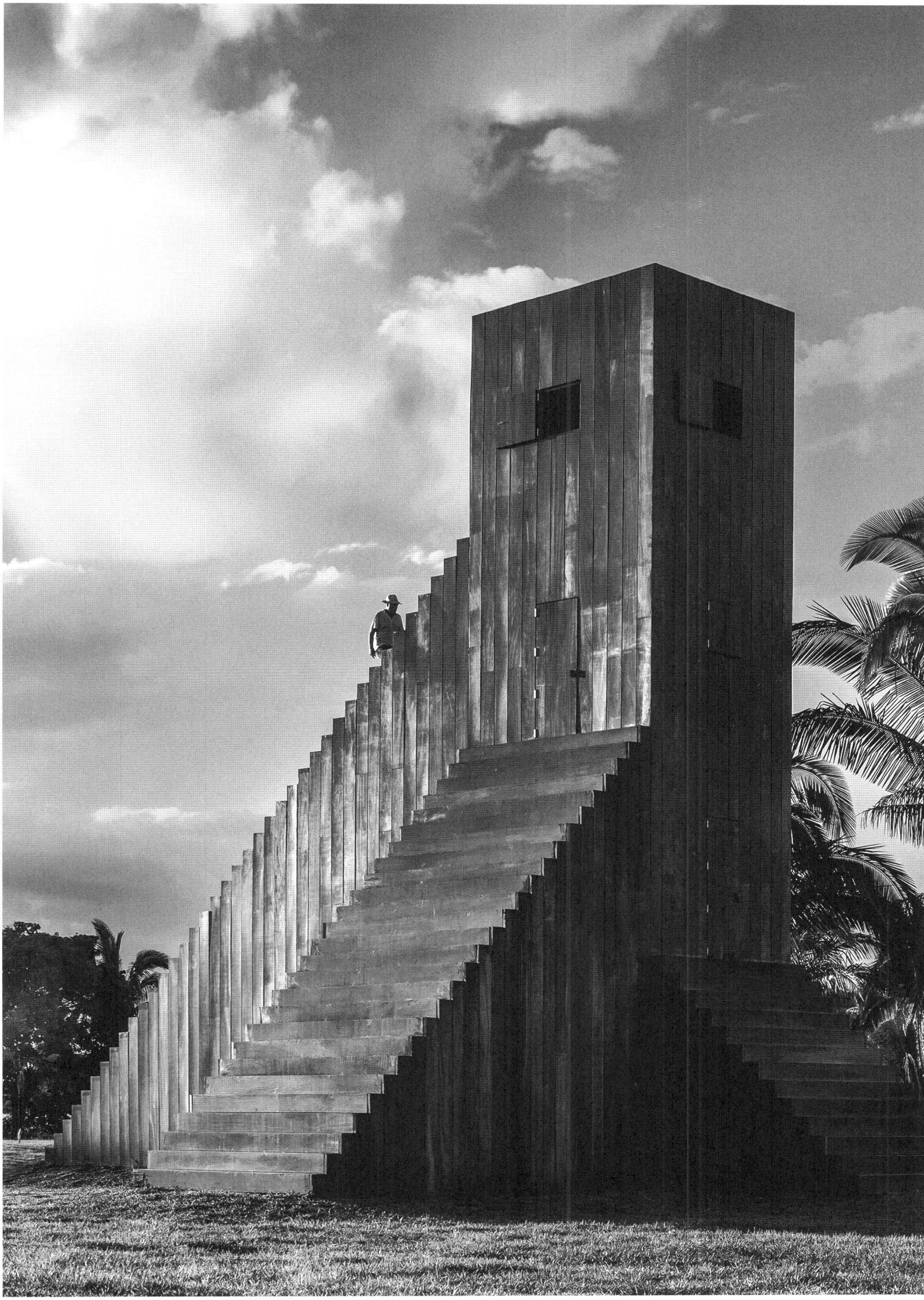

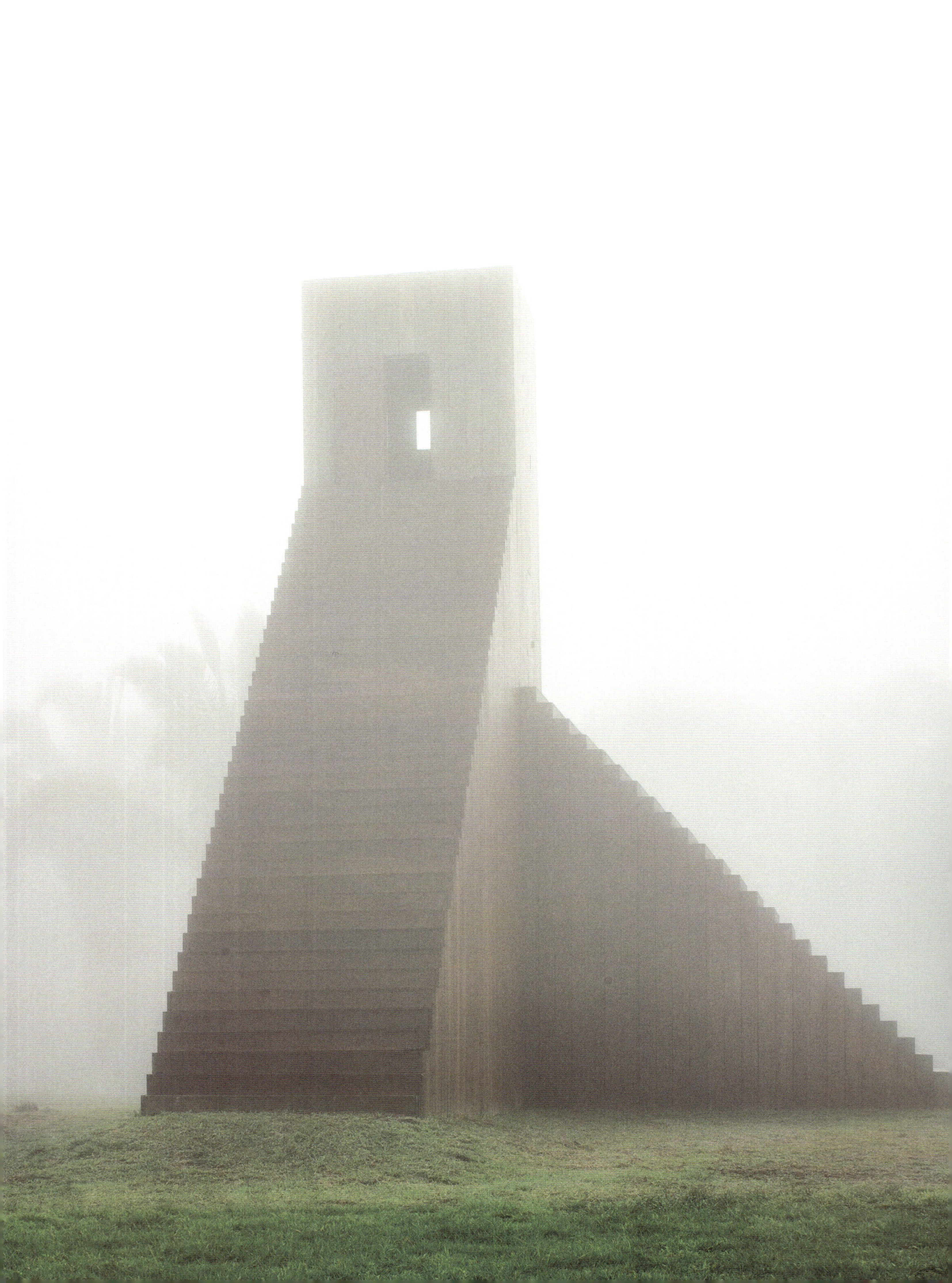

House to Watch the Sunset
2016

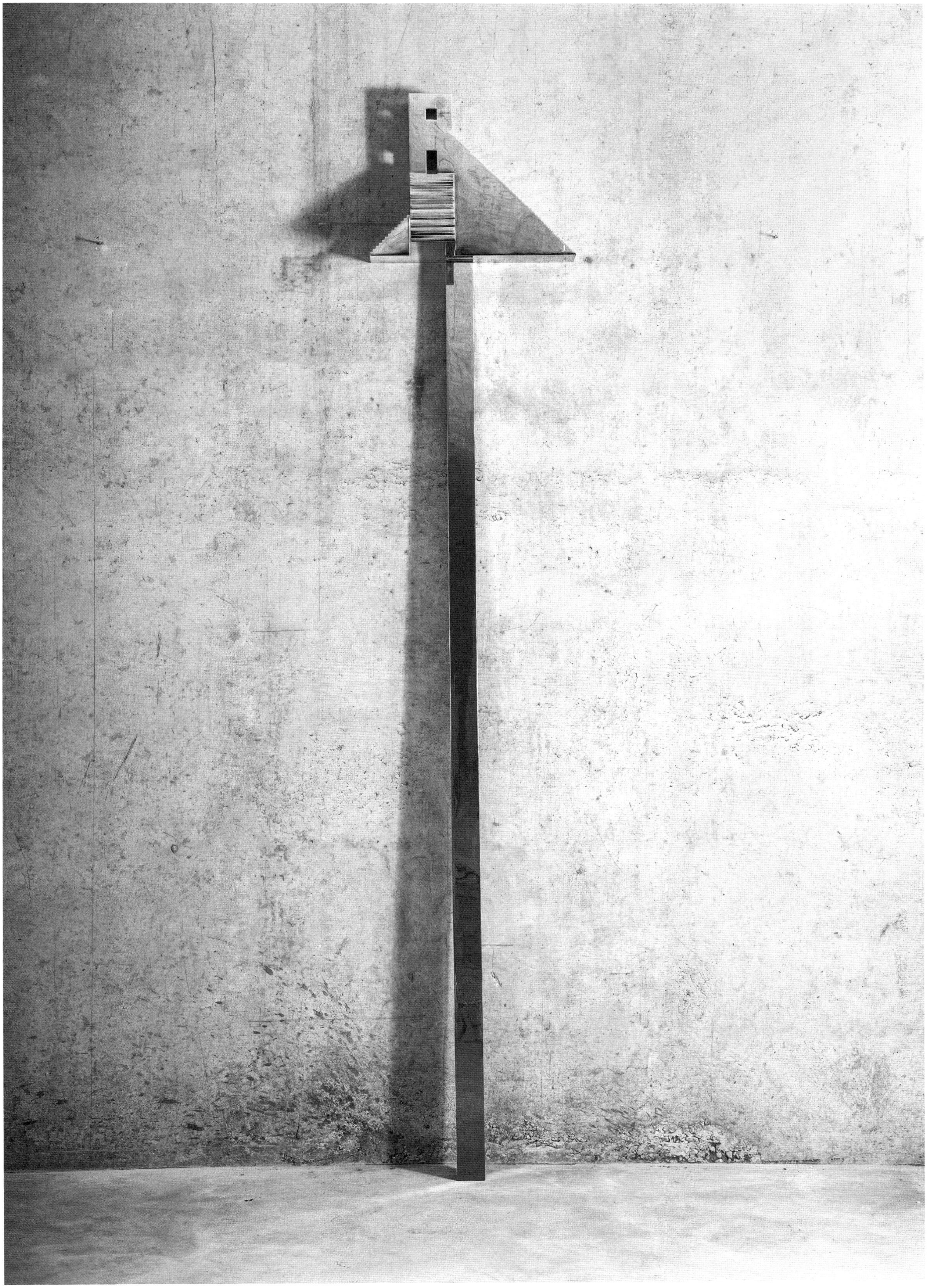

House with No Doors
Paraná do Mamori, Brazil
2016

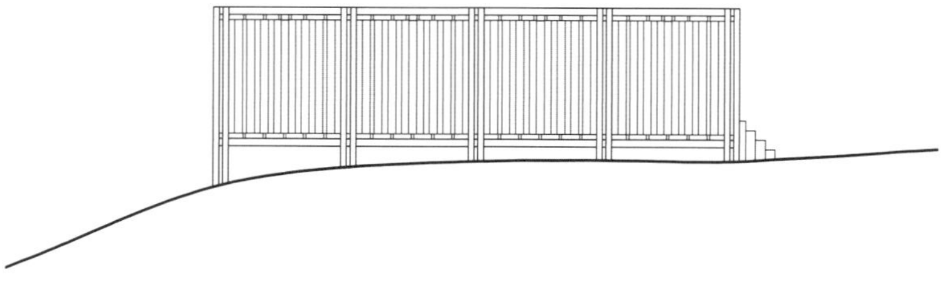

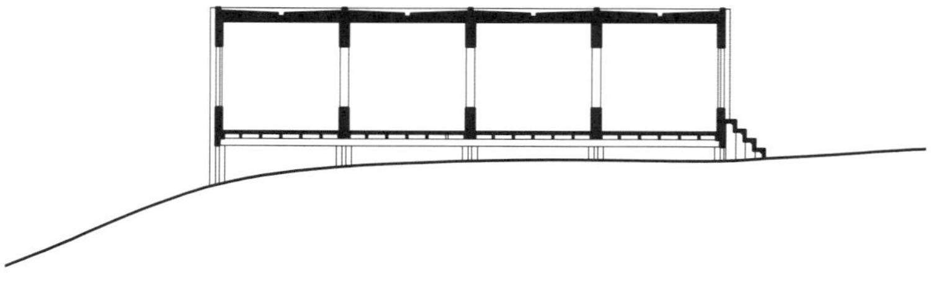

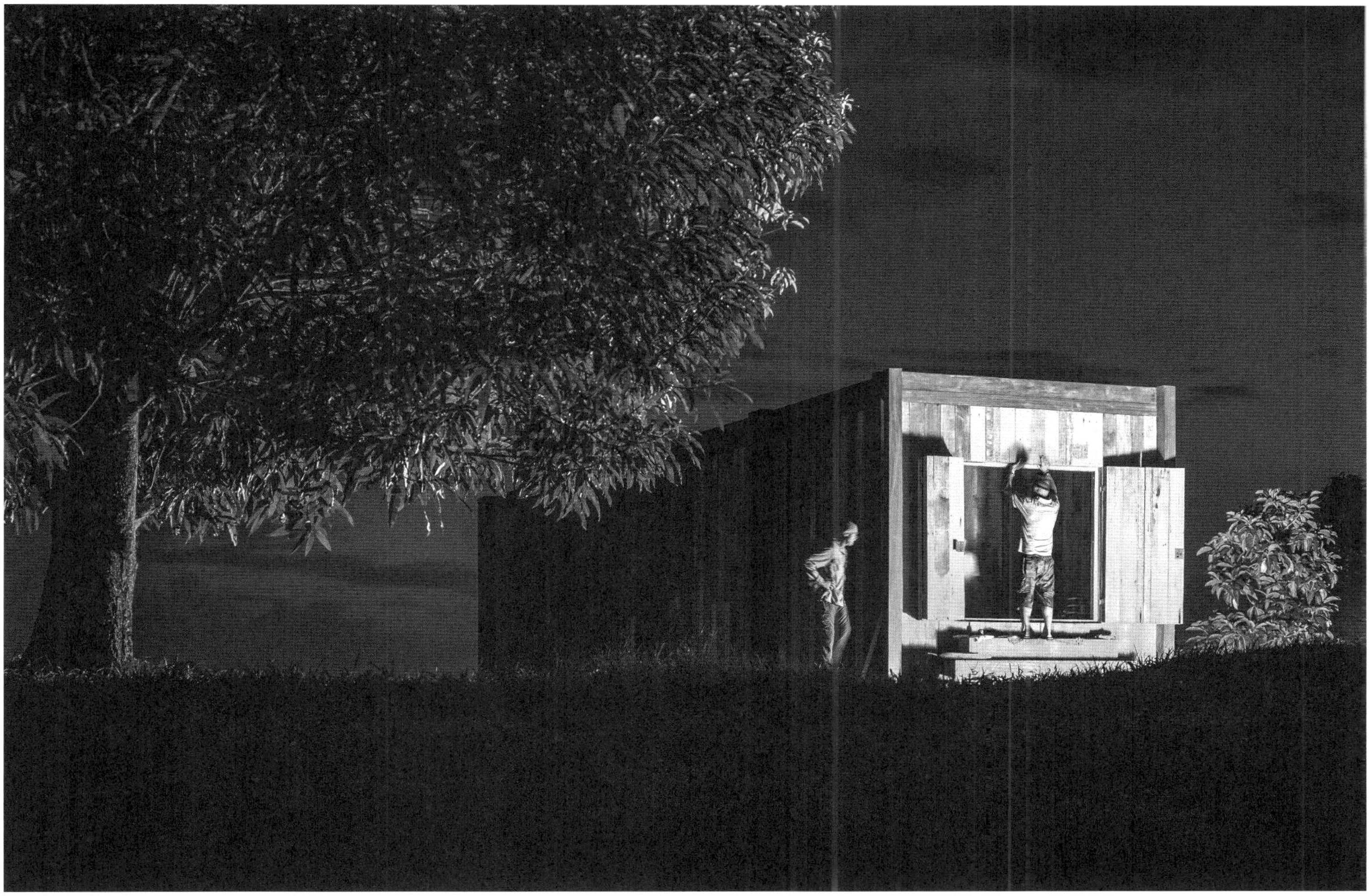

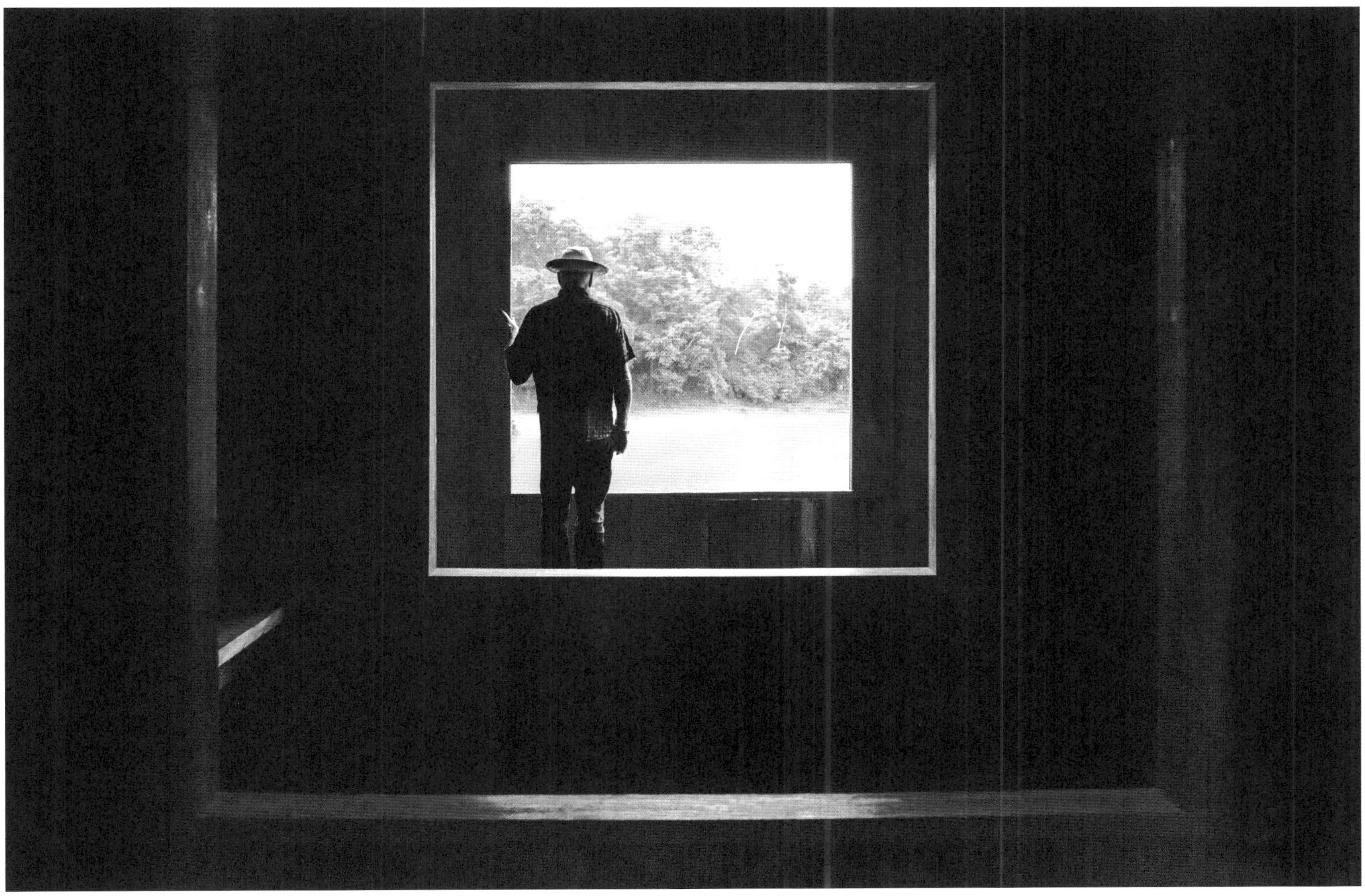

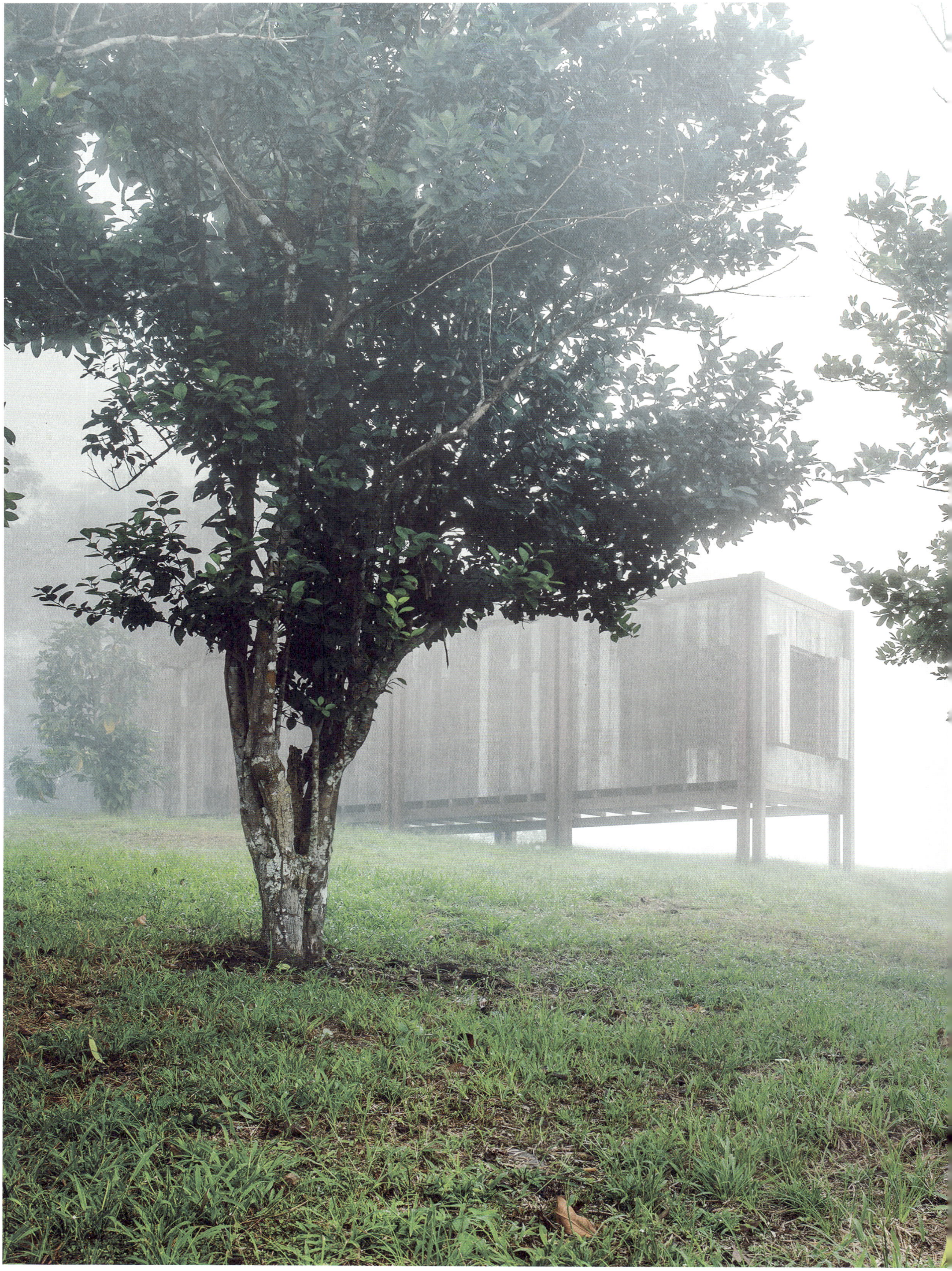

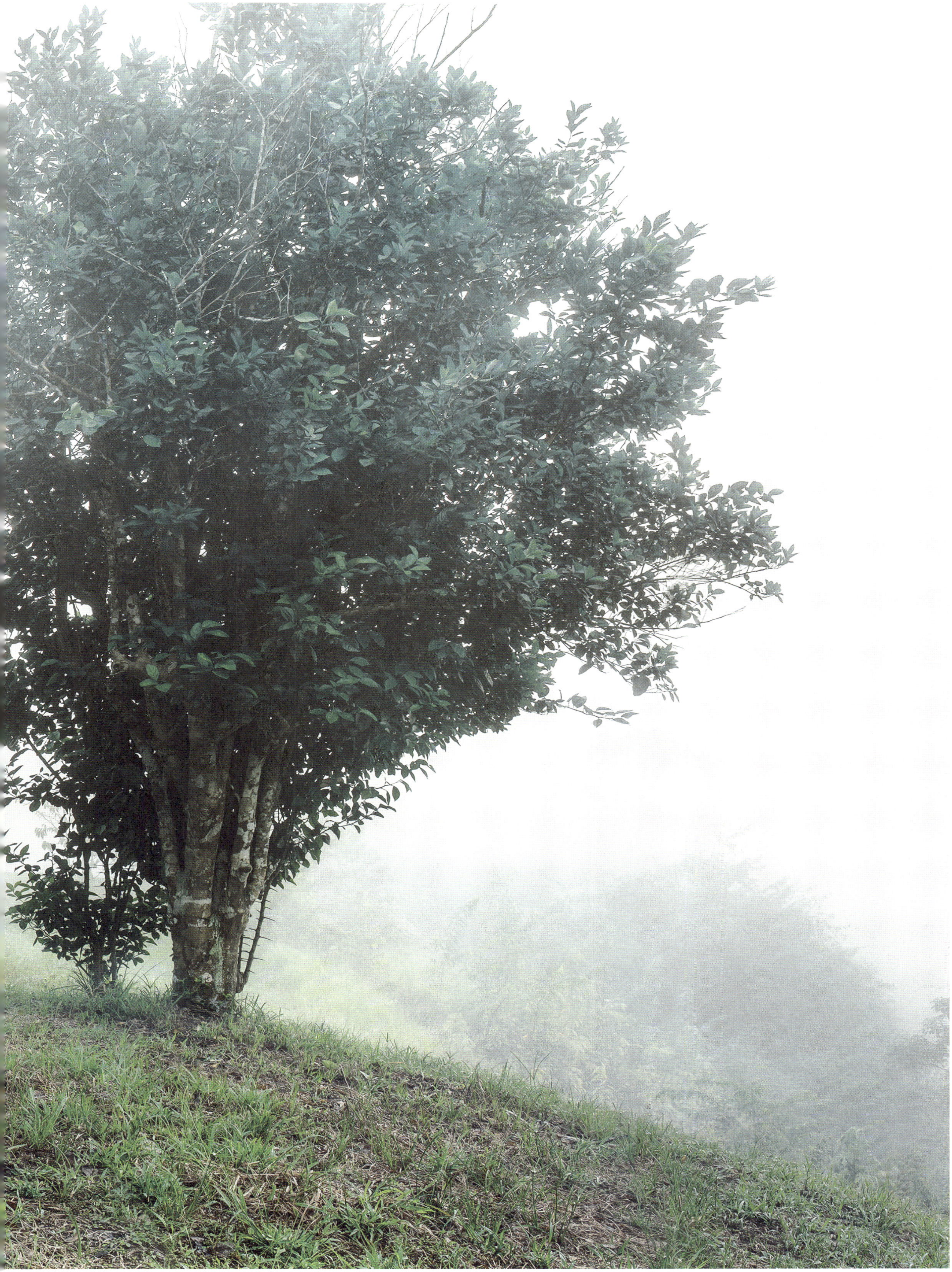

Cathedral
Paraná do Mamori, Brazil
2016

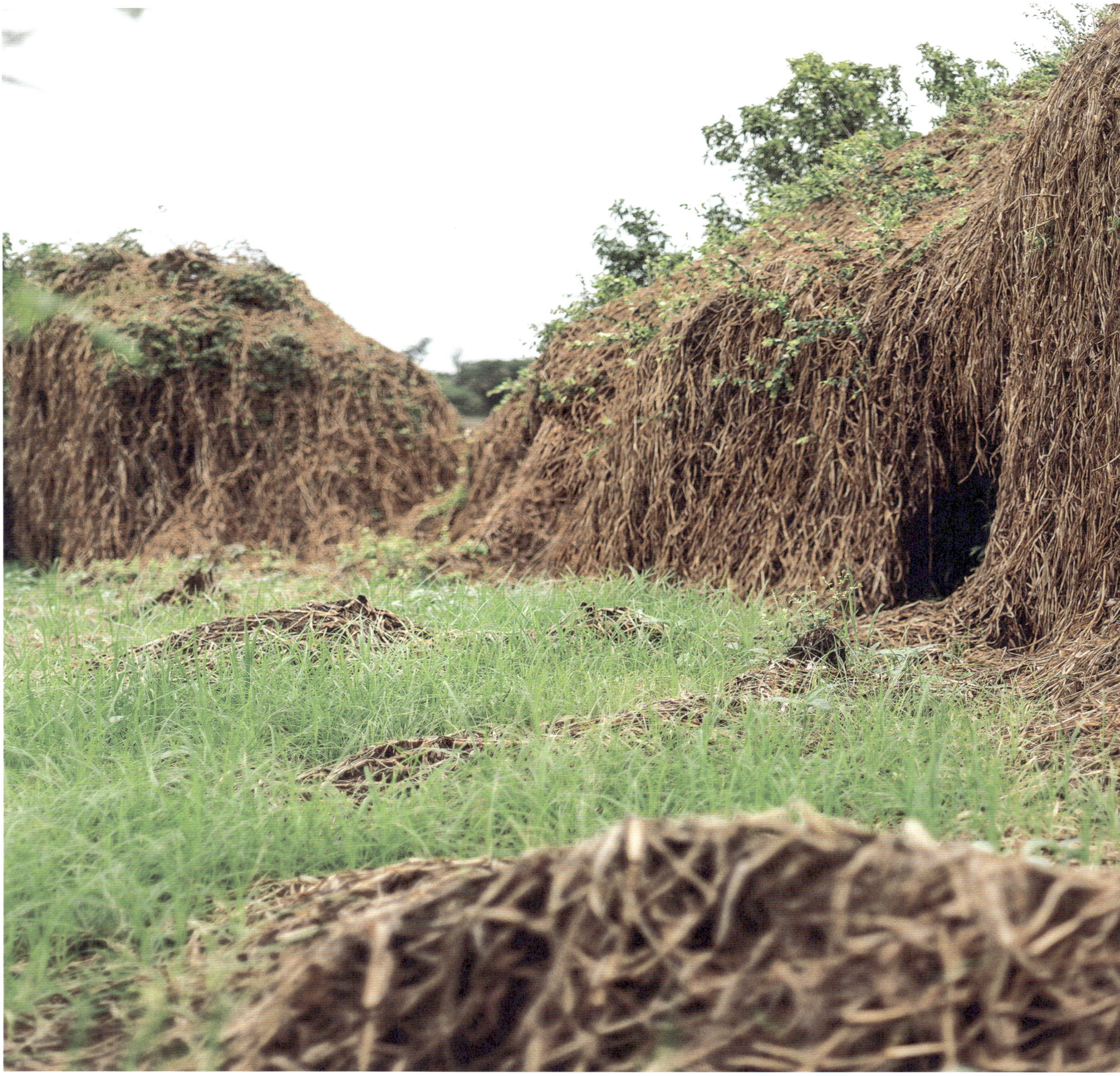

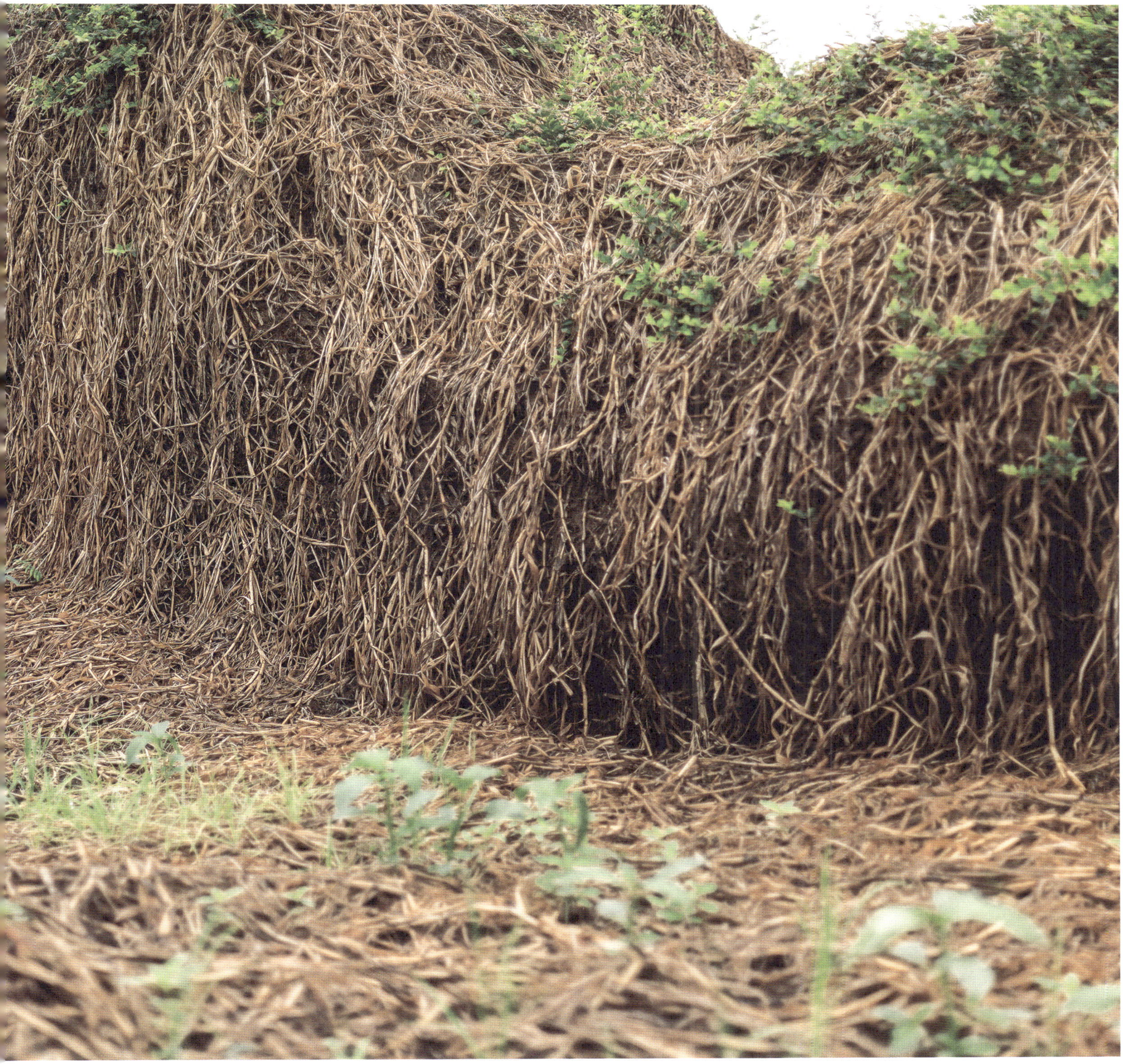

Indonesia

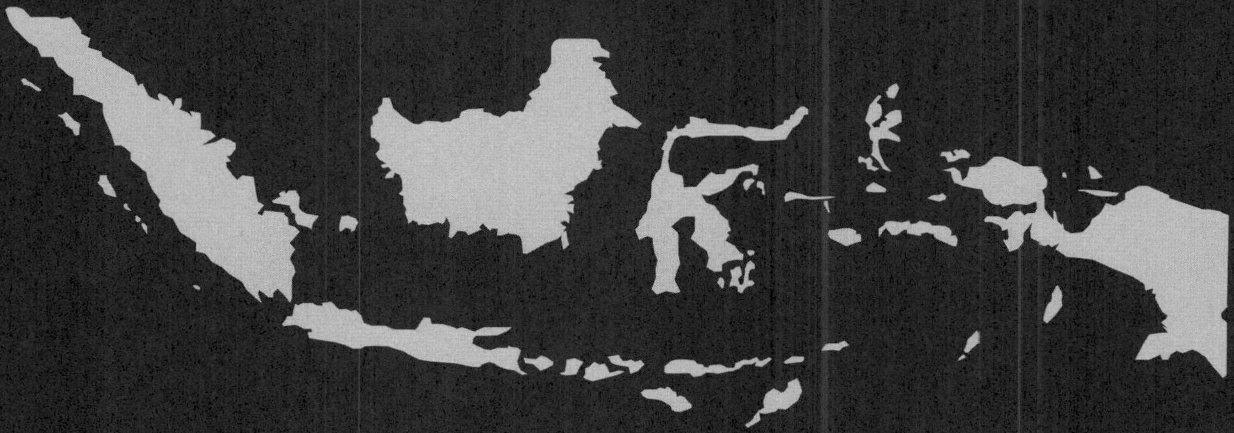

Roof House
Moni, Flores, Indonesia
2016

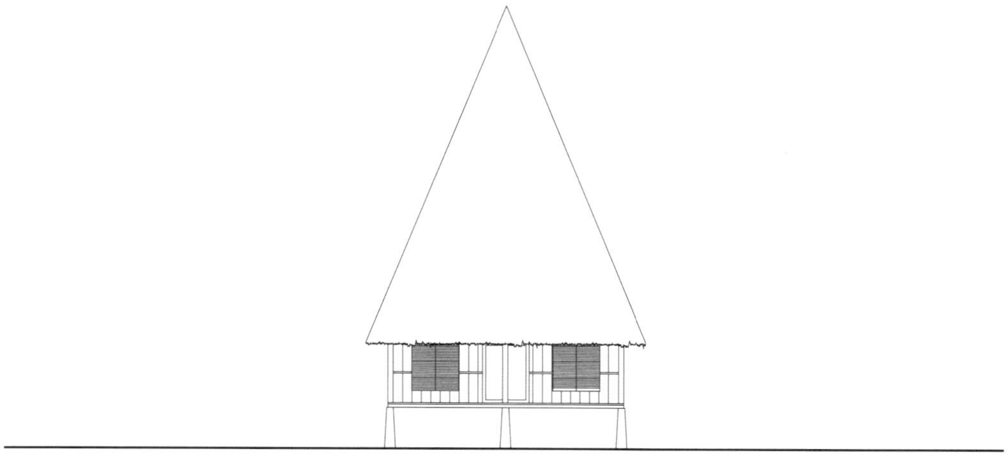

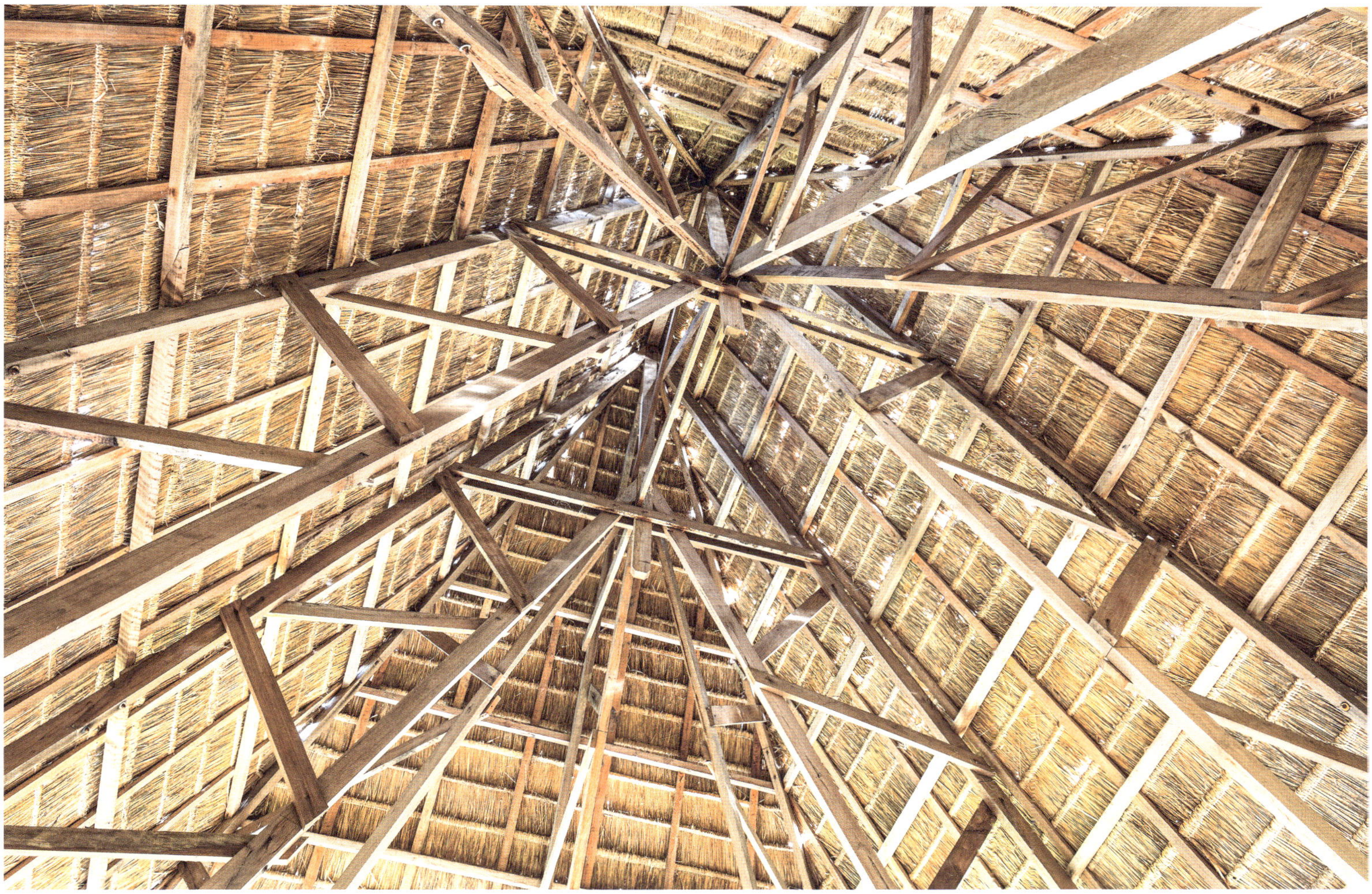

House to Watch the 3 Volcanoes

Moni, Flores, Indonesia
2017

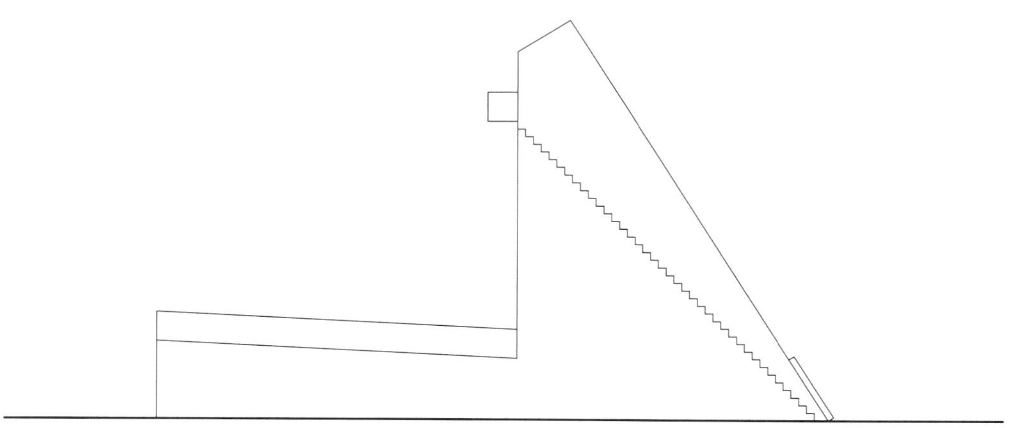

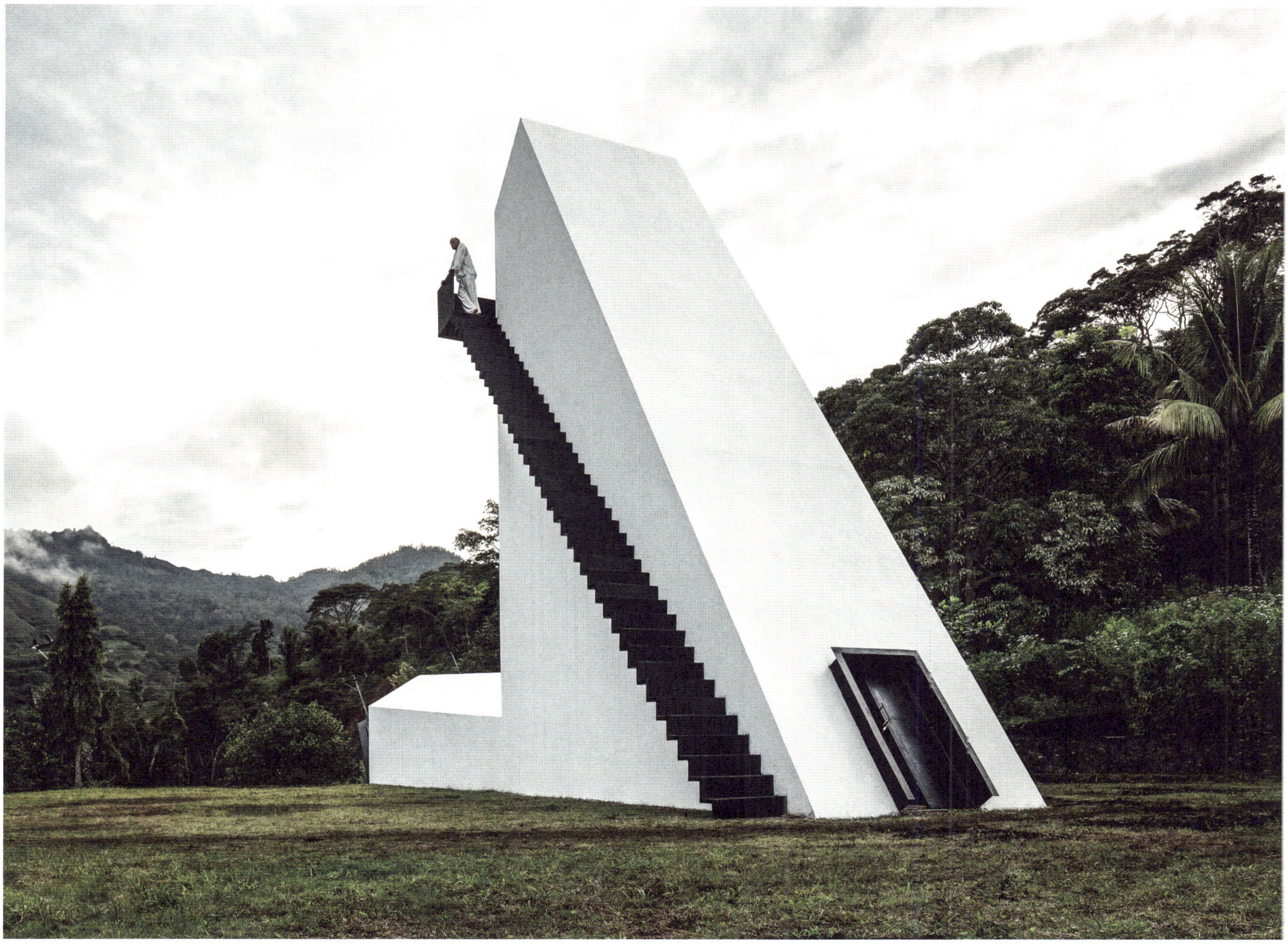

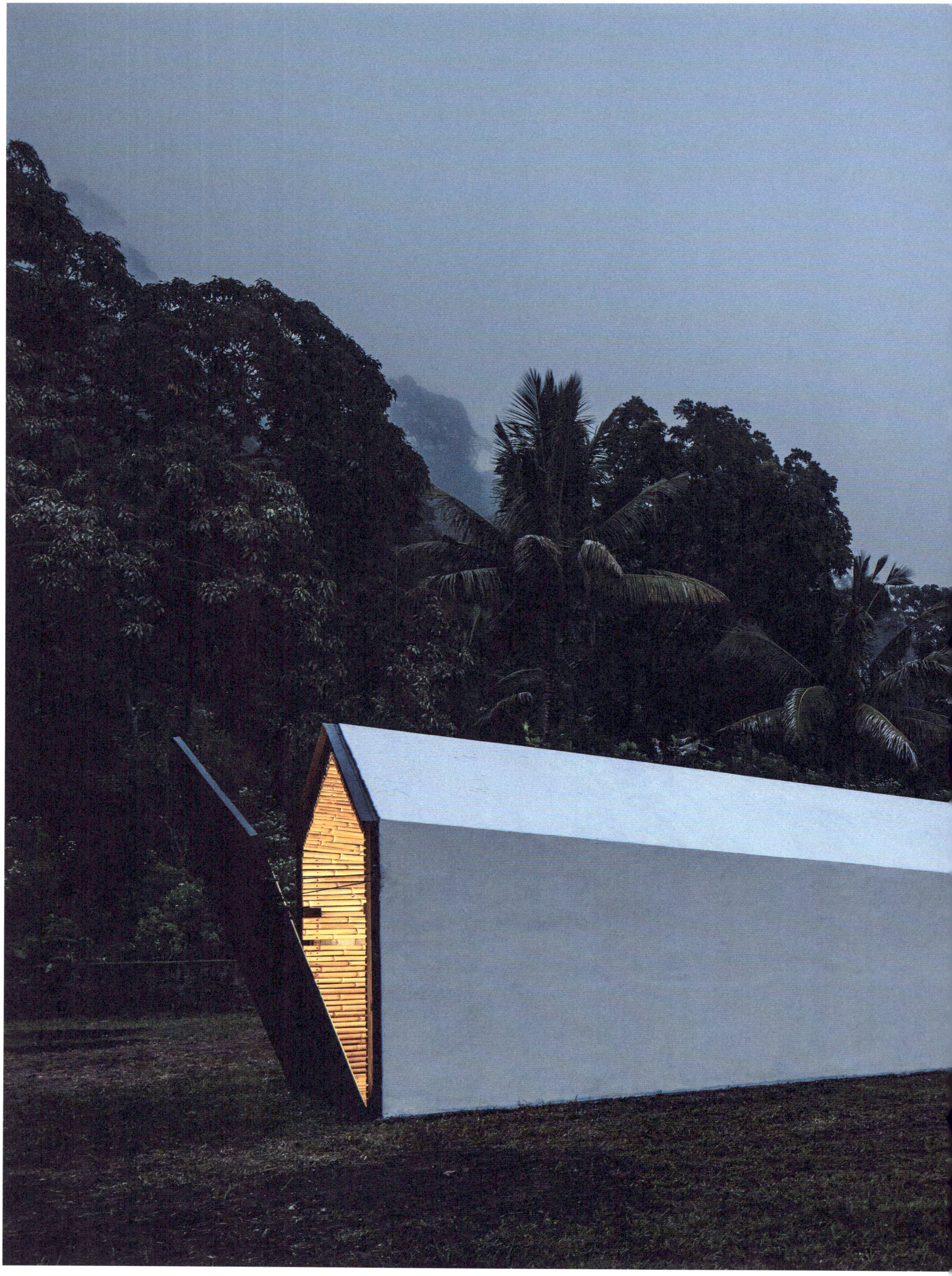

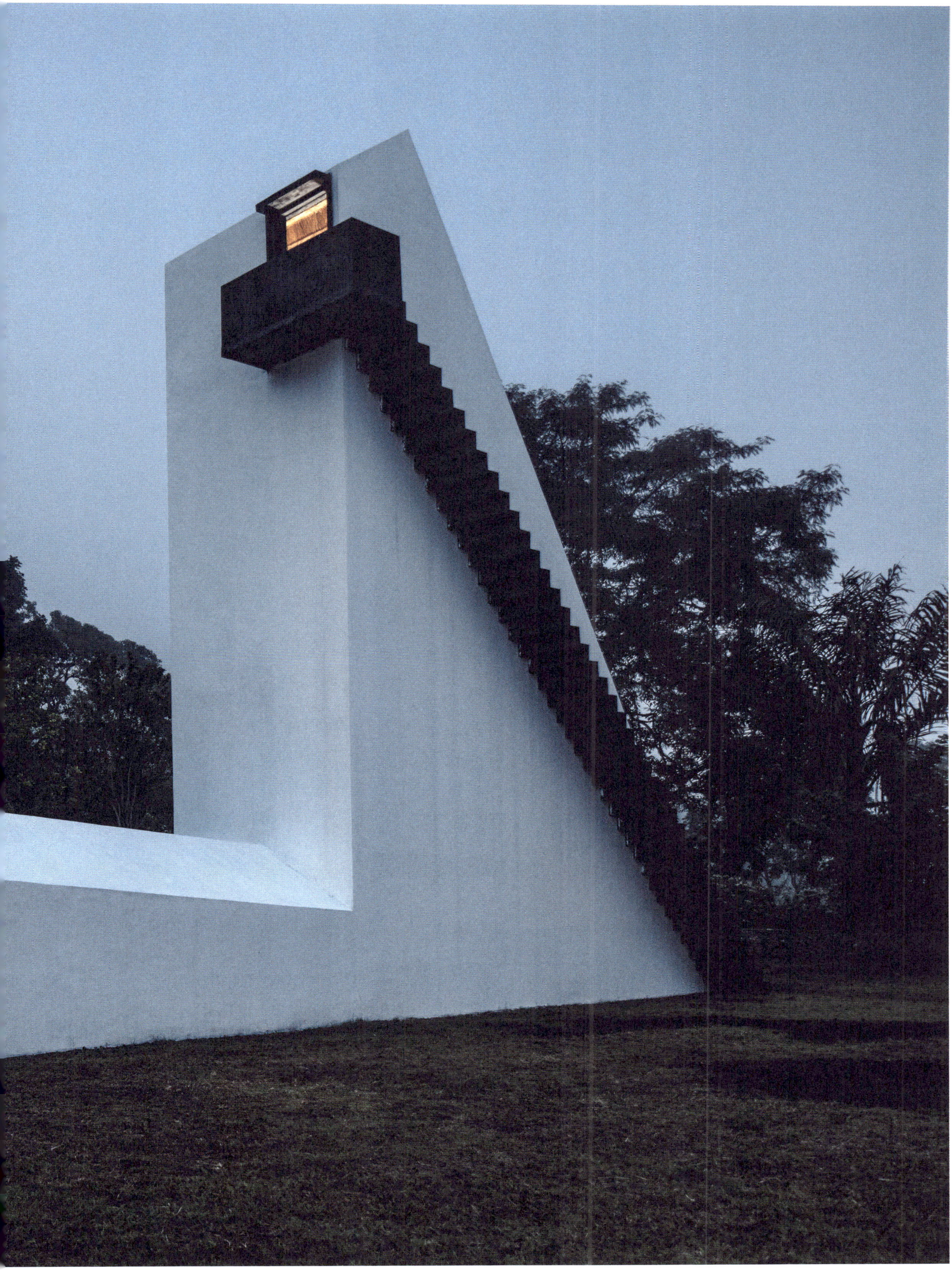

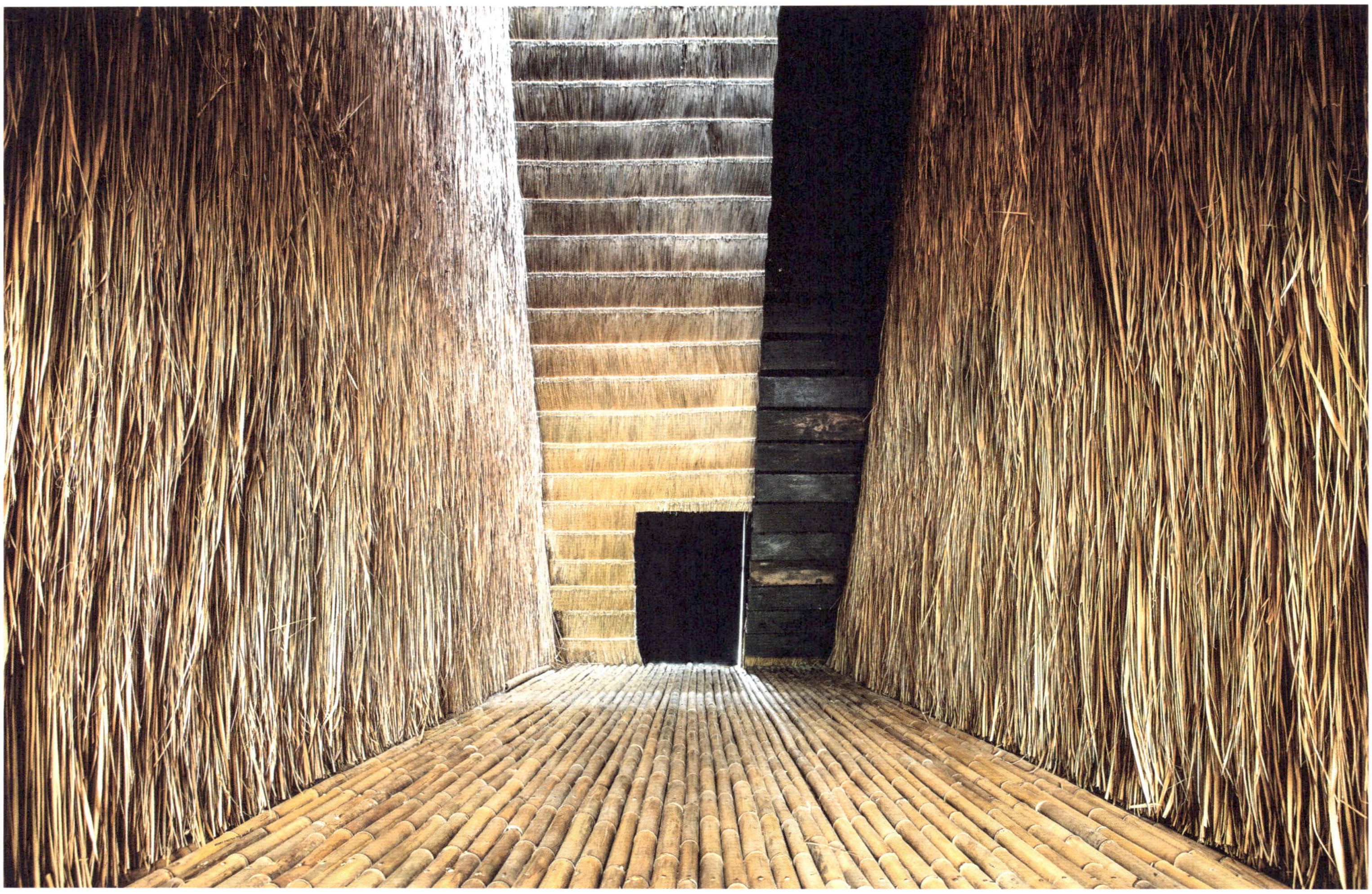

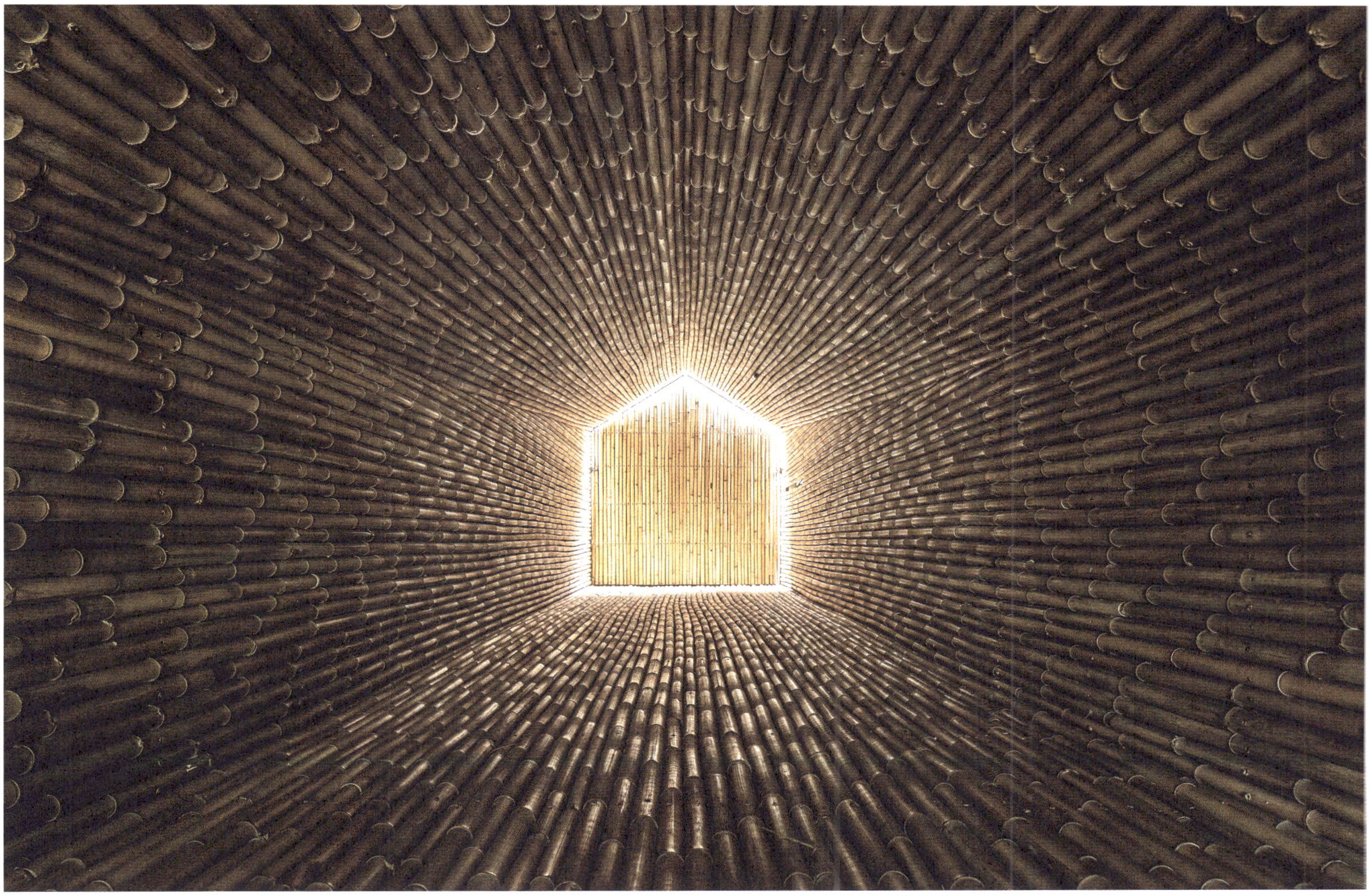

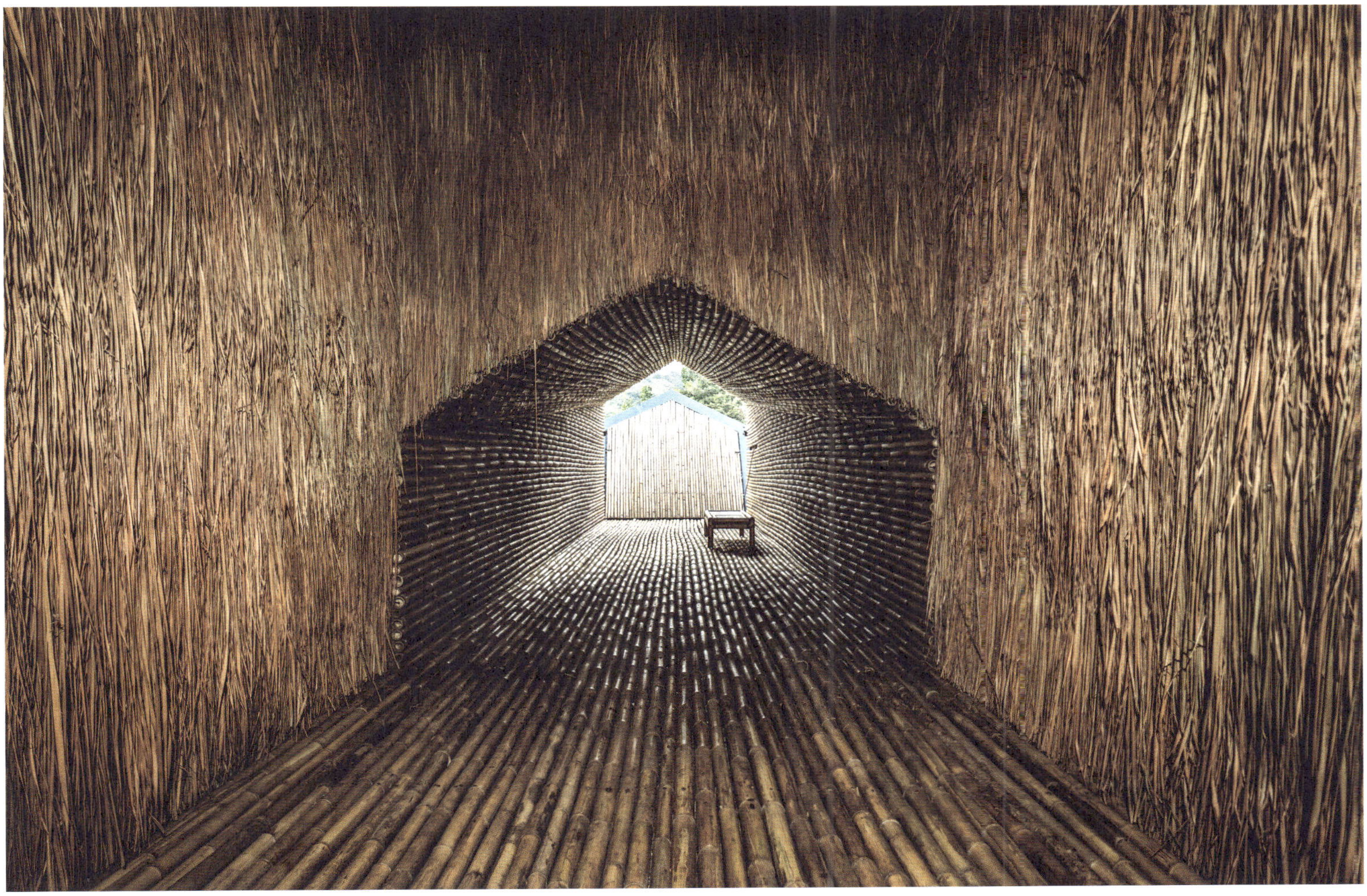

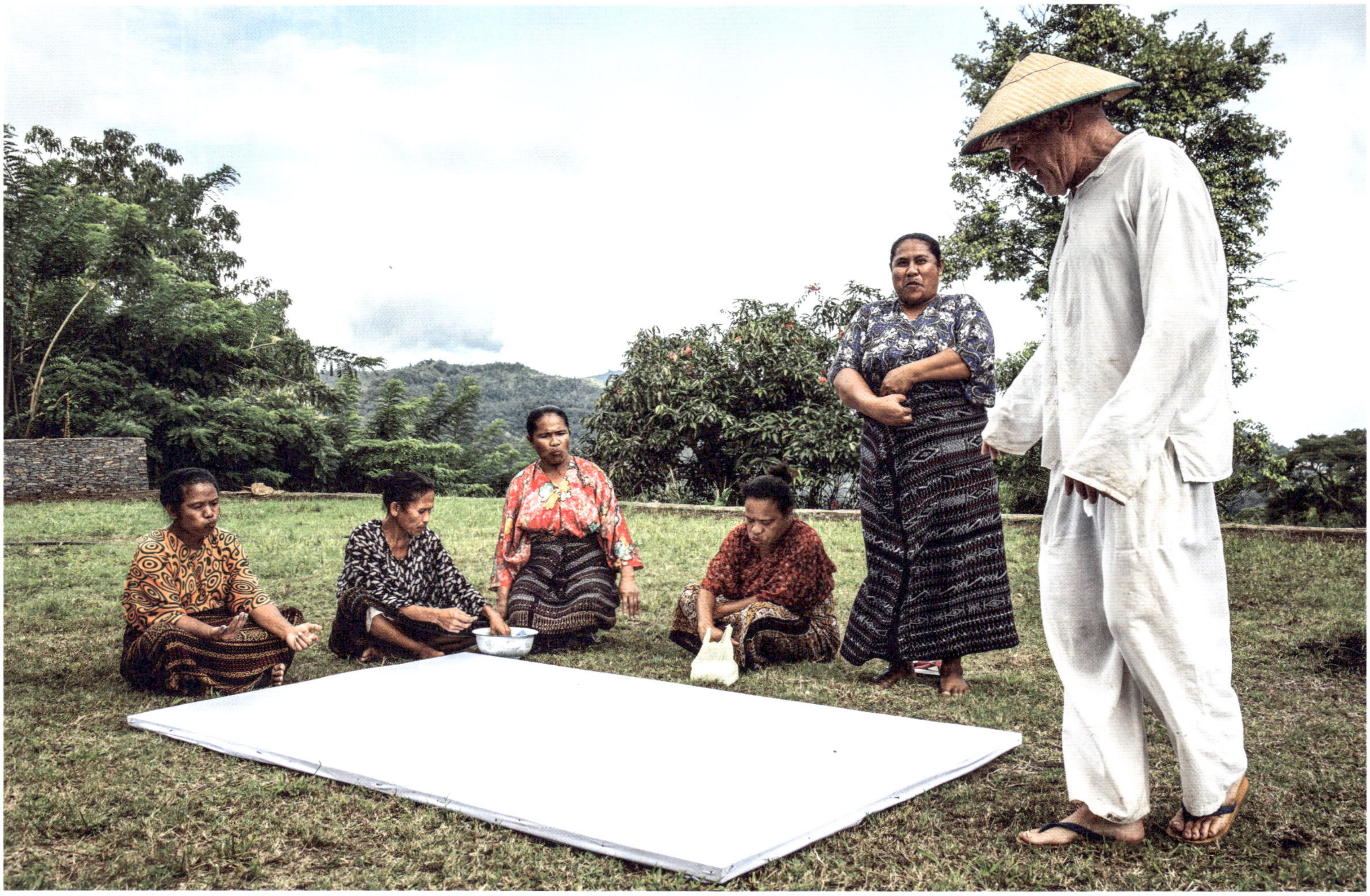

Not Vital making a community-based artwork with the women of Moni. The piece, made by spitting betel nut juice onto canvas, is a study for a larger project: one day, the women will participate in painting the façade of *House to Watch the 3 Volcanoes*.

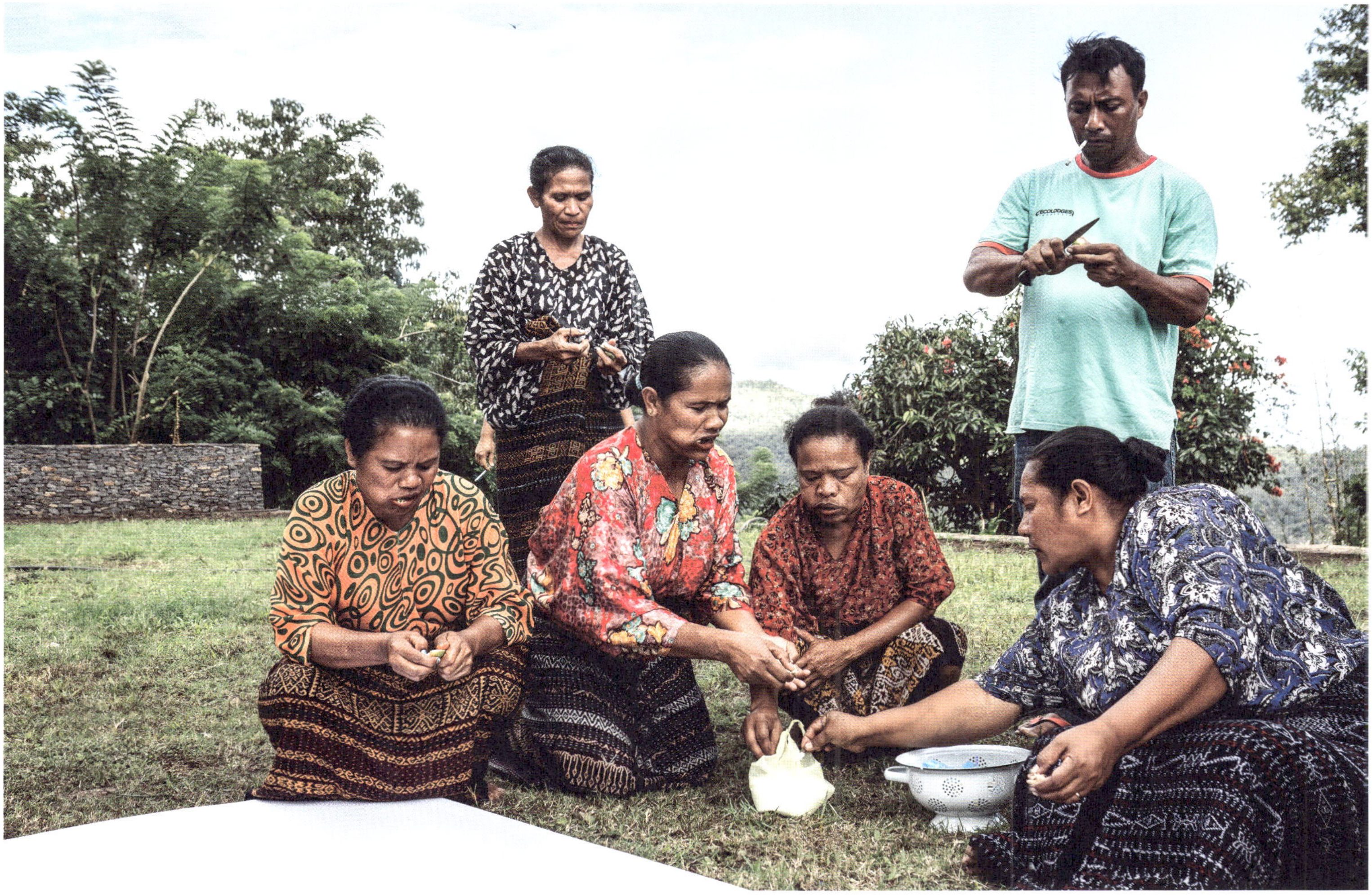

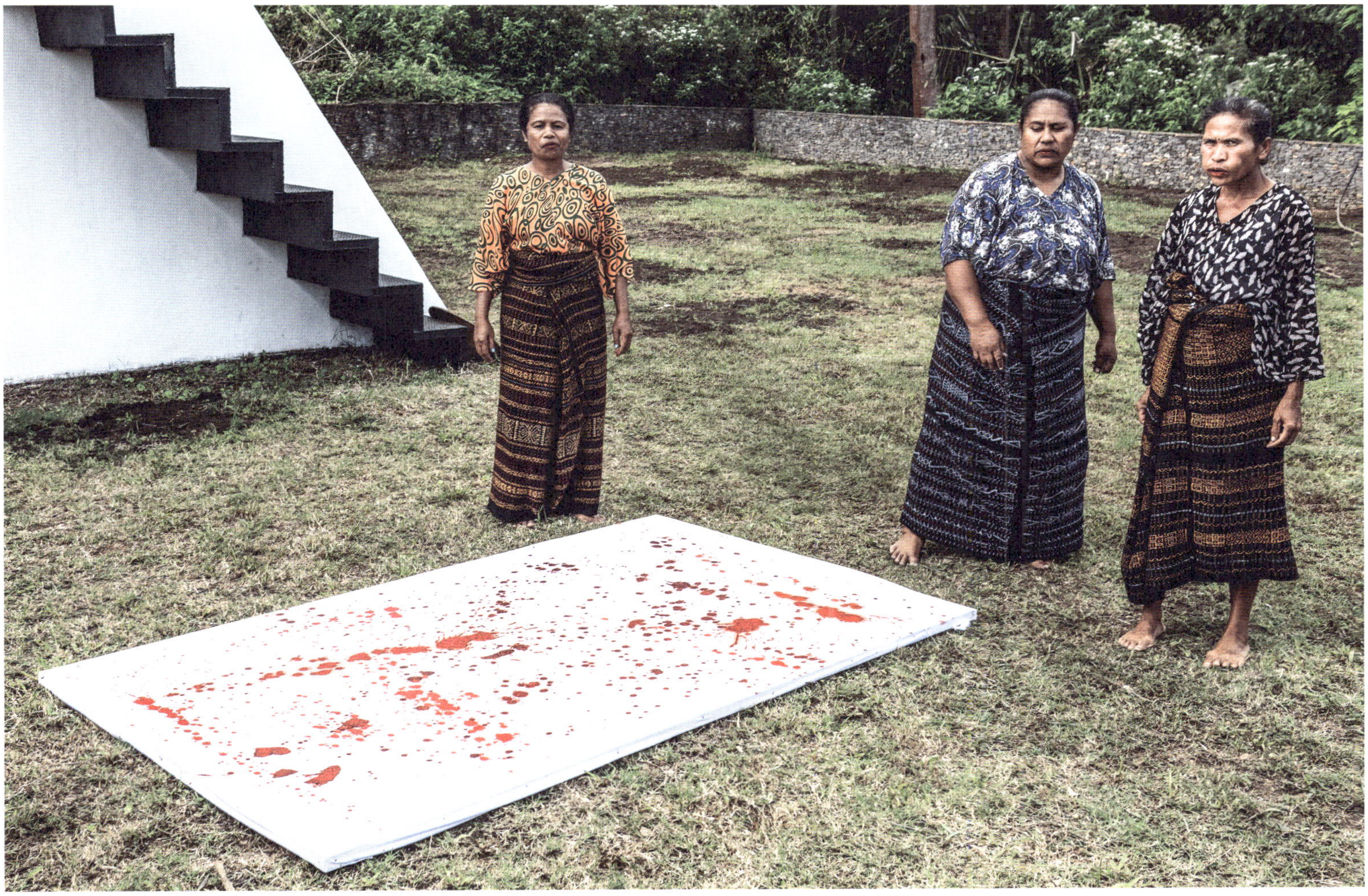

House to Watch the 3 Volcanoes
2013

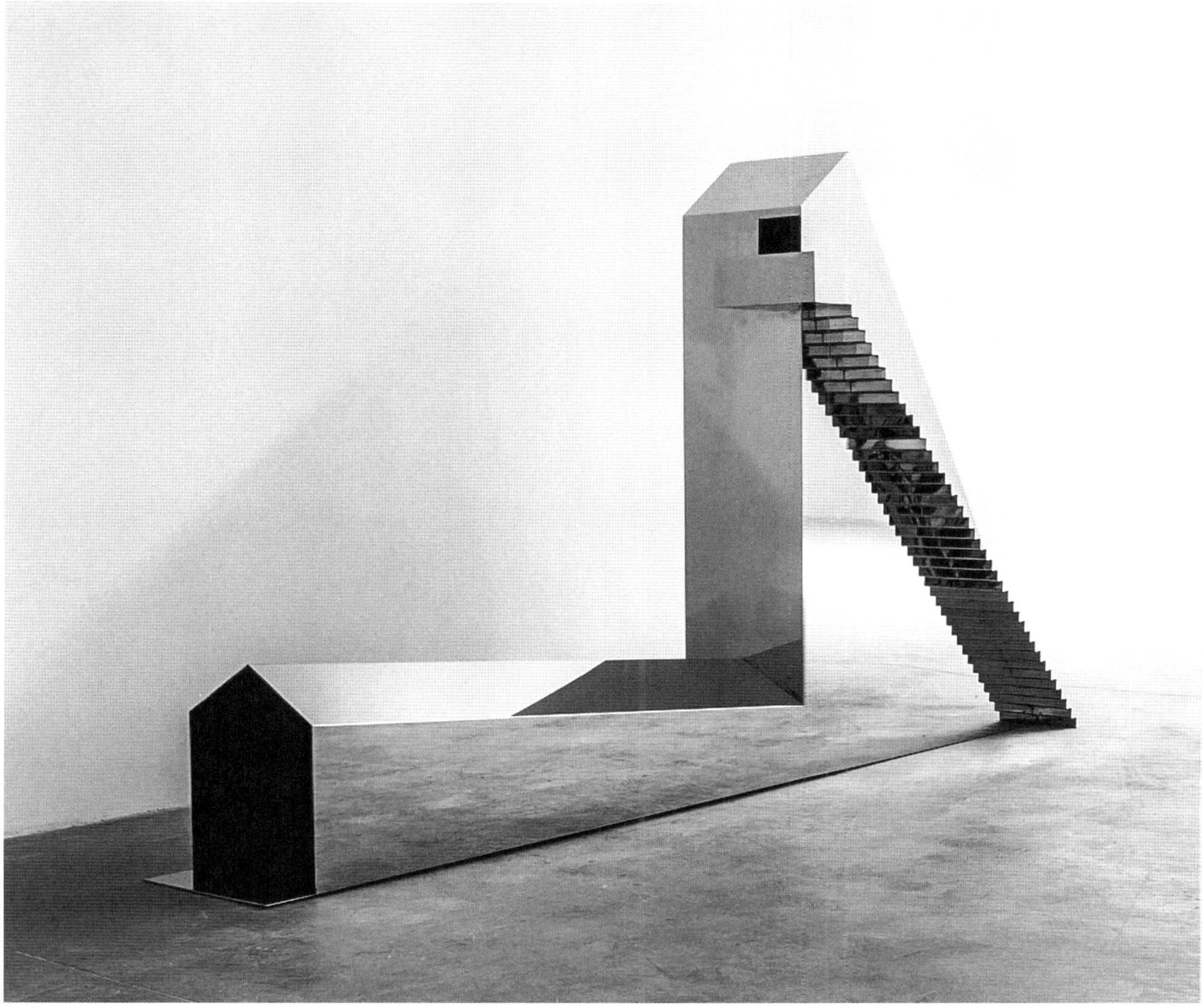

The houses are a project on which I have worked for a long time. & now, they have come to form the center of my activities. Mostly, I work alone on them. I do hire people who help me to execute these projects, such as architects, but basically, I am alone in designing them & in finding the places to build them & in financing them.

At times, I feel like I am giving birth to a child. I actually know nothing about giving birth. But I guess that when you give birth, you have no idea what comes out. & that's how I feel with my houses.

Mostly, everything related to these projects just falls into place. It's like watching a film of a house exploding, but backward. Sometimes the projects are so exciting that I cannot sleep at night. In other instances, they vanish like a fart.

The most exciting period in the course of these projects has been the African desert. That was the beginning of it all. I couldn't really anticipate the outcome. I worked with Hausa & Tuareg workers for months. Taking 1 day at a time, just like drinking tea. It was a novel experience for all of us. When realizing these projects, the workers were pushed further than ever before. So was I.

1 of the most fascinating things about it was how fast everything evolved. To commence a project sometimes only took a few minutes, like in the case of *Makaranta*. It was simply a necessity to build the school. The *House to Watch the Sunset* also grew out of necessity, but it was a necessity of another nature. Actually, every project is born out of a different necessity.

Most often, many people are involved not only in the execution of the project, but also in the building's maintenance & usage. On the island of Flores, for example, the house that I am building is, of course, a house for me. Yet, it is simultaneously a house for the people of Flores. On top of the tower, they can look at what they always had & always will have: the 3 volcanoes of Mount Kelimutu.

The kids sometimes look at me with surprise when I watch the sunset from the house in Aladab, Niger. Aboubakar, a child of 7, asked me once why I am watching something I can see every single day. My answer was that I am watching it precisely because of that. Because it happens every day. In his dark eyes, I saw a spark.

To find the right places to build these houses usually takes little time since I am not really searching for them. I find them. Nietzsche once said that if you are tired of searching, you should relearn to find. & that's what happens just about every time I do a project.

I am in Flores. On an island in Indonesia, working on a house from which I can see the sunset over Mount Kelimutu's volcanoes. It is a very complex project. The iron, the cement & basically any material needed for the construction of this house has to be imported from Java. It takes weeks for the material to arrive in Moni, the place where this 13-meter-high, 23-meter-long house is being built. The many workers all wear flip-flops, just like in Africa. Their skills might be minimal, but their smiles are not. The work here started in April & now it is November & we will still need many more months to erect the tower.

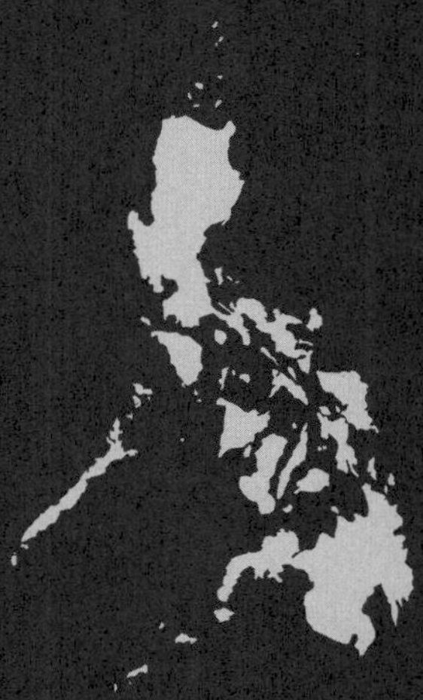

Chapel

Bataan, Philippines
2016

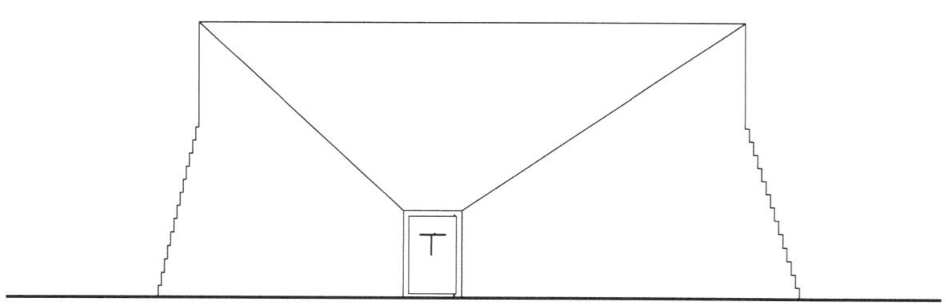

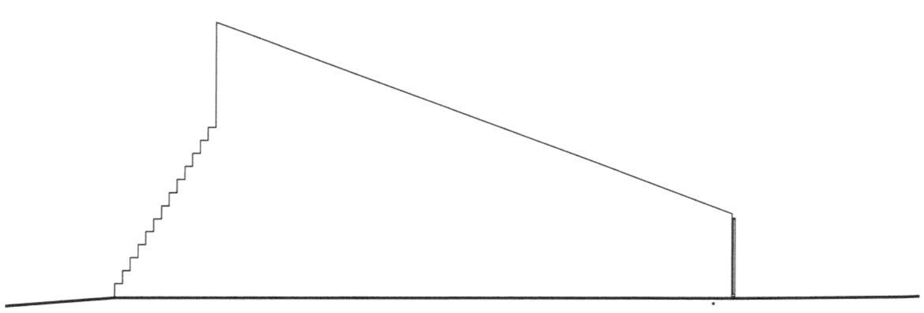

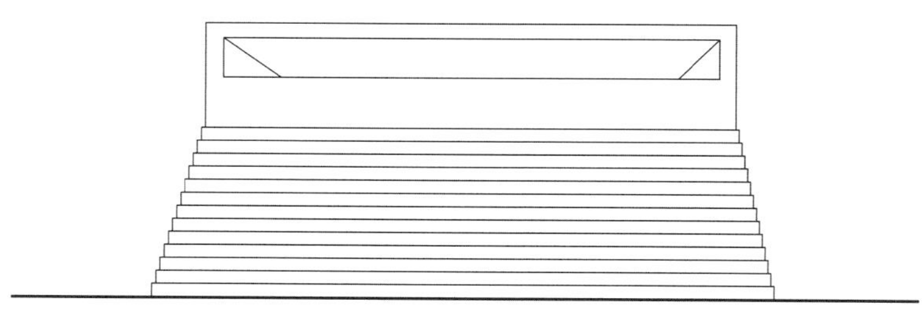

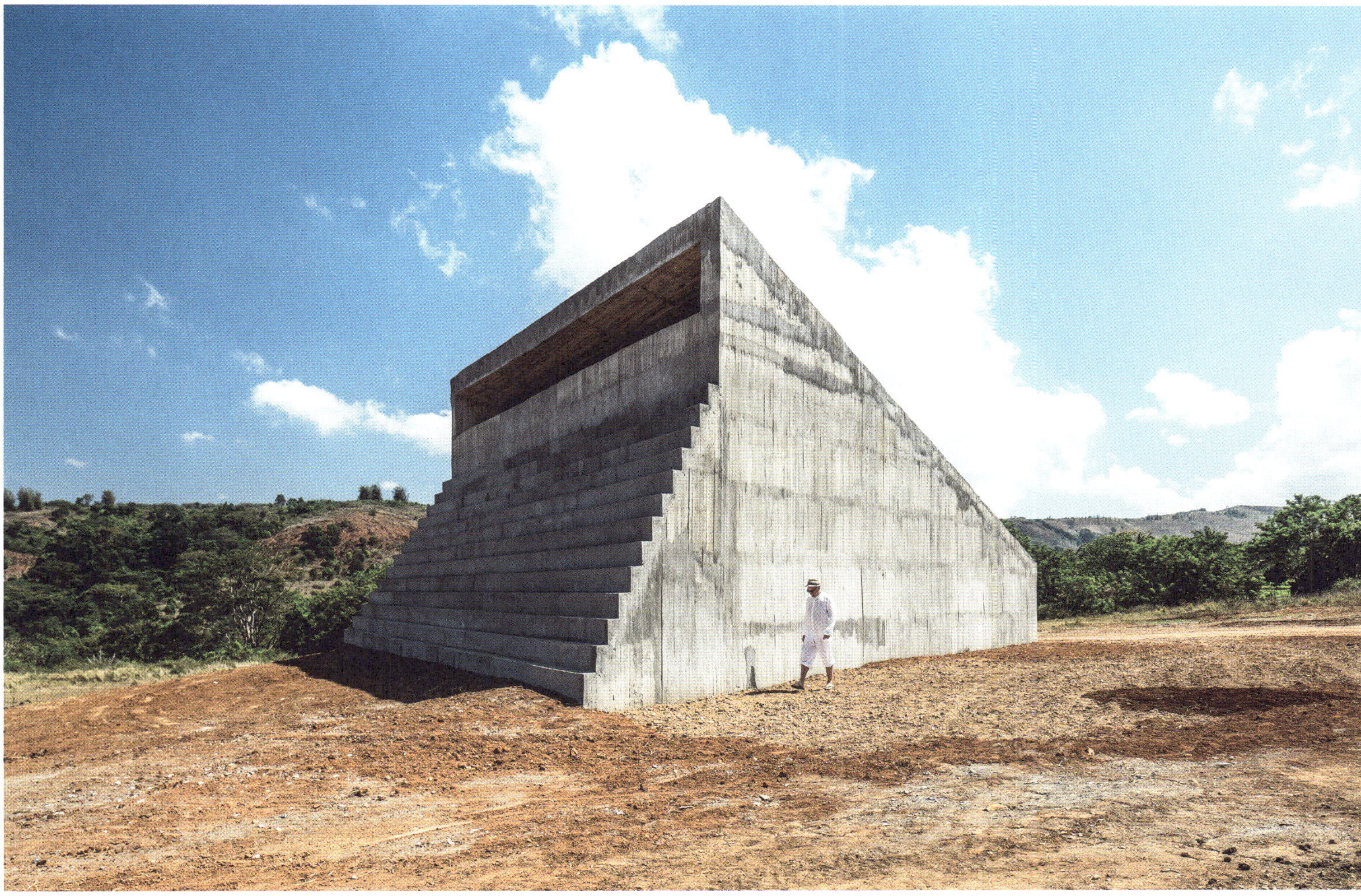

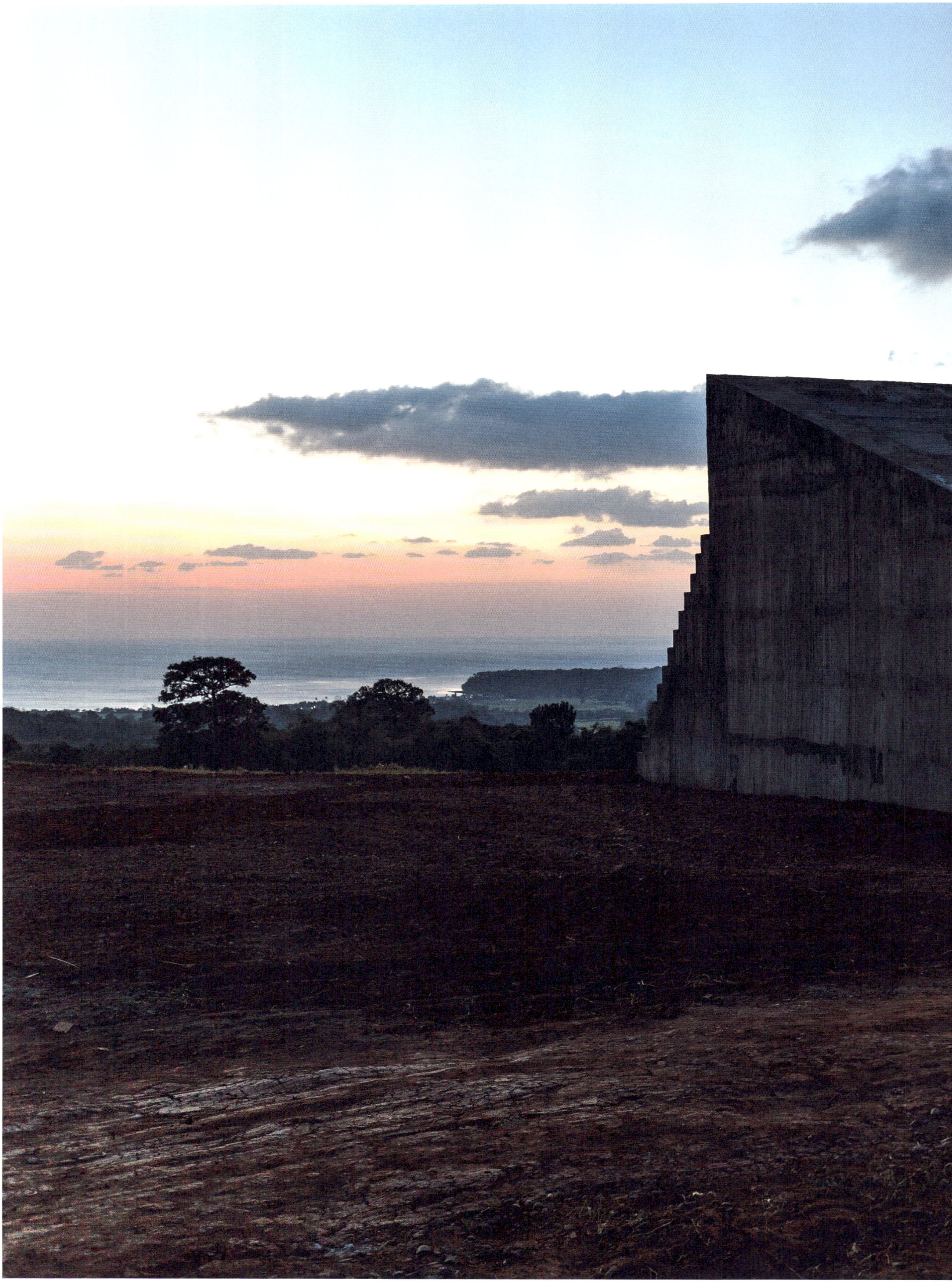

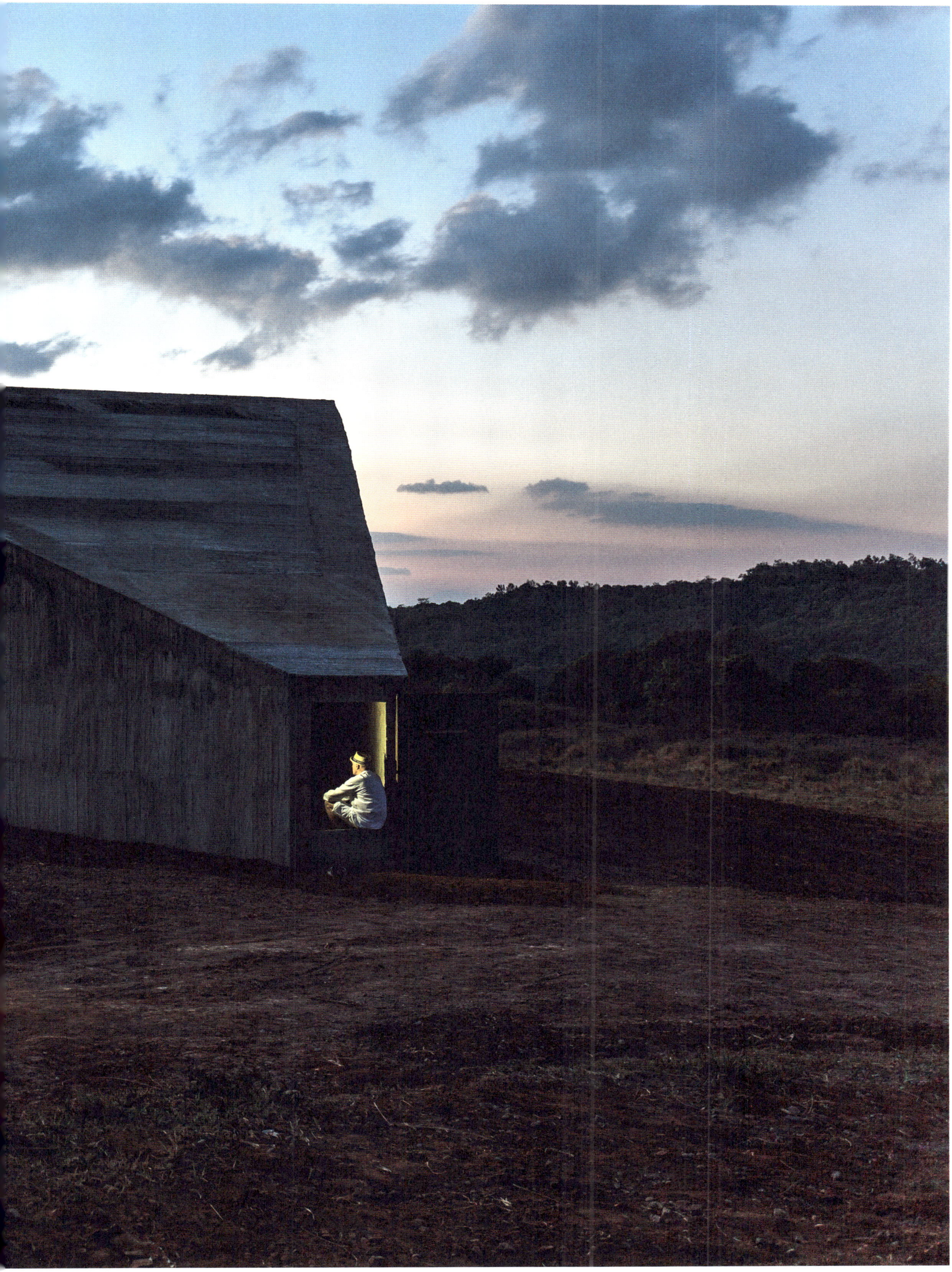

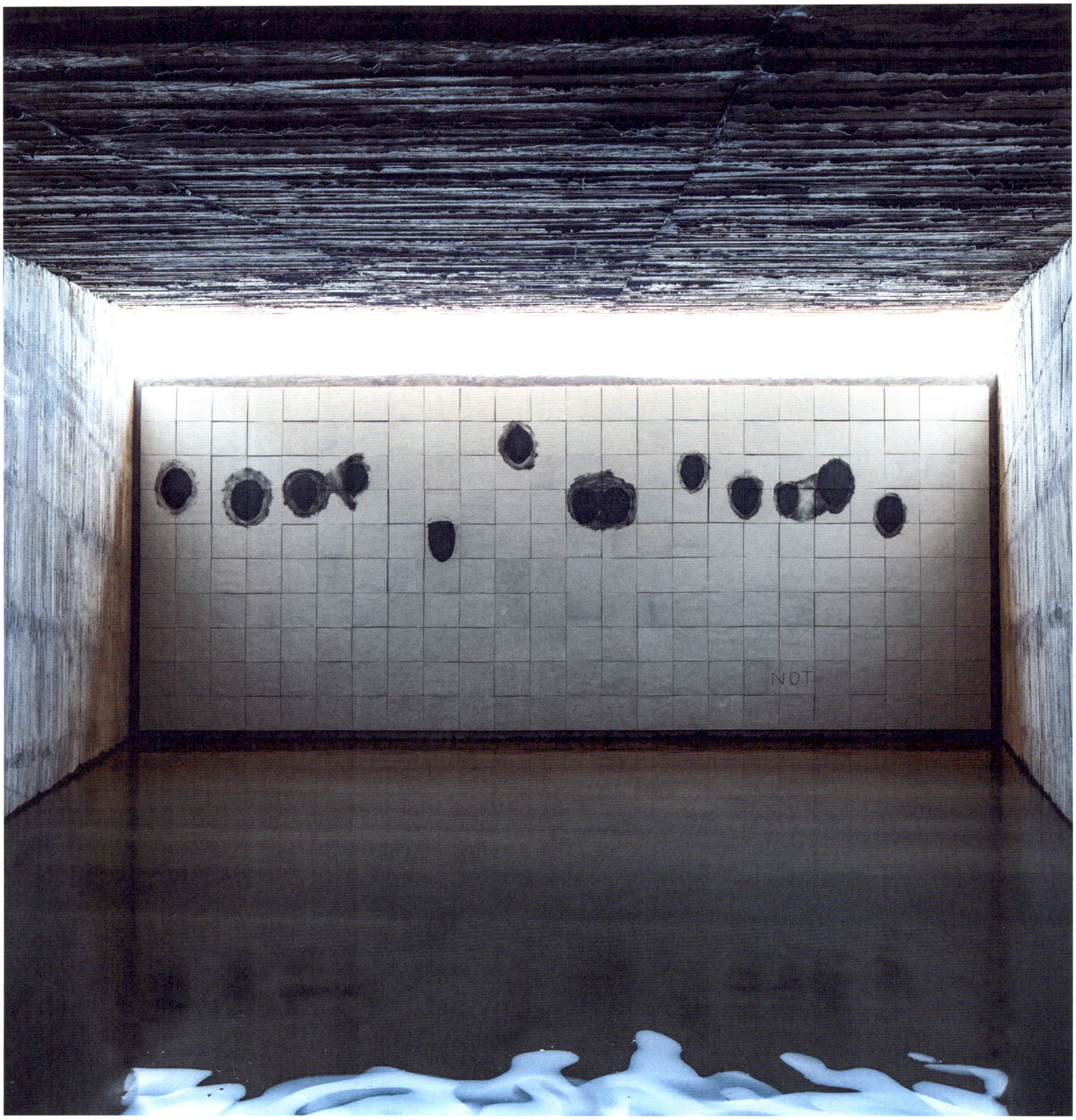

The Last Supper (2014), installed inside *Chapel*

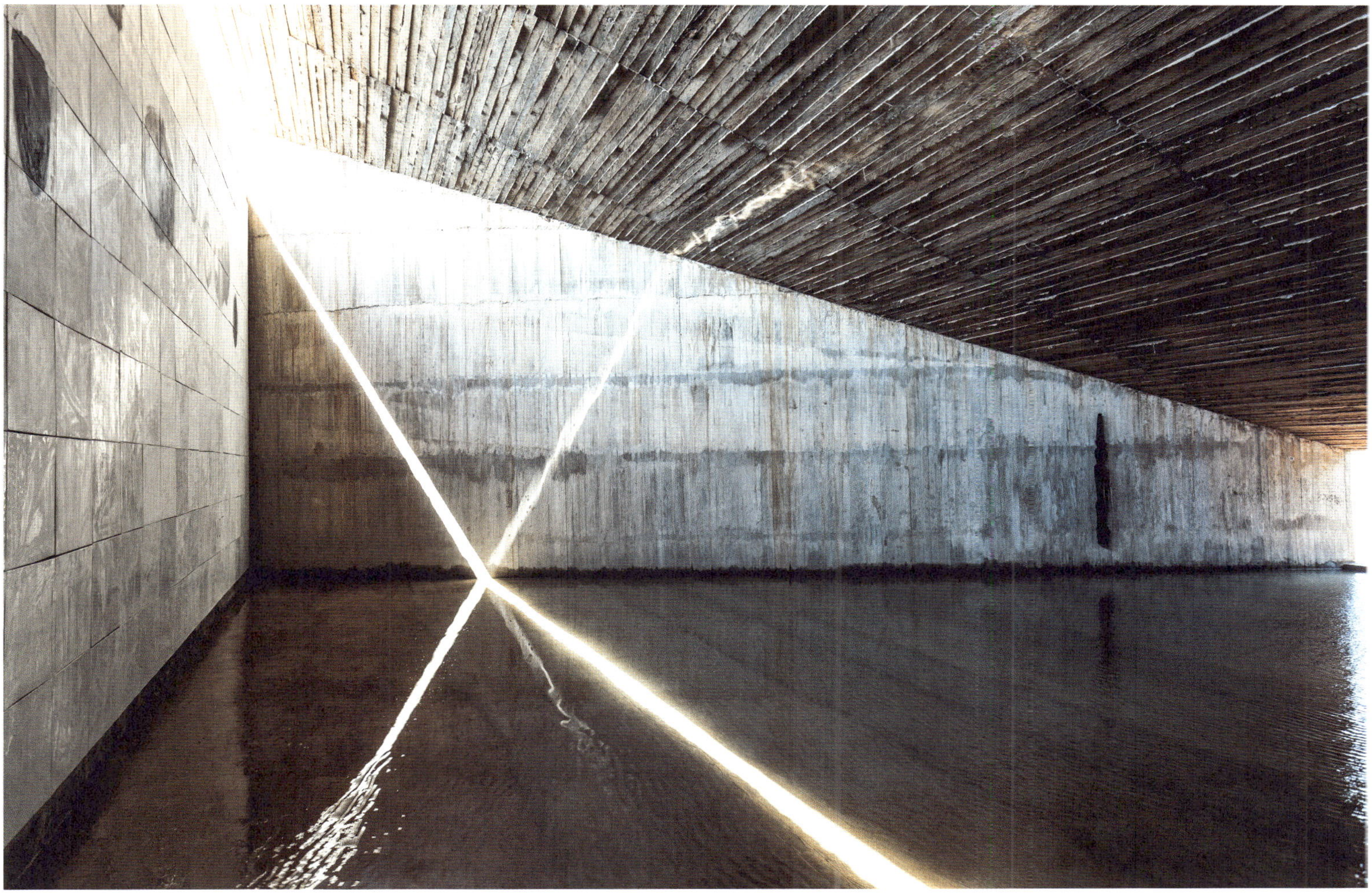

The Chapel
2016

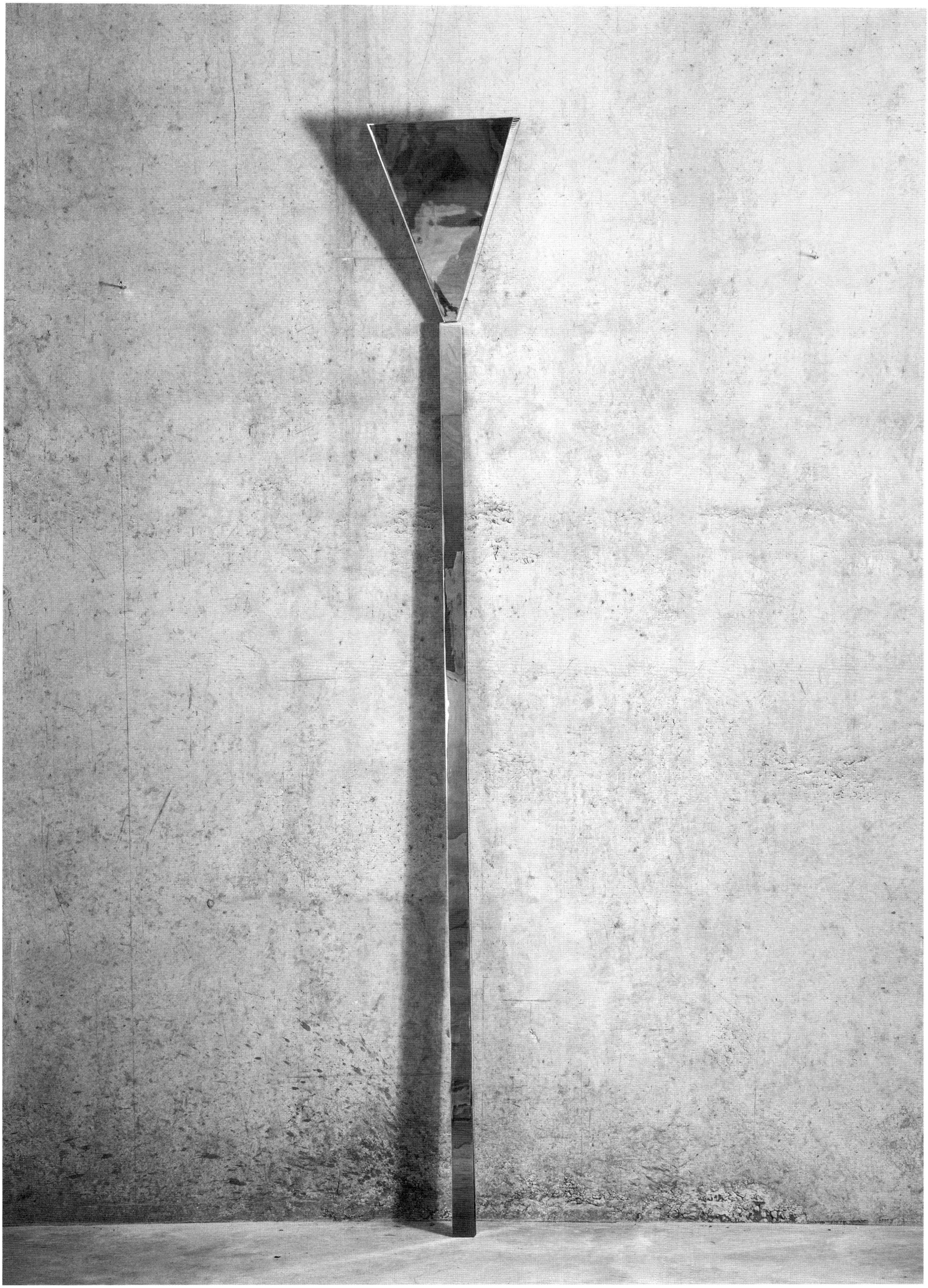

Switzerland

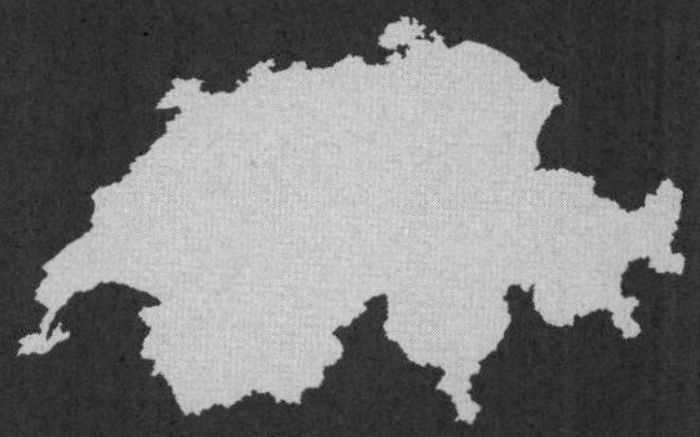

Painting Studio
Sent, Switzerland
2015

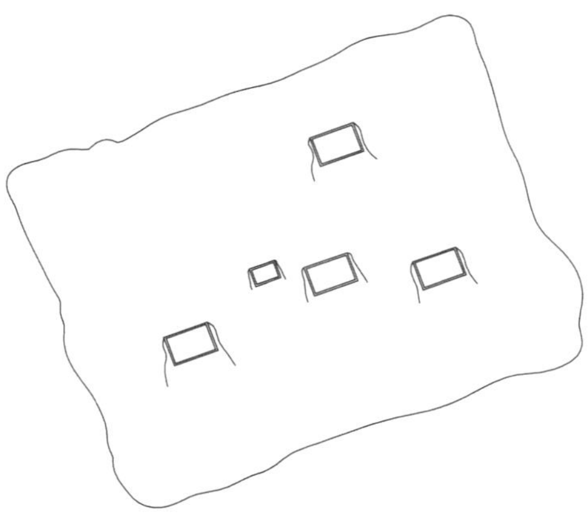

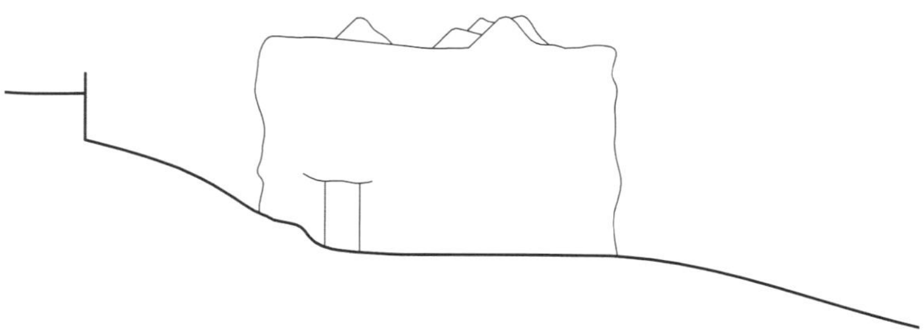

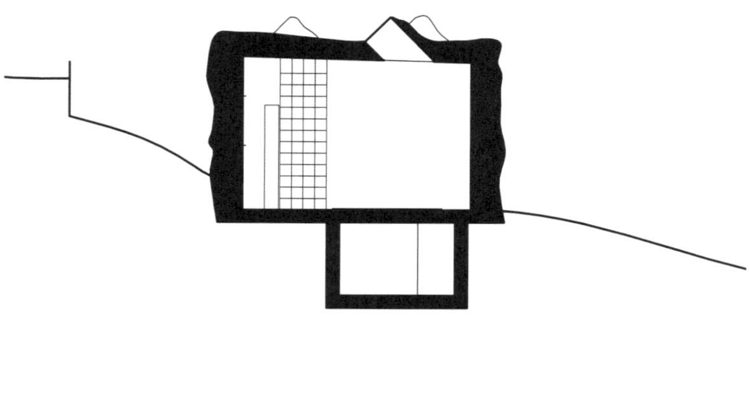

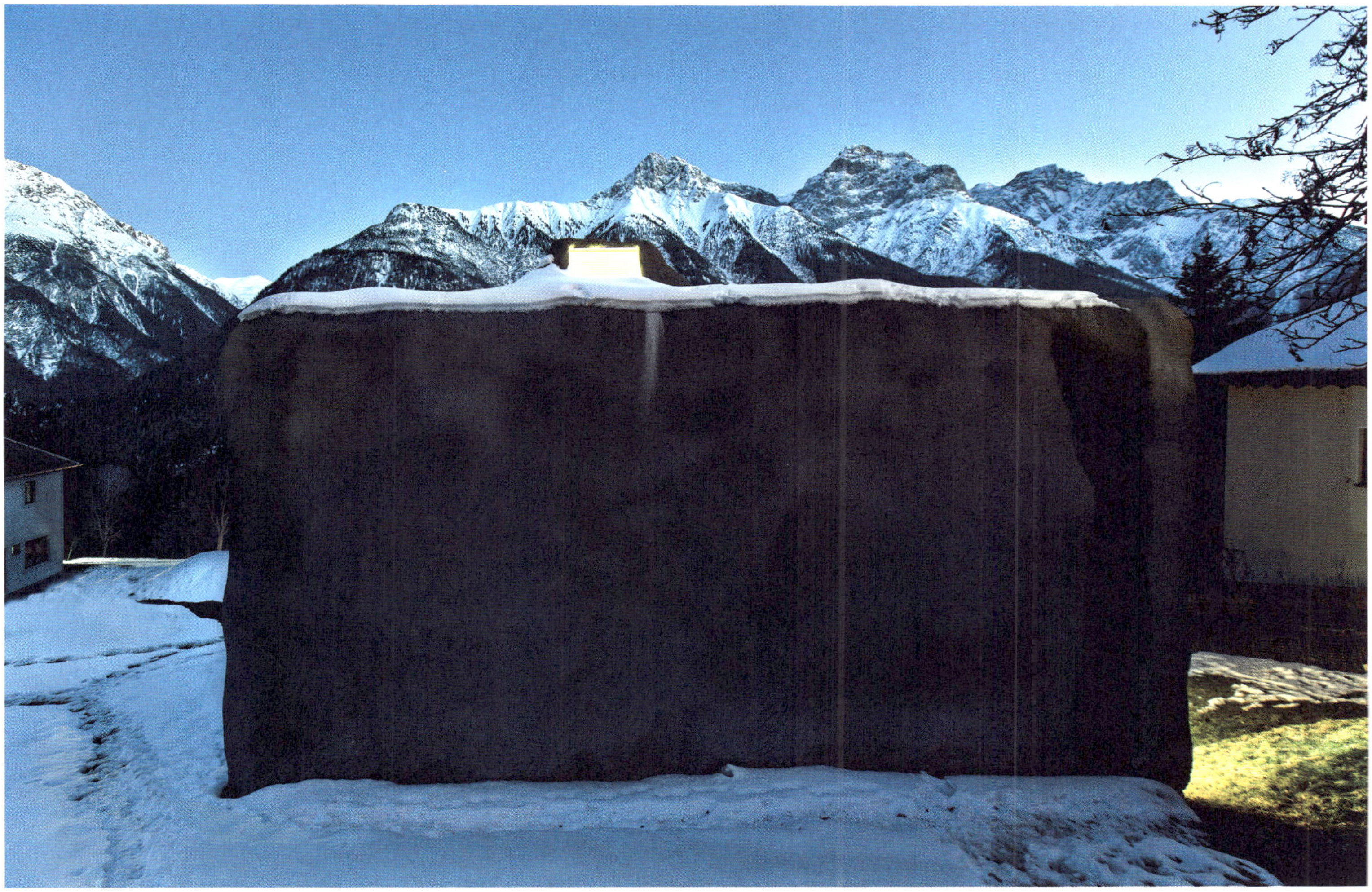

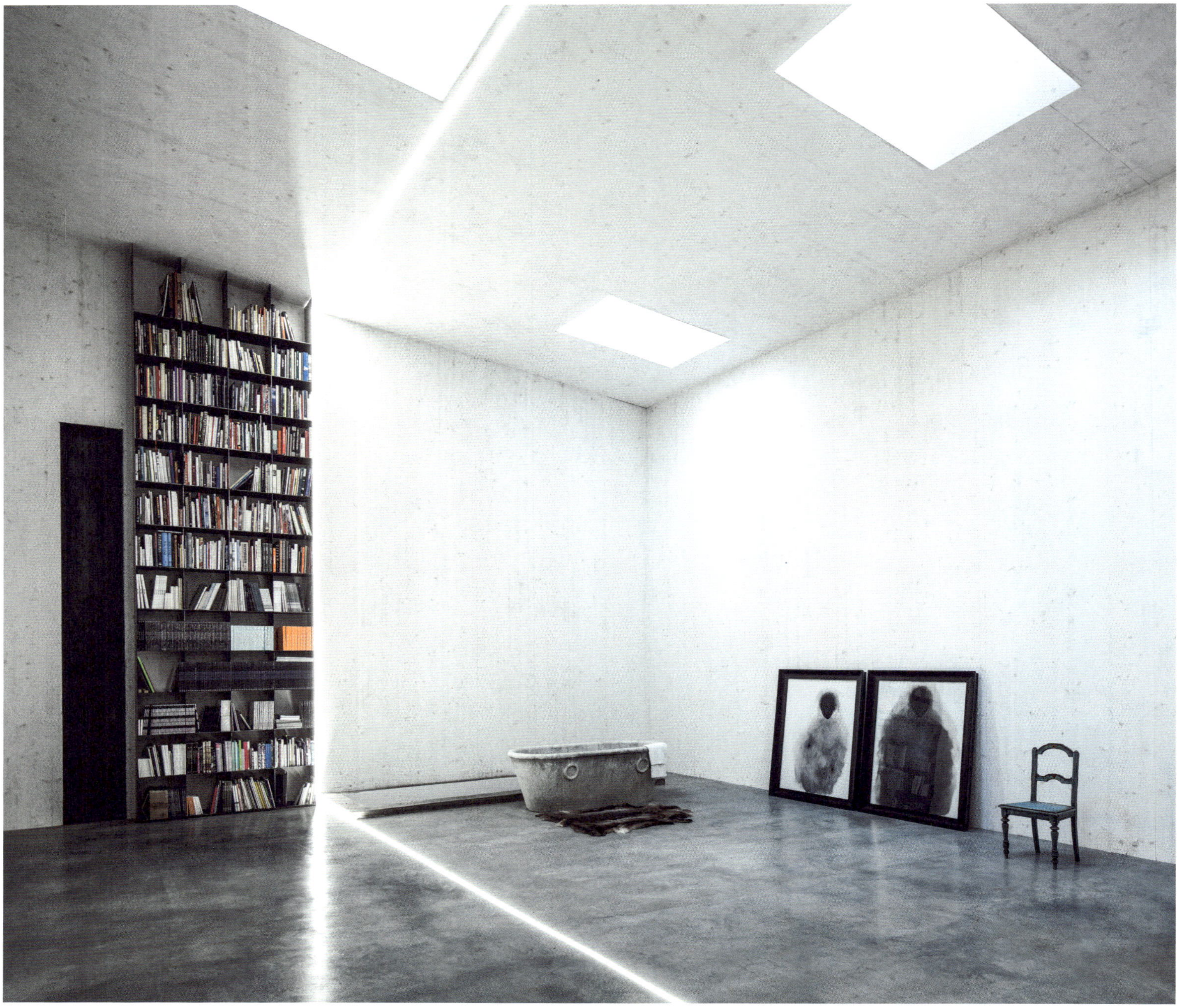

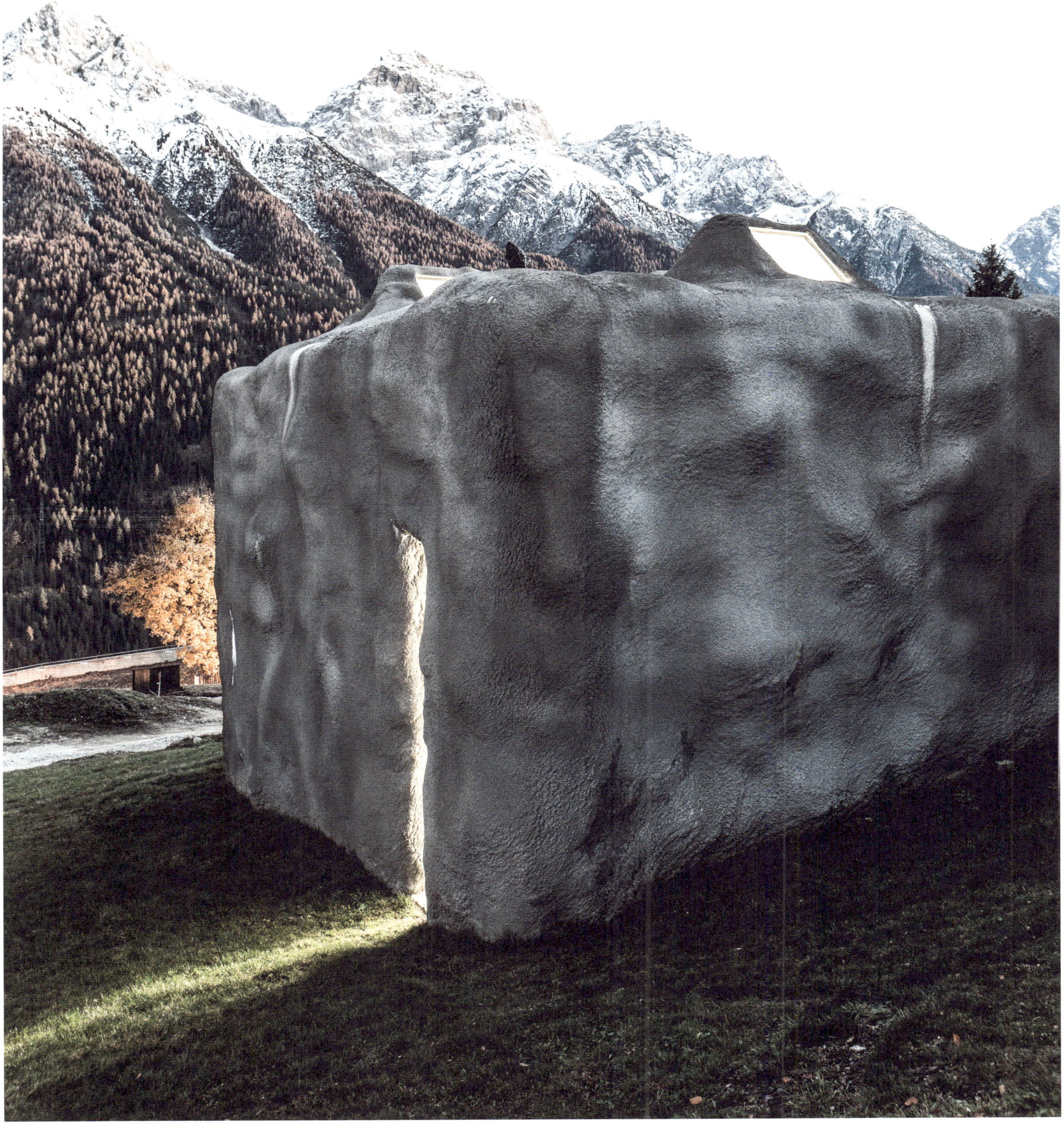

Pole on House
2016

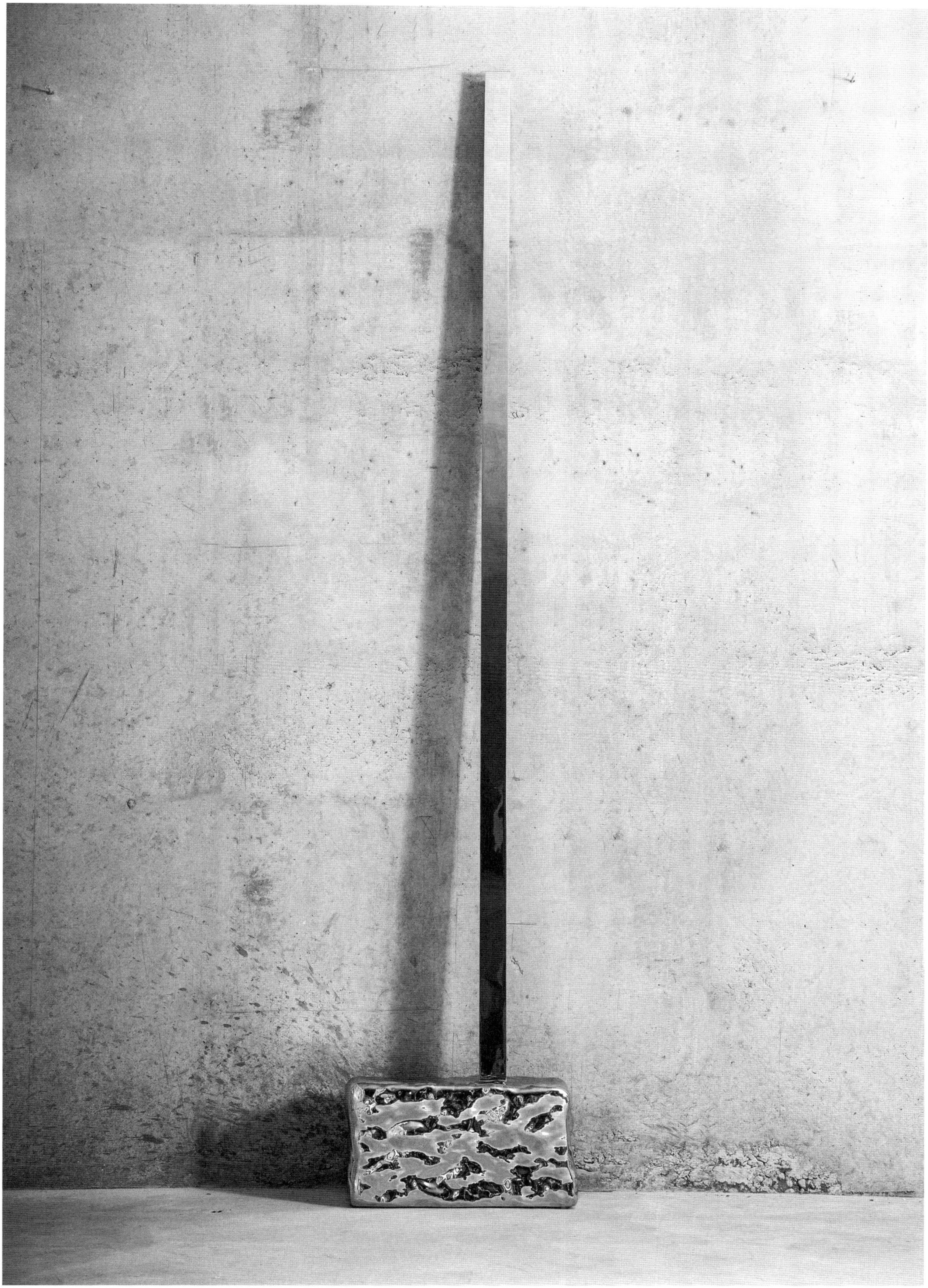

House to Watch the Sunset
Tarasp, Switzerland
2018

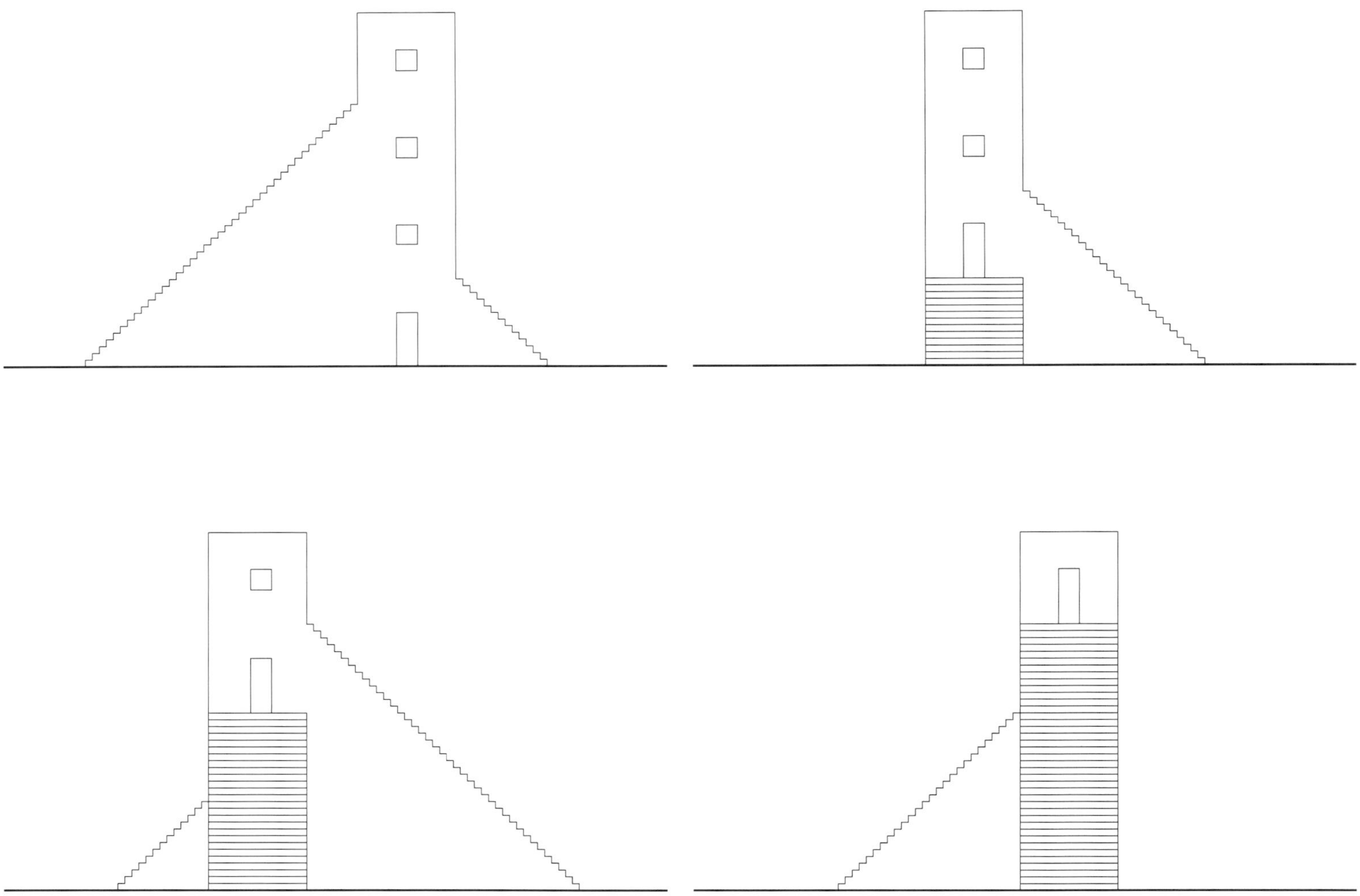

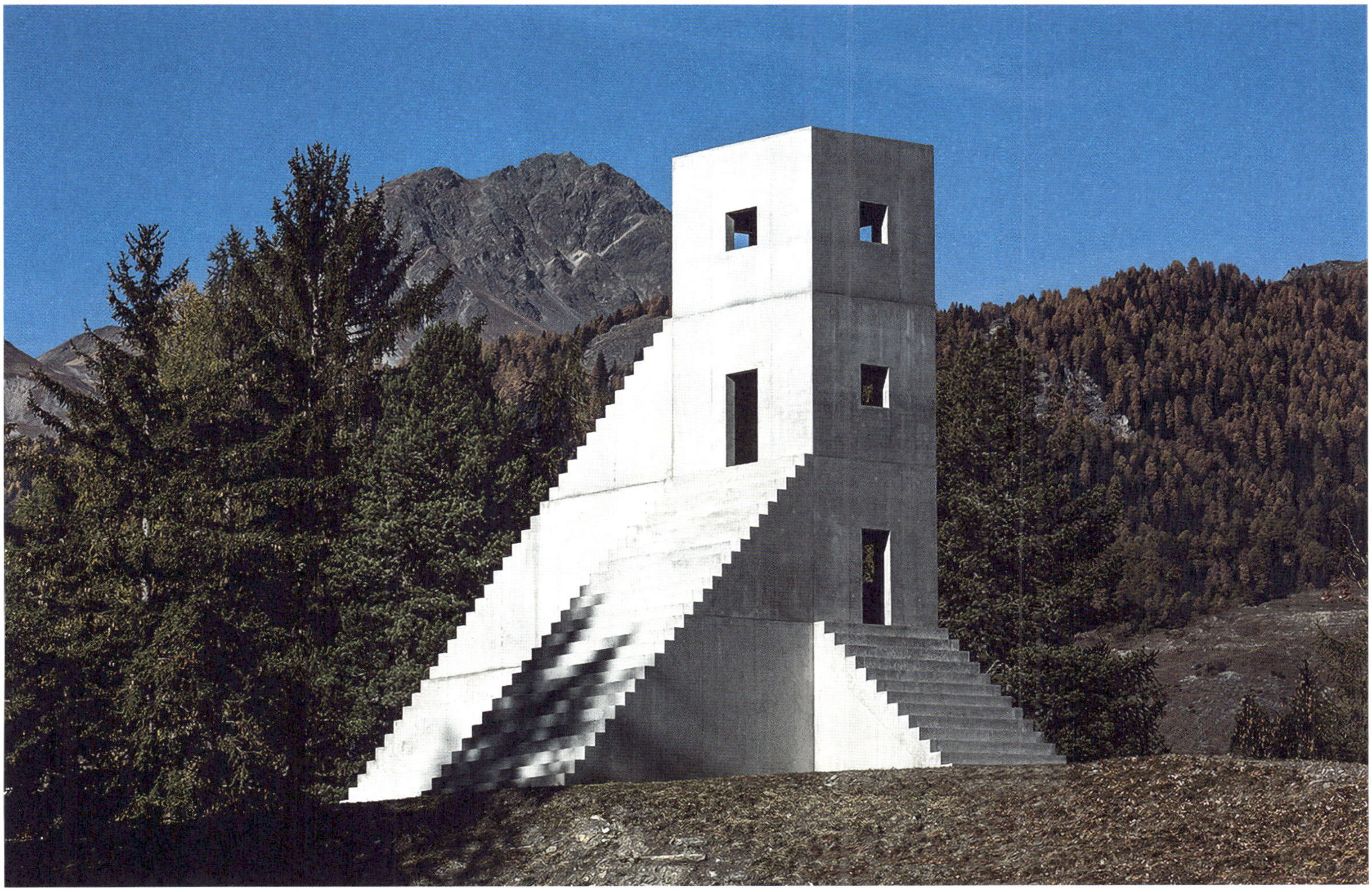

House to Watch the Sunset
Not Vital, 2015

tower 13 × 3.40 × 3.40 m

3 outside stairs

1 with 13

1 with 26

1 with 39 steps

each 1 is 25 × 25 cm +

45 degrees

the 1st floor has 1 door

the 2nd 1 door + 1 window

the 3rd 1 door + 2 windows

the 4th 1 door + 3 windows

4 rooms 3 × 3 × 3 m

+ 1 bed + 1 table + 1 chair

no water or electricity

just enough

to make the sun set

Poetry, Unique and Intense
Tilla Theus

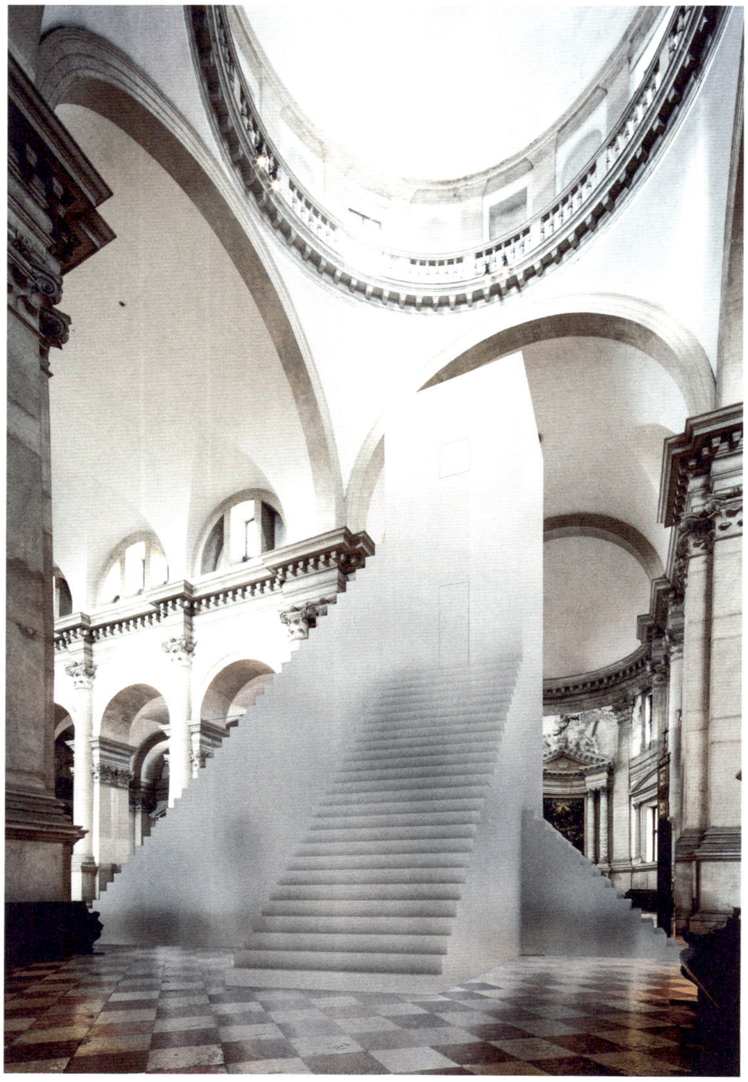

Rendering for the installation of *House to Watch the Sunset* in the Abbey of San Giorgio Maggiore, Venice, Italy

Not Vital coined the word SCARCH, a portmanteau word, to describe his works between sculpture and architecture. They are conceived and executed transcendentally, with no infrastructure. In other words, they are neither practical nor utilitarian but intensely poetic. Vital, who leaves nothing to chance, developed a clear-cut concept for SCARCH. Everything is meticulously worked out and formulated from beginning to end, as illustrated by the following excerpt of the "list" that he wrote in a 2015 poem:

> 4 rooms 3 × 3 × 3 m
> + 1 bed + 1 table + 1 chair
> no water or electricity
> just enough
> to make the sun set

SCULPTURE AND ARCHITECTURE

The project *House to Watch the Sunset* is a quintessential SCARCH, which the artist intends to construct on every continent in the world, much like U.S. military bases, but for the peaceful purpose of watching the sunset.

These four-story SCARCHes all have the same dimensions. Three separate staircases at an angle of 45 degrees with 13, 26, and 39 steps, each measuring 25 centimeters in height and breadth, lead on three sides to one of the four stacked rooms, which are in turn each three square meters in size. If you want to enter all of the rooms you have to climb up and down three times. Every room is furnished with a bed, a table, and a chair—nothing else; no water, no electricity, but it is adequately equipped to watch the sun set.

Using the stairs requires great concentration. Climbing them is a challenging act. The descent calls for an even greater sense of balance. The windows on every floor reveal only a section of the surroundings. That focuses the gaze: "to make the sun set," as Vital writes in his poem, in order to permit your sun to go down.

EFFORT, A PREREQUISITE FOR THE EXPERIENCE

This SCARCH is not a work of art for viewing. It has to be climbed and in this way—and only in this way—it sharpens our perception. "To watch the sunset" bestows an experience, a memory of the great and consciously laborious call to concentrate. Climbing the stairs prepares the climber to look at the sunset. Only through this action does ordinary nightfall become a new experience, exerting a profound impression that is stored in memory.

After Vital has created the idea and finds the place—or rather, the place finds him—he verifies his idea on-site with reference to available materials. He observes the people living there, their habits and their techniques. In short, he develops the specific implementation of his idea in harmony with local resources, possibilities, inhabitants, and techniques. The abstract poetic idea is thus interwoven with local realities and completed as a new reality.

As mentioned, dimensions of the *Houses to Watch the Sunset* are identical, but they are executed in different materials depending on where they are built. They have been planned for all of the continents in isolated locations shrouded in myth; they are hard to reach. Visitors are compelled to communicate and enter into an exchange with local people in order to find a SCARCH.

A *House to Watch the Sunset* was built of mud, straw, and dung in 2005 in an oasis in Aladab, Niger; another was built in 2016 out of angelim vermelho, a native tropical hardwood, in the Amazonian jungle near Paraná do Mamori, Brazil; and a third in 2018 in Tarasp, Switzerland, out of concrete using sand from the River Inn.

This year Vital has been working on a *House to Watch the Sunset* made of iron in the Mongolian steppes and another—out of aluminum—for the island of Fangasito in Tonga. The latter will first be installed in the Abbey of San Giorgio Maggiore during the 2020 Architecture Biennale in Venice.

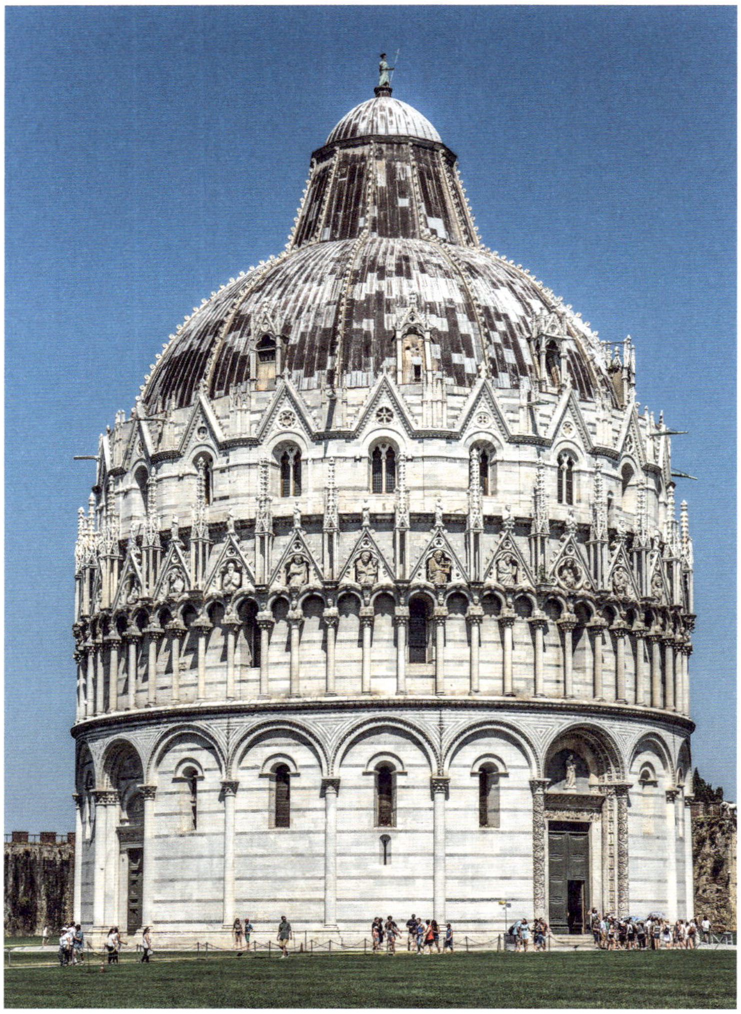

Pisa Baptistery of St. John in Pisa, Italy

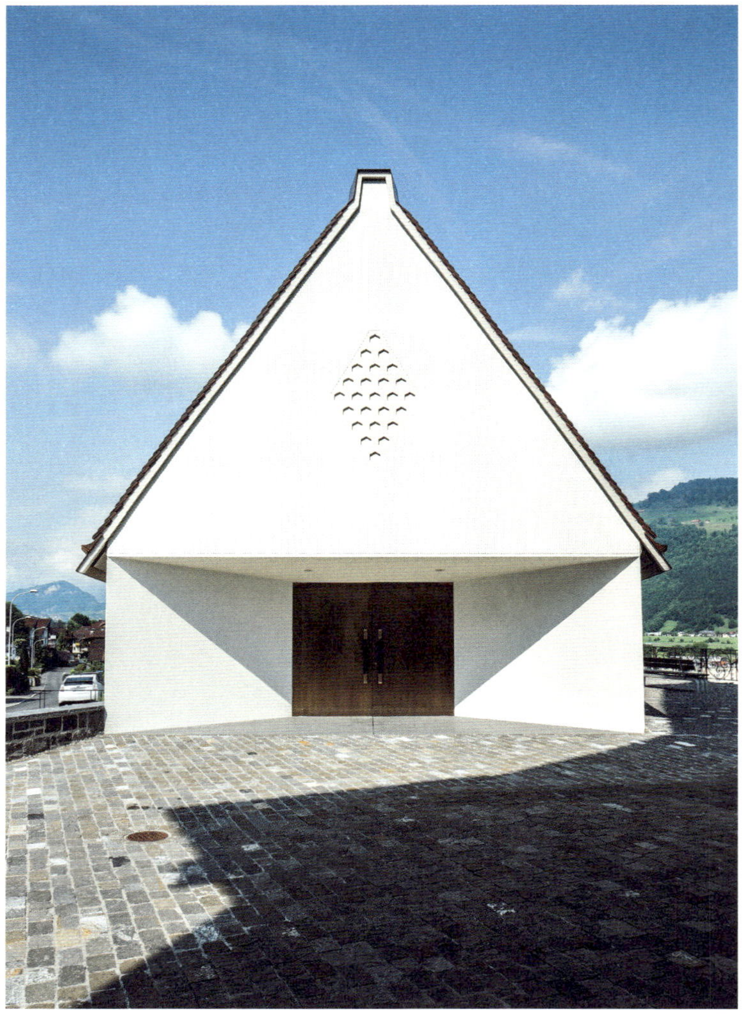

Chapel of the Dead in Buochs, Switzerland

ARCHITECTURAL COMPARISONS

Seeking architectural comparisons to the SCARCH structures that are likewise exclusively monofunctional, I think of religious buildings erected for important stages in life—namely, for baptism and death. Artists recognized the significant singularity of these events and created spaces for them that aroused strong emotions.

Magnificent, intensely moving baptisteries are found in the Lateran in Rome (4th century), in Riva San Vitale (5th century), in Florence (11th century), in Pisa (12th century [p. 246]), and in Parma (13th century).

Just as baptism, signaling active entry into a religious community, was assigned a room of its own, death (and entry into eternal life) was honored with an exclusive architectural space as well, as illustrated by St. Michael in Fulda, Germany (9th century), and the chapels in Schwaz, Austria, and Loreto, Italy (both 16th century). Contemporary masterpieces are the chapel in Buochs, Switzerland [p. 246], and the chapel by Carlo Scarpa, completed in 1978, in the Brion Cemetery in San Vito d'Altivole near Treviso, Italy [p. 247].

In addition to being monofunctional, the *Houses to Watch the Sunset* feature a distinctive treatment of light. Comparable projects, in this respect, are James Turrell's *Skyspaces*, with sky windows precisely calculated to experience nightfall and the dawn of day [p. 248]; and Walter De Maria's *The Lightning Field*, made of steel rods with slanted tips laid out in the landscape to catch and reflect the light of dawn [p. 248].

INSTEAD OF A HOUSE, AN ISLAND IS TRANSFORMED

One *House to Watch the Sunset* steps out of line: *NotOna* in Patagonia [pp. 160–73]. Vital had intended to build one on this island but then changed his mind after spending time with the terrain. Instead, he has transformed the entire island into a house. A tunnel, approximately 180 feet long, leads to a window from which "to watch the sunset." The tunnel was carved out of a mountain of white marble and all of the excavated material was packed into one large cube at the entrance to the island, so as to leave nothing behind, neither natural nor designed.

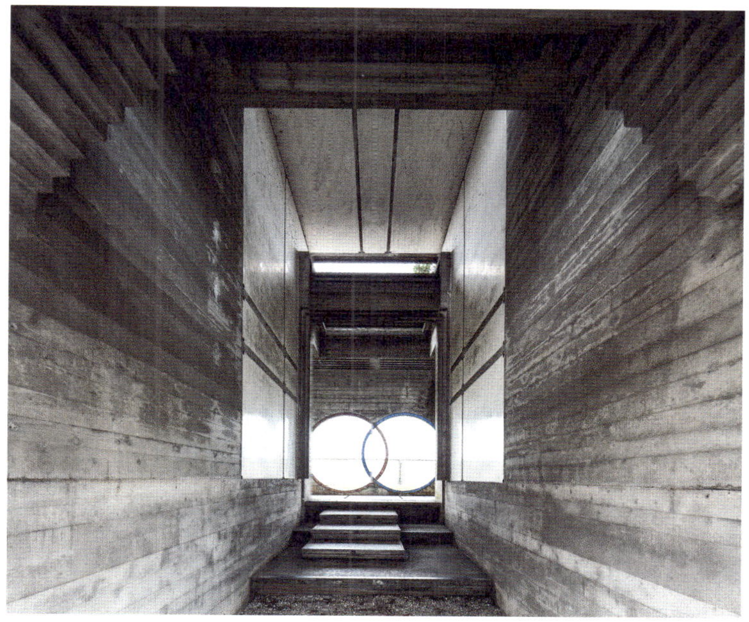

Chapel in Brion Cemetery in San Vito d'Altivole, Italy, by Carlo Scarpa

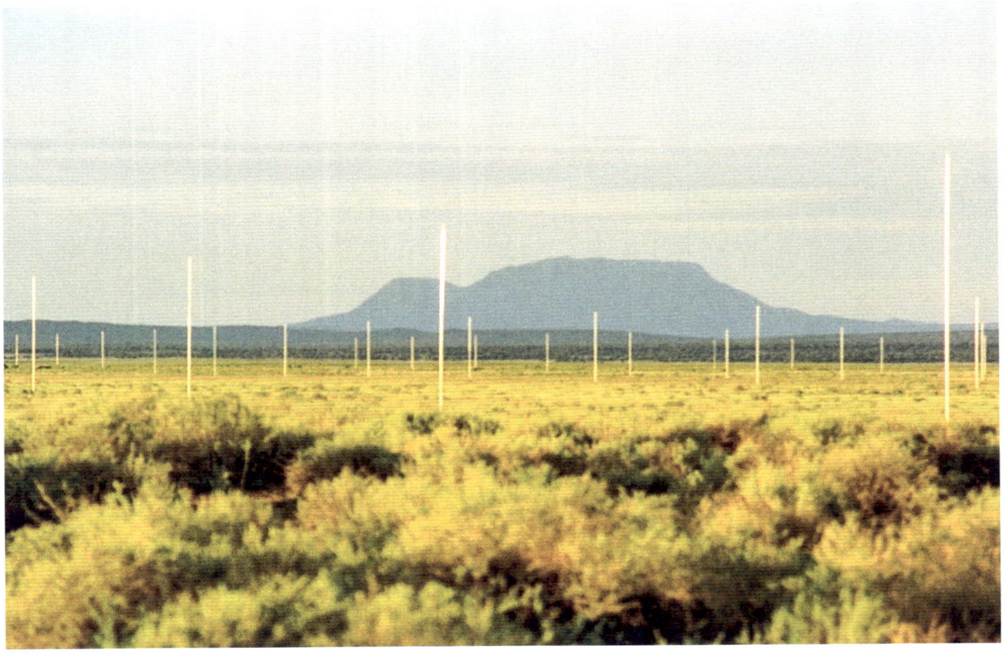

Walter De Maria, *The Lightning Field*, 1977

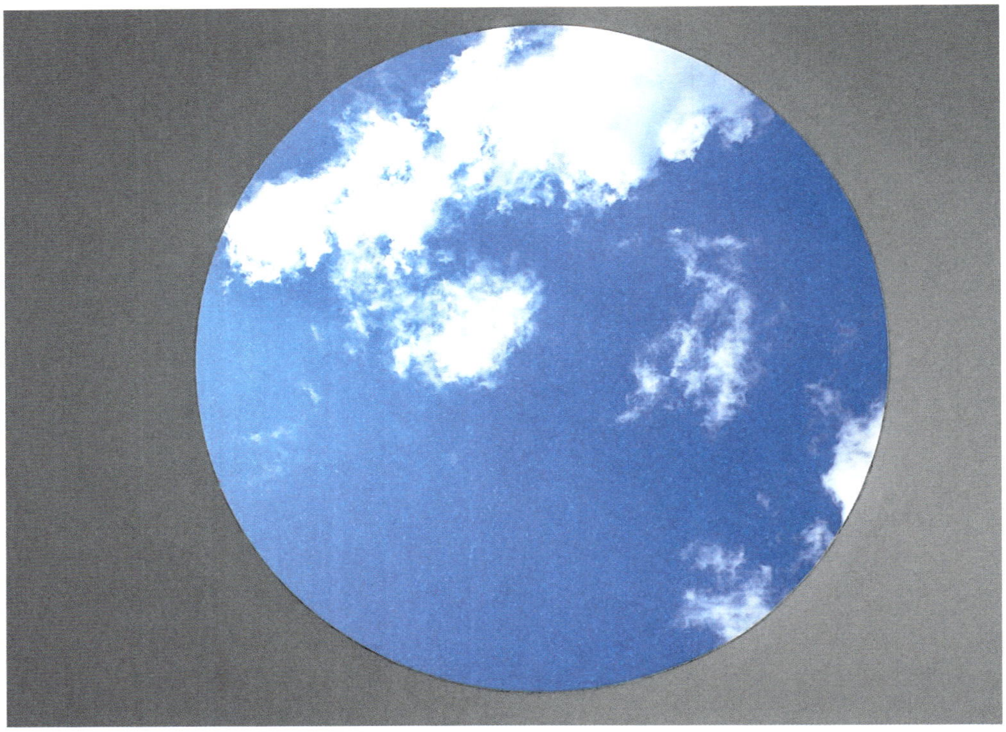

James Turrell, *Skyspace Piz Uter*, 2005, Hotel Castell Zuoz

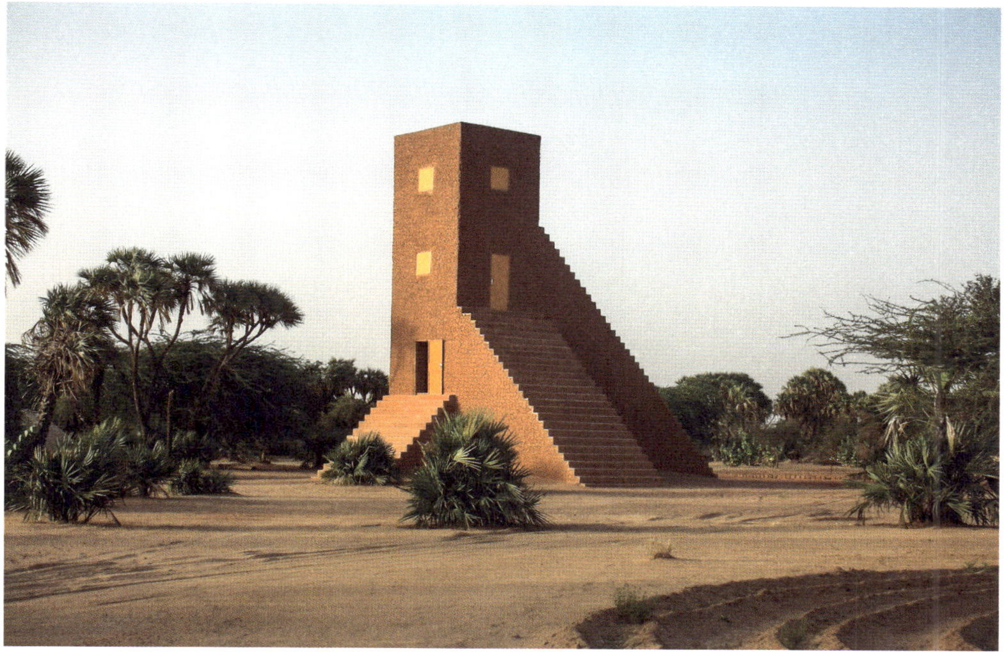

House to Watch the Sunset, 2005, Aladab, Niger

The best way to visit *NotOna* is to fly to Puerto Montt. Then, at the Lago General Carrera, a man named Chely must be found. He ferries the visitors to and from *NotOna* in a small boat. These instructions underscore the necessity of speaking with the locals to receive vital information—namely, to take food, water, wood, and a lighter along. These are the requisites for an unforgettable experience entirely in the spirit of Vital, who often says: "Go there alone. Get to know yourself. Become your own friend."

To me, the experience around De Maria's *The Lightning Field* is similar. The task consists of discovering the only house in the village that is one story higher than the others, entering it through a wooden door, walking into the courtyard, then through a dark hallway, and finally through three consecutive rooms. In the last one, a man wearing a cowboy hat and boots is sitting at a table; he will take you to *The Lightning Field*. This may sound disconcerting but it corresponds to reality. We were deposited in the desert and picked up again 24 hours later. The experience is overwhelming and is indelibly impressed upon memory—exactly like Vital's *Houses to Watch the Sunset*.

Or Turrell's *Roden Crater* in Texas. After a bumpy ride through volcanic terrain near Flagstaff, Arizona, past herds of cattle, you climb into the work of art hollowed out of the volcano: an incredible atmosphere and distilled concentration meet you there in the oval space with its stairs leading to a precise angular opening on the sky. The changes in light as darkness falls open the mind to unprecedented shifts in color and a new perception of the sky.

There is one significant difference between the *Roden Crater* and the *Houses to Watch the Sunset*. Turrell often adds sequences of colored lights to his *Skyspaces*, while Vital relies exclusively on natural light. And the rooms in Vital's "houses" are so small that visitors are encouraged to watch the sunset alone, whereas in Turrell's case, several persons can experience the *Skyspaces* together.

INGENIOUS CREATIVITY AS AN ENTHRALLING GIFT

This sensitivity to the natural world generates art that is exclusively poetic and reliant upon the cosmos. With his ingenious creativity, Vital bequeaths us an enthralling gift—in Niger, Tarasp, Brazil, Patagonia, soon to come in Mongolia, then in Venice, and finally in Tonga—"to watch the sunset," or rather, as the artist insists, "to make the sun set."

Translated by Catherine Schelbert

Window + Door
1965

Acknowledgments

We would like to thank all the people who have been involved in the realization of Not Vital's SCARCH projects, working with utmost dedication in often remote locations. Together with 55 workers from Agadez, the Haïdara brothers, especially Akhmed and Mohamed, contributed to the realization of all of the projects in Niger. Mitsunori Sano and Cristián Orellana Terrsy were Not's assistants in Sent for several years, working on a multitude of projects, some of them located in the sculpture park in Sent, such as *Biotop* (2007) and *Bridge* (2008). In addition, they were also instrumental in two other projects: Sano designed and built the artist's studio in Beijing, and Orellana Terrsy was responsible for the conception and realization of *NotOna* (2008–14), working in Patagonia for six years. Chely Hernandez also played an important role in Chile by bringing the workers, amongst them Eliezer Vasquez and Jorge Jimenez, to *NotOna* via boat every day and subsequently taking care of the island's maintenance. *Marble Tower* (2009), which traveled from Italy to Belgium, would not have been possible without the courage and determination of Umberto Togni, who labored on this monumental sculpture for years. Paulo dos Sousa made the projects in Brazil possible: in the Amazon forest, he oversaw the construction of *House to Watch the Sunset* (2016) and *House with No Doors* (2016). All the architectural drawings that are included in this book are reconstructions made by dos Sousa. Currently, dos Sousa is working with the artist on two new projects for the Amazon forest. In Brazil, Leuson Caetano and Everton Lamartine also play an important role since they not only take care of Not's house in Rio de Janeiro but also helped to build projects in the Amazon. In Indonesia, Saiful Rachman Fugu Soba Boro and his son Jeli, together with Abubekar Arhustam, made the construction of *House to Watch the 3 Volcanoes* (2017) and *Roof House* (2016) possible. *Chapel* (2016) would not have been possible without the generosity and support of Jam, Jerry, and Tess Acuzar, who provided both the land and the materials for this project in the Philippines. It was Alma Zevi, Not's former assistant, who introduced him to the Acuzar family. Dos Sousa was the architect who worked on the realization of *Chapel*. Photographer Eric Gregory Powell went around the world and shot many of these projects, providing us with important images for this publication. He also photographed all of the drawings included in this book. Aitor Ortiz went to Chile to photograph *NotOna* and to the Amazon in Brazil to photograph *House to Watch the Sunset* and *House with No Doors*.

Li Gao, Not's assistant, not only oversees all that happens at the Beijing studio but also accompanies the artist on his travels. Gao always takes care of the people around him and has the sharpest eye when it comes to details. Annatina Miescher, known as Cüqa, is another frequent travel companion; she takes care of people's mental health and finds the bones that later become sculptures. Cüqa also helped in the making of *Tower of Silence* (2003) by carrying up all the branches for the nest in order to cure her fear of heights. In Beijing, Zhenqian Liu and his wife Lizhe Zhao oversee the production of sculptures in stainless steel and aluminum, such as *Date* (2016), *Pole on House* (2016), and *Bridge* (2017). Tian Tian Li makes most of the models for these sculptures, which are later materialized in metal. Dongxu Liu worked for several years realizing sculptures, such as *Minaret for Agadez* (2009). In Jingdezhen, Jiangzhong Wu makes all of the ceramic works, such as *The Last Supper* (2014), which is installed in *Chapel* in the Philippines. In Switzerland, Not's brother Duri Vital not only helped with the realization of all structures at the sculpture park but also oversaw the design and construction of the *Painting Studio* (2015) in Sent, as well as the construction of *House to Watch the Sunset* (2018) in Tarasp. The latter was built by Armon Thomas, who used local sand from the River Inn to mix the concrete for this building.

In Switzerland, Mario Riatsch, Hannes Ortner, and Franz Tragust are in charge of maintaining the sculpture park. Ortner also went to Chile to help with the construction of *NotOna* and to Indonesia to help build *House to Watch the 3 Volcanoes*. Engineers such as Jürg Buchli and Florian Patsch make sure that sculptures and buildings like *JOSÜJO* (2007) and *House to Watch the Sunset* (2018) can be realized. Then, metalworkers and woodworkers across Italy, Switzerland, and Austria—for example, Walter and Patrick Vaghi, Hubert Brunner, Cla Riatsch, and Impraisa Buchli—materialize many of these pieces, mastering each new challenge with inventiveness and precision. Jean-François Brecq was responsible for the realization of *Stage* (2011). Laetitia Gauden, the shipment coordinator in China, and Daniele Agostini, the studio's registrar in Switzerland, ensure that all of the artworks are safely transported to and from all regions of the world. No matter what a sculpture's size or weight may be, Gauden and Agostini make sure that everything goes seamlessly. Without all of these people mentioned here, without their dedication, vision, belief, and hard work, the projects that together comprise SCARCH would not have been possible.

We have long shared a vision for a survey publication that brings together these far-flung works for readers, and thanks to the support of Manuela and Iwan Wirth and Marc Payot, this vision has, at last, been astutely realized. It is fitting that we celebrate this milestone publication at the opening of an exhibition of Not's work at Hauser & Wirth Somerset, where the hard work and passion of the team led by Alice Workman and Dea Vanagan introduce SCARCH to this landscape for the first time. We are grateful for Damien Saatdjian's clear, responsive visualization of the global nature of Not's work in the book's design. Lastly, gratitude is due to Hauser & Wirth Publishers and the resolute dedication of publisher Michaela Unterdörfer and managing editor Jennifer Magee for shepherding this book to print and into your hands.

Not Vital, Giorgia von Albertini, and Olivier Renaud-Clément

About the Artist

Not Vital is a Swiss sculptor and painter from the mountain village of Sent, located in the Engadine valley of Switzerland. He currently lives and works in Rio de Janeiro, Beijing, and Sent. Vital's multifaceted oeuvre, which encompasses drawing, painting, sculpture, and built structures, is reflective of his quasi-nomadic way of life. In order to give a name to his built structures of monumental scale that bridge sculpture and architecture, Vital coined the term SCARCH in 2009.

Contributors

Akhmed Haïdara lives and works in Agadez, Niger. Together with his brothers, he assisted Not Vital in the realization of SCARCH projects in Niger.

Philip Jodidio studied economics and art history at Harvard. He was editor in chief of the leading French art monthly *Connaissance des Arts* from 1980 to 2002. He is the author of more than 150 books, mainly about contemporary architecture, published by Taschen, Thames & Hudson, Rizzoli International, Prestel, Actes Sud, and others.

Olivier Renaud-Clément has organized exhibitions and acted as an adviser to artists and estates in the United States, Europe, Brazil, and Japan for many years. He works frequently with Hauser & Wirth and has collaborated with Takesada Matsutani, the estate of Fabio Mauri, Lygia Pape, August Sander, and Mira Schendel, among others.

Tilla Theus is an architect and designer based in Zurich and Graubünden, Switzerland. She holds a diploma in architecture from ETH and is a member of the Swiss Society of Engineers and Architects and the Federation of Swiss Architects. Some of her key projects include Zurich's Widder Hotel, the Swiss Re headquarters, and Jelmoli, as well as the Nikolai Monastery in Chur and the Suvretta House in St. Moritz.

Giorgia von Albertini is an independent curator and writer based in Switzerland. Von Albertini's most recent curatorial projects include *Not Vital: Saudade*, Galeria Nara Roesler, São Paulo; *Martin Soto Climént: In the Shadow of an Invisible Thread*, Hessel Museum of Art, New York; *Bethan Huws*, Galerie Tschudi, Zuoz; and *DREAM MACHINES: Salvatore Scarpitta and Panamarenko*, Fundaziun Not Vital, Tarasp. Working closely with Vital since 2016, she manages his studio and foundation and has written extensively about Vital's work.

List of Works

Chanala da tet
(*Rainwater Gutter*), 1964
Tin and white paint
85⅞ × 5⅛ × 8¼ in.,
218 × 13 × 21 cm
p. 13

Door + Window, 1965
Wood and chicken wire
85⅜ × 39⅜ in.,
217 × 100 cm
pp. 10–11

Fatschada (*Façade*), 1965
Sand and acrylic on canvas
37¾ × 30¾ in., 96 × 78 cm
p. 14

Window + Door, 1965
Asphalt on paper
76 × 60 in., 193 × 152.5 cm
pp. 250–51

Chasa i bogn
(*House and Bathtub*), 1970
Tin
House: 39⅜ × 24 × 9½ in.,
100 × 61 × 24 cm
Bathtub: 20⅞ × 31½ × 28½ in.,
53 × 80 × 72.5 cm
p. 14

Wheel Animal, 1982
Bronze
Diameter: 39⅜ in., 100 cm
Courtesy of Rubell Family
Collection, Miami
p. 16

Paw Pow, 1984
Bronze
77⅛ × 46⅛ × 18⅛ in.,
196 × 117 × 46 cm
Edition of 5
p. 16

Arabia, 1985
Bronze and marble
Each: 129⅞ × 11¾ × 3⅞ in.,
330 × 30 × 10 cm
Edition of 5
Private collection, Switzerland
p. 17

Handrail and Waterpipe, 2000
Iron and rubber
Length: 1,003⅞ in., 25.5 m
Parkin, Sent, Switzerland
Courtesy of Fundaziun Not Vital
pp. 86–87

Mekafoni, 2001
Mud, straw, and dung
Height: 511¾ in., 13 m
Agadez, Niger
pp. 120–25

Punt dals asens (*Donkey Bridge*),
2001
Aluminum
275⅝ × 1,378 in., 7 × 35 m
Parkin, Sent, Switzerland
Courtesy of Fundaziun Not Vital
pp. 88–91

Tuor per ir pella bos-cha
(*Hair Tower*), 2001
Wood and synthetic hair
Height: 669¼ in., 17 m
Parkin, Sent, Switzerland
Courtesy of Fundaziun Not Vital
pp. 92–93

Chasa barcha / Chamonna
süll'aua (*House by the River*),
2002
Stone pine
155½ × 149⅝ × 189 in.,
3.95 × 3.8 × 4.8 m
Parkin, Sent, Switzerland
Courtesy of Fundaziun Not Vital
pp. 96–99

Chasa da glatsch
(*Glass House*), 2002
Glass
74¾ × 39⅜ × 59 in.,
1.9 × 1 × 1.5 m
Parkin, Sent, Switzerland
Courtesy of Fundaziun Not Vital
pp. 94–95

Makaranta, 2003
Mud, straw, and dung
Height: 255⅞ in., 6.5 m
Agadez, Niger
pp. 126–31

Tuor da silenzi
(*Tower of Silence*), 2003
Animal skin, wood, and steel
Height: 614⅛ in., 15.6 m
Parkin, Sent, Switzerland
Courtesy of Fundaziun Not Vital
pp. 100–01

Bremer Stadtmusikanten
(*Musicians of Bremen*), 2004
Four silver boxes, each
containing a sun-dried animal
(a donkey, a dog, a cat, and a
rooster)
Overall: 29½ × 29½ × 17¾ in.,
75 × 75 × 45 cm
Private collection
p. 122

Camel, 2004
16 silver spheres containing
one sun-dried camel
Diameter of each sphere
(approx.): 9 in., 23 cm
p. 121

Chamonna spanada
(*Board House*), 2004
Wood and salt
141¾ × 102⅜ × 189 in.,
3.6 × 2.6 × 4.8 m
Parkin, Sent, Switzerland
Courtesy of Fundaziun Not Vital
pp. 74, 102–03

Model for a Water Tower, 2004
Black marble and water
28⅜ × 18½ × 14⅝ in.,
72 × 47 × 37 cm
Courtesy of the artist and
Galerie Thaddaeus Ropac,
London • Paris • Salzburg
pp. 132–33

Water Tower for Agadez, 2004
Cotton, tape, and pencil
on paper
17 × 14 in., 43.2 × 35.6 cm
p. 29

House to Watch the Sunset,
2005
Mud, straw, and dung
Height: 511¾ in., 13 m
Aladab, Niger
pp. 138–39, 249

The 10th House, 2005
Rock
Tigidit, Niger
pp. 142–43

House Against Heat and
Sandstorms, 2006
Mud, straw, and dung
Height: 511¾ in., 13 m
Aladab, Niger
pp. 144–45

House for 8 Brothers, 2006
Mud, straw, and dung
118⅛ × 618 in., 3 × 15.7 m
Alarsas, Niger
pp. 150–51

House to Watch the Night Skies,
2006
Mud, straw, dung, and iron
Height: 255⅞ in., 6.5 m
Aladab, Niger
pp. 148–49

Mountain House, 2006
Tape and pencil on paper
17 × 14 in., 43.2 × 35.6 cm
Courtesy of Barbara
Garberson-Schmid,
Switzerland
p. 30

Biotop, 2007
Painted wood
27½ × 570⅞ in., .7 × 14.5 m
Parkin, Sent, Switzerland
Courtesy of Fundaziun Not Vital
pp. 104–05

JOSÜJO (*Disappearing House*),
2007
Steel with fluorescent varnish
147⅝ × 252¾ × 201⅝ in.,
3.75 × 6.42 × 5.12 m
Parkin, Sent, Switzerland
Courtesy of Fundaziun Not Vital
pp. 106–09

Bridge, 2008
Stainless steel
91 × 236¼ × 78¾ in.,
2.31 × 6 × 2 m
Parkin, Sent, Switzerland
Courtesy of Fundaziun Not Vital
pp. 74, 110–11

NotOna, 2008–14
Marble island
General Carrera Lake,
Patagonia, Chile
pp. 160–73

Hotel for Aa, ZH, 2009
Stickers, tape, and pencil
on paper
17 × 14 in., 43.2 × 35.6 cm
p. 32

Hotel for Ardez, 2009
Cotton, glue, and pencil
on paper
17 × 14 in., 43.2 × 35.6 cm
p. 31

House for Sent, 2009
Cotton, tape, and pencil
on paper
17 × 14 in., 43.2 × 35.6 cm
p. 35

Marble Tower, 2009
Marble
Height: 362¼ in., 9.2 m
Walloon Brabant, Belgium
Courtesy of Lhoist Group
Collection, Limelette, Belgium
pp. 186–89

Minaret for Agadez, 2009
Fiberglass, textile, and
plastic tubing
118⅛ × 47¼ × 39⅜ in.,
3 × 1.2 × 1 m
pp. 154–55

Pavilion for NotOna Island,
2009
Dental floss, tape, and
pencil on paper
17 × 14 in., 43.2 × 35.6 cm
p. 33

School for Agadez, 2009
Fiberglass and plaster
40⅛ × 88⅝ × 74¾ in.,
102 × 225 × 190 cm
pp. 152–53

Synagogue for Tel Aviv, 2009
Straws, tape, and pencil
on paper
17 × 14 in., 43.2 × 35.6 cm
p. 36

Weekend House for Tallinn,
2009
Molding paste, tape, and
pencil on paper
17 × 14 in., 43.2 × 35.6 cm
p. 34

*Entrance + Exit to the Tunnel
at NotOna,* 2010
Plastic bag, glue, and pencil
on paper
17 × 14 in., 43.2 × 35.6 cm
Courtesy of Wilde Gallery,
Geneva, Switzerland
p. 37

House for Upsala, 2010
Straws, tape, and pencil
on paper
17 × 14 in., 43.2 × 35.6 cm
p. 38

Sleeping House, 2010
Stainless steel and varnish
31½ × 11¼ in., 80 × 28.5 cm
Edition of 18
Courtesy of the artist and
Galerie Thaddaeus Ropac,
London • Paris • Salzburg
pp. 146–47

NotOna, 2011
Marble
11¾ × 51⅛ × 59 in.,
30 × 130 × 150 cm
pp. 174–75

Palc (*Stage*), 2011
Iron
144⅞ × 98⅜ × 472½ in.,
3.68 × 2.5 × 12 m
Parkin, Sent, Switzerland
Courtesy of Fundaziun Not Vital
pp. 116–17

Tower of Cheese, 2012
Cheese
Dimensions variable
pp. 180–81

House for CS (Bread), 2013
Wood and bread
66⅞ × 36⅝ × 36⅝ in.,
170 × 93 × 93 cm
pp. 182–83

House to Watch the Sunset,
2013
Stainless steel
41 × 20½ × 45⅝ in.,
104 × 52 × 116 cm
pp. 156–57

*House to Watch the 3
Volcanoes,* 2013
Stainless steel
51⅛ × 15¾ × 93¼ in.,
130 × 40 × 237 cm
pp. 216–17

Mosque, 2013
Metal and cement
236¼ × 472½ in., 6 × 12 m
Agadez, Niger
p. 18

Gordon Matta-Clark, 2014
Silver
2 boxes
2⅜ × 8⅝ × 8⅝ in.,
6 × 22 × 22 cm
16⅞ × 7½ × 7½ in.,
43 × 19 × 19 cm
(overall: 19¼ × 8⅝ × 8⅝ in.,
49 × 22 × 22 cm)
p. 176

The Last Supper, 2014
Glazed ceramic
196⅞ × 472½ in., 5 × 12 m
p. 228

Painting Studio, 2015
Concrete and wood
218⅞ × 448⅞ × 326¾ in.,
5.56 × 11.4 × 8.3 m
Sent, Switzerland
pp. 234–37

Cathedral, 2016
Bushes
Paraná do Mamori, Brazil
pp. 202–03

Chapel, 2016
Iron and concrete
287⅜ × 629⅞ × 511¾ in.,
7.3 × 16 × 13 m
Bataan, Philippines
pp. 224–29

The Chapel, 2016
Stainless steel
131⅞ × 26¾ × 9⅞ in.,
335 × 68 × 25 cm
Edition of 3 + 1 artist proof
pp. 230–31

Date, 2016
Stainless steel
118⅛ × 60¼ × 49⅝ in.,
300 × 153 × 126 cm
p. 21

House to Watch the Sunset,
2016
Angelim vermelho (wood)
Height: 511¾ in., 13 m
Paraná do Mamori, Brazil
pp. 192–95

House to Watch the Sunset,
2016
Stainless steel
139 × 26⅜ × 15¾ in.,
353 × 67 × 40 cm
Edition of 5 + 2 artist proofs
pp. 196–97

House with No Doors, 2016
Wood
133½ × 133½ × 527⅛ in.,
3.39 × 3.39 × 13.39 m
Paraná do Mamori, Brazil
pp. 198–201

100 Architects, 2016
Black granite
Dimensions variable
pp. 73, 78–81

Pole on House, 2016
Stainless steel
122½ × 23⅝ × 15¾ in.,
311 × 60 × 40 cm
Edition of 3 + 1 artist proof
pp. 238–39

Roof House, 2016
Straw, wood, and bamboo
Height: 511¾ in., 13 m
Moni, Flores, Indonesia
pp. 206–07

3 Brothers, 2016
Stainless steel
138¼ × 11⅜ × 11⅜ in.,
351 × 29 × 29 cm
138¼ × 11⅜ × 11⅜ in.,
351 × 29 × 29 cm
129½ × 20⅛ × 11⅜ in.,
329 × 51 × 29 cm
Edition of 3 + 1 artist proof
pp. 112–13

Bridge, 2017
Aluminum
98⅞ × 267¾ in., 251 × 680 cm
pp. 114–15

Empire State Building, 2017
Aluminum tape and pencil
on paper
17 × 14 in., 43.2 × 35.6 cm
p. 41

House, 2017
Dental floss, tape, and
pencil on paper
17 × 14 in., 43.2 × 35.6 cm
p. 42

House to Watch the 3
Volcanoes, 2017
Cement, iron, straw, and
bamboo
Height: 511¾ × 895⅝ in.,
13 × 22.75 m
Moni, Flores, Indonesia
pp. 208–15

School House for Timbuktu,
2017
Straws, glue, and pencil
on paper
17 × 14 in., 43.2 × 35.6 cm
Courtesy private collection,
Switzerland, and Galerie
Tschudi, Zuoz, Switzerland
p. 39

Tower, 2017
Foam board and pencil
on paper
17 × 14 in., 43.2 × 35.6 cm
Courtesy of Roger Boltshauser,
Switzerland
p. 40

Tower, 2017
Tape and pencil on paper
17 × 14 in., 43.2 × 35.6 cm
p. 43

Bamako, 2018
Tape, pencil, and glue on paper
17 × 14 in., 43.2 × 35.6 cm
p. 56

Cabana, 2018
Starch and pencil on paper
17 × 14 in., 43.2 × 35.6 cm
p. 48

Casa de palafita para Purucuru
Amazonia Brasil, 2018
Tape and pencil on paper
17 × 14 in., 43.2 × 35.6 cm
p. 54

Central do Brasil, 2018
Tape and pencil on paper
17 × 14 in., 43.2 × 35.6 cm
p. 50

Centro do Rio, 2018
Foam board, silicone, and
pencil on paper
17 × 14 in., 43.2 × 35.6 cm
p. 55

Editors
Olivier Renaud-Clément and
Giorgia von Albertini

Publisher
Michaela Unterdörfer

Managing editor
Jennifer Magee

Project assistant
Mélanie Letoré

Book design and typography
Damien Saatdjian

Copyediting and proofreading
Georgia Bellas

Pre-press
LUP AG, Cologne

Production coordination
Christine Stricker

Printing and binding
DZA Druckerei zu Altenburg
GmbH

Cover: Paradise linen
Endpaper: f.color glatt 409
Tiefschwarz
Paper: Blocker (Lakepaper),
135 gm
Typeface: Neue Haas Grotesk

Photo credits
p. 8: Baron/Boisanté Editions; p. 247: © 2020 Darren Bradley; p. 18 (bottom): Canadian Centre for Architecture, Gift of Estate of Gordon Matta-Clark; p. 133: Charles Duprat; p. 246 (left): © Michael Evans/stock.adobe.com; p. 147: Ulrich Ghezzi; pp. 11, 13–14, 113, 197, 231, 239, 251: Joschi Herczeg; p. 248 (bottom): courtesy Hotel Castell; p. 246 (right): © Douglas Mandry; pp. 161–63, 165–66, 171, 173, 176, 193–95, 199–03: Aitor Ortiz; pp. 15, 17, 74 (bottom), 87, 89–91, 93, 95, 98–99, 101, 103, 105, 107–09, 111, 117, 131, 155, 175, 187–89, 207, 209–15, 217, 225–29, 236–37: Eric Gregory Powell; pp. 121–22: © Foto Florio Puenter; pp. 76, 97, 183: Stefan Ruiz; pp. 74 (top), 235, 241: Filippo Simonetti; p. 248 (top): Tilla Theus; pp. 16 (bottom), 18 (top), 115, 127–29, 139, 143, 149, 151, 249: Not Vital; p. 21: Giorgia von Albertini; pp. 123–25: Deidi von Schaewen

Every effort has been made to trace copyright ownership and to obtain reproduction permissions. Corrections brought to the publisher's attention will be incorporated in future reprints or editions of this book.

Cataloging-in-Publication Data is available from the Library of Congress.

Distribution:
Europe and the UK
Buchhandlung Walther König
Ehrenstrasse 4
50672 Köln
Tel +49 221 20 59 6-53
Fax +49 221 20 59 6-60

All other territories
ARTBOOK | D.A.P.
75 Broad Street, Suite 630
New York, NY 10004
Tel +1 212 627 1999
Fax +1 212 627 9484

ISBN: 978-3-906915-50-0
Printed and bound in Germany